A Prosodic Model of Sign Language Phonology

Language, Speech, and Communication

Statistical Language Learning, Eugene Charniak, 1994

The Development of Speech Perception, edited by Judith Goodman and Howard C. Nusbaum, 1994

Construal, Lyn Frazier and Charles Clifton, Jr., 1995

The Generative Lexicon, James Pustejovsky, 1996

The Origins of Grammar: Evidence from Early Language Comprehension, Kathy Hirsh-Pasek and Roberta Michnick Golinkoff, 1996

Language and Space, edited by Paul Bloom, Mary A. Peterson, Lynn Nadel, and Merrill F. Garrett, 1996

Corpus Processing for Lexical Acquisition, edited by Branimir Boguraev and James Pustejovsky, 1996

Methods for Assessing Children's Syntax, edited by Dana McDaniel, Cecile McKee, and Helen Smith Cairns, 1996

The Balancing Act: Combining Symbolic and Statistical Approaches to Language, edited by Judith Klavans and Philip Resnik, 1996

The Discovery of Spoken Language, Peter W. Jusczyk, 1996

Lexical Competence, Diego Marconi, 1997

Finite-State Language Processing, edited by Emmanuel Roche and Yves Schabes, 1997

Children with Specific Language Impairment, Laurence B. Leonard, 1997

Type-Logical Semantics, Robert Carpenter, 1997

Statistical Methods for Speech Recognition, Frederick Jelinek, 1997

WordNet: An Electronic Lexical Database, edited by Christiane Fellbaum, 1998

Investigations in Universal Grammar: A Guide to Experiments on the Acquisition of Syntax and Semantics, Stephen Crain and Rosalind Thornton, 1998

A Prosodic Model of Sign Language Phonology, Diane Brentari, 1998

A Prosodic Model of Sign Language Phonology

Diane Brentari

A Bradford Book
The MIT Press
Cambridge, Massachusetts
London, England

This book was set in Times New Roman on the Monotype "Prism Plus" PostScript Imagesetter by Asco Trade Typesetting Ltd., Hong Kong and was printed and bound in the United States of America.

Library of Congress Cataloging-in-Publication Data

Brentari, Diane.
  A prosodic model of sign language phonology / Diane Brentari.
    p.   cm. — (Language, speech, and communication)
  "A Bradford Book."
  Includes bibliographical references and index.
  ISBN 0-262-02445-4 (alk. paper)
  1. Sign language. 2. American Sign Language. 3. Grammar,
Comparative and general—Phonology. I. Title. II. Series.
HV2474.B44   1998
419—dc21   97-50053
                                                    CIP

For Arnold

Contents

Preface   xiii

Notational Conventions and
Abbreviations   xvii

Chapter 1

Goals of the Model   1

1.1   General Introduction   1

1.2   Introduction to Sign Structures
3

1.3   Overview of the Prosodic Model
22

Chapter 2

**The Use of Constraint-Based
Frameworks and Prosodic Units in
Analyses of Sign Languages   53**

2.1   General Assumptions   53

2.2   How Constraint-Based Models
Operate   55

2.3   Feature Geometry and
Dependency Phonology   63

2.4   The Phonetics-Phonology Interface and Enhancement Theory   69

2.5   Markedness   69

2.6   The Syllable and the Prosodic
Word   70

2.7 The Relationship between Native and Nonnative Components of the ASL Lexicon   81

2.8 The Prosodic Model in the Context of Other Models of Sign Language Phonology   83

Chapter 3

Inherent Features   93

3.1 A Feature Geometry for ASL 93

3.2 The Traditional ASL Parameters and Their Relationship to Class Nodes   96

3.3 The Structure of the Inherent Features: Articulator and Place   97

3.4 Handshape Inventories, Redundancy, and Markedness   117

3.5 Place of Articulation   119

3.6 The Orientation Relation   123

3.7 Nonterminal Features   126

3.8 Conclusion   126

Chapter 4

Prosodic Features   129

4.1 Introduction to Movement Types 129

4.2 Movement Migration: Proximalization and Distalization   133

4.3 Path Features   136

4.4 Setting Changes   151

4.5   Orientation Changes   155

4.6   Handshape Changes   158

4.7   An Articulator-Free Feature: [Trilled Movement]   164

4.8   Nonmanual Prosodic Features 173

4.9   Conclusion   174

Chapter 5

Timing Units   177

5.1   Definition of Timing Units in the Prosodic Model   177

5.2   Three Segment Slots or Two? 180

5.3   Two-Movement Stems   186

5.4   Phonological Operations Involving Timing Units: Phrase-Final Lengthening   193

5.5   A Morphophonemic Operation Using Timing Units: A Linearly Ordered Affix in ASL—[Delayed Completive]   196

5.6   Sequential Movements Are Syllables   205

5.7   Conclusion   211

Chapter 6

Complexity, Sonority, and Weight in ASL Syllables   213

6.1   Complexity in Inherent and Prosodic Branches of Structure   213

6.2   Prosodic Complexity as Visual Sonority   216

6.3   Grammatical Uses of Visual
Sonority in Syllables   224

6.4   Subsyllabic Units of Prosodic
Analysis   237

6.5   Weight Units and Their Interaction with Syntactic Constituents
244

6.6   Conclusion   245

Chapter 7

The Structure of Two-Handed Signs
247

7.1   The Importance of Two-Handed
Signs in a General Description of Sign
Language Phonology   247

7.2   Alternative Accounts of H_2
251

7.3   Arguments Supporting a Single
Structure for Two-Handed Signs
256

7.4   The Prosodic Model's Structure
for H_2 260

7.5   An Optimality-Theoretic Account
of Weak Drop   265

7.6   Alternative Accounts of H_2
Revisited   277

7.7 H_2 as a Prosodic Unit   279

7.8   Conclusion and Residual Issues
282

Chapter 8

Contributions of Sign Language
Phonology to Phonological Theory and
Cognitive Science   285

8.1   The Prosodic Model Revisited
285

8.2   Constraints, Inventories, and the Lexicon   292

8.3   Units of Phonological Analysis 303

8.4   Similarities between the Architecture of the Visual System and the Prosodic Model   306

8.5   Conclusion   313

Appendix A

The Letters of the ASL Manual Alphabet Labeled [Flexed] or Nonflexed 315

Appendix B

Verb Forms That Do and Do Not Allow the [Delayed Completive] Aspect   317

Appendix C

Forms That Undergo Reduplicative Nominalization   319

Appendix D

Descriptive Categories of Two-Handed Signs According to Their Ability to Undergo Weak Drop   321

Notes   325

References   335

Index of Illustrated Signs   353

General Index   355

Preface

A major goal of this book is to function as a point of access to the field of sign language phonology for researchers who are working in closely related disciplines but who have not yet learned to sign. For instance, for those readers who have attended a conference session on sign languages and would like to learn more, this book will provide a first immersion into current questions in the phonology of sign languages. To aid in this, I have included images that will serve as an anchor for the book's arguments based on sign language forms.

In addition to introducing the field, the book has several other goals, which have shaped its structure. Chapters 1 and 8 are a framing device for what is contained in chapters 2 through 7. Chapter 1 concisely articulates the major claims of the Prosodic Model and the grounds on which I will argue for them. It also describes and gives example images of the canonical types of signs used in phonological analyses more generally, providing background for the more detailed analyses to follow. Chapter 8 shows how the Prosodic Model incorporates elements of other models of sign language phonology and how it differs from them. This chapter also uses the well-formedness constraints developed on independent grounds in the rest of the book to propose a means for delineating lexical strata in American Sign Language. Finally, it places the Prosodic Model into the context of current discussions of higher-order visual processing. This research on vision has gone virtually untouched by sign language phonologists, yet its findings could be useful in making arguments about sign language phonological structure based on perception. I also believe that sign language data, and analyses of them, provide categories of visual forms used in some of the experimental work on vision.

Chapter 2 is aimed at sign language researchers and linguists who are not phonologists who may benefit from some background in the specific theories drawn upon for the analyses in this book. Although the discussions in this chapter do not cover these theories in their entirety, they do explain the context in which particular concepts developed and how they are being used to analyze sign language within the Prosodic Model.

Chapters 3 through 7 are the heart of the book. Sign language phonology is no longer in its infancy, and researchers have come to a consensus about some of the questions that launched the field. My intention is to highlight these areas of consensus wherever possible so that future work can build upward and outward from them. The central idea of the Prosodic Model of sign language phonology, which distinguishes it from other models, is that two kinds of phonological features can be systematically identified in core lexical items: those that are necessary for describing a sign's movement (the prosodic features) and those that describe properties of the sign that do not participate in movement (the inherent features). The latter express many of the paradigmatic contrasts of a sign; the former capture phonological contrasts as well, but they also are important for syllable construction and syllable weight. To date, no other model has isolated movement features in this way—a way that allows their uniform behavior in phonological operations to be expressed.

This book was completed only with the help of many friends and colleagues. I would like to thank the University of California-Davis for a leave in 1994–1995, which allowed me to complete a full first draft; the anonymous reviewers of MIT Press for their helpful comments; and John Goldsmith and Wendy Sandler for reading the manuscript in an earlier form. I am grateful to Steven Lapointe for co-teaching a seminar on Optimality Theory with me in the fall of 1996, which helped me crystallize the analyses in this book that employ that framework. I am also thankful to Karen Emmorey, Bruce Hayes, Harry van der Hulst, Robert Johnson, Judy Kegl, Scott Liddell, Carol Padden, David Perlmutter, Kelly Stack, and Ronnie Wilbur for many discussions about earlier stages of analyses during linguistic colloquia and at conferences. For the opportunity to work in a laboratory integrally involved in studying the effects of neurological damage on motor control, and for helpful conversations and guidance in these areas, I thank Howard Poizner. The analyses in this book also benefited a great deal from conversations at the 1994 Workshop on Sign Language Phonology in Trondheim, Norway, and the 1995 Linguistic Institute in Albuquerque, New Mexico; to their organizers and participants go my heartfelt thanks.

The photographic images throughout the text were made possible by plunging into the world of photo CDs, photography techniques specific to sign languages, and relevant computer software, and for help in this area I am thankful to the professional staff of the Center for German Sign Language, in particular Thomas Hanke. I am grateful to Sigmund Prillwitz for making the resources of the Center available to me while I was in Germany and to Joel Snyder for helping me reconstruct them "on a budget" when I came back to the United States. I also acknowledge the Richard and Nancy Robinson Fund for its support. I also owe special thanks to David Landan for proofreading and figure preparation, to James Williams for constructing the index, and to Anne Mark for her excellent copyediting assistance.

I also wish to thank members of the Deaf community for their patience and acceptance, for their help as informants, and for discussions about particular signs in these analyses; Drucilla Ronchen deserves warm thanks in this regard. Finally, I am indebted to Stefan Goldschmidt and Robin Shay for serving as the models for the signs.

Notational Conventions and Abbreviations

Notional conventions used in the text:

MOTHER	(all capital letters) ASL sign glossed to its nearest English equivalent
ALIGNMENT	(capital and small capital letters) a constraint label within Optimality Theory
TO-FILM	(words separated by a hyphen) an ASL sign that expresses all the English words connected by the hyphens
THINK ^ SELF	(words separated by a circumflex) ASL compound
S-O	(letters separated by a hyphen) fingerspelled borrowing
INDEX$_1$	(index with a numeral subscript) deictic point toward a particular anaphoric locus
INDEX$_a$	(index with a letter subscript) deictic point toward a particular spatial locus
HOUSE$_a$	(lexical item with subscript) articulation of a sign at a particular locus in the signing space, which is within a system of anaphoric reference
$\overline{\text{MOUN}^t\text{TAIN}}$	(overline with 't') topicalized constituent marked with raised eyebrows, head back
$\overline{\text{MOUN}^q\text{TAIN}}$	(overline with 'q') interrogative marker extending over a constituent marked with raised eyebrows, head forward
$_3$GIVE$_1$	(numerical subscripts) stem and incorporated person inflections

$_0$GIVE$_{-0}$	('0' subscripts) default specifications used with stems that allow incorporated person inflection, but in which no inflectional morphology is present ($_0$ indicates a default locus at the signer; $_{-0}$ indicates a default locus away from the signer)
[contact]	([. . .]) distinctive feature or a morphological structure, such as a person, number, or aspect category
[direction: >|]	([. . . : . . .]) distinctive feature with a particular value
[open], [closed]	([. . .], [. . .]) temporal ordering of one feature before another
∅	null pronoun or, in a feature tree, no specification
'word'	English translation of an ASL gloss

Abbreviations used in the text:

A	articulator
GSS	global signing space
H	hold
HC	hand configuration
HP	hand prism
HS	handshape
I	index (finger)
IF	inherent features
L	location
LSS	local signing space
M	movement; (with respect to fingers) middle
NM	nonmanual
O	orientation
P	position; (with respect to fingers) pinkie
POA	place of articulation
PF	prosodic features
R	ring (finger)
RAFI	radial side of fingers
SF	selected fingers
T	thumb

A Prosodic Model of Sign
Language Phonology

Chapter 1
Goals of the Model

1.1 General Introduction

In this book I present a theory of the phonological structure of sign languages. In general, my goal is to integrate the insights of work by myself and others into a unified account, the Prosodic Model. Descriptively, I focus on the grammar of American Sign Language (ASL), the language of the Deaf community in the United States and in the English-speaking portions of Canada, but because the model makes empirically falsifiable predictions, wherever possible I check the analyses against forms from other sign languages and suggest broader generalizations. In addition to addressing problems that are well known to sign language phonologists, I analyze the conventional sign language "parameters" of handshape, movement, orientation, and location (i.e., place of articulation) as manipulable feature groups, and I demonstrate their relationship to more abstract units, specifically segments, syllables, and prosodic words. To phonologists who work on either signed or spoken languages, this analysis of sign language data offers a new perspective on the definition of these traditional abstract units: it suggests concrete ways of defining them so that they can encompass both spoken and signed languages. If these are units of universal grammar, such definitions must be within our grasp.

The assumption that phonology is inextricably bound to gestures made by the vocal apparatus and perceived by the auditory system gradually has been replaced with the understanding that phonology is a level of grammatical analysis. Gestures made using the arms and body in sign languages and those made using the tongue, velum, glottis, and palate in spoken languages are equivalent from the point of view of the grammar. Phonology is the level of grammatical analysis where primitive structural units without meaning are recursively combined to create an infinite number of meaningful utterances. It is the level of grammar that has a direct link with the articulatory and perceptual phonetic systems, either a visual/gestural pair or an auditory/vocal pair of peripheral systems.

There is a body of literature to support the claim that those aspects of neurological structure used in language production and language processing evolved into their current states by complex interactions between areas of the brain used to control movements of the vocal apparatus and sound perception more generally, and the accompanying physiognomic changes in the vocal apparatus and structures of the inner ear (see Mattingly and Liberman 1988 for a good introduction to this literature based on human and animal models).[1] Today, the extent to which neurological systems used for language encoding and formulation are disassociated from those concerned with more general peripheral functioning is still a matter of debate (Kimura 1993; Lieberman et al. 1992; Damasio and Damasio 1980; Damasio 1994). What is clear is that, in the absence of useful auditory input, these language areas of the brain are used by visual/gestural languages, and that subjects with similar lesion sites due to brain damage in the left hemisphere demonstrate similar language deficits, regardless of whether the language is spoken or signed (Poizner, Klima, and Bellugi 1987). Furthermore, a clear distinction exists between nonlinguistic gesture and sign language in native language acquisition (Petitto 1987; Reilly, McIntire, and Bellugi 1990) and in language breakdown (Poizner, Klima, and Bellugi 1987; Corina et al. 1992).

Because of this special nature of gesture in sign language phonological systems, one goal of this work is to account for aspects of sign and spoken language representations with the same abstract phonological structures. Since most theoretical work in phonology deals with spoken languages, phonologists who work on sign languages must read reports of such work with an eye toward a discussion that is one step more abstract. We must try to imagine spoken languages stripped of their substantive phonetic link to the vocal apparatus and auditory system in order to consider the type of work that the units in question do for the grammar as a whole, and to consider their instantiations in a visual/gestural language. The goal of accounting for spoken and sign language phonological structure with one set of mental constructs does not mean that sign phonologists should take spoken language units and find analogues to them in sign languages. We must bring our background as phonologists and our experience with sign language equally to the task of developing a phonological model for sign. It is rash to behave either as if methods of analysis for uncovering the sound pattern of a spoken language are useless for sign, or as if our hypotheses about sign should be shaped exclusively by them. My hypothesis is that the closer our analyses are to the phonetics, the more apparent the differences are between sign language and spoken language, and that the closer our analyses are to grammatical function, the more apparent the similarities become. As phonologists, we have a strong disciplinary history that has developed using spoken language forms, and my position is that, even at this early stage in the disciplinary history of sign linguistics, an ongoing dialogue between spoken and sign language phonologists would be more mutually beneficial than would separate, parallel lines of inquiry.[2]

The principle guiding the approach taken in this book is that phonological theory offers several innovative frameworks, each covering different conceptual problems in phonology. If one's aim is to account for a language-specific grammar, as mine is here, one must draw on insights arising from several frameworks. In chapter 2 I will point out why each of the theories listed here is useful in this project. In addition to the theories of autosegmental phonology and feature geometry, principles from constraint-based theories, primarily Optimality Theory (Prince and Smolensky 1993; McCarthy and Prince 1993b) and Harmonic Phonology (Goldsmith 1989, 1990, 1991, 1993), Dependency Phonology (Anderson and Ewen 1987; Dresher and van der Hulst 1994), and Phonetic Enhancement (Stevens, Keyser, and Kawasaki 1986; Stevens and Keyser 1989) will play a role in the book. I also make use of a model of the lexicon that Itô and Mester (1995a,b) propose for Japanese to show the relationship between the native component of the lexicon and the peripheral components.

Spoken language terms such as *syllable*, *segment*, and *mora* have been used in quite disparate ways in the literature, confusing readers interested in spoken language phonology and sign language phonology alike. I will therefore begin each analysis by referring only to weight units and timing units. That is, I will begin discussing sign units without referring to spoken language counterparts, saving discussion of overlap and nonoverlap with comparable units in spoken languages (e.g., syllable, mora, and segment) until the conclusion.[3]

1.2 Introduction to Sign Structures

Before giving an overview of the Prosodic Model in section 1.3, I describe here the eight types of ASL signs that will figure prominently in the analyses in later chapters. These eight types form a kind of canonical set of structures for which any complete phonological model must be able to account. Because it is difficult to find minimal pairs, a key strategy for ascertaining the units of sign structure is to observe the alternations in output forms due to morphological and phonological operations in the various types of signs. The assumption made here is that if a unit must be referred to in phonological operations, it must be a part of the phonological representation.

From the monomorphemic forms in the ASL lexicon, any framework must minimally be able to account for restrictions on

1. simple one-handed signs,
2. two-handed signs, and
3. fingerspelled borrowings.

From the set of polymorphemic forms, any framework must be able to account for the formation of

4. derived nominals,
5. agreement affixation,
6. compounds,
7. derived words containing grammatical aspect affixes,[4] and
8. "classifier forms" (Supalla 1982) or "polymorphemic verbs" (Engberg-Pederson 1993; Wallin 1994).

1.2.1 Monomorphemic Forms: One-Handed Signs
Simple one-handed signs display a wide range of phonological behavior that any framework of sign phonology must account for. Some of the systematic behaviors of these forms, and the terms I will use to describe them, are as follows.

All monomorphemic signs contain a movement, either a path movement or a local movement (Wilbur 1987, 1990; Brentari 1990b,c; Stack 1988; Perlmutter 1992). In this book *path movements* are movements made primarily with the elbow or shoulder. Formally, a path movement may be specified as either a movement feature (e.g., a path shape or a direction-of-movement feature) or a change in setting (i.e., a change in feature specification, such as ipsilateral/contralateral, top/bottom, or proximal/distal, within a major body region). *Local movements* are those made by the wrist, knuckles, or finger joints. Formally, they are expressed as a change in one or more features specified in the articulator branch of structure.

Figure 1.1
UNDERSTAND contains a local movement.

Figure 1.2
SIT contains a path movement.

For example, UNDERSTAND (figure 1.1) contains a local movement, SIT (figure 1.2) contains a path movement, and THROW (figure 1.3) contains both a path movement and a local movement.

Most monomorphemic signs have one major *place of articulation* (Mandel 1981; Battison 1978; Sandler 1987a). UNDERSTAND, SIT, and THROW all have one major place of articulation. The sign UNDER-STAND has two specifications for *aperture* (the degree to which the hand is open or closed): both hands are located at the forehead (the place of articulation), but the first handshape is closed and the second is open. The place of articulation for both SIT and THROW is *neutral space* (the area directly in front of the signer at the level of the torso), but each is articulated with respect to a different plane within neutral space. The plane of

Figure 1.3
THROW contains both a path and a local movement.

articulation of SIT is the horizontal plane in front of the signer. The plane of articulation of THROW is the midsagittal plane.

There is a tendency for words in ASL, especially monomorphemic forms, to be composed of a single movement; this has been referred to as *monosyllabicity* (Coulter 1982; Wilbur 1987, 1990). The number of syllables is roughly isomorphic with the number of sequential movements in a sign. Two-movement forms (disyllabic signs), although less numerous, reveal much about phonological structure in ASL. A rough guide to counting syllables, based on previous studies of sign language syllables (Chinchor 1978; Coulter 1982; Wilbur 1987, 1990; Brentari 1990b,c,d, 1993; Perlmutter 1992; Sandler 1993c), is given in (1).

(1) *Syllable-counting criteria (Brentari 1994)*

    a. The number of sequential phonological dynamic units in a string equals the number of syllables in that string.

        i. When several shorter dynamic units co-occur with a single dynamic element of longer duration, the longer unit is the one to which the syllable refers.

        ii. When two or more dynamic units are contemporaneous, they count as one syllable.

    b. If a structure is a well-formed syllable as an independent word, it must be counted as a syllable word-internally.

These criteria have several practical implications for counting syllables. (1a) excludes phonetic or redundant movements from the syllable count, and it covers both cases where *trilled movements* (TMs; a term coined by Sandler (1993c) and discussed by Padden and Perlmutter (1987)) are layered contemporaneously with a path or local movement and cases where any local movement and path movement co-occur. In such cases co-occurring dynamic elements count as one syllable. (1b) requires any single place of articulation that co-occurs with a TM to be counted as a syllable, whether it is word-internal or word-final.

There is also a restriction on *selected fingers* (the fingers of a handshape that can move during the production of a sign, or that can touch the body—the "active fingers" (Mandel 1981)).[5] This restriction, on which there is some consensus, is that only one set of selected fingers is allowed in a given minimal domain. This minimal domain has been formulated as the sign itself (Mandel 1981), the morpheme (Sandler 1987b), and the syllable (Brentari 1990b; Perlmutter 1992). In later chapters I will place this restriction on the prosodic word—a revision of my earlier proposals, and closer to what Mandel (1981) originally proposed.

Finally, Corina (1990b) has proposed a restriction on changes in handshape aperture, which he formulates roughly in terms of the sonority distance between the two aperture settings. The restriction states that there must be a minimum specified distance between two aperture settings of a handshape change. In Brentari 1990b I have proposed a constraint on aperture that restricts the number of partially open or partially closed handshapes in a phonological word.

1.2.2 Monomorphemic Forms: Two-Handed Signs

The hand/arm used to articulate fingerspelled forms and one-handed signs is called the *dominant hand* (abbreviated H_1 throughout this book); in two-handed signs, the other hand is the *nondominant hand* (abbreviated H_2). Battison (1978) has proposed three types of two-handed signs. In *type 1 signs* both hands are active and perform identical motor acts. The hands may or may not contact each other, they may or may not contact the body, and their pattern of movement may be either synchronous or alternating. For example, SINCE has a synchronous pattern of movement (figure 1.4), and BICYCLE has an alternating pattern. In *type 2 signs* one hand is active and one hand is passive, but both hands have the same handshape (e.g., REMEMBER (figure 1.5), SIT (figure 1.2)). In *type 3 signs* one hand is active and one hand is passive, and the two hands have different handshapes (e.g., TOUCH (figure 1.6)). (Battison also proposed a fourth type, *type C signs*, for compounds that combine two or

Figure 1.4
SINCE is a type 1 two-handed sign with synchronous (i.e., nonalternating) movement.

Figure 1.5
REMEMBER is a type 2 two-handed sign.

Figure 1.6
TOUCH is a type 3 two-handed sign.

Figure 1.7
An impossible two-handed monomorphemic sign

more of the above categories.) Example signs in each category are listed in the table that follows, and an impossible two-handed sign is shown in figure 1.7.

Examples of type 1, type 2, and type 3 two-handed signs

Type 1	Type 2	Type 3
SINCE	TRAIN	HELP (H_2 HS: 'B'; H_2 contact: inside surface of fingers)
HEALTHY	WORK	FIRST (H_2 HS: 'A'; H_2 contact: finger/thumb tip)
BODY	SCHOOL	TOUCH (H_2 HS: 'S'; H_2 contact: back of palm)
SUNDAY	SIT	COMMUNIST (H_2 HS: 'C'; H_2 contact: radial thumb)
NAVY	MONTH	PRACTICE (H_2 HS: '1'; H_2 contact: radial surface of finger)

Some constraints on two-handed signs are as follows. There may not be two distinct regions of the body or two distinct movements in a two-handed sign (from Battison 1978). If H_2 moves at all, it must articulate a version of the movement of H_1, executed either identically or in 180° asynchrony (alternating movement). H_2 may have a different handshape than H_1, but it must be selected from a limited set, the members of which are variations of selected finger groups 'B' and '1'. (There are seven handshapes altogether (Battison 1978): 'B', 'A', 'S', 'C', 'O', '5', and '1'.) All signs with two different handshapes are type 3 signs. There are eight discrete places of articulation where H_2 contact can be made in type 3 signs. 'B' may be specified for all eight; '1' may be specified for five

(Battison 1978). H_2 has two distinct roles in phonological structure: as a place of articulation and as an articulator (Sandler 1987b, 1989, 1993a). How these two roles should be represented, and other types of restrictions on two-handed signs, are the subject of chapter 7.

The restrictions outlined above are for monomorphemic, core, two-handed signs and do not cover all uses of H_2. A signer need not use the same hand as H_1 in all linguistic contexts, but can systematically shift between hands under certain conditions, such as in narrative storytelling, in poetry, or for particular lexical emphasis (there is wide idiolectal variation on this last point). Also, H_2 can perseverate while H_1 continues to articulate an utterance (2). The restrictions on H_2 in two-handed signs will be taken up at length in chapter 7.

(2) *Perseveration of H_2 in an utterance (Brentari and Goldsmith 1993)*

H_1: $\overline{\text{PHOTO}\overset{\text{t}}{\overline{\text{GRAPH}}}}$, MY MOTHER. INDEX$_1$ SEE SELF
       INDEX$_a$ ... GOOD AND BAD
H_2: - - - - - - - - - - - - CL:B in PLACE$_a$ - - - - - - - - - - - -
       -

1.2.3 Monomorphemic Forms: Fingerspelling and Lexicalized Fingerspelled Borrowings

Fingerspelling, which is the representation of the letters of an alphabetic writing system via signs, is one way for sign languages to borrow words from spoken languages. The ASL manual alphabet is the set of names for the English orthographic letters. I include the ASL manual alphabet here among the monomorphemic forms, but their morphological status is somewhat ambiguous. Just as spoken languages have words for letters (e.g., for *y*: [wai] in English, [igʀɛk] in French, [ipsilõw] in Portuguese, [ipsolon] in Italian), so the fingerspelled letters are words in their own right when uttered as single words. In some sign languages, this is the limited role that fingerspelled letters play, used as infrequently as speakers spell out words in English. Thus, in many sign languages (e.g., French, Dutch, German, Danish, Italian, Japanese, Chinese), words are not borrowed from the dominant surrounding language primarily by fingerspelling, but by some other means. In fact, ASL signers are thought to overuse fingerspelling by some members of such Deaf communities.

Fingerspelling serves many other purposes in ASL, however, more than spelling does in spoken languages; I will describe four of these. First, fingerspelling is used when no ASL sign exists, in order to introduce a concept (e.g., local proper names) used outside a community of signers. For example, there is a sign for the town name *Stockton, California*, but only local area residents would recognize it; when the town is mentioned by or to a nonresident, its name is fingerspelled. Second, fingerspelled forms may be used to emphasize a word for which an ASL lexical item does exist. For example, it would be appropriate to fingerspell the word 'home' in the following sentence if the signer is tired and is anxious to leave: WE-2 GO H-O-M-E! Third, there are fingerspelled forms that are completely assimilated into the lexicon; BREAD and NO are two such forms. These forms obey all constraints placed on words in the core lexicon.

Finally, in specific academic disciplines, fingerspelled forms are sometimes preferred over coined signs in order to highlight a technical versus nontechnical semantic distinction between uses of the same term (Padden 1995); or they may refer to domains of knowledge where consensus on the use of a specific sign has not been achieved. Fingerspelled forms of this type undergo a rapid lexicalization process, *local lexicalization*, whereby in a single discourse the fingerspelled form comes to represent, not each of the letters of the borrowed word, but the concept that word has in the source language. Local lexicalization of fingerspelled forms will be used as evidence in chapters 5 and 6.

The ASL fingerspelling alphabet is given in figure 1.8.

1.2.4   Polymorphemic Forms: Nominals
In this book I will discuss two kinds of nominalizations. Both are formed from verb stems: one by reduplication of a verb stem, and the other by adding a "trilled" feature to the movement of the stem. In chapter 5 I will argue that in addition to semantic requirements, the phonological shape of the stem of both types of nominals determines whether nominalization can occur.

1.2.4.1   Reduplicated Nouns   The *reduplicated nouns* in ASL were first described by Supalla and Newport (1978). For each reduplicated noun there is a corresponding verb.[6] The two signs are related in meaning, and the verb expresses the activity performed with or on the object named by the noun. The movement of the stem is repeated, and both movements are produced in a "restrained" manner (e.g., CLOSE-WINDOW/WINDOW (figure 1.9)). These forms have been given a segmental analysis, but in chapters 5 and 6 I will propose an analysis that includes both syntagmatic and paradigmatic components.

Figure 1.8
The ASL manual alphabet. Reprinted with permission from *A Basic Course in American Sign Language, Second Edition*, by T. Humphries, C. Padden, and T. J. O'Rourke. Copyright 1994. T. J. Publishers, Inc., Silver Spring, Md.

Figure 1.9
Two signs showing the operation of reduplication in nominalization: CLOSE-WINDOW/WINDOW. In CLOSE-WINDOW (left), there is a single path movement. In the noun WINDOW (right), there are two restrained path movements.

(3) *Reduplicated nominals in ASL (from Supalla and Newport 1978)*

   SIT/CHAIR
   CALL/NAME
   HIT-WITH-HAMMER/HAMMER
   GO-BY-PLANE/AIRPLANE
   GO-BY-BOAT/BOAT
   GO-BY-ROCKET/ROCKET
   GO-BY-FLYING-SAUCER/FLYING-SAUCER
   GO-BY-SHIP/SHIP
   GO-BY-TRAIN/TRAIN
   PUT-ON-BACKPACK/BACKPACK
   GO-TO-BED/BED
   COVER-WITH-BLANKET/BLANKET
   PUT-ON-BRACELET/BRACELET
   PUT-ON-BROOCH/BROOCH
   CLOSE-WINDOW/WINDOW
   CLOSE-GATE/GATE

1.2.4.2 Activity Nouns The class of derived nominals known as *activity nouns* was first discussed by Padden and Perlmutter (1987). They might be seen as a type of gerund, since they function in this way. The derived form contains a trilled movement (TM). TMs have been defined as small, rapidly repeated, uncountable movements (Liddell 1990b) and

Figure 1.10
An example of trilled movement affixation forming a derived activity noun:
READ/READING. In the verb READ (left), there is a single path movement. In
the derived activity noun READING (right), a trilled movement feature is affixed
to the stem.

have also been referred to by other names: local movement, oscillation
(Liddell 1990b), secondary movement (Perlmutter 1992; Brentari 1993),
and secondary path (Brentari 1990c). Semantically, the verb stems that
undergo this operation denote atelic activities (Vendler 1967). The forms
in (4a) may undergo this operation, and those in (4b) may not; figure 1.10
shows the acceptable pair READ and READING. Even though the verbs
BAT and THROW, GIVE and TAKE denote similar types of activities,
native informants respond differently to their derived activity nouns,
rejecting THROWING and TAKING but accepting BATTING and
GIVING.

(4) *Distribution of activity nouns*

    a. *Examples of verbs and their derived activity nouns*

READ	READING
RAP	RAPPING
CHAT	CHATTING
DRIVE	DRIVING
DRAW	DRAWING
WRITE	WRITING
SHOP	SHOPPING
BAT	BATTING
GIVE	GIVING

b. *Examples of verbs that have no derived activity noun*

SIT	*SITTING
SMILE	*SMILING
STAND	*STANDING
WANT	*WANTING
DESIRE	*DESIRING
LOVE	*LOVING
LIKE	*LIKING
THROW	*THROWING
TAKE	*TAKING

1.2.5 Polymorphemic Forms: Agreement

One morphologically complex group of signs that has been studied at length using both internal and external linguistic evidence is the so-called agreement forms. If one were to describe in general how agreement works in sign languages, given research on Langue des signes québecoise (Nadeau 1993; Desouvrey 1994), Danish Sign Language (Engberg-Pederson 1993), Japanese Sign Language (Fischer 1996), Sign Language of the Netherlands (Bos 1990), Taiwanese Sign Language (Smith 1990), Swedish Sign Language (Wallin 1994), Italian Sign Language (Pizzuto 1987), Swiss German Sign Language (Boyes-Braem 1990), and ASL, it would be that referents for persons or objects are assigned a locus in the signing space that remains constant throughout a stretch of discourse.[7] Whether these forms ought to be called agreement forms at all, or whether they should be considered to be outside the linguistic system altogether, is currently under debate. Liddell (1995) argues against calling spatial reference "agreement" because of the apparently infinite allomorphy of these forms. Engberg-Pederson (1993) argues that these references to objects in the signing space ought to be called "agreement," because loci cannot be established randomly in the signing space. Instead, she argues (p. 80), the number of *deictic lines of reference* used by sign language grammars— the deictic, anaphoric sequence, and mixed time lines, and the calendar plane—is limited.[8] If one accepts that these phenomena are linguistic, then another question arises: do these phenomena constitute one system of reference where all types are treated alike, two distinct systems of reference with different properties, or a category of subsystems that share overlapping properties but cannot be treated completely alike? Padden (1983, 1990) has argued for two distinct systems (one of person agreement,

Figure 1.11
DRIVE-TO is considered a typical spatial agreement verb, in which the initial and
final loci refer to a spatial map.

Figure 1.12
HELP is considered a typical person agreement verb, in which the initial and final
loci refer to grammatical subject and object, respectively.

the other of spatial agreement), and there is neurolinguistic evidence that
supports a distinction between person-inflection use of loci and spatial use
of loci in the signing space (Poizner, Klima, and Bellugi 1987). Engberg-
Pederson argues for a category of subsystems that share overlapping
properties but cannot be treated completely alike, rather than the binary
split of spatial versus grammatical. Figure 1.11 illustrates a typical verb
of the spatial agreement class (DRIVE-TO); figure 1.12, a typical verb of
the person agreement class (HELP). Comparison of figure 1.12 and figure
1.13 shows the difference in direction of the path movement between a

Figure 1.13
REQUEST is considered a "backward" agreement verb, in which the initial and final loci refer to grammatical object and subject, respectively.

verb (HELP) exhibiting typical (or forward) agreement and a verb (REQUEST) exhibiting backward agreement (Padden 1983; Kegl 1985; Brentari 1988; Meir 1995). Sentences exemplifying these types of verbs are given in (5)–(7). A case where the spatial and person systems of reference are mixed is shown in (8); here, the locus at the end of GO-TO is the same as the locus at the end of HELP, even though in the first case it expresses spatial agreement, and in the second case it expresses person agreement.

(5) *Spatial agreement verb*

a. *No spatial agreement loci*

$\emptyset$ $_0$DRIVE-TO-$_0$
'I drive.' (I drive (i.e., rather than walk, bike, or take the bus).)

b. *Final spatial locus only*

$\emptyset$ $_0$DRIVE-TO$_a$, DROP-OFF KIDS, SHOW-UP$_c$ WORK 9:30.
'I drive there, drop off the kids, then show up for work at 9:30 a.m.'

(6) *Person agreement verb*

a. *Subject and object agreement loci*

INDEX$_1$ $_1$HELP$_3$ J-O-H-N INDEX$_3$.
'I help John.'

b. *Subject and object agreement loci*

INDEX$_2$ $_2$HELP$_1$.
'You help me.'

c. *Object agreement locus only*

INDEX$_3$ J-O-H-N $_0$HELP$_4$ INDEX$_4$ M-A-R-Y.
'John helps Mary.'

(7) *Contrast between "forward" and "backward" verb agreement*

a. *Subject and object agreement loci*

J-O-H-N INDEX$_3$ $_3$HELP$_4$ INDEX$_4$ M-A-R-Y. (typical class)
'John helps Mary.'

b. *Object agreement locus only*

J-O-H-N INDEX$_3$ $_4$REQUEST$_0$ M-A-R-Y INDEX$_4$. (backward class)
'John requested [it of] Mary.'

(8) *Mixed spatial and person agreement*

INDEX$_1$ $_3$REQUEST$_0$ J-O-H-N, "WHERE GO?" INDEX$_3$ SAY, "GO-TO$_a$ M-A-R-Y HER$_a$ HOME. PROMISE $_0$HELP$_a$."
'I ask[ed] John, "Where are you going?" He said, "To Mary's house. I promised I'd help her."'

The phonological representations of such forms, and their impact on a feature system for ASL, are issues addressed by the Prosodic Model. In my earlier work, forms such as HELP, REQUEST, and DRIVE-TO are used to argue for a feature [direction] in the underlying representation of such signs.

1.2.6 Polymorphemic Forms: Compounds

Compounds in ASL are limited to two stems. Specifying the grammatical class of the input stems of the compound is problematic because, as Supalla and Newport (1978) have argued for noun-verb pairs, the underlying structure may not be specified for class (in Supalla and Newport's case, it may not be specified as either a noun or a verb), but is assigned the appropriate class by the morphology or syntax. Distinguishing between verbs and adjectives is also difficult in ASL, since almost all adjectives may appear as syntactic predicates with no change in phonological structure. Examples of compounds appear in the table that follows; the compound operation for THINK^SELF 'decide for oneself' is shown in figure 1.14. There are monosyllabic forms and disyllabic compounds, using the syllable-counting criteria listed in (1).

Examples of ASL compounds (V = verb; N = noun; A = adjective) (examples from Svaib 1992)

Stem order	Examples	Grammatical category after compounding
VN	SLEEP^DRESS 'nightgown'	noun
	THINK^SELF 'decide for oneself'	sentence
NV	WATER^RISE 'flood'	noun
	GIRL^MARRY 'wife'	noun
VV	THINK^FREEZE 'faint'	predicate
VA	NAME^SHINE[9] 'good reputation'	noun
AV	NUDE^ZOOM 'streak'	noun
AA	GOOD^ENOUGH 'barely adequate'	predicate
AN	BLUE^SPOT 'bruise'	noun/adjective
	YELLOW^HAIR 'blond'	noun/adjective
NA	FACE^STRONG 'resemblance'	noun
NN	GIRL^WEDDING 'bride'	noun

Several segmental analyses of compounding have been proposed (Liddell and Johnson 1986; Sandler 1987b, 1989, 1993c); in chapter 5 I will add a paradigmatic component—one that I have previously sketched in Brentari 1990d, 1993—to the traditional analysis of compounding.

1.2.7 Polymorphemic Forms: Grammatical Aspect

ASL has a complex system of grammatical aspect and very little grammatical tense morphology (although some has been reported (Jacobowitz and Stokoe 1988; Aarons et al. 1995); also, auxiliary verbs have been described in Taiwanese Sign Language (Smith 1990)). The system of grammatical aspect in ASL encodes descriptions of both the temporal unfolding of an event and the distributional properties of the objects and persons involved in the event. Examples of the distributional and temporal aspects described in the literature are given in the table that follows. Klima and Bellugi 1979 remains the most comprehensive discussion of aspect; other

Figure 1.14
THINK (top left) and SELF (top right) are shown as single words and in the compound THINK^SELF (bottom).

work includes Liddell 1984b, Wilbur, Klima, and Bellugi 1983, Sandler 1990, and Brentari 1996b.

Examples of temporal and distributional aspect categories in ASL

Temporal	Distributional
protractive (Liddell 1990b)	multiple (Klima and Bellugi 1979)
unrealized-inceptive (Liddell 1984b)	exhaustive (Klima and Bellugi 1979)
delayed-completive (Brentari 1996b)	internal apportionative (Klima and Bellugi 1979)
habitual (Klima and Bellugi 1979)	
durative (Klima and Bellugi 1979)	external apportionative (Klima and Bellugi 1979)

Figure 1.15
A polymorphemic form in ASL, which means 'two, hunched, upright-beings, facing forward, go forward, carefully, side-by-side, from point "a," to point "b"'

These categories provide fertile ground for paradigmatic and syntagmatic morphophonemic alternation, and they are used as evidence to support various analyses throughout the literature (e.g., Sandler 1993c; Brentari 1990c, 1992, 1993). Each category mentioned in the table has its own particular phonological shape, and these will be discussed when relevant for a particular analysis in later chapters.

1.2.8 Polymorphemic Forms: Classifier Predicates

In the part of the ASL lexicon known as "verbs of motion and location" (Supalla 1982, 1985, 1990), words are constructed of many morphemes, each morpheme often consisting of a single feature or cluster of features.[10] What is remarkable about these forms is that they may also be monosyllabic. The ASL word in figure 1.15 contains nine morphemes and one syllable. It means 'two, hunched, upright-beings, facing forward, go forward, carefully, side-by-side, from point "a" to point "b"'. These forms have been discussed in some depth from a morphological point of view (Supalla 1982, 1985, 1990; Wallin 1994; McDonald 1982; Kegl 1985; Schick 1990), but little has been written about constraints on their phonological structure. They are syntactically verb phrases or sentences. Constraints that are unviolated in other parts of the native lexicon are relaxed in these forms; for example, the H_2 restriction on handshape does not apply to classifier forms. I consider these forms in this book because any phonological model proposed for sign languages must show the potential of being expanded to include them.

1.3   Overview of the Prosodic Model

The goal of the Prosodic Model is to integrate into one model the insights
about systematicity in paradigmatic structure and syntagmatic structure
in sign. This work was initiated by Stokoe (1960) and Klima and Bellugi
(1979). Specifically, the model articulates a set of constraints in ASL that
must refer to paradigmatic structure and complexity: co-occurrence pro-
hibitions among features, redundancies among co-occurring features, and
so on. Sign languages do not require different units of analysis or different
kinds of constraints than do spoken languages; indeed, this model does
not propose units or types of constraints that are unattested in spoken
languages. What is claimed, however, is that ASL exploits paradigmatic
constraints in a greater range of phenomena than do spoken languages.
To take one example, it has been argued that H_2 is a weak branch of
prosodic structure similar to a coda or a word-level appendix in spoken
languages (Brentari and Goldsmith 1993). In ASL, however, this constituent is expressed simultaneously with the core syllable rather than
sequentially as it is expressed in spoken languages.

In this section I will sketch the guiding principles and general claims
of the model and give five central arguments for conceptualizing ASL
phonological structure this way. The Prosodic Model makes a fundamental distinction between *prosodic features* and *inherent features*.

(9)   *Definition of* inherent features

   Inherent features are those properties of signs in the core lexicon
   that are specified once per lexeme and do not change during the
   lexeme's production (e.g., selected fingers, major body place).

(10)   *Definition of* prosodic features

   Prosodic features are those properties of signs in the core lexicon
   that can change or are realized as dynamic properties of the signal
   (e.g., aperture, setting).

As will become clear, for many reasons inherent features and prosodic
features should be separate branches of structure. There is a systematic
many-to-one relation between prosodic and inherent features; inherent
features have more complex hierarchical structure than do prosodic features; inherent features are realized simultaneously, whereas prosodic
features are realized sequentially.

This conceptual division draws on the distinction between inherent and prosodic features made by Jakobson, Fant, and Halle (1972 [1951], 13):

The opposition grave vs. acute, compact vs. diffuse, or voiced vs. unvoiced, and any other opposition of inherent distinctive features appears within a definite sequence of phonemes but is, nevertheless, definable without any reference to the sequence. *No comparison of two points in a time series is involved* [emphasis mine]. Prosodic features, on the other hand, can be defined only with reference to a time series.

As examples of prosodic features, Jakobson, Fant, and Halle note that in Old Czech the feature [syllabic] is contrastive in the pair /br̥du/ versus /brdu/, and that in Polish [length] is contrastive in vowels (e.g., /prava:/ vs. /pra:va/). In both examples it is clear that these features differ from features, such as [voice] and [nasal], that can be identified within a single segment by their articulatory or acoustic correlates. [Syllabic] and [length] must be placed in a context where their properties can be measured with respect to other segments in the local domain. In current theories the properties of length and syllabicity are aspects of segmental or syllabic structure rather than features; but my point here focuses on how these two types of contrast differ from one another.

Although the distinction between inherent and prosodic features used here draws most directly on the basic distinction made by Jakobson, Fant, and Halle (1972 [1951]), the term *prosody* or *prosodic* has had several somewhat overlapping uses in linguistics, and a discussion of some of these may be helpful here. Firth (1957) uses the term *prosody* to describe phonological properties that extend beyond the segmental unit to the syllable; examples include tone melodies in tone languages and register in Mon Khmer languages. This Firthian type of prosodic unit is developed by Haugen (1949), who expands on ideas in Firth's unpublished work of the 1930s. Haugen uses the term *prosodeme* as a variant of Jakobson, Fant, and Halle's *prosodic phoneme* to describe alternations in speech sounds involving tone, stress, and duration. Autosegmental phonology (Goldsmith 1976) has developed in contemporary theory a formal way of expressing the relative independence of such properties as tone, stress, and duration in phonological representations. McCarthy and Prince (1986), Itô (1986), Selkirk (1984), Selkirk and Tateishi (1988), and Nespor and Vogel (1986) use the term *prosodic structure* to talk about canonical shapes of the syllable, prosodic word, prosodic phrase, and so on, which interact with other components of the grammar and with each other.

The goal of the Prosodic Model is to develop this line of inquiry for sign languages.[11]

Properties from these works that are important in the Prosodic Model are listed in (11).

(11) *Properties of prosodies, such as "tonal melodies"*

   a. Prosodies are timed with respect to units larger than the segment.

   b. Prosodies have a restricted set of abstract patterns.

   c. Prosodies have autosegmental status.

   d. Prosodies can carry lexical contrast.

In tone languages, tonal prosodies are often called tonal melodies, and tone patterns within stems are often drawn from a restricted set. Venda, for example, exhibits a wide range of surface tone patterns, arising from a small set of underlying primitive tone patterns: (L), H, (L)-H, H-(L)-H, and H-(L). (Low tones are not specified underlyingly.)

"Tonal melody" inventories for Venda stems (Cassimjee 1983)

Underlying representations		Surface forms	
		(Post L-tone)	(Post H-tone)
thamaha	L	thamaha	thámâha
madzhi	H	mádzhîe	mádzhie
danana	LHL	danána	dánâna
khokhola	HLH	khókhôla	khókholá
phaphana	LHH	phapháná	pháphâna
dukana	LLH	dukaná	dúkâná
dakalo	HHL	dákálo	dákalo

In itself this is unremarkable, since distinctive features do the same thing. But Goldsmith (1976) has convincingly shown that tone is not just another set of distinctive features, but maintains a type of autonomy and stability within the system, since a restricted inventory of abstract patterns is involved. This autonomy is expressed by placing tone on a separate autosegmental tier, which allows a much more explanatory account of tonal phenomena than was previously possible. In the Prosodic Model, movement is claimed to behave in ways strikingly similar to the way that tones behave in Venda.

The arguments for placing all movement features on a separate branch of structure in ASL will take the form shown in (12). All movement features share the same behavior with respect to these characteristics.

(12) *Arguments for placing movement features on a separate branch of structure are based on*

   a. the timing of movement features within and between words,

   b. the ability of movement features to "migrate" by means of phonetic proximalization or distalization,

   c. the distribution of prosodic-to-inherent features,

   d. the distribution of disyllabic movement patterns,

   e. the mutual exclusivity of inherent features and prosodic features (movement features).

Regarding timing evidence: the specific temporal relationship among parallel aspects of lexical movement makes it clear that they are linked to timing units and that they are linked to these timing units in similar ways, distinct from those aspects of handshape, orientation, and location that are not part of the movement parameter. Regarding the ability of movement features to "migrate": phonetic arguments will show that underlying movement melodies are executed on the surface by a "default joint" in the absence of any impetus to the contrary, or by another joint by means of "translation statements" that allow a movement to spread or be displaced to a joint more proximal to the body or to a more distal joint of the arm or hand. This reinforces the position that abstract properties of movement are realized in a variety of phonetic forms. Regarding distribution of prosodic-to-inherent features: I will argue that handshape, orientation, and place of articulation each contain prosodic features—properties that change throughout the articulation of a lexeme—and inherent features that do not change. This division has been demonstrated convincingly with respect to handshape and can be extended to place of articulation and orientation. Regarding distribution of disyllabic movement patterns: the prosodic features in disyllabic forms (i.e., signs with two-movement sequences) that are executed by handshape change, location change, and orientation change can be shown to come from the same set of combinatoric possibilities. Thus, movement prosodies span all of the traditional parameters, and the argument supports grouping handshape changes, orientation changes, and location changes together. Regarding the argument that the inherent and prosodic features constitute mutually exclusive sets, with the exception of [ipsilateral] and [contralateral] no feature of the model appears in both the inherent and the prosodic branches of structure. The structure that I will propose is shown in (13).

(13) *Overall structure of inherent and prosodic features in ASL*

    a. *Feature organization*

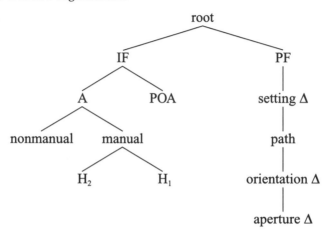

    b. *Parameters in the model*

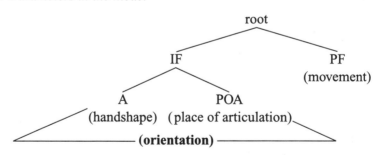

New aspects of the model since Brentari 1990c include an explicit proposal for a feature tree, an explicit proposal for segmental structure, and a more explicit definition of sonority and how it works in ASL phonology. In earlier work I divided the phonological grammar into three levels of structure: the M(orphological) Level, which contained the underlying structure and the sonority hierarchy; the W(ord) Level, which contained the syllable template and constraints on distinctive features; and the P(honetic) Level, which added redundant features to strings and expressed constraints dealing with timing units. Here I have abandoned this division

Figure 1.16
FALSE

into levels, because the structural units themselves and constraints among them can achieve the necessary contrasts and perform the operations to construct the phonological grammar.[12] The structure for FALSE (figure 1.16) argued for in this book is given in (14).

(14) *Prosodic Model representation of FALSE*

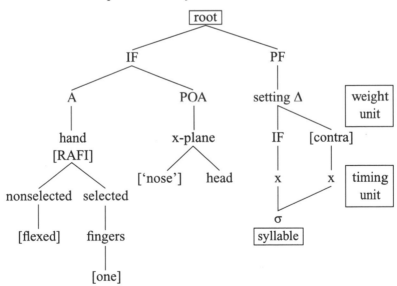

In the Prosodic Model, sonority will be defined phonetically both perceptually and articulatorily. Perceptually, it is defined as the property that enhances the ability of a property of a sign to be perceived at greater distances; in this regard, perceiving a property of a sign, discriminating it from other similar properties, and identifying it are taken to be separate operations in the act of comprehension. Articulatorily, sonority is defined and measured on the basis of the joint(s) used to articulate a single movement. The specific claim that the Prosodic Model makes about sonority is that it is expressed differently in sign languages than in spoken languages, but that in both cases it involves perceptual salience. The formal difference between sonority in spoken languages and sonority in sign languages is that in the former sonority can be calculated from the presence of a single feature, which is an inherent property of the sound in question, whereas in the latter it must be calculated from the difference between two prosodic features in a sequence. Furthermore, sonority in sign languages is subsumed under the notion of phonological complexity. Phonological complexity, described in Dependency Phonology (Anderson and Ewen 1987; Dresher and van der Hulst 1994), is based on the number and type of branching structures contained in a given form. This notion captures a grammatical preference for economy of structure in grammars, and also allows for a grammar to distinguish between structures of greater or lesser complexity. For example, stress phenomena in spoken languages often co-occur with the most complex unit at a specific level of structure (i.e., foot or syllable structure); therefore, it becomes important for a grammar to make such complexity distinctions.

The Prosodic Model also makes an explicit proposal regarding segmental structure, defining segments as the minimal concatenative units of the system. As in earlier versions of the model, a mora fulfills the minimal requirement for a well-formed syllable, and moras are weight units that may occur simultaneously with one other. One advance of the current version is to show how moras and segments interact with one another and how they play a role in constraining phonological outputs.

1.3.1 Support for a Unified Group of Movement Features: Timing Evidence

The first argument in (12) is based on the timing of handshape change, orientation change, location change, and path movements within words, and how it aids in independently establishing the binary branching structure of movement features (or prosodic features) and inherent features.

In studies focusing on a measure called the *handshape change duration/ movement duration ratio* (abbreviated HSΔ/Mov ratio), Brentari and

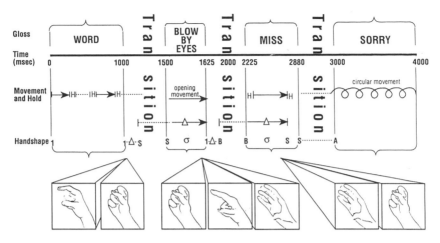

Figure 1.17
Temporal relations of WORD BLOW-BY-EYES MISS SORRY (from Brentari, Poizner, and Kegl 1995)

Poizner (1994) and Brentari, Poizner, and Kegl (1995) found an interesting type of systematicity in all prosodic features. The HSΔ/Mov ratio measure is the amount of time a subject takes to execute a given handshape change simultaneously with a given movement. Consider the example in figure 1.17. In the ASL sentence WORD BLOW-BY-EYES MISS SORRY 'The word went by too quickly. I missed it, sorry', the handshape remains the same throughout the signs WORD and SORRY; that is, there is no word-internal handshape change. There is a word-internal handshape change in the signs BLOW-BY-EYES and MISS. Between WORD and BLOW-BY-EYES and between BLOW-BY-EYES and MISS there is also a handshape change, but it is a transitional one between signs. In frame-by-frame analysis of recorded, spontaneous signing and elicited signed sentences by signers with Parkinson's disease and by age-matched controls, we found that in the productions of control signers the HSΔ/Mov ratio is very high word-internally and very low between words. Examination of the first and second handshape changes reveals this difference. Between WORD and BLOW-BY-EYES the handshape change takes only a small portion of the time that the movement takes and is not temporally linked to the beginning and end of the movement (i.e., a low HSΔ/Mov ratio—approximately 40%); the word-internal handshape change in BLOW-BY-EYES occurs simultaneously with the movement and is temporally linked with the beginning and end of the movement (i.e., a high HSΔ/Mov ratio—approximately 100%). Further measures of orientation changes reveal the same co-temporal relationship.

The systematic coupling and decoupling of handshape changes and movements has an important theoretical implication: namely, it constitutes evidence that the representation of word-internal movements includes timing units. In purposeful nonlinguistic gesture, the joints are systematically coordinated but not necessarily co-temporally so (Poizner et al. 1990; Poizner 1990).[13] Because ASL is a system of purposeful gestures, coordination between local and path movements (Sainburg et al. 1995), but not co-temporal linking, would be expected here as well. The crucial point is that syllable-internal movement components within ASL words are unexpectedly co-temporal when contrasted with nonlinguistic complex movements of the same type. The features grouped together as prosodic features in the model are all temporally linked in the same manner with units on the timing tier. This is support for grouping these features together in the phonological representation, and it is an important step in establishing the fact that changing features are alike in the way they behave toward timing units.

1.3.2 Support for a Unified Group of Movement Features: Distalization and Proximalization of Movement

The next argument in (12) is that abstract movement categories govern the production of movement and therefore should be dominated by a single node in the feature tree. Movements are phonetically realized by "default joints" that execute handshape changes (i.e., finger joints), orientation changes (i.e., wrist and forearm), path features (i.e., elbow), and setting changes (i.e., shoulder). However, a sign is often executed by joints in addition to those specified by its default joint by a process of movement spread, or by joints other than those that execute it in the default case. The table that follows lists five signs, each with three variants: a *citation form*, a *reduced* (or *distalized*) *form*, and an *enhanced* (or *proximalized*) *form*.[14] (Distal joints are smaller joints, closer to the extremities; proximal joints are larger joints, closer to the torso.) Figure 1.18 shows two versions of the one-handed form of TAKE, a sign with a path movement and a handshape change: the citation form, using the default joints, and the reduced form, in which the movement has been distalized from the elbow to the wrist.

Figure 1.18
The citation form of TAKE (left), which is a sign with a path movement and a handshape change, and the reduced form of TAKE (right), with a handshape change and a movement that has been distalized from the elbow to the wrist

Examples of signs with movements executed by their default joints and by atypical joints

	Default joint(s)	Reduced form ("distalized form")	Enhanced form ("proximalized form")
REFER	wrist	knuckles	+elbow
SEND	fingers/elbow	fingers/wrist	∣shoulder
TAKE	fingers/elbow	fingers/wrist	+shoulder
ASK	fingers/elbow	fingers/wrist	+shoulder
GIVE	fingers/elbow	fingers/wrist	+shoulder

The next few paragraphs discuss the anatomical and physiological underpinnings of proximalization and distalization. Figure 1.19 (left) shows the *fundamental standing position* (hands at sides, palms in). The Prosodic Model defines the *fundamental signing position* as shown in figure 1.19 (right); it consists of the fundamental standing position, with the addition that the elbows are flexed.[15] In figure 1.20 the three dimensions and planes in which movements are executed are shown with respect to the body: the x dimension projecting forward from the body, the y dimension projecting vertically from the top of the head, and the z dimension projecting from the sides (Luttgens and Hamilton 1997, 38). Since a plane can be defined by the dimension running perpendicular to it, the planes shown in figure 1.20 are described as the frontal (i.e., x-) plane, the transverse (i.e., horizontal, y-) plane, and the midsagittal (i.e., z-) plane; these are the terms I will later use in referring to planes of articulation. In the table that follows I list the joints of the arm and hand (omitting the thumb joints, because they do not bear on this discussion). Figures 1.21–1.23 illustrate the movement types based on the various joint possibilities.[16]

Articulatory correlates—joint capabilities

Common name	Anatomical name	Type of joint	Degrees of freedom	Utilization in ASL movement types
shoulder	glenohumeral	ball & socket	3-axial	(path movement)
elbow	humeroulnar	hinge	1-axial	(path movement)
	humeroradial	ball & socket	3-axial	(path movement)
forearm	prox. radioulnar	pivot	1-axial	(orientation Δ)
	distal radioulnar	pivot	1-axial	(orientation Δ)
wrist	radiocarpal	ovoid	2-axial	(orientation Δ)
fingers	metacarpophalangeal	ovoid	2-axial	(handshape Δ)
	prox. interphalangeal	hinge	1-axial	(handshape Δ)
	distal interphalangeal	hinge	1-axial	(handshape Δ)

The names and types of joints are of more anatomical and physiological interest than phonological interest. What is of phonological interest is that movements of signs can be executed in similar manners by a number of joints of the hand and arm. One example is that the fingers, wrist, elbow, and shoulder all allow vertical flexing movements; therefore, given a particular palm orientation, these joints can execute many phonetic variants of direction-of-movement features. Another example is that any of the following combinations of joint movements result in a circular movement: abduction/adduction and flexion/extension of the fingers, flexion/extension of the wrist and rotation of the forearm, flexion/extension and abduction/adduction of the wrist, horizontal flexion/extension of the shoulder and vertical flexion of the elbow, flexion/extension and abduction/adduction of the shoulder.

In the case of phonetic enhancement, the movement spreads from the default joint to a more proximal joint; in the case of phonetic reduction, movement migrates to a more distal one. The spread of joint extension

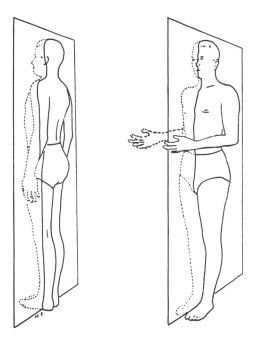

Figure 1.19
The fundamental standing position (left), with hands at sides and palms oriented
inward toward the midsagittal plane. In the fundamental signing position (right),
the elbows are flexed, and the three dimensions and planes in which movements
are executed with respect to the body are taken into consideration. (Based on
Luttgens and Hamilton 1997, 38, fig. 2.8; by permission.)

from wrist to elbow is an effect that cannot be easily captured if orientation and path movement are in separate portions of the representation, as
they are in other current models of sign phonology. In the models proposed by Sandler (1989), Wilbur (1993), and Uyechi (1995), changes in
handshape, orientation, and place of articulation are represented in separate places. In the Prosodic Model this type of enhancement or reduction can be straightforwardly handled by adding an association line within
the prosodic branch of structure, since orientation and path movements
are dominated by a single node in the representation. Furthermore, abstract features of movement such as [direction] and [tracing] show the common basis of movement classes, regardless of whether they are articulated
by the shoulder, elbow, wrist, or hand joints.

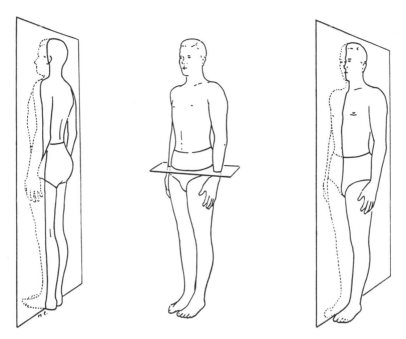

Figure 1.20
The planes of articulation are described as the ventral (i.e., frontal, x-) plane (left),
the transverse (i.e., horizontal, y-) plane (middle), and the midsagittal (i.e., z-)
plane (right) (from Luttgens and Hamilton 1997, 38; by permission).

1.3.3 Support for a Unified Group of Movement Features: Many-to-One Relation in the Core Lexicon

The third argument in (12) is that all four parameters of sign languages
—handshape, orientation, location, and movement—exhibit a many-to-
one autosegmental relationship between prosodic features and inherent
features based on their distribution. The various representations proposed
for sign languages (see (15)–(21)) suggest generalizations about the way
features have been grouped. (The details of these models will be explained as needed later; at this point only the number of parameters
represented and the relations among the tiers of features are important.)
In the models proposed by Stack (1988), Uyechi (1995), and van der
Hulst (1996)—(15)–(17)—handshape, orientation, and location are the
only parameters, and these are dominated by the root node of the feature
tree. In the models proposed by Ahn (1990), Wilbur (1993), and Liddell
and Johnson (1989)—(18)–(20)—movement or manner of movement is

on a separate tier from handshape, orientation, and location, but movement in these models is defined as path movement only, and local movements are dominated by the place, handshape, and orientation class nodes. The Hand Tier Model proposed by Sandler (1989), a schema of which is given in (21), separates handshape and orientation from movement and location. Sandler argues that hand configuration features form a unified group and should be separate from location and movement features, and that location and movement features form the bases of segmental structure.

(15) *Model of feature organization proposed in Stack 1988*
 (HS, O, L//∅)

 FALSE

 LOC [nose, ipsi] [nose, contra]
 PO [to nose]
 HC [1, open]

(16) *Model of feature organization proposed in Uyechi 1995*
 (HS, O, L//∅)

 FALSE

$$
\text{LSS in GSS} \begin{bmatrix} \text{Loc: } [+\text{base-LSS:nose-GSS}] \\ \text{Or: } [\text{``anchored (default)''}] \\ \begin{bmatrix} \text{HP Loc} \\ \text{in} \quad [\text{base-HP:}+\text{base } [+\text{center}]] \\ \text{LSS Or} \quad \begin{bmatrix} \text{front-HP:contra side-LSS} \\ \text{top-HP:}+\text{local-LSS} \end{bmatrix} \begin{bmatrix} \text{front-HP:local-LSS} \\ \text{top-HP:contra side-LSS} \end{bmatrix} \\ \text{HP} \begin{bmatrix} \text{Or} \\ \begin{bmatrix} \text{palm:front-HP} \\ \text{fingertips:top-HP} \end{bmatrix} \\ \text{HS} \begin{bmatrix} +\text{SEL } [\text{I:open}] \\ -\text{SEL } [\text{TMRP:closed}] \\ \text{THUMB } [+\text{opposed}] \end{bmatrix} \end{bmatrix} \end{bmatrix} \end{bmatrix}
$$

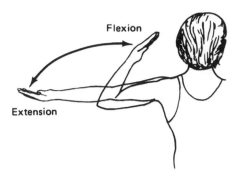

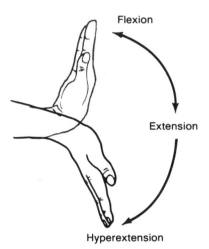

Figure 1.21
Movement types and possible joints of execution: vertical or horizontal extension
or flexion (from Luttgens and Hamilton 1997, 142, 153, 158; by permission)

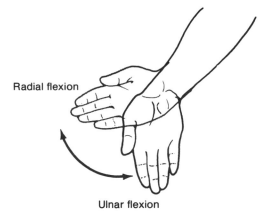

Radial flexion

Ulnar flexion

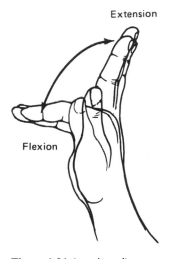

Extension

Flexion

Figure 1.21 (continued)

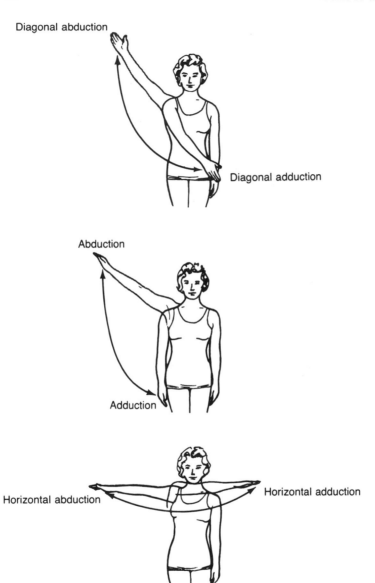

Figure 1.22
Movement types and possible joints of execution: abduction or adduction (from
Luttgens and Hamilton 1997, 116, 158; by permission)

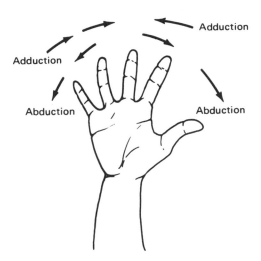

Figure 1.22 (continued)

(17) *Model of feature organization proposed in van der Hulst 1996*
    (HS, O, L||∅)

   FALSE

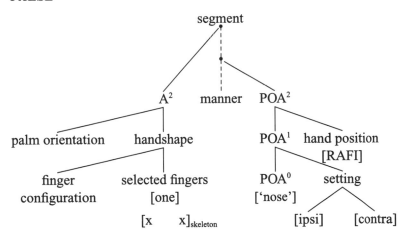

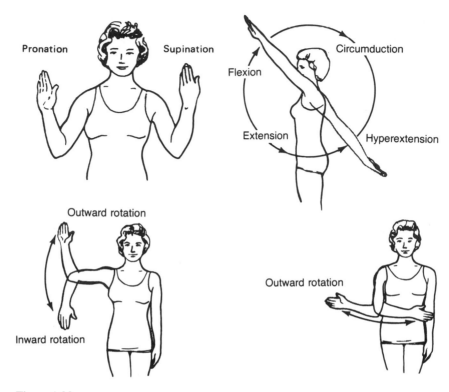

Figure 1.23
Movement types and possible joints of execution: rotating movement (from
Luttgens and Hamilton 1997, 116, 142; by permission)

(18) *Schematic model of feature organization proposed in Ahn 1990*
      (HS, O, L|| Manner)

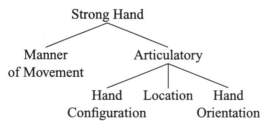

(19) *Schematic model of feature organization proposed in Wilbur 1993*
(HS, O, L||Manner)

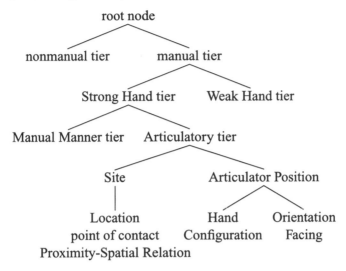

(20) *Model of feature organization proposed in Liddell and Johnson 1989*
(HS, O, L||M)

FALSE

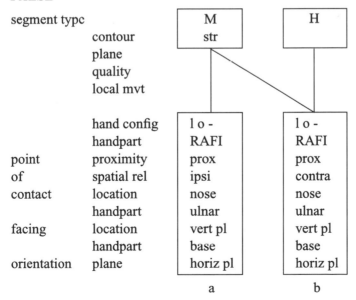

(21) *Model of feature organization proposed in Sandler 1989*
      (HS, O||L, M)

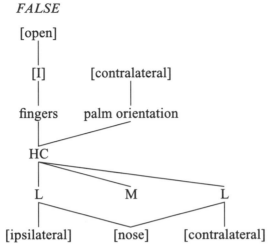

Within the hand configuration tier, following insights by Mandel (1981) and Stokoe (1960), Sandler argues that "selected fingers" should be separated in the representation from "position" ("aperture" in the Prosodic Model). She bases her argument on the distribution of the two types of features in monomorphemic signs, such as those in (22) (see figure 1.3 for photograph of THROW): signs of this class use just one set of selected fingers but may exhibit more than one position.

(22) *Signs with two aperture features and one set of selected fingers*

THROW	closed 'H' → open 'H'
ASK	open '1' → curved '1'
INFORM	flat 'B' → open 'B'

The same argument concerning the division of labor between selected fingers and position can be extended to major body place ("place" in the Prosodic Model) and major body position ("setting" in the Prosodic Model). Features of place and setting are distributed in monomorphemic signs in the same way as selected fingers and aperture. There is typically only one place of articulation, even though the setting within that place may change. Example signs are given in (23); figure 1.24 illustrates the sign DEAF. Sandler (1987a) analyzes this phenomenon as place harmony, rather than proposing a unified analysis for handshape and loca-

Figure 1.24
DEAF

tion, even though in her representation of location, major body place and setting are on separate tiers dominated by the Location feature tree, just as position (i.e., aperture) and selected fingers are dominated by the hand configuration node.

(23) *Signs with two setting features and one place*

FLOWER	contra ['nose'] → ipsi ['nose']
BODY	top ['torso'] → bottom ['torso']
DEAF	top ['cheek'] → bottom ['cheek']

The next step is to extend the notion of the division of labor between inherent and prosodic features within sign handshape and location to the orientation parameter. As Crasborn (1995) makes clear in his description of joint movement, the orientation parameter is quite complex to represent, because the joints in the forearm are responsible for prone/supine rotation, and the wrist is responsible for both vertical and horizontal extension/flexion and abduction/adduction. Although all three movements are physiologically possible, for any given lexeme at least one and more often two of them remain constant, and if two movements involving orientation change within a sign, they change in sequence rather than in parallel. Examples are given in (24); figure 1.25 illustrates the use of each type of orientation change in the signs REBEL, INSULT, and YES.

Figure 1.25
Possible types of movements involving changes in orientation. In REBEL (top
left), the movement involves pronation of the forearm, an orientation change from
[supination] to [pronation]; in INSULT (top right), the movement involves radial
flexion (or [abduction]); in YES (bottom), the movement involves [flexion] of the
wrist.

(24) *Signs with an orientation change*

HAPPEN, REBEL: supination → pronation (IF → [pronation])
    no side-to-side or vertical movement
INSULT, ALL RIGHT: adduction → abduction
(IF → [abduction])
    no vertical movement or rotation
YES, FIGHT: extension → flexion (IF → [flexion])
    no side-to-side movement or rotation

In HAPPEN and REBEL, there is no side-to-side or vertical movement, only rotation; in INSULT and ALL RIGHT, there is no vertical movement or rotation, only radial flexion (or abduction); in YES and FIGHT, there is no side-to-side movement or rotation, only vertical flexion. These facts can be captured as shown in (25) by allowing the types of movement possible with the forearm and wrist to be expressed as features dominated by the prosodic feature branch of structure; the constant properties are captured by features dominated by the inherent feature branch. By employing a two-part relation between the relevant handpart of a given handshape and the major body place of articulation, the Prosodic Model account stabilizes the relevant aspects of inherent orientation. This is all that is necessary to capture the constant properties of orientation. The details of this analysis are given in chapter 3.

(25) *Representation of inherent and prosodic aspects of orientation*

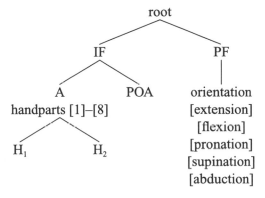

That orientation should be treated as a relation between two aspects of phonological structure has been proposed by Liddell and Johnson (1989), Uyechi (1995), and Crasborn and van der Kooij (1997). In the Hand Tier Model, Sandler (1989) proposes the use of features, but these are not sufficient to capture orientation because they are based on palm orientation alone; this creates ambiguities in the lexicon. Consider forms like OLD, LOVE-SOMETHING (i.e., 'kiss'), and CHERISH. The place of articulation is the chin, and if the handparts are specified with respect to it, only one feature is needed to capture the contrastive orientation of the hand: radial for OLD, back of palm for LOVE-SOMETHING, and back of fingers for CHERISH. The eight places on the hand used to specify underlying orientation (figure 1.26) are the same eight places on the hand

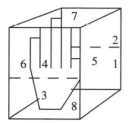

Figure 1.26
Schema of places on H_2

that are needed to express the places of contact on H_2 in type 3 two-handed signs.

Hand places[17]

	Role in two-handed signs	Role in underlying orientation
[1] Palm of hand	LEARN	MY
[2] Finger fronts	DISMISS	LABEL
[3] Back of palm	TOUCH	LOVE-SOMETHING
[4] Back of fingers	EASY	CHERISH
[5] Radial side of selected fingers	WOOD	OLD
[6] Ulnar side of selected fingers	TICKET	BROKE (i.e., 'no money')
[7] Tip of selected fingers/thumb	TOP	COMPLAIN
[8] Heel of hand	CHEESE	SLIP

1.3.4 Support for a Unified Group of Movement Features: Movement Sequences in Disyllabic Signs

The fourth argument in (12) in favor of analyzing movements as prosodies is that disyllabic signs contain the same limited set of movement sequences, regardless of whether they are path, handshape change, orientation change, or location change movements. This unified distributional behavior further supports placing all movements in a single phonological group, rather than having movements of separate phonological parameters in different branches of structure. ASL contains a reasonably large number of disyllabic signs, but these signs exhibit relatively few permissible combinations of movement types, just as tonal languages exhibit a relatively small set of tonal melodies. The following table lists ten different types of movement, along with the ways in which movement types are expressed in path movement (or location change), handshape change, and orientation change. Possible monosyllabic movements as well as disyllabic sequences are included. Signs showing the realization of one two-movement sequence ([O], [—]) are given in figure 1.27.

Abstract movement types and their expression

	Path (location Δ)	Handshape Δ	Orientation Δ
1-movement types			
straight: from [‖>]	TELL	WAKE-UP	OPEN
straight: to [<‖]	SIT	SAY-NO	CLOSE
tracing [—]	BLACK	****	LONG
circle [O]	YEAR	BEAUTY	ALL
2-movement sequences			
repeat	MILITARY	MELON	BETRAY
repeat: 90° '7'	DETROIT	REMOVE	****
repeat: 90° 'X'	CANCEL	****	HOSPITAL
repeat: set.ᵢ set.ⱼ	CHILDREN	NAVY	GO/RETURN HERE
repeat: 180° (bidirectional)	JUMP	WHITE (race)	COOK
alternating	BICYCLE	JESUS	COMPETITION
[O], [—]	WHEN	APPOINTMENT	LOCK

Among disyllabic signs, the widest range of movement sequences is found in path movements. Both handshape change and orientation change display a subset of the sequence types that path movements display. If handshape change, orientation change, and place-of-articulation change were functioning as independent branches of structure, we would expect to find a few places where these three different types of movement fail to overlap—but we don't. Some ill-formed combinations of handshape and orientation movement sequences are given in (26). Figure 1.28 shows an impossible monomorphemic lexeme combination, containing an ill-formed straight+circular movement.

(26) *Nonoccurring disyllabic sequences in monomorphemic words*

    a. *wrist extension of open 'B', followed by a closing 'B'

    b. *prone 'B' → supine 'B' → abducted 'B'

    c. *straight movement → circular movement

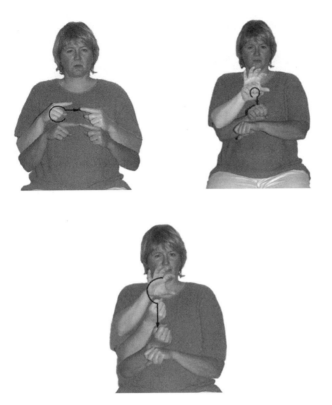

Figure 1.27
Signs showing realization of a two-movement, circular+straight combination
(i.e., [O] [—]) sequence. The circular movement is realized as a path movement
in WHEN (top left), as a handshape change in APPOINTMENT (top right), and
as an orientation change in LOCK (bottom).

The fact that orientation and handshape disyllabic sequences are proper
subsets of the set of path movement disyllabic sequences is evidence that
these sequences constitute one set of abstract phonological categories
that cut across these different sorts of realizations. On the basis of this
evidence, I conclude that the prosodic node of structure dominates all
features of this type.

1.3.5 Support for a Unified Group of Movement Features: Exclusivity of Feature Sets

The fifth argument in (12) for the binary split in structure between inherent and prosodic features is that the two sets of features are mutually ex-

Figure 1.28
An ill-formed two-movement, straight+circular sequence for monomorphemic signs. It occurs legitimately in the phrase $_2$GIVE$_1$, SORRY 'Give [it] to me, sorry'.

clusive, except for two features [ipsilateral] and [contralateral]. I list the members of each set in (27)–(28); I will justify and further define them in subsequent chapters.

(27) *Inherent features*

    a. *Articulatory features*

> [symmetrical]: analogous parts of the hand oriented toward each other (e.g., WITH, REQUEST, BICYCLE)
> [spread]: fingers contrastively spread (e.g., JAIL, FOOTBALL, WANT)
> [flexed]: fingers bent at specified joints (e.g., GIVE, WANT, SNAKE)
> [stacked]: fingers in a position, one above the other as in a "squash racket grip," with the index finger on top and pinkie finger on the bottom (e.g., FEW, 'K')
> [crossed]: fingers crossed middle over index (e.g., ROPE, CIGAR)
> [opposed]: thumb in a plane perpendicular to the palm
> [unopposed]: thumb in the same plane as the palm
> [all]: all fingers selected
> [one]: one finger selected
> [ulnar]: reference made to the pinkie side of the hand
> [mid]: reference made to the middle finger
> [extended]: nonselected fingers extended rather than flexed
> [2-handed]: sign articulated with two hands

b. *Place-of-articulation features*

[1]–[8]: vertical strips that divide the head, arm, or torso into eight regions, and H_2 into eight places
[ipsilateral] ([ipsi]): same side of the body as H_1
[contralateral] ([contra]): opposite side of the body from H_1
[contact]: contact with a place of articulation or between the two hands

(28) *Prosodic features*

[ipsilateral] ([ipsi]): same side of the body as H_1 within a place of articulation
[contralateral] ([contra]): opposite side of the body from H_1 within a place of articulation
[top]: the upper portion of a place of articulation
[bottom]: the lower portion of a place of articulation
[arc]: an arc movement shape
[distal]: a setting relatively far from the body within a y-plane or a z-plane
[proximal]: a setting relatively close to the body within a y-plane or a z-plane
[straight]: a (contrastive) straight movement shape
[circle]: a circular movement shape
[trilled movement]: an uncountably, rapidly repeated movement
[alternating]: a movement in two-handed signs in which the hands are 180° out of phase
[pivot]: a movement that maintains one fixed point around which the movement occurs
[repeat]: a movement that is repeated (e.g., MILITARY, COUGH)
[tracing]: a movement that takes place within a plane
[direction]: a movement that takes place perpendicular to a plane
[extension]: a movement extending the wrist
[flexion]: a movement flexing the wrist
[pronation]: a movement to a prone position of the palm
[supination]: a movement to a supine position of the palm
[abduction]: radial flexion of the wrist
[open]: a handshape change to an [open] allophonic handshape
[closed]: a handshape change to a [closed] allophonic handshape

The mutual exclusivity of feature sets in the Prosodic Model introduces several innovations. The first, which I adopt from van der Hulst 1995, separates the features specifying the joints [flexed] in underlying hand-shapes and the aperture settings [open] and [closed]. Previous work on handshape has conflated these two roles, but separating them achieves a more comprehensive account of underlying handshapes and a more pre-dictive account of handshape change (for more detail, see chapters 3 and 4). Second, in the parameter of orientation, the functions served by the inherent and prosodic features are strikingly different. As an inherent property, orientation is relational; it is a relation between a handpart and a place, and the only features that must be added to account for this are the specifications for the eight surfaces of the hand. Prosodic features of orientation are not relational; they specify absolute values such as [supi-nation], [pronation], [flexion], and [extension], which capture the way the wrist can move. Third, the feature [contact] is an inherent feature in the Prosodic Model. In previous work (Brentari 1988, 1990c) I have argued that [tracing] is a path feature that predicts continuous contact through-out a movement, whereas [direction] is a path feature that predicts contact at either the beginning of a path movement ([direction: |>]) or the end ([direction: >|]). Thus, [contact] no longer needs to be a property of both place of articulation and movement; instead, it can be seen as an inherent feature in a system in which its phonetic realization can be predicted on the basis of path features.

There are, however, two features that are both inherent and prosodic: [ipsilateral] and [contralateral]. There is at least one pair of signs for which [ipsilateral] and [contralateral] are contrastive—namely, PITTS-BURGH and LEATHER. These features function also as settings in a very productive way—FLOWER, CONGRESS, NAVY. Note also that [flexed] is an inherent feature of handshape, whereas [flexion] is a prosodic feature of orientation. Likewise, [extended] is an inherent feature of handshape, whereas [extension] is a prosodic feature of orientation. To date I have not been able to solve these problems, and I leave them for future research.

In sum, these five arguments justify only the initial split into inherent and prosodic features. In order for the model to work, the sub-branches forming the internal structure of each branch must be cohesive, and their relation to segmental and syllable structure must be spelled out. In later chapters I will make proposals in these regards. I will address the phono-logical function of each substructure, and in chapter 8 I will compare each with its spoken language counterpart, so that future research can reexamine the definition of these fundamental phonological units.

Chapter 2

The Use of Constraint-Based Frameworks and Prosodic Units in Analyses of Sign Languages

2.1 General Assumptions

In this chapter I will highlight the aspects of phonological theory that will be relevant for my analyses, and I will point out aspects of other researchers' work on sign language phonology that the Prosodic Model draws upon. First, however, I would like to explicitly state a few basic assumptions, since they are part of the specific tacit knowledge about the field that helps to shape the problems and analyses taken up here.

General assumptions
1. Lexical entries are determined by eliminating all possible redundancy due to grammatical operations; they should minimize abstract elements to the greatest extent possible (see Halle 1959; Chomsky and Halle 1968 (*SPE*), 12).[1]
2. A grammar should operate on the principles of simplicity and economy. It should contain the fewest number of constraints, and these constraints and the representations referred to in them should contain the fewest number of "marks" possible. The grammar should cover as many forms as possible with the fewest number of exceptions. Frequent operations should be easy to express; infrequent or nonoccurring operations should be difficult to express (see *SPE*, 330–335; Clements 1985).[2]
3. The phonological word is subject to all phonological operations, and morphological and phonological boundaries are visible to the phonology (see *SPE*, 371; Goldsmith 1989).[3]
4. Phonological words are constructed out of the underlying representations of their component morphemes in one step (*SPE*, 13; Goldsmith 1989).

5. Surface forms seek to meet the well-formedness conditions of the language to the greatest extent possible (Goldsmith 1989; Prince and Smolensky 1993; McCarthy and Prince 1993b).

6. Units of analysis can be uncovered by internal linguistic evidence (e.g., by finding minimal pairs and by observing the units referred to in phonological operations) and supported by external linguistic evidence (e.g, diachronic change, language acquisition, language breakdown).

Assumptions 1–2 are very general and have been accepted in the field at least since *SPE*. The seeds of assumptions 3–5 are found in *SPE*, but during the period dominated by Lexical Phonology, these ideas were reconfigured. For example, assumptions 3–4 express ideas about boundaries that have attracted renewed attention in constraint-based models, ideas that resonate more with their original formulation in *SPE*: that is, the boundaries themselves are always straightforwardly visible to the phonology rather than being visible only during a specific portion of the derivational process. In the analyses developed in this book, I will adopt the following principles and formalism specific to Optimality Theory:

Principles of Optimality Theory adopted in this book (from Prince and Smolensky 1993; McCarthy and Prince 1993b)

1. Each possible output candidate that is generated is evaluated for its well-formedness with respect to the ranked set of constraints.

2. Constraints on forms are ranked with respect to one another in a constraint tableau. This indicates the extent to which a constraint is violable (i.e., it exhibits surface exceptions).

3. Constraints are intended to be universal; hence, they are expressed in the most general possible terms rather than in language-particular ways.

4. The principle of *Local Constraint Conjunction* holds and is defined as follows: A and B are each ranked lower than constraint C (C≫A,B), and this no longer holds true when both A and B are violated. This allows A+B to be ranked higher than either A or B alone.[4]

Constraints in Optimality Theory should not look like language-particular rules, but instead they are instantiations of the more general families of phonological operations that are known to exist. In the Prosodic Model, two such constraint families are important for analyzing ASL: ALIGNMENT and FAITHFULNESS. The ALIGNMENT constraints align the edges of prosodic units, such as syllables, with morphological or morphosyntactic units, such as stems; they play a role in the analysis of fingerspelled borrowings in chapters 5–6. The FAITHFULNESS constraints require that the input should look like the output as much as possible. Features in the input should appear in the output; this is ensured by PARSE constraints (i.e., there should be no deletion). Features in the output should have a corresponding feature in the input; this is ensured by FILL constraints (i.e., there should be no epenthesis).[5] PARSE constraints play a role in the analysis of two-handed signs and fingerspelled forms. Local Constraint Conjunction is needed to account for the distribution of the optional operation of Weak Drop (Padden and Perlmutter 1987), in which a two-handed input surfaces as a one-handed output.

2.2 How Constraint-Based Models Operate

In this book I adopt a constraint-based approach to phonological operations rather than a derivational one. In Optimality Theory (Prince and Smolensky 1993; McCarthy and Prince 1993a,b) and Harmonic Phonology (Goldsmith 1989, 1990, 1991, 1993), as well as in other constraint-based theories such as Declarative Phonology (Scobbie 1991, 1993) and Theory of Constraints and Repair Strategies (LaCharité 1993; Paradis 1988; LaCharité and Paradis 1993), surface forms are arrived at using nonderivational constraints. These models differ in many ways, but they all have the result of displacing the derivation—which had been a cornerstone of phonological theory since *SPE*, and in linguistics as a whole since the late 1950s (Chomsky 1957)—from its central role in phonology. Although the constraint mechanisms needed to describe spoken languages have been shown to be quite complex, the constraints proposed by these nonderivational models can perform much, if not all, of the temporal work performed by the derivation, and even by the cycle as it was formulated in Lexical Phonology (Kiparsky 1979, 1982).

Sign language phonology is a fertile context for addressing issues of abstract representations, because sign language presents fresh challenges to an architecture of phonology theory based on spoken languages. The interaction of sign language phonology with the phonology of spoken languages is advantageous to both enterprises. Sign languages benefit from an enhanced range of structure, since abstract prosodic units such as the mora, the minimal word, and the syllable provide new tools for addressing sign-specific problems. Spoken language phonology models can benefit from the test of submitting the definitions of these units to the challenges that sign languages present. Since the definition and use of units of analysis and phonological architecture have become focal points in spoken language phonology, sign language research has a better chance to contribute to general conceptions about phonological structure than it had when the focus was on rule interaction. This shift began with advances made by autosegmental phonology (Goldsmith 1976) and can be described as follows: "In general, more enriched representations and a more articulated conception of the grammar's internal architecture have taken over much of the explanatory burden that was borne by the rules in earlier generative analyses" (Kenstowicz 1994, 103). In other words, phonological operations can be stated much more simply if the structure is expressed accurately, in sufficient detail. This refocusing of research energy on structures, in both spoken and sign phonology, has provided richer sets of mechanisms in phonological representations (feature geometry, the syllable, and the mora, to name a few) and made the conception of constraint-based theories possible. The enriched set of structures developed in spoken language phonology provides more points where insights about sign language structure can be brought together with insights about spoken language structure. Instead of elaborate mechanisms for the interaction of rules, the grammars of both types of language need a more useful set of structures. Because of this emphasis on structures and their interaction, rather than on rules and their interaction, it becomes important to consider which units are imported into analyses of sign languages, and how.

The current constraint-based approach to the architecture of phonological theory contrasts with derivational approaches, such as that of Lexical Phonology (Kiparsky 1982; Mohanan 1986). In Lexical Phonology three kinds of ordering are possible in a phonological derivation. First, there is the ordering of the word-building or derivational rules (called the lexical component) before the purely phonological rules (called the postlexical component). Second, there is the ordering of strata within the lexical component, so that different kinds of morphemes can be subject to particular rules at particular points in the derivation. Third, there is the ordering of rules within a given cycle (a set of rules that may apply on each stratum); this is a mechanism that allows certain rules to apply before others, wherever that set of rules becomes operative. Padden and Perlmutter (1987), considering Lexical Phonology, point out that ASL does not need the second and third types of ordering. In all of the cases they discuss, derivational rules (lexical rules) feed phonological rules

Figure 2.1
The citation form of QUIET (top left) is a type 1, two-handed sign. QUIET-ish (top right) affixes a [trilled movement] feature to the stem. 'Characteristically' QUIET (bottom left) affixes a [repeat] feature and a [circle] feature to a two-handed stem. [['Characteristically' QUIET]-'ish'] and ['characteristically' [QUIET-'ish']] (bottom right) both look the same in the output, containing the features of both affixes.

(postlexical rules) straightforwardly, and the outputs of derivational rules may feed each other.

A case in which derivational rules feed each other is the stem QUIET, which has the derived forms QUIET-'ish', with trilled movements, and 'characteristically' QUIET with circular movements. Either derived form can feed the other, to produce [['characteristically' QUIET]-'ish'] or ['characteristically' [QUIET-'ish']] (figure 2.1). Neither the rules themselves nor different strata of the lexical phonology need to be ordered. Because Padden and Perlmutter use the stem as the base to which lexical phonological rules apply, these operations are viewed as processual, but they can easily be reformulated as morphological combinations of forms that yield expected outputs when subjected to the phonology. In Optimality Theory and in Harmonic Phonology, mutually feeding operations such as these need no rule ordering at all; such forms are subject to well-formedness constraints on outputs.

One such constraint on surface forms has been formulated by Wilbur, Klima, and Bellugi (1983); it is a structure-preserving constraint, which prevents derivational forms from feeding one another if doing so will disturb the phonological integrity of the shape of the movement of particular affixes. An example based on, but not identical to, those given by Wilbur, Klima, and Bellugi (1983) is shown in figure 2.2. The stem GIVE allows, among others, three simple derivational forms. In GIVE [iterative], the stem movement is rapidly repeated tensely with a hold at the end of each repetition; the form means 'give over and over again' (multiple events). GIVE [durative] affixes concave arcs between each of the convex arcs of the stem; the form means 'give over a long time' (single event). GIVE [multiple] alters the form of the stem movement to form a smooth arc; the form means 'give to all'. The complex derivational forms GIVE [[multiple] iterative] and GIVE [[durative] multiple] are possible, but *GIVE [[[durative] iterative] multiple] is ill formed, because the form GIVE [[durative] iterative] disrupts the smooth arc of the multiple. Notice that it is only the iterative affix whose structure has holds *during* the production of the affix, rather than between affix structures and stem structures, or between affixes. The holds that are a part of its structure disrupt the smooth, unbroken movement structure of the durative and multiple affixes. A constraint preventing such combinations can therefore be formulated as a constraint on output.

Padden and Perlmutter (1987) do conclude that the type of rule ordering that orders the lexical before the postlexical component of the phonology is needed for ASL. Their evidence comes from the fact that one-handed signs and two-handed signs yield different 'characteristically' X outputs. One-handed signs have an alternating reduplicated movement, and two-handed signs have a nonalternating reduplicated movement. This difference has an interesting result when a two-handed form undergoes the optional rule of Weak Drop, whereby a type 1 two-handed nonalternating form optionally surfaces as one-handed. QUIET, 'characteristically' QUIET, and QUIET-'ish' all meet the structural description for Weak

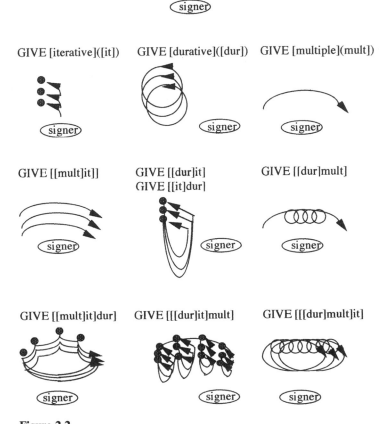

Figure 2.2
Three grammatical aspect affixes on the stem GIVE and their combinatorial possibilities. (Filled circles indicate a period of stasis. [it] = [iterative], [dur] = [durative], [mult] = [multiple])

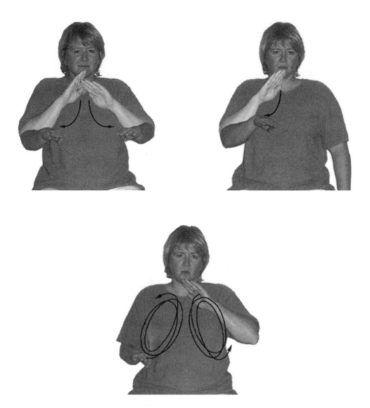

Figure 2.3
The two-handed input form QUIET (top left) can have a well-formed one-handed
output (i.e., a Weak Drop form) (top right). However, a form of 'characteristically' QUIET with alternating movement is ungrammatical (bottom); this is a
well-formed output only when the input is a one-handed sign.

Drop to apply, and all three forms may surface as one-handed. What is
not possible, though, is for the one-handed surface form of QUIET to
then feed the 'characteristically' X morphological operation, as shown in
figure 2.3.

   This prohibition against using a one-handed form of QUIET as an input
to a derivational rule can be predicted in a constraint-based approach
without appealing to a lexical versus postlexical distinction. The one-
handed form is not in the lexicon and therefore is not a possible input
form; and well-formedness is determined by comparing underlying representations (i.e., inputs) with members of a candidate set of forms (i.e.,

outputs). This is called *input-output correspondence* in Optimality Theory (McCarthy and Prince 1995). The one-handed form of 'characteristically' QUIET with an alternating movement is ill formed given that its input is two-handed. A model containing well-formedness constraints that compare an input and a candidate output is all that is needed to account for these forms in ASL.

There is one set of ASL forms for which a two-level model of phonology that compares input forms and output candidates with respect to a set of ranked constraints is inadequate. This type of phonological interaction, in which there is an output constraint that refers to a structure other than the input, is fairly common.[6] An account of such facts, known as opacity, requires reference to a level of structure other than the input. This intermediate level of structure has been called the Word-level in Harmonic Phonology (Goldsmith 1989, 1990, 1991, 1993, 1996). Goldsmith (1993, 1996) discusses several cases of opacity in detail; one such case occurs in Mituku, a Bantu tone language. Mituku has a strong prohibition against contour tones; however, it allows them in the output if the input (but not the output) contains a bimoraic syllable. A relevant form is shown in (1).

(1) *Mituku verb form illustrating the need for an intermediate level of representation*

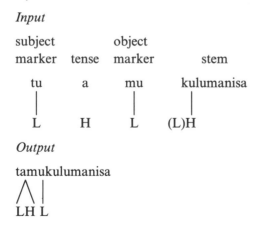

Input

subject marker	tense	object marker	stem
tu	a	mu	kulumanisa
L	H	L	(L)H

Output

tamukulumanisa

LH L

The facts about this example that make its importance clear are (1) as the floating unassociated low tone (L) indicates, there may be only one tone per tone-bearing unit (TBU); the phenomenon of "downstep" results when the unassociated low tone intervenes between two associated high tones (e.g., 'bátú'kúlumanisa'); (2) there is constraint against bimoraic surface syllables (*CVV) that results in outputs such as 'ta' rather than 'tu-a'; (3) the contour tone on 'ta' surfaces only when the two tones of the subject marker + tense marker have TBUs in the input. Crucially, the presence of the contour tone depends on there being a TBU in the input, but that vowel is deleted by an independent constraint, creating the need for three separate representations: the input where both two tones and two TBUs exist, the intermediate form where the 'u' still exists while the contour tone is created, and the output where the contour tone is in place and the 'u' has been deleted.

The ASL case, a complete analysis of which is given in chapter 5, consists of disyllabic output forms resulting from specification of a setting change (a change in place of articulation within a single plane or major body area) in the input. Some of these forms have two settings and one handshape (e.g., DEAF, CONGRESS, MEMBER, FLOWER); some have two settings and two handshapes (e.g., BACKGROUND, BOARD OF TRUSTEES). Although these signs are treated as entirely disyllabic by Liddell and Johnson (1989) and Johnson (1986), only one of their variants is disyllabic: the variant that contains movement to each of the settings, and a transitional movement from the contact of the first setting to the initiation of the second straight movement, as shown in figure 2.4. The other variant of these signs is monosyllabic and contains an arc movement between the two points of contact. (See section 4.4 for a detailed discussion of setting changes and section 5.3 for the evidence for treating

Figure 2.4
The disyllabic form of WE containing a setting change

this group of signs as disyllabic.) The settings in the input forms of these signs are given in (2); WE is illustrated in figure 2.4.

(2) *Disyllabic forms with a setting change*

DEAF [top] → [bottom] of cheek
BACKGROUND [top] → [bottom] of hand (palm side)
WE [contra] → [ipsi] of torso
CONGRESS [contra] → [ipsi] of torso
MEMBER [contra] → [ipsi] of torso
BOARD OF TRUSTEES [contra] → [ipsi] of torso
FLOWER [contra] → [ipsi] of nose

In chapter 4 I will argue that a grammar that accounts for these disyllabic forms and their metathesis-like behavior, whereby the first setting assimilates to be maximally similar to the place of articulation of the preceding sign (Johnson 1986), must treat the two movements to contact as epenthetic. On this account, the settings must be associated to the timing units (by the Association Convention) *before* the epenthetic movements are inserted, and the handshape and location features must spread to the epenthetic movements *after* the epenthetic movements are inserted, as shown schematically in (3).

(3) *Three structures in disyllabic forms*

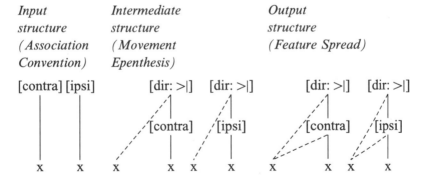

Input	*Intermediate*	*Output*
structure	*structure*	*structure*
(Association	*(Movement*	*(Feature Spread)*
Convention)	*Epenthesis)*	

2.3 Feature Geometry and Dependency Phonology

Feature geometry (Clements 1985; Sagey 1986) and Dependency Phonology (Anderson and Ewen 1987; Dresher and van der Hulst 1994) each play an important role in chapters 3 and 4 on feature organization.

Unlike in Brentari 1990c, where I assumed no feature geometry in the organization of features, in this book I will argue for an explicit feature geometry for both inherent and prosodic features. This feature geometry shares many characteristics with those of Sandler (1986, 1989), Ahn (1990), Wilbur (1993), and van der Hulst (1993). Like others who have studied feature geometry, I will examine the ways in which features cluster in phonological operations in order to establish the dominance relationships between terminal features and class nodes, between class nodes and class nodes, and between class nodes and the root node. I will specifically address the relationships between feature structures in the tree and phonological constituent structure (segments, moras, syllables, etc.). In recent work on feature geometry, Halle (1995) has investigated a less rigid adherence to articulator-bound features (i.e., those that can be articulated by one and only one structure); we will see that some features in ASL—especially the feature [trilled movement]—are not articulator-bound, but articulator-free (i.e., they specify properties of the entire structure).

The structural conventions of feature geometry (Clements 1985, 1991; Sagey 1986; Halle 1986) include the following: All features of a given tree are dominated at the top by a *root node*; at the bottom of the structure are the *terminal nodes*, where most features are located (4). Root and terminal nodes are mediated by the *class nodes*; in spoken languages the root node has a direct relation to the *timing* or *skeletal tier*, which contains either segments (Levins 1985) or moras (Hyman 1985; Hayes 1989).

(4) *Architecture of a feature tree*

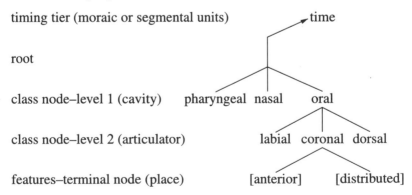

One important difference between the structure in (4) for spoken languages and a comparable structure for ASL concerns the relation between the root node and the timing slots of the structure. Consider the examples in (5).

(5) *Root-to-segment relations in spoken languages*

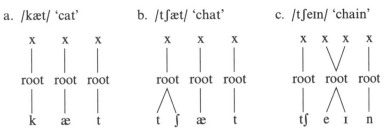

    a. /kæt/ 'cat'   b. /tʃæt/ 'chat'   c. /tʃeɪn/ 'chain'

In (5a) each root node terminates in a single set of paradigmatic features without ordering. In (5b) the affricate /tʃ/ has two linear parts, but crosslinguistically affricates are overwhelmingly "stop+continuant," not "continuant+stop"; hence, despite having two specifications for the feature [continuant]—[−cont], [+cont]—explicit ordering is not necessary (Lombardi 1990). In (5c) the diphthong /eɪ/ does require a change in the specification of [high], and although all English diphthongs end in the [+high] specification, this is not universal, so features of vowel height may be ordered with respect to one another. For example, in Spanish the diphthong is /ie/, not /eɪ/ (Harris 1983). The affricate and diphthong cases in which a root node branches, although by no means rare, are considered atypical in spoken languages. In *SPE* the formalism actually built in a one-to-one relationship between features in a matrix and segments; structural changes involving quality and quantity were both handled in this way. With the advent of autosegmental phonology, this one-to-one relationship became much less rigid; however, it is important to recognize that, despite this flexibility, the default case is still one timing slot per autosegmental tier. The Association Convention expresses this well, since in the absence of any specification or rule effects to the contrary, the association of tones to tone-bearing units (i.e., vowels) proceeds one to one, either right to left or left to right.

If root nodes have this relation to timing slots in sign, this canonical one-to-one relationship between features and segments does not hold, since in ASL the canonical shape corresponds closely to that of a diphthong. Although few ASL core lexemes require linear ordering, cases such as TAKE with an open to closed aperture change and DROP with a

Figure 2.5
Two pairs of signs illustrating the importance of order in representing handshape: one-handed forms of TAKE (i.e., a class; top left) and DROP (i.e., a class; top right), and SEND (bottom left) and SHUT-UP (2sg. imperative form; bottom right)

closed to open aperture change, and SEND with a flat to open aperture change and the imperative form of SHUT-UP with an open to flat aperture change, illustrate the contrast (see figure 2.5). For this reason I take the position that the minimal concatenative unit is not identified with the root, but with the terminal features (6). (IF stands for all of the handshape features that express the underlying handshape—for TAKE-UP and DROP, the closed handshape, for SEND and SHUT-UP, the flat handshape; PF = prosodic features.)

(6) *Root-to-segment relations in sign languages*

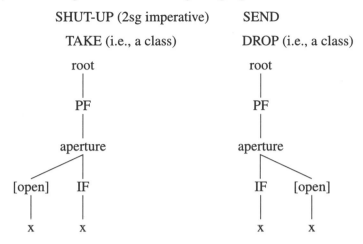

SHUT-UP (2sg imperative)   SEND

TAKE (i.e., a class)   DROP (i.e., a class)

For the work on sign language reported here, I have adopted several theoretical concepts from Dependency Phonology (Anderson and Ewen 1987; van der Hulst 1993; Dresher and van der Hulst 1994). The first concept is *binarity*. Even though some languages have ternary syntactic and phonological structures, Dresher and van der Hulst (1994) argue very convincingly that phonology can be analyzed in terms of recursive headedness and that there is a strong preference for such structures to be binary branching. Although not exceptionless, the principle of binarity can be exploited for a variety of phonological operations, most notably stress assignment (Anderson and Ewen 1987; Kager 1989; Mester 1994).

The second Dependency Phonology concept relevant to this work is *head-dependent asymmetry*. This notion captures the differences in behavior between the two branches of a binary-branching structure and allows for head-dependent relations, corresponding to a notion of "prominence" in other theories (such as Harmonic Phonology). Heads determine how the whole constituent combines at higher levels of structure. Heads exhibit two identifiable properties. First, head features remain unchanged within a given domain or phonological operation. The more structure preserving a set of features is, the more likely it is to be a head. Second, heads are more "complex" than their corresponding dependents (see below). For example, in spoken languages the stressed syllable of a foot is the head, and it is in the coda of this syllable that more complexity is typically found; in addition, stressed syllables of a foot often allow more distinctions within subsyllabic constituents (e.g., a greater range of vowels is possible in stressed than in unstressed syllables). Selected finger groups in sign and places of articulation on the body are argued to have just these properties with respect to constituent structure in sign (van der Hulst 1993). Conversely, dependent properties may change within a given domain, just as prosodic features may have two values.

Head-dependent relations can be of two types. A head and a dependent can be constituents of the same type, or they can be constituents of different types. Alpha-alpha dependency relations hold between like structures, such as a series of feet in a word, of which one is the head and the others are dependents, or a series of syllables in a foot, or a series of phonological p-phrases in an intonational phrase. Alpha-beta dependency relations hold between heterogeneous constituents, such as a nucleus and a coda, or a rhyme and its onset. An example at the segmental level would be manner and place nodes if these enter into a dependency relation (Dresher and van der Hulst 1994).

The third Dependency Phonology concept relevant to this work is *complexity*, whereby branching structures are more complex than non-branching structures, and forms with more hierarchical structure are more complex than forms with less hierarchical structure. Structures with and without a daughter are shown in (7a); the structure with a daughter is more complex. Structures with a branching daughter and a nonbranching daughter are shown in (7b); the structure with a branching daughter is more complex.

(7)   *Schema for complexity in phonological structures in Dependency Phonology (from Dresher and van der Hulst 1994)*

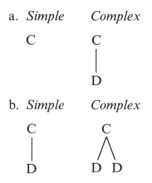

In Dependency Phonology heads are more complex than dependents.

2.4   The Phonetics-Phonology Interface and Enhancement Theory

A major task of research on sign language phonology is to come up with a set of features that effectively represents all contrasts in the language (i.e., distinctive features) and is able to express all phonological alternations (i.e., both redundant and distinctive features). Another is to draw the distinction between phonetics and phonology. These matters are taken up in Enhancement Theory (Stevens, Keyser, and Kawasaki 1986; Stevens and Keyser 1989). Enhancement Theory argues that a subset of distinctive features for spoken languages are primary features; other features are argued to be secondary features that may enhance the primary features. [Continuant], [sonorant], and [coronal] are argued to be the primary features; the strength with which each of these properties is expressed is influenced by the combination of secondary features that co-occur with the primary features. Secondary features—for example, [voice], [consonantal], [strident], [nasal], and [distributed]—have values that may enhance the properties of the primary features based on their ability to enhance the acoustic properties and articulatory correlates of the primary features. For example, [+voice] and [−consonantal] enhance [+sonorant]; [−voice] and [+consonantal] do not. In sections 6.2 and 6.3 I argue that aperture features such as [open] and [closed], typically expressed by the more distal joints of the hand, are enhanced by the more proximal joints of the wrist, elbow, or shoulder. Enhancement Theory is an important tool that the Prosodic Model uses to explain alternative surface forms involving changes in joint movement that have no differences in meaning.

2.5   Markedness

In the analyses in this book, feature specifications will occasionally be termed *default* or *unmarked*, as opposed to others that are relatively marked, with respect to a given context or substructure. In chapters 3–4 I will discuss markedness criteria for handshape, and in chapter 6 I will propose an "unmarked" syllable structure.

My definition of markedness is based partially on the observations of Battistella (1990, 26–27) and of Moravcsik and Wirth (1986, 3). Their definition relies on three types of criteria: (1) simplicity of structure (i.e., less marked elements are simpler); (2) elaboration in terms of subtypes (i.e., less marked elements allow a greater number of subtypes); and (3) distribution of elements (i.e., less marked elements are more widely distributed).

These three criteria of markedness originated in the Prague School. Basing markedness on physical (i.e., phonetic) or formal simplicity was first proposed by Jakobson (1968 [1941]) and elaborated in other of his works (e.g., Jakobson and Halle 1971 [1956]); by this criterion, the vowel /a/ is unmarked or least marked, because it needs to be specified only by the feature [low]. Basing markedness on number of subtypes is related to distribution of elements and amount of structure in overlapping parts of a grammar (for detailed discussion, see Jakobson 1984 [1939], 154). Finally, by far the most important criterion for markedness is a structure's patterns of distribution. This criterion was first developed by Trubetzkoy (1939); according to his formulation, for any two allophones, the one that appeared in contexts where neutralization could occur was unmarked, and the other one was marked. This method of observing patterns of distribution to determine markedness, and particularly to determine unmarked structures, has been taken up by Optimality Theory (McCarthy and Prince 1994), where unmarked prosodic structures in a given language can be identified by their appearance in reduplicated forms. It is this method that I use in chapter 6 to determine the unmarked syllable structure in ASL.

2.6 The Syllable and the Prosodic Word

There are certain well-formedness conditions that hold at the syllable level and others that hold at the level of the prosodic word. Most prosodic words are monosyllabic in ASL (Coulter 1982);[7] however, 25% of the lexical items listed by Stokoe, Casterline, and Croneberg (1965) are disyllabic (i.e., they contain two sequential movements). This figure is especially interesting when compared with the percentage—only 18%—of signs containing "complex movements"—signs that have two parallel, co-occurring movements, such as a handshape change and a co-occurring path movement (e.g., THROW). The constraints that hold on the quantity (i.e., number) and quality (i.e., complexity) of movements across disyllabic signs are constraints on prosodic words. The constraints that hold on the quality and quantity of single sequential movements are constraints on syllables. Enumerating and defining these constraints is the subject of chapters 5–7. Calling a single sequential movement a "sign language syllable" is not very informative, since there are at least three ways of conceiving of a syllable for sign, each of which draws on generalizations that are rooted in different aspects of phonological theory developed for spoken languages; we must examine these sources of inspiration to see if it makes sense to talk about syllables in sign languages.

2.6.1 Definitions of the Syllable

Let us begin with a functional definition of the syllable, that is, by looking at the kinds of work that it does in the grammar. Support for this strategy comes from the fact that, developmentally, there appears to be a single neurological substrate in the supplemental motor area that causes children to play with repetitive vocal and gestural articulatory movements (i.e., babble) (Meier and Willerman 1995). Furthermore, even without a consensus phonological definition of the syllable, syllabic babbling in Deaf infants of Deaf parents is readily identified (Petitto and Marentette 1991).

Formally, the syllable might be defined as a unit that is the domain of well-formedness constraints that refer to smaller units of structure, such as segments, features, and moras (i.e., the syllable organizes these smaller units), and, at the same time, as a unit subject to constraints from larger domains of structure, such as the foot, the phonological word, and the phrase (i.e., the syllable is organized by larger units of structure). This level of structure was not discussed in *SPE*; there, the segment was the fundamental domain of rule application. Very soon, however, the syllable regained its prominence in phonological analyses; it was argued to offer a more perspicuous way of expressing certain phonological rules, such as syllable-final devoicing in German (Vennemann 1972; Hooper 1972; van der Hulst and Smith 1982). The different sorts of phonological work the syllable is claimed to perform, and discussions of its internal structure, have proliferated since the early 1980s (e.g., Itô 1986; Zec 1988; Christdas 1988; Hayes 1989; Bosch 1991; Wiltshire 1992; Ziolkowski, Noske, and Deaton 1990). In the earliest writings, when authors argue for the existence of the syllable, they do so not on the basis that a theory without the syllable cannot handle the data in question, but on the basis that using the syllable allows the generalizations to be expressed more simply. The later metrical theory developed by Hayes (1981) and Prince (1983), however, crucially requires the syllable to express its insights.

It is worthwhile, then, to consider the functions that the syllable has in spoken language and to inquire whether comparable functions exist for sign.[8] There are some clear parallels and some that are not so clear; comparison is all the more difficult because competing models of syllable structure exist for both sign and spoken language phonology. Most of the formal comparisons that can be made at this point for sign involve the syllable's function in organizing subsyllabic structures (i.e., "downward-looking" operations). The reason why comparisons between the function of sign language syllables and the function of spoken language syllables as units organized by larger or "higher-level" phonological structure is so difficult is that so little is clear about the metrical structure of sign. Much of the discussion about the role of spoken language syllables in higher phonological structure centers around metrical structure (i.e., stress systems).

The one crucial difference between the definition of the sign syllable in the Prosodic Model and its definition in the Hand Tier Model (Sandler 1989) or the Moraic Model (Perlmutter 1992) is that the Hand Tier and Moraic Models—to be discussed in the next section—provide only a syntagmatic definition of the syllable, whereas the Prosodic Model contains both syntagmatic and paradigmatic components.[9]

2.6.2 The Need for Syllable Structure

The first question sign phonologists must ask is, "Do we need any unit of phonological structure smaller than a word, but larger than a segment?" The answer is clearly yes, because a phonological unit smaller than the word, but larger than the segment, is needed to capture differences between monomorphemic signs with one phonological movement (8a) and signs with a sequence of two phonological movements (8b), and to express constraints on signs with two sequential movements (8b) (as opposed to cases where two adjacent signs in a phrase display a sequence of two movements (8c)). For example, a circle+straight movement is allowed in ASL stems (e.g., WHEN, LOCK, GOVERNMENT) but a straight+circle movement is not (Uyechi 1995); see figure 2.6.

(8) *Monomorphemic monosyllabic and disyllabic signs, and two-sign sequences*

   a. *Monosyllabic signs*

      THROW
      UNDERSTAND

Figure 2.6
The two-movement, circle+straight sequence in the phrase $_2$GIVE$_0$ #SORRY. This two-movement combination is well formed in a phrase, but ill formed in a single word.

b. *Disyllabic signs*

PROJECT
DESTROY

c. Two-sign sequences

$_2$GIVE$_0$ #SORRY
ORANGE #OLD

Stokoe (1960) first observed that all signs have a movement, handshape, and location, but of these three, only movement is optional. For a sign to be pronounceable, it must physically have a handshape and a location, but conceivably movements could play no role in phonological operations—in other words, they could be a phonetic effect. However, this is not the case.[10] An account that expresses these generalizations about ASL word structure without movement misses the analogous roles that vowels and movements play as syllabic units in spoken and signed languages and fails to capture the systematic behaviors of movements as phonological entities. Although some segmental accounts, such as those of Liddell and Johnson (1989) and Sandler (1989), sketch the similarities between vowels and movements, analyses within the Prosodic Model specifically build a case for the role that movements play in prosodic structure as syllable nuclei, and in constraints on well-formed words.

Some well-formedness constraints that make use of the syllable are summarized in (9); each will be discussed further in later chapters. They are not restricted to constraints on movements.

(9) *Examples of constraints that refer to the syllable*

    a. There are restrictions on the types of handshape and movement sequences that can occur in disyllabic monomorphemic signs, as compared with a sequence of two signs or polymorphemic forms (Uyechi 1995, 104–106).

    b. No monomorphemic sign is well formed unless it has a movement of some type (Wilbur 1987; Stack 1988; Brentari 1990b,c).

    c. The phonetic temporal coordination of handshape changes with respect to movements occurs at the level of the syllable, not at the level of the lexical item or morpheme.

    d. The notion of sonority, defined as "visual perceptual salience," is relevant for syllable-internal operations in sign.

2.6.3 Parallels between Signed and Spoken Language Syllables

2.6.3.1 The Minimal Word All words consist of at least one syllable, but canonical words in a language are commonly bimoraic (Prince and Smolensky 1993). One kind of grammatical work that syllables do in signed and spoken languages is that of expressing constraints on the *minimal word*, or canonical word shape. The minimal word also differs from the "unmarked syllable," since unmarked syllables often contain more than minimal information; that is, in spoken languages unmarked syllables have been argued to be consonant-vowel (CV) syllables, even though most (though not all) languages allow V syllables as well. In the expression "CV syllable" or "V syllable," the "V" must be understood as a cover symbol for the sounds in a given language that exceed a certain threshold of sonority, not simply vowels (Zec 1988). Some languages— English, for example—allow sonorant consonants (nasals and liquids) to serve as "V"s under some conditions, and other languages (e.g., Bella Coola; Bagemihl 1991) allow even obstruents to do so. "V syllables," then, are syllables composed of a single sound that meets this threshold of sonority. Only a member of this set of sounds and no other can compose a syllable of just one sound, and spoken languages will modify structures if a sound that does not meet this sonority condition would otherwise surface as a syllable nucleus (regarding syllable nuclei, see section 2.6.4.1). A common structural modification is the addition of some unmarked vowel to a local domain that lacks a sufficiently sonorous segment (i.e., epenthesis; Itô 1986).

In ASL a well-formed syllable is sufficient to be a well-formed word. All monomorphemic signs must have a movement; and since movements are syllable nuclei, they are also well-formed syllables (Stack 1988; Brentari 1990b,c; Perlmutter 1992; Sandler 1993c). In cases where an underlying form consists of only a single place and a single handshape (e.g., THINK, KNOW, body part signs, the numbers 1–10), a movement is inserted to ensure that the structure is well formed. Evidence for this claim is based on contrasting the output of signs that contain a short movement to contact in citation form, such as THINK and KNOW, with the output of the same signs in compounds, a context where these short movements to contact are absent (Brentari 1990d).

2.6.3.2 Sonority These types of observations about both signed and spoken languages led researchers to work toward developing a hierarchy of perceptual salience; the grammatical role this perceptual salience plays in phonology is called *sonority*.[11] Ohala (1990), Dell and Elmedlaoui (1985), Zec (1988), Goldsmith and Larson (1990), Prince and Smolensky (1993), and Kenstowicz (1994), among others, have studied this issue with respect to spoken languages; Sandler (1993c), Perlmutter (1992, 1993), Corina (1990b), and I (Brentari 1990b,c, 1993), among others, have studied it with respect to sign. Researchers working on both types of language use phonetic arguments and phonological alternations to argue that certain properties are relatively more sonorous than others. In general, a sound articulated with a relatively more open nasal or vocal tract is more sonorous than one articulated with a relatively less open nasal or vocal tract. This allows the sound to be perceived at greater distances; for example, an [a] can be heard at a greater distance than an [n] or an [l]. In general, a gesture (i.e., a movement) articulated with a relatively more proximal joint is more sonorous than one articulated with a more distal joint. This allows the gesture to be perceived at greater distances; for example, a path movement (a gesture articulated by the elbow or shoulder) can be seen at a greater distance than handshape change (a gesture articulated with the finger joints). The articulatory sonority hierarchy is stated in (10). How this hierarchy of articulatory structures is expressed as a sonority hierarchy of different kinds of phonological properties of sign is taken up in chapter 6.

(10) *Proposed sonority hierarchy on articulatory principles*

  shoulder > elbow > wrist > base joints > nonbase joints

(The base joints of the hand are the metacarpal joints where the hand and fingers meet; the nonbase joints are the interphalangeal joints of the fingers and thumbs (i.e., the knuckles).)

2.6.4 Controversial Issues Concerning the Sign Language Syllable

We now move away from the less controversial parallelisms between the sign language and spoken language syllable to the more controversial ones. The issues addressed here arise from taking detailed work on the syntagmatic syllable structure in spoken language and applying it to sign. The first issue is whether or not sign structure is subject to a sonority sequencing constraint; the second concerns syllable-internal constituency; the third concerns metrical structure.

2.6.4.1 The Sonority Sequencing Constraint

The Sonority Sequencing Constraint (SSC) is a principle for which there is a great deal of support in spoken language (Ohala 1990; Ohala and Kawasaki 1984; Clements 1990; Selkirk 1982). Generally, the SSC ensures that sonority values within a syllable follow a kind of curve, with specified sonority distances being required between adjacent sounds, and that sonority values rise during the first half of the syllable (or demisyllable; Clements 1990) and fall during the second. The two lines of argument for the SSC in spoken languages are as follows. First, the syllable peak (syllable nucleus) is invariably the sound with the local maximum of sonority, and much work has conclusively demonstrated that processes of syllabification begin by sequentially scanning a string for such absolute sonority maxima, then establish syllable margins wherever possible (Dell and Elmedlaoui 1985; Goldsmith 1989, 1992b; Itô 1986; Prince and Smolensky 1993). Second, consonant clusters in the onset of the syllable are governed by language-specific principles, but these principles always follow the universal generalization that sonority values rise from one consonant to the next in an onset cluster and that sonority values fall from one consonant to the next in a coda cluster (Ohala 1990; Ohala and Kawasaki 1984; Clements 1990; Selkirk 1982). The stronger arguments for the SSC are those of the second type, since they show a clear gradual rise in sonority, and not simply a peak-nonpeak dichotomy. Unfortunately, ASL has nothing that could resemble consonant clusters, so these arguments cannot be used for sign. Regarding a sonority sequencing constraint in sign, there are competing views. Sandler (1993c) and Perlmutter (1992) argue that sign does use a syntagmatic scanning method across entire segments to assign syllable nuclei in strings. Corina (1990b) and I (Brentari 1990c, 1993) argue that sign uses a different method to scan for syllable nuclei, one that scans individual paradigmatic properties that occur simultaneously. I consider this matter in depth in chapter 6.

2.6.4.2 Syllable-Internal Constituency Let us now turn to the issue of hierarchical structure within the sign language and spoken language syllable. This is one of the most difficult problems concerning parallelisms between the two types of syllable, and it is the basis for a few innovative claims that I make here, both for sign language itself and for possible contributions of this work to phonological theory more generally. There is convincing evidence for an asymmetry between parts of syllable structure in spoken language syllables, and it matters a great deal what parts we are referring to when we think about these issues in sign.

Several structures that have been proposed for spoken language syllables are shown in (11).

(11) *Spoken language syllable structures (σ = syllable; o = onset;*
r = rime; n = nucleus; c = coda; μ = mora)

a. *Hierarchical structure (Selkirk 1982)*

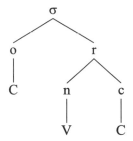

b. *Moraic structure*

    i. *(Hayes 1989)*   ii. *(Hyman 1985)*

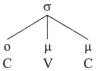
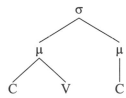

c. *Combined structures*

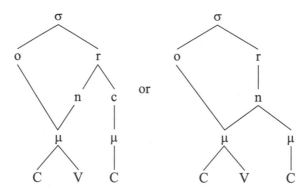

The first is a traditional hierarchical syllable structure ((11a); Selkirk 1982). The syllable branches into rime and onset constituents; the rime branches into nucleus and coda. Two types of asymmetries are present in syllable structure. One concerns the ability to carry phonological contrast. The first half of the syllable can carry all possible phonological contrasts that exist in a language; the second half can often express only a subset of these (Prince 1984; Goldsmith 1989; Itô 1986; Paradis 1989; Paradis and Prunet 1991; Wiltshire 1992). With respect to this dimension, which can be called *information-bearing capacity*, the beginning of the syllable is stronger and the end is weaker. The other type of asymmetry concerns *metrical structure*, the subsystem of phonology that deals with stress and with the distinction between heavy syllables (generally CVV or CVC), which attract stress, and light syllables (CV), which do not.[12] Here, the rime of the syllable (located in the second half of the syllable) is more important than the onset (located in the first half of the syllable); in fact, in some models the onset plays no role at all in metrical structure (Hayes 1989, 1995). Each kind of asymmetry, then, picks out a different part of syllable structure as its focus.

Under the hierarchical view, the information load asymmetry might be seen as existing either between the onset and the rime or between the onset and the coda, the latter capturing the fact that it is the consonants, rather than the vowels, of the syllable that primarily participate in this dichotomy. Also under the hierarchical view, metrical asymmetry exists between the onset and rime constituents. If one were to apply this view of the syllable to sign, there is no information load asymmetry in sign because the beginning and end of a sign syllable, defined thus far as a sequential movement, can bear equal amounts of phonological information.

With respect to metrical structure, the rime is the constituent that carries "weight" in the hierarchical view. Light syllables are assigned one mora and heavy syllables two moras, the term *mora* being defined as a weight unit, but being understood to have a phonetic correlate expressed primarily in durational terms. In other words, relatively speaking, a CV syllable is shorter in duration and "light"; a CVC or a CVV syllable is longer and "heavy."[13] This distinction, perspicuously captured in structures (11bi) (Hayes 1989) and (11bii) (Hyman 1985), is crucial in languages that are quantity sensitive—that is, languages that assign stress on the basis of counting from a word edge to the first heavy syllable to assign word stress. There is no basis on which to draw an onset-rime distinction for sign, either on the basis of metrical structure or on the basis of information load, at least not under the syntagmatic definition of these units developed in the spoken language literature.

There is, however, another way to divide the syllable, not according to the hierarchical view, but according to the moraic view. Moraic syllable structure cannot always replace hierarchical structure for spoken languages (Davis 1990; Steriade 1982, 1990), and moraic structure and hierarchical structure are not mutually exclusive, as illustrated in (11c), where moraic and hierarchical structures are combined in one representation. It has been convincingly established that moras play a role in syllabification (Zec 1988) and related prosodic processes, and this unit is an uncontroversial part of the phonological grammar of quantity-sensitive languages (Prince and Smolensky 1993; Hayes 1989; Hyman 1985; Trubetzkoy 1939). There are different views about how feature material of subsyllabic structure links up with moraic structure. Hayes (1989, 1995) allows the onset to be virtually invisible to moraic structure; see (11bi), where the syllable onset is undominated by any mora, associated only to the syllable. In contrast, Hyman (1985) associates the onset to the first mora as shown in (11bii), thereby dividing the syllable into two parts: the first C and V, which he calls a *core syllable*, and the second V or the C of the coda. This structure would also be consistent with the view that the syllable has two half-syllables or demisyllables (Clements 1990) or the view of Harmonic Phonology (Goldsmith and Larson 1990). Under this view, the first C and V together can bear all possible phonological contrasts; the first mora functions as a core syllable, and the coda alone is the weak branch of the syllable in terms of information load. The coda is less complex than the core syllable, and as such is a dependent branch of structure. This distinction—that is, between "core" and "complex" syllables—is more useful for sign, and it will play a role in analyses presented in chapter 6.

2.6.4.3 Metrical Structure   Let us pursue one final point about the moraic view of the syllable—namely, the distinction between "heavy" (more than one mora) and "light" (one mora). This distinction plays a crucial role in word stress assignment and higher metrical structure of quantity-sensitive languages, among them English, Spanish, Italian, Margi, and many others. In chapter 6 I will argue that there is a heavy-light distinction in ASL, one that is expressed paradigmatically rather than syntagmatically. This distinction is based on the simple versus complex syllable distinction mentioned above. "Heavy" syllables contain complex movements (i.e., those with parallel submovements), and "light" syllables contain simple movements (i.e., those with a single handshape change, path movement, orientation change, or setting change). The contrast can be seen in the pair UNDERSTAND (figure 1.1), which contains a single simple path movement, and THROW (figure 1.3), which contains a path movement and a handshape change. The heavy-light distinction in sign bears little formal similarity to the distinction in spoken language phonology, since the weight units are expressed paradigmatically. The heavy-light syllable distinctions in sign language and spoken language do, however, bear a strong *functional* similarity to one another. To give just a brief example, in spoken languages there is often a phonological context that attracts heavy forms, either in a phonological phrase or in a single word (Zec and Inkelas 1990). Phrase-final position is just such a context that attracts heavy forms in ASL (Brentari 1990a). It is important to mention that such a paradigmatically expressed notion of weight is also found in spoken languages. One example comes from Bantu languages, which often undergo a historical change from a tone language to an accent language. When this occurs, vowels that originally bore high tones often attract prominence, which is later exhibited as accent. A second example comes from Llogoori, where both long vowels and vowels bearing high tones are treated as heavy for purposes of assigning accent (Goldsmith 1992a). These two examples show that high tones, which are paradigmatic properties of the syllable, contribute to its weight or prominence. The claim I am making is that ASL has not invented something new; rather, it only more heavily exploits grammatical options that best suit the visual perceptual system—options that are also found, although more sparsely, in spoken languages. This distinction between simple movements and complex movements plays a role in identifying possible candidates for the operation of nominalization in ASL. Simple movements can be thought of as analogous to light syllables, and complex movements as analogous to heavy syllables, given the structures argued for in chapter 6 and shown in (12).

(12) *Representations for simple and complex movements in the Prosodic Model*

    a. *Simple movement*   b. *Complex movement*

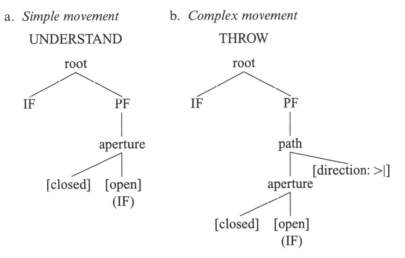

Clearly, whether sign does or does not have a syllable unit as a part of its phonological grammar is not an easy question to answer. Throughout chapters 3–6 I will not rely on a notion of the syllable, per se, but analyses will show that basic prosodic units, such as the syllable and the prosodic word, are needed on empirical grounds.

2.7 The Relationship between Native and Nonnative Components of the ASL Lexicon

Most work on the phonology of sign languages has focused primarily on what is often called the "frozen" (or *native*) component of the lexicon, the part whose forms (1) are monomorphemic and (2) show no synchronic traces of elements borrowed from English through fingerspelling. This eliminates from consideration all initialized forms, forms that have evolved from reduced fingerspelled forms, and forms that are the result of concatenating classifier forms and movement roots; yet it is in these components that expansion of the lexicon primarily takes place. In the Prosodic Model, the ways that the productive components of the lexicon are systematically related to the native component to the greatest extent possible can be explicitly expressed. In the native lexicon of ASL, there are three overlapping sets of items that have been part of the language since its beginnings (13): (1) the fingerspelled letters of the manual alphabet; (2) the productive polymorphemic classifier predicates; and (3) a set of core lexical stems fed directly by part 2 and indirectly by part 1.

(13)   *Schema for the native and nonnative (or peripheral) components of the ASL lexicon*

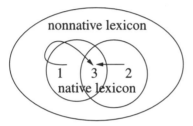

The so-called core lexemes are those that may exhibit appropriate derivational and inflectional morphology (Padden, in press) and that obey all phonological constraints proposed in later chapters. Core forms do not all come from a particular historical period of the language. For example, the recently coined form for POETRY or POEM, which is produced at mid-torso and contains a handshape change (i.e., flat to open 'B') and an orientation change (i.e., prone to supine) would be a core lexeme under the definition developed here.

Itô and Mester (1995a,b) have proposed a model of the Japanese lexicon based on principles that are directly relevant to an analysis of the ASL lexicon. In Japanese the Yamoto forms constitute the native component; the Sino-Japanese, Foreign, and Mimetic components are peripheral. Itô and Mester (1995a,b) argue that many of the constraints that hold for the native component cease to hold or are weakened in systematic ways in the peripheral components. They also predict (1) that the components of the lexicon do not behave like nonoverlapping entities within the grammar, but rather that principles of the core lexicon are weakened in peripheral components; (2) that peripheral components do not add or strengthen a constraint; and (3) that the components should be identifiable by differences in segmental inventories and exploitation of constraints. These predictions are empirically supported by forms in ASL. In chapter 8 I will analyze the way in which adherence or lack of adherence to a set of independently motivated well-formedness constraints provides evidence for three strata of the peripheral lexicon.

2.8   The Prosodic Model in the Context of Other Models of Sign Language Phonology

In developing the Prosodic Model of sign language phonology, I have built upon and learned from many insights by other sign phonologists. In this section I will briefly highlight the aspects of other models of sign language phonology most relevant for the Prosodic Model.

2.8.1   The Cheremic Model
Over thirty years ago, when William Stokoe published the first pieces on ASL phonological structure, the task he set for himself was to take sign-sized units and analyze them for their phonological components (Stokoe 1960; Stokoe, Casterline, and Croneberg 1965). At that time he concluded that there were three phonological components: the shape of the hand(s) when articulating a sign, which he called *dez*; the location on the body or in space where the sign is articulated, which he called *tab*; and the movement of the hand(s) in the course of changing locations or handshapes, which he called *sig*. Although these sublexical phonological components of signs were equivalent to phonemes as the notion had been developed in the American structuralist tradition (e.g., Bloomfield 1933; Hockett 1954), Stokoe purposely avoided terms that already had a use within linguistics, instead calling the components *cheremes* (from Greek *xeír* 'hand'). Like Stokoe's early proposals, the Prosodic Model holds that there are three structural parameters—handshape, place of articulation, and movement; underlying orientation (the fourth parameter introduced by Battison (1978)) is expressed as a two-part relation between a part of the hand and a place of articulation.

2.8.2   The Hold-Movement Model
The Hold-Movement (HM) Model (Liddell 1984a,b, 1990a,b, 1993; Johnson 1986, 1990, 1993; Liddell and Johnson 1983, 1986, 1989; Johnson and Liddell 1984) divides signs into articulatory bundles whose component features operate without hierarchical arrangement (i.e., there is no feature geometry), weighting, or independent status. The division of the

sign stream into units of stasis (holds) and movement is a concept developed by Chinchor (1978) and Supalla (1982), which Liddell and Johnson have elaborated into a complete model. The major elements are Movement segments (Ms—the hand's activities) and Hold segments (Hs—postures of the hand that are held in a steady state for ≥.1 second). Movements are specified by two feature bundles and may contain any type of feature; Holds may contain a subset of these features. The underlying representations of signs contain both Hold and Movement segments; Holds predictably delete between movements in a phrase by means of a pervasive rule of Hold Deletion. The HM Model representation of the sign FALSE (figure 1.16) is given as an example, articulated in isolation (14) and in the string FALSE STATEMENT (15). In the phrase, feature cluster "b" does not exhibit a segmental Hold.

(14) *HM Model representation of FALSE in isolation*

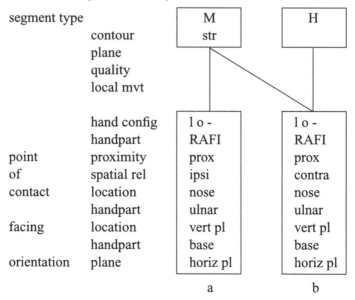

(15) *HM Model representation of FALSE in a string*[14]

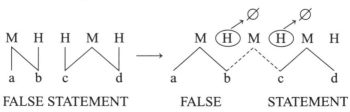

The clusters of features (i.e., point of contact, hand configuration, facing, and orientation) have no formal status in the HM Model; the unified entities of handshape, location, and movement lose the phonemic status they had in Stokoe's model in favor of smaller units of contrast. This shift is analogous to the change in the definition of a minimal pair in spoken languages after the publication of Jakobson, Fant, and Halle 1972 [1951]. Previously the English words [kɪd] ('kid') and [bɪd] ('bid') were considered a minimal pair, because they differ by only one phoneme. After the notion of distinctive features was introduced, [kɪd] and [bɪd] were no longer considered a minimal pair because they differ by more than one feature: [voice] and [place of articulation]. Only pairs such as [kat] ('cot') and [gat] ('got') retained the status of minimal pairs.

One weakness of the HM Model is its inability to pick out minimal pairs, and this weakness prompted me to seek another type of representation. Bloomfield, and the American structuralists who followed him (including Stokoe), believed in the principle "Once a phoneme, always a phoneme"; that is, if there was even one lexically contrastive pair of signs for two opposing values of a feature, this feature became phonemic for the entire language. If this notion were pushed to its logical conclusion in the HM Model—that is, if every proposed feature were a phoneme— ASL would have 299 phonemes. However, not all features in this model are established by the diagnostic of lexical contrast, since it is obviously very difficult to hold 298 features constant and vary just one.[15] Instead, the following grammaticality judgment by native signers is used in the HM Model: if a particular property of a sign is produced using an alternative, phonetically similar feature value other than the one used in citation form, is the sign still grammatically well formed? If it is not, the feature used in the citation form is contrastive. The possible phonetic variants to employ when forms are presented to native signers for grammaticality judgments are not clear, and this creates difficulties for this diagnostic, since sometimes allophonic variation can involve forms that are not very similar. For example, all English vowels become schwa [ə] in unstressed syllables, even though this reduction neutralizes a large number of features, and it could be argued that from a phonetic perspective, [ü] is more similar to [u] than [ə], even though [ü] and [u] are not allophones. In ASL point of articulation behaves in a similar way. The 'forehead' and the 'chest' are in allophonic variation in RABBIT, even though these places are not very similar phonetically. The question of which features of the HM Model are lexically contrastive has never been completely answered.

In the Prosodic Model, contrastive features are those for which minimal pairs exist or those that must be referred to in phonological operations. The inherent features are pulled out of the two feature bundles of the HM Model and placed on a separate branch of structure, and the features involved in all types of movements are aligned with two segmental timing slots.

2.8.3 The Hand Tier Model

The Hand Tier (HT) Model (Sandler 1986, 1987a,b, 1989, 1990, 1993a,b,c, 1996a,b) is the first model to place hand configuration on a separate autosegmental tier. With this representation, the HT Model gives handshape a more prominent status than it has in the HM Model; namely, hand configuration can be seen as a unified entity by the phonological grammar. The notion of hand configuration as an autosegmental tier revives the formal status of the group of handshape features, which gives hand configuration a role similar to the one it had in Stokoe's model as a chereme.[16] Features are organized into two distinct feature trees in the HT Model, a Hand Configuration tree (16) and a Location feature tree. Movements (Ms) and Locations (Ls) share the same features except for the shape feature [arc]; Ms associate to L features as necessary. Thus, the L feature tree can be used for Ms and Ls, and it is shown in (17) as an X slot since it can serve both roles, except for the [arc] feature.

(16) *Hand Configuration tree*

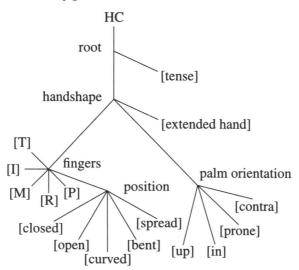

(17) *Location tree*

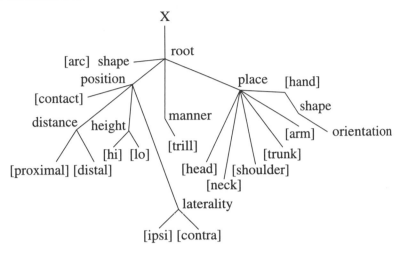

(18) *HT Model representation for FALSE*

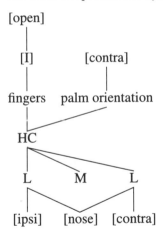

One difference between the HT Model and the HM Model is that instead of Hold segments, the static units in the HT Model are Locations (Ls). Rather than defining an L in terms of duration of stasis as the HM Model does for Holds, the HT model defines it as "a segment that is present when the dominant hand (i.e., the hand that articulates one-handed signs) obligatorily reaches [a specific] location in the course of executing a sign" (Sandler 1989, 133). An L need not actually be static, since a hand can be in motion when it reaches such an obligatory location; an L functions more as an obligatory place of articulation than as a static unit per se.

The first proposed feature geometry for sign came from the HT Model. Various modifications have been proposed to this account for the Hand Configuration tree (Corina 1990a, 1993; Johnson 1994) and for other clusters of features as well (Wilbur 1993; Ahn 1990; van der Hulst 1993, 1995; Johnson 1994).

The Prosodic Model acknowledges the need for feature geometry first noted in the HT Model, but differs from the HT Model in three ways. First, with respect to timing units, the Prosodic Model has a two-slot structure rather than a three-slot structure for forms with single movements, such as FALSE. Second, the two models differ with respect to the internal structure of the feature geometry. Third, in the Prosodic Model movements are not segments, but primitive prosodic units.

2.8.4 The Moraic Model

The Moraic (μ) Model (Perlmutter 1990, 1991a, 1992, 1993) adds a type of moraic structure to the phonological representation. It also argues for a type of syllable that is the domain for a number of phonological constraints, such as those on changes in handshape—both changes in selected fingers (called *handshape contrasts*) and changes in aperture setting (called *handshape contours*). These constraints were also noticed in early versions of the Prosodic Model. Another innovation of the μ Model is the use of the concept of sonority to explain the pattern of distribution of phonological properties of sign, such as trilled movements. The addition of moraic structure has the effect of replacing segmental timing units with moraic timing units, but the μ Model also includes segments—Movements (Ms) and Positions (Ps)—in the representation of the sign. Ms are path movements; Ps are nonpath movements or places of articulation; both Ms and geminate Ps are moraic. The μ Model makes no specific proposals for features. The moraic timing units of the model have the advantage of being generic; that is, they can arise from either P units or M units. For example, in the case of Mora Insertion, a phrase-final operation argued for by Perlmutter (1992, 1993), the mora inserted at the end of the phrase will associate to whatever the final segment of the word happens to be. In DANCE the duration of the M is lengthened since DANCE has no final P.[17] In signs that do have a final P, however, two types of hold emerge from this analysis: short holds and long holds. Signs with a word-final P phrase-medially (e.g., FALSE) have a short hold phrase-finally; phrase-medially they have no hold. Signs with a geminate P phrase-medially (e.g., GERMANY) have an accompanying short hold;

phrase-finally they have a long hold. These types of signs before and after the rule of Mora Insertion are represented as in (19).

(19) *μ Model representations of DANCE, FALSE, and GERMANY before and after Mora Insertion (cf. Perlmutter 1992)*

    a. *Phrase-medially (before Mora Insertion)*

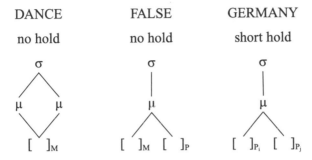

    b. *Phrase-finally (after Mora Insertion)*

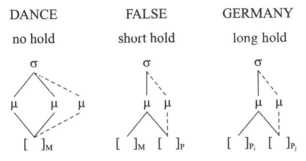

In the μ Model, as in phonological theories of spoken languages, a mora is the minimal subsyllabic unit required of a well-formed syllable. Both the Prosodic Model account and the μ Model account of moras claim this, but there are differences between the uses of the mora in the two models that I will discuss in chapter 6.

2.8.5 The Dependency Phonology Model

Several core notions of Dependency Phonology make it useful for sign phonology. One is complexity, which can refer both to complexity in feature geometry or in constituent structure (moras, syllables, feet, words, etc.) and to the relative complexity among phonological structures within the same category. In addition, Dependency Phonology employs the earlier-mentioned principles of binarity and head-dependent asymmetry, argued for in Dependency Phonology research on spoken language (Dresher and van der Hulst 1994; Anderson and Ewen 1987). Van der Hulst (1993, 1995, 1996) has also employed Dependency Phonology to build a model of sign language phonology. He has not proposed a syllable unit for this Dependency Phonology (DP) Model, arguing that because sign has no onset-rime distinction, its basic prosodic unit should not be called a syllable (Harry van der Hulst, personal communication); instead, the fundamental prosodic unit is simply the segment. The schematic structure proposed for this segmental unit is given in (20).

(20) *Segmental unit of FALSE in the DP Model (cf. van der Hulst 1995)*

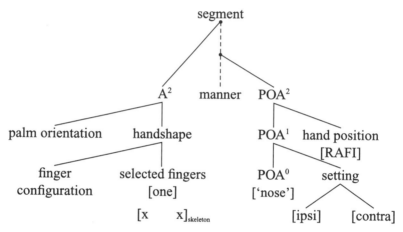

Although independently motivated, the dominance relations in this representation are similar to those in the Prosodic Model. The Prosodic Model draws upon the representation of timing slots used by the DP Model and the concepts of complexity and binarity both in its representations and for many of the dependency relations among the class nodes. The Prosodic Model and the DP Model differ in one major way, namely, in their handling of movement features. All movement features are grouped together in the Prosodic Model. The DP Model currently contains no movement features, although the manner tier could potentially dominate such features.

2.8.6 The Visual Phonology Model
In the Visual Phonology (VP) Model (Uyechi 1994, 1995), mathematical geometry is chosen to express many generalizations about sign language phonology, particularly those related to the physiological capabilities of

the articulators. The articulatory joints are considered pivot points within a two-dimensional coordinate system, and signing space is a system of four three-dimensional cubes: one for the hand, called the *hand prism* (HP); one for simple signs with one major body place or neutral space, called *local signing space* (LSS); one for complex signs, called *global signing space* (GSS); and one for larger constituents, called *discourse signing space* (DSS). Each of these cubes contains six *articulatory planes*. The notion of articulatory planes has been adopted in the Prosodic Model. The nested spaces are illustrated in figure 2.7; the VP Model representation for the sign FALSE is given in (21).

(21) *Representation of FALSE in the VP Model*

$$
\begin{array}{l}
\text{LSS} \\
\text{in} \\
\text{GSS}
\end{array}
\left[
\begin{array}{l}
\text{Loc: } [+\text{base-LSS:nose-GSS}] \\
\text{Or: } [\text{``anchored (default)''}] \\[4pt]
\begin{array}{l}
\text{HP} \\
\text{in} \\
\text{LSS}
\end{array}
\left[
\begin{array}{l}
\text{Loc} \\
[\text{base-HP:}+\text{base } [+\text{center}]] \\
\text{Or} \\[4pt]
\begin{bmatrix}
\text{front-HP:contra side-LSS} \\
\text{top-HP:}+\text{local-LSS}
\end{bmatrix}
\begin{bmatrix}
\text{front-HP:local-LSS} \\
\text{top-HP:contra side-LSS}
\end{bmatrix} \\[12pt]
\text{HP} \\
\begin{bmatrix}
\text{Or} \\[4pt]
\begin{bmatrix}
\text{palm:front-HP} \\
\text{fingertips:top-HP}
\end{bmatrix} \\[8pt]
\text{HS} \\
\begin{bmatrix}
+\text{SEL } [\text{I:open}] \\
-\text{SEL } [\text{TMRP:closed}] \\
\text{THUMB } [+\text{opposed}]
\end{bmatrix}
\end{bmatrix}
\end{array}
\right]
\end{array}
\right]
$$

The VP Model is a movement-free model, as is the model proposed by Stack (1988); it contains neither movement features nor movement segments. Movements are analyzed as "transition units" arising from "rigid body transformations" of the sign articulators. Despite the apparent shift in focus in the VP Model from previous work, there are points of similarity. For example, transition units in the VP Model are handshape changes, orientation changes, and location changes that may be expressed paradigmatically; this construct is similar in function to the weight units argued for in the Prosodic Model, because they have a distinct formal role

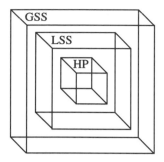

Figure 2.7
Hand prism (HP), local signing space (LSS), and global signing space (GSS)
(Visual Phonology (VP) Model; Uyechi 1995)

in the phonological structure, and because they are important in determining the overall complexity of the sign.

In addition, orientation in the VP Model is not expressed by means of a
single set of specifications for the orientation of the hand, palm, or fingers.
Rather, it is a set of relations between different signing spaces: the articulatory planes of the hand prism to those of the local signing space, those
of the local signing space to those of the global signing space, and those of
the global signing space to those of the discourse signing space. Inter-
estingly, orientation is expressed by a similar set of relations in the HM
Model. In the HM Model representation of the sign FALSE (14), the
radial side of the fingers (RAFI; i.e., index finger side) is facing a surface
proximal to the nose. This is roughly the same relation that is expressed in
the VP Model's relation between the hand prism and the local signing
space. Likewise, the HM Model's relation of the ulnar side of the hand
(i.e., the pinkie finger side) toward the vertical plane, and the base of the
hand toward the horizontal plane, is roughly equivalent to the relation
expressed in the VP Model between the planes of the local signing space
and those of the global signing space. In chapter 3 I will make a distinction
between relational, or relative, orientation and orientation changes; these
two phenomena are handled by different parts of the representation.

As this brief overview makes clear, the Prosodic Model, although proposing many innovations for the phonological representation of signs, by
no means starts with a tabula rasa; it is deeply indebted to a number of
existing proposals, and it incorporates areas of consensus among previous
models whenever possible.

Chapter 3
Inherent Features

3.1 A Feature Geometry for ASL

The input structure of a sign contains features that spell out the underlying handshape, orientation, and place-of-articulation features of a core lexeme; these are called the *inherent features*. Both inherent and prosodic features (discussed in chapter 4) are needed to achieve all lexical contrasts in ASL, but there is a consistent many-to-one relationship between prosodic and inherent features in the core lexicon. In this chapter I will present arguments for a specific organization of the inherent features. These features are realized paradigmatically, similar to the way that place, manner, and voicing in consonants are all realized paradigmatically in spoken segments, except that the realization occurs over the course of a lexeme rather than a single segment. Manual, nonmanual, H_1, H_2, and place features that do not change are all dominated by the inherent features branch of structure.

Every model of sign phonology is intimately linked with the feature specifications and their structural relations, because the feature system contributes to the execution of the phonological grammar in a significant way. The feature structure presented here and in chapter 4 divides features into two branches of structure, as shown schematically in (1).

(1) *Proposed feature tree for ASL*

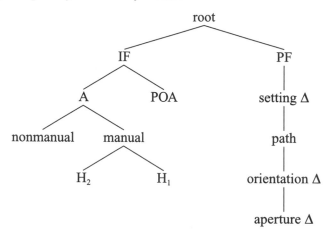

The inherent features class node dominates the following hierarchical structure. First, it branches into the *articulator* node, which includes the arm(s) and hand(s) used in the execution of a sign, and the *place-of-articulation (place)* node; the articulator node then branches into *manual* and *nonmanual* tiers. Inherent handshape features of the *dominant hand* (H_1) and the *nondominant hand* (H_2) are dominated by the manual and articulator nodes. Inherent place-of-articulation features are dominated by the place node. Inherent orientation is a relation between a set of specific handshape features and a place of articulation.

As stated in chapter 2, the HT Model was the first to use feature geometry for sign, and Sandler (1989) gives further arguments for doing so. The grammar of ASL requires a feature geometry because the major phonological parameters (handshape, location, movement) need to be referred to by the grammar as units themselves (e.g., the morphology ascribes meanings to specific handshapes), and because these groups of features display unified behavior with respect to phonological operations. Handshape, place, and movement can be used as rhyming elements in ASL poetry (Valli 1990) and as manipulable units in language games (e.g., ABC stories, number stories; Bienvenu and Colonomos 1990); as such, they should be recognized as important units in the structure of the phonological grammar. Furthermore, sign errors reported by Klima and Bellugi (1979, 102–104) argue for the integrity of place of articulation, handshape, orientation, and movement as manipulable units. For these reasons, these sets of features are given an intermediate status within the structure between the individual features and the root node; they are known in feature geometry as *class nodes*. Arguing for the use of feature geometry in spoken languages, Clements (1985) states that if certain sets of features behave as units with respect to assimilation and resequencing operations, their behavior is evidence that they are units of phonological representation. With respect to the role of class nodes within the theory of feature geometry as a whole, Sagey (1986) argues that, all things being equal, a theory that takes the physical system into account in addition to phonological alternations will be more explanatory than a theory that is concerned only with formal properties of the system. One must be careful, however, not to argue for the feature geometry too much on the basis of articulatory structure and too little on the basis of phonological operations. The number of parts of the body that are actively involved in the articulation of signs (i.e., in the body, hands, arms, and face) is larger than the number referred to by the grammar. Although knowledge of the anatomy and physiology of the articulators is necessary to understanding the phonetics of sign language gestures, too heavy a reliance on these aspects of articulation could lead to an explosion of class nodes within the system. For example, although there is a relatively self-contained set of joints and muscles that correspond to an inventory of contrastive handshapes, a much wider range of physical structure is involved in the movement and orientation parameters. The identification of class nodes must be guided primarily by phonological behavior and only secondarily by physical structure.

Features may be located at any node in the feature tree; for example, major class features, such as [consonantal] and [sonorant], have been argued to be located at the root node. Despite the apparent flexibility of such a feature tree, only one member of a given type of feature is specified at any given moment in a spoken language feature tree. The features of the inherent branch of the sign phonology are realized at the same time; each is a different sort of feature. For example, the features [one] and [spread], which will be proposed later in the chapter, are realized at the same time. This is similar to the execution of features in a spoken language feature tree, such as [nasal], [voice], and [labial]; each expresses a different aspect of the articulatory mechanism. Another similarity between feature geometries of spoken language and sign language involves dominance. In Dependency Phonology (Anderson and Ewen 1987; Dresher and van der Hulst 1994), sister features dominated by the same class node can be in a dominant/dependent relation with respect to one another. In the front vowel series of English, [high] can exist alone (i.e., an /i/), but it can be in a dominant relationship with the feature [low], which will result in a mid-vowel. This is what happens between the features [all] and [one], which are dominated by the fingers node (Brentari et al. 1996).

My proposal regarding features also adopts from Dependency Phonology the notion of head-dependent asymmetry, which allows for heads and dependent branches of structure, whose features display different patterns of distribution. According to Dresher and van der Hulst (1994), the direction of assimilation is most often from heads to dependents, and heads are typically more complex than dependents. Head-dependent asymmetries clearly exist in several places in the representation argued for here, such as between H_1 and H_2 features and between manual and nonmanual features.

3.2 The Traditional ASL Parameters and Their Relationship to Class Nodes

Regarding the four major parameters of sign structure in Battison 1978—handshape, movement, place, and orientation—the goal of the Prosodic Model is to capture the different role that each plays in the phonology and to posit different structures according to these roles. These structures must be shown to be more explanatory than a proposal that handles the four parameters as equal but separate structural entities. The way the orientation parameter is represented in the Prosodic Model differs most strikingly from the way it is represented in other models.

In chapter 1 it was shown that orientation features, like place and handshape features, play a role in both the inherent and the prosodic branches of structure. Different models have offered conflicting ways of representing orientation features. Some, such as the HT Model, express orientation as a set of features; others, such as the HM and the VP Models, represent orientation as a relation or set of relations. In the Prosodic Model, basic orientation of core lexemes (i.e., underlying or input orientation) is a relation between a part of the hand and a place of articulation in the inherent features branch of structure, whereas orientation change is a set of features that constitute a type of movement, and they are therefore expressed in the prosodic features branch of structure. This captures the fact that CHILDREN and THING are contrastive for inherent orientation; the handpart specified for CHILDREN is the palm, whereas the handpart specified for THING is the back of the hand

Figure 3.1
A pair of example signs illustrating a contrast in inherent orientation. In
CHILDREN (left) the palm is oriented toward the y- (i.e., horizontal) plane;
in THING (right) the back of the hand is oriented toward the y- plane.

(figure 3.1). The handpart is specified with respect to the superior surface
of the horizontal plane in all cases. These inherent orientation specifications do different phonological work than the features of orientation
change—[supination], [pronation], [flexion], and [extension].

3.3 The Structure of the Inherent Features: Articulator and Place

In this section I will propose a binary branching structure for the inherent
features tier, dividing it into *articulator* and *place* features (2). This is
similar to the structure developed in the DP Model (van der Hulst 1993).

(2) *Articulator and place daughters of the inherent features branch*

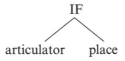

In arguing for this binary structure and then for specific features on each
branch, I will show how orientation in core lexemes emerges out of a
relation between the head of the place branch and the head of the
articulator branch (H_1). The articulator branch of structure captures the
underlying (i.e., input) features of the hand(s)/arm(s), and nonmanual
behaviors that are involved in producing a sign. It can be thought of as
the set of active articulators (an idea suggested in van der Hulst and Mills

1996). By far, handshape is the most complex of the active manual articulators, and it is here that we will focus most of our attention. It is clear
that both *place* and *articulator* can be established as autosegmental tiers
using the same type of phonological evidence as Sandler (1986) has convincingly shown for handshape.[1] This is true whether we are referring to a
hand/arm configuration or to a nonmanual posture such as an eye-gaze
or mouth position. Place meets Sandler's criteria in the following ways.
There may be many-to-one association in forms with a setting change but
with a single place (e.g., DEAF has one place and two settings). Place
may have morphological status (e.g., coreference of place for objects of
possession (van Hoek 1992)). Place also meets the criterion of stability,
since in most monomorphemic signs only one major body place is specified (Mandel 1981; Sandler 1987a). Also, in partial assimilation in compounds, the handshape of the second stem sometimes spreads to the
first stem (Sandler 1989). For example, in the compound THINK ^ SELF
'decide for oneself', the extended thumb present in the place of articulation of the first stem remains (figure 3.2).

The place and articulator branches also perform similar tasks in the
phonology; both have a large number of possible paradigmatic contrasts.
Encoding them as sisters expresses this similarity. Further, as van der
Hulst and Mills (1996) point out, handshape is the prominent active articulator in sign (analogous to the tongue in spoken languages), whereas
place is the passive articulator, and these structures function just as
their spoken language counterparts do. Just as the passive articulators
of spoken language specify where contact is made, so the place branch
specifies these contrasts in sign. Just as the active articulators of spoken
language specify what is moving toward a specific target, so the articulator branch specifies what is moving in sign. The difference is that in sign
the active articulator can assume many different shapes and has many
more possibilities for contact than do the active articulators of speech;
hence, the articulator branch has a more complex structure than its
spoken language counterpart. In sign the entire front of the head and
torso, as well as the sides of the head and arms, can serve as the passive articulator; however, place is complex in both signed and spoken
languages.

3.3.1 Manual and Nonmanual Branches of the Articulator Tier

In the remainder of section 3.3 I discuss the proposal in (3) for the internal structure of the articulator tier:[2]

Figure 3.2
The compound THINK^SELF, illustrating the property of stability for place of
articulation. In the citation form of THINK (top left), the handshape is '1' and
the place of articulation is the ipsilateral side of the forehead. In the citation form
of SELF (top right), the handshape is 'A' and the place of articulation is an x-
plane (i.e., ventral plane) in front of the signer. In the compound THINK^SELF
(bottom), the thumb extension of the 'A' handshape has regressively assimilated,
but the places of articulation of both signs remain distinct.

(3) *The articulator branch of structure*

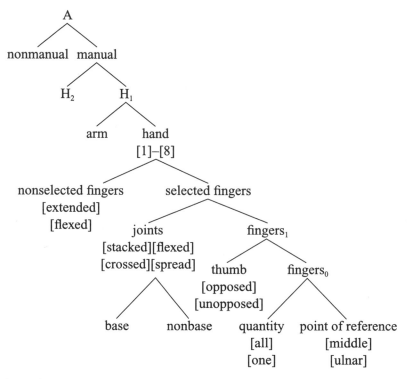

The articulator node branches into *manual* (head) and *nonmanual* (dependent) tiers. Nonmanual behavior has been shown to have the same ability to carry lexical contrast as features of handshape, place, orientation, and movement. For example, in work on ASL and Danish Sign Language, eye gaze has been shown to function like manual pointing that refers to a location in space identified with a noun phrase in specific contexts (Engberg-Pederson 1993; Bahan 1996). A clear case of allomorphy involving a manual and a nonmanual component is discussed in chapter 5. In the affix meaning 'prolonged' (Davies 1983), which is also used in the aspect form 'delayed completive', finger wiggling and tongue wagging are allomorphic (Brentari 1996b). If the input contains an [all] handshape, then finger wiggling is used, as in RUN-OUT-OF. If the input contains any other handshape, the rapidly repeated movement associates to the tongue and is realized as tongue wagging. This allophonic articulatory behavior of eye gaze and indexical pointing, and of finger wiggling and tongue wagging, shows that nonmanual behaviors can be seen as systematic variants of handshapes, and can be used in a way similar to the way parts of the hand are used in relational orientation. Such behavior is therefore represented, like manual behavior, as a daughter of the articulator node.

There are prosodic and inherent nonmanual features; the prosodic features will be discussed in chapter 4.

3.3.2 H_1 and H_2 Branches of the Manual Tier

As shown in (3), the manual tier branches into the *dominant hand* (H_1) and the *nondominant hand* (H_2) branches. In chapter 7, I give a full account of H_2 as a dependent branch of the articulator tier. There are three reasons for taking H_1 to be the head. The first two were originally argued for in Brentari 1990c, the third in van der Hulst 1995, 1996. The first argument is based on the asymmetry in H_1's and H_2's ability to carry contrast. The features dominated by the H_2 node are a proper subset of the features dominated by H_1. The handshapes (i.e., 'B', 'A', 'S', 'C', 'O', '1', '5') are a subset of all possible handshape contrasts. The second argument is based on direction of assimilation. There is an asymmetry in the direction of feature assimilation between H_1 and H_2 branches of structure; in historical change, H_1 features have more commonly spread to H_2 than the reverse, though there have been a few exceptions.[3] The third argument is based on the degree of hierarchical complexity in H_1 and H_2. The structure dominated by H_2 is much simpler than that dominated by H_1.

A feature [2-handed] generates an H_2 structure. The H_2 node has two daughters: place and handshape. In ASL, H_2 cannot exhibit independent orientation or movement features. H_2 exhibits the orientation features of the sign as specified on H_1, discussed below. Regarding movement, H_2 has two choices: either to copy the movement of H_1 or to exhibit no movement at all. Battison (1978) noted that contact on H_2 in two-handed signs can occur at eight different places. These eight places are the same as the places that specify one-half of the underlying orientation relation. Perlmutter (1991a) has argued that the handshape of H_2 is predictable from the place where it is contacted by H_1, but there are exceptions to this; for example, one cannot predict the handshape in TRY-ON or PUT-ON-SHOE (figure 3.3) from the place of articulation. The fact that there are counterexamples to Perlmutter's claim supports the conclusion that the H_2 node has both place and handshape as daughters. See chapter 7 for a complete analysis of the role of H_2 in higher-order prosodic structure.

Figure 3.3
The pair of signs TRY-ON (left) and PUT-ON-SHOE (right) show that the handshape of the nondominant hand (H_2) cannot be predicted from the place of contact between the two hands. In both signs the place of contact on H_2 is the front surface of the fingers.

3.3.3 The Dominant Hand

The dominant hand (H_1) is the head of the articulator branch of structure. In this section I argue for a specific internal organization of this structure, complete with distinctive features as terminal nodes. The H_1 branch of structure in (3) contains many innovations, but it also draws on insights in work by Ann (1992), Boyes-Braem (1981), Brentari (1988, 1990c), Liddell and Johnson (1989), Sandler (1989, 1995, 1996b), Uyechi (1995), van der Hulst (1995, 1996), and Wilbur (1993). It captures all handshape contrasts, as well as contrasts involving the wrist, the arm, and the handpart involved in specifying underlying orientation.

The H_1 node can be defined as shape and selection of the hand or arm specified in the underlying representation. The H_1 node branches into the nodes *arm*, for those signs that use the whole arm as the articulator (e.g., DAY, OVERNIGHT, TREE), and *hand*. The hand branch of structure is more complex than the arm branch (i.e., it has more branches), and it has more possibilities for carrying lexical contrast (i.e., it contains more features). The hand node branches into the nodes *selected fingers* (head) and *nonselected fingers* (dependent), and selected fingers branches into *fingers₁* and *joints*.

Whenever the arm node is a part of the structure of the articulator branch, the whole forearm is involved in the articulation of the sign; there are relatively few signs that are produced in this way. In all signs that

Figure 3.4
The signs DAY (left) and REBEL (right) illustrate the presence of a [pivot] path movement feature.

specify the arm as the articulator, the elbow is fixed in space and functions as a pivot point for movement (e.g., MORNING, DAY, AFTERNOON, TREE, DARK, DINOSAUR, REBEL; DAY and REBEL are shown in figure 3.4).

3.3.4 The Hand Node

Hand is the part of structure that spells out the details capturing underlying handshape contrasts. Of the handshapes in figure 3.5, only the one on the right is contrastive. The position taken here is that this is the most unmarked of the contrastive handshapes. Neither the handshape on the left nor the one in the middle is a member of the contrastive set of handshapes in ASL. Figure 3.5 (left) is the position assumed "at rest," in both signers and nonsigners (Ann 1992, 1996); the fingers are slightly curved, rather than extended. This handshape is often substituted for a target handshape in productions of signers with Parkinson's disease. Figure 3.5 (middle) is the open handshape assumed in a redundant open position in a handshape contour environment (Uyechi 1995); the fingers are slightly spread and slightly flexed at the metacarpal joint. There are phonetic reasons for this choice in this environment that are due to ease of articulation, and phonological reasons due to patterns of distribution.

3.3.5 Selected Fingers and Nonselected Fingers

In the Prosodic model the hand node has two branches: one for nonselected fingers and one for selected fingers. In ASL "extended" non-

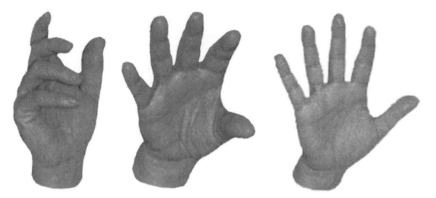

Figure 3.5
Three open handshapes: the 'at rest' handshape (left), in which the fingers are slightly spread and slightly curved; the allophonic [open] handshape (middle), which appears in handshape contour environments; the fully open handshape (right), which is a member of the contrastive set of ASL handshapes

selected fingers are phonetically realized as slightly spread and not quite fully extended (i.e., [extended]); otherwise, the nonselected fingers are realized as flexed (i.e., [flexed]). The realization of the nonselected fingers is generally predictable from the selected fingers' joint specification (explained in section 3.3.6), except in the case of a selected closed index finger, which can be realized with either extended or flexed nonselected fingers (e.g., FIND vs. PRINT). This generalization is expressed in the constraint calling for maximal perceptual contrast between selected and nonselected fingers (4).

(4) *Maximize finger contrast (Redundancy rule)*

If selected fingers are [α flexed], nonselected fingers are [−α flexed].

Nonselected fingers contact each other when they are closed, and the thumb closes around the other nonselected fingers when it is also non-selected. In cases such as 'M' and 'N' where the selected fingers are flat, the thumb contacts the other nonselected fingers by being tucked under the selected fingers, since otherwise contact between the thumb and the other nonselected fingers is impossible.

The selected fingers branch of the hand node is more complex than the nonselected fingers branch. Selected fingers has two branches: *joints* and *fingers₁*. Detailed work on the physiology of the hand (Uyechi 1995; Ann

1996) and psycholinguistic work on distinctive features of handshape (Boyes-Braem 1981) help to clarify the roles that these aspects of structure play in the representation. The separation of fingers$_1$ and joints was first proposed by van der Hulst (1995). It has four major advantages.

First—and this is the biggest advantage of separating fingers$_1$ and joints—it allows handshape contours to be represented more easily than models that specify the two handshapes in contour environments.[4] The separation of fingers$_1$ and joints is necessary in order to see clearly the systematic differences between handshapes that occur in the contrastive inventory and those that appear only in *handshape contour* environments— namely, those environments with a handshape change involving two allophonic handshapes (the term was coined in Perlmutter 1992). The inventory of handshapes in a given sign language is a combination of these two very different types of information. The fingers$_1$ branch of structure specifies which of the fingers and thumb are selected; the joints branch specifies which particular joints are involved in specifying a given underlying handshape. Specifying the two types of information independently also makes it possible to predict more accurately which groups of fingers and which kinds of joint configurations are likely to be more frequent crosslinguistically, and where gaps in the overall pattern of distribution will be, without overrepresenting handshapes such as 'S' or '5' by virtue of their similarity to open and closed allophones of many handshapes in contour environments. This proposal therefore distinguishes more clearly between handshapes that occur in the contrastive inventory and those that appear only in *handshape contour* environments.

Second, this proposal provides a way of identifying which handshape in a contour is the more basic handshape; that is, it captures the fact that in signs with handshape contours, one is phonologically more salient, and one is the open or closed variant of this handshape. This has been demonstrated in asymmetries in the persistence of one of the handshapes in a handshape contour. For example, when the [multiple] affix (a sweeping arc) is added to two different stems with handshape contours, one handshape of each of the stems is used during the articulation of the arc (Corina 1993). As figure 3.6 illustrates, in the sign HATE [multiple] the first handshape is used to articulate the arc, whereas in ASK [multiple] the second handshape is used; thus, we cannot predict whether it will be the first or the second handshape that will persist. Moreover, we cannot generalize that it is either the relatively more open or the relatively more closed handshape that will be chosen, since the more closed handshape is chosen

Figure 3.6
The signs HATE [multiple] (left) and ASK [multiple] (right) illustrate that the
handshapes in a handshape contour are predictable neither from order (1st or 2nd)
nor from aperture specification (open or closed). In HATE the first, closed handshape appears in the [multiple] affix; in ASK the second, open handshape appears.

in HATE [multiple], and the more open handshape in ASK [multiple].
Neither an explanation based on order nor one based on aperture can
capture this phenomenon.

Third, the proposed representation captures constraints on handshape
contrasts. Although handshape contours are the most common type of
handshape change in core lexemes, another type does occur. These are
called *handshape contrasts*, following Perlmutter (1992), because they
involve two contrastive handshapes, and they involve either joints or
fingers[1]. Separating these two elements captures the more marked nature
of handshape changes involving selected fingers or joints.

Fourth, the proposed representation captures the distribution of thumb
position in core lexemes—that is, the semi-independence that thumbs can
display in signs.

3.3.6 Joints
Turning first to the *joints* branch of the selected fingers node, we can see
that the phonological system of ASL encodes only joint flexion, rather
than flexion versus extension, as Uyechi (1995) and Ann (1996) have
claimed. All seven contrastive joint postures can be distinguished by considering a privative dimension (flexed) rather than the two-dimensional
physiological fact (flexed vs. extended). Using the notion of flexion alone
will make the phonology simpler, even though physiologically both types

of muscle movements are at work. In (5) the possible joint and [flexed] specifications are shown; in figure 3.7 example signs are also given. In the examples the selected fingers specifications are held constant (all fingers are selected). The representations are stipulated as follows. For *open* handshapes, no joints are specified, and in fact they are represented with no joints branch at all; this is taken as the unmarked joint posture for any selected finger group. *Closed* handshapes are represented using a joints branch and a [flexed] feature; this is interpreted by the system as having all joints flexed. *Flat* handshapes have one further branch of structure, the base joint; ASL has an open, flat handshape (e.g., SHOWER, TO-FILM) without a [flexed] feature, and a closed, flat handshape (e.g., TEACH, KISS) with a [flexed] feature. In *curved* handshapes both the base and the base joints are specified. There are open, curved handshapes (e.g., CUP, ENVISION) without a [flexed] feature, and closed, curved handshapes

(5) *Structure for the seven contrastive joint specifications in ASL*

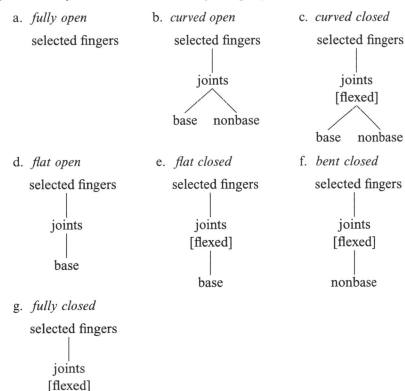

Figure 3.7
Signs illustrating the seven possible, contrastive joint specifications in ASL: (top: left to right) fully open (e.g., SUNDAY); curved open (e.g., ENVISION); curved closed (e.g., KNOW-NOTHING); (bottom: left to right) flat open (e.g., TO-FILM); flat closed (e.g., KISS); bent closed (e.g., WANT); fully closed (e.g., SATURDAY)

(e.g., KNOW-NOTHING) with a [flexed] feature. For *bent* handshapes, the nonbase joints are specified, but the base joints are not; these hand-shapes have a closed, bent variant only (i.e., one with a [flexed] feature). This classification—the branching structure plus the feature [flexed]—captures all necessary contrasts in the native lexicon, including the classifier predicates.

All of the joint specifications in (5) are contrastive; this is clear since in all of the signs in figure 3.7, either the handshape in question is not part of a contour (SUNDAY, SATURDAY, TO-FILM, KNOW-NOTHING), or it may appear without the handshape contour in particu-

Figure 3.7 (continued)

lar morphological contexts (KISS, ENVISION, WANT). It is important that the system be able to capture those handshapes that do not participate in handshape contours, and it is equally important that it in some way be able to identify those handshapes that do participate in handshape contours. That there is a difference between the underlying representation for TO-FILM and the open allophonic handshape in a sign, such as KISS, can be argued on grounds similar to those used in distinguishing between coronal obstruents in English (i.e., /d, t/). Crosslinguistically it has been argued that coronals, especially the coronal obstruent [t], should be underspecified, since they exhibit the following characteristics: they are involved in common substitution errors in aphasic speech and in the speech of children; they are often "transparent" in vowel harmony (i.e., they do not block the spread of a harmonizing feature); they are often inserted in operations involving epenthesis; they may appear in codas when no other consonant may do so (Paradis and Prunet 1991). For these reasons, coronals are often not specified for a place of articulation. Yet in other cases coronal obstruents must be more fully specified underlyingly (Davis 1991). For example, there is a constraint that prohibits homorganic consonants from occurring in the same root morpheme. If coronals are unspecified for place of articulation, this constraint should allow a sequence of two coronals, yet coronals are indeed subject to the constraint; they are accorded no special status in this context. In ASL the appearance of the open, flat handshape in TO-FILM is not predictable, whereas in KISS it is (see chapter 4).

In addition to [flexed], the joints node dominates the features [spread], [stacked], and [crossed] (see figure 3.8). [Spread] is self-explanatory (i.e., the fingers are spread apart; e.g., SEE, STAND); [stacked] involves placing the fingers on top of one another, with the pinkie finger at the bottom—roughly speaking, in the position needed to grip a racquet (e.g., FEW, SALAD, MELT; Greftegreff 1993; Johnson 1994). 'K' and 'P' are open [spread] and [stacked]. The position in which the middle finger crosses over the index finger, specified by the feature [crossed], occurs only with an 'H' handshape (e.g., CIGAR). It must be noted that in the phonetic realization of SEE in figure 3.8, the handshape is both [spread] and [stacked]. The [stacked] feature is supplied by a redundancy rule not discussed here.

3.3.7   Fingers$_1$ and Fingers$_0$

In this section I discuss the *fingers$_1$* branch of selected fingers, isolated from the joint specification of these fingers. This is where the fingers that are selected are specified. Drawing on basic insights in Boyes-Braem 1981 and Sandler 1996b, we can translate finger selection into phonological categories based on structural and perceptual economy. When all of the fingers are selected, they are assigned the feature [broad] in Sandler 1995, 1996b, which is similar to the category 'broad' proposed in Boyes-Braem 1981. When a single finger is selected, it is assigned the feature [digitated], which is in some ways similar to the category 'extended' proposed in Boyes-Braem 1981. In Sandler's and Boyes-Braem's systems, such features attempt to capture both joint and finger selection; in doing so, they differ from the Prosodic Model, where such features capture only finger selection. Furthermore, Sandler's analysis does not distinguish between the handshapes with three adjacent fingers selected (e.g., fingerspelled

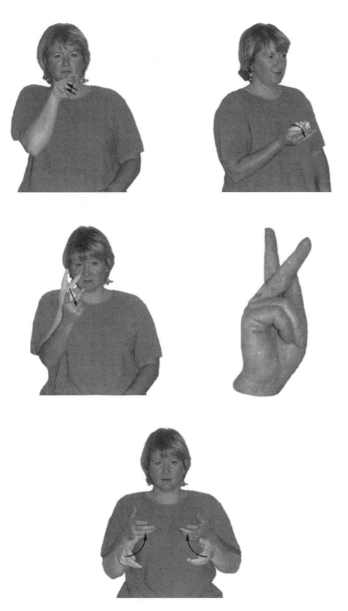

Figure 3.8
Signs illustrating the features [crossed], [stacked], and [spread]: CIGAR [crossed]
(top left); FEW [stacked] (top right); SEE [spread] (middle left); 'K' [spread]
[stacked] (middle right); SALAD [spread] [stacked] (bottom)

'M') and two fingers selected (e.g., fingerspelled 'H' or 'N') for ASL, which are contrastive in core lexemes (e.g., DOCTOR vs. NURSE).

In the Prosodic Model, when no $fingers_1$ branch is present, the form is realized as an 'S'. When a $fingers_1$ node is present with no daughters, the form is realized as a '5'. The Prosodic Model structure may involve a thumb branch of $fingers_1$, as needed, as well as a $fingers_0$ branch of structure. In some (but not many) signs, the thumb is an independent structure, but we will see that it needs to be such only under certain systematic conditions.

$Fingers_0$ dominates four features, [all], [one], [mid], and [ulnar], either individually or in a dependency relation (as in Sandler's model); for work on three of these, see Brentari et al. 1996. In Dependency Phonology, features can sometimes dominate one another to produce intermediate forms; in this way, two features can produce a four-way contrast. To see how features in a dependency relation work, consider the English front vowel series: a [high] feature alone is realized as /i/; a [low] feature is realized as [æ]; a [high] feature dominating a [low] feature is realized as [ɪ]; and a [low] feature dominating a [high] feature is realized as [ɛ]. Leaving aside the thumb for a minute, the features [all] and [one] specify the number of selected fingers: [all] is defined as all four fingers, and [one] is defined as one finger. [Ulnar] and [mid] specify where the point of reference for the selected fingers occurs: [ulnar] specifies that the pinkie finger side of the hand is used as the reference point; [mid] specifies that the middle finger is used; otherwise, the radial or index finger side of the hand is assumed. [One] may appear with [mid], which is realized as the '8' handshape, or with [ulnar], which is realized as the 'I' handshape.

If the two quantity features [all] and [one] and the two point-of-reference features [mid] and [ulnar] are allowed to enter into dependency relations, all possible selected finger handshapes can be accounted for. When [all] dominates [one], all possible handshapes with three adjacent fingers selected are specified; when [one] dominates [all], all handshapes with two adjacent fingers selected and two closed are specified (hence the distinction between 'N' and 'M'). The quantity feature [one] can combine with [ulnar] dominating [mid], which is realized as '7' (i.e., in '7' the ring finger is selected). The point-of-reference feature [ulnar] can combine with [one] dominating [all], which is realized as the 'horns' handshape (e.g., MOCK, SARCASTIC). Specifications for some problematic handshapes are given in (6).[5]

(6) *Possible selected fingers combinations*

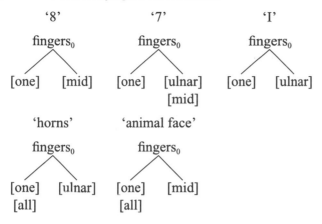

3.3.8 Thumb

Thumb is a branch of fingers₁ and sister to fingers₀. It is the dependent branch: it is simpler than fingers₀, since it dominates only one feature, [opposed]; and, when assimilation occurs, the specifications for the other fingers spread to the thumb from fingers₀. An observation about handshapes that has been difficult to express is that in the majority of cases the thumb behaves like the other selected fingers with respect to joint specification and handshape posture in members of the handshapes, yet in some signs it operates as a semi-independent articulator. These variations of thumb behavior can be handled using the joints node.

One insight gained from separating selected fingers from joint specification is that if we understand that the thumb may be specified in a limited number of ways in ASL—selected or nonselected, opposed or unopposed— we can characterize this distinction with a single feature [opposed] (i.e., a specification of the base joint). Let us consider each of these thumb specifications in turn.

When the thumb is not selected, there is no thumb branch under fingers₁. It has the same specification for [extended] or [flexed] as the other nonselected fingers, with the added specifications for phonetic realization shown in (7). (7a) is a direct result of the fact that the "no joints selected" option is realized as a flat, open hand (i.e., extended), and (7b) is an extension of the statements in sections 3.3.5 and 3.3.6 about nonselected fingers.

(7) *Redundant thumb behavior when the thumb is* not *selected*

    a. If the nonselected fingers are [extended] and [unopposed], the thumb is open and unopposed (e.g., WHY, FEEL).

b. If the nonselected fingers are [flexed], the thumb contacts the other nonselected fingers.

    i. The thumb does not contact the selected fingers, except when contact with the selected fingers is unavoidable (e.g., the first handshape in THROW).

    ii. In flat handshapes ('M', 'N'), the preference to contact the other nonselected fingers requires that the thumb rest beneath the selected fingers.

When the thumb is a selected finger, it is represented as an empty node if it behaves like the other selected fingers, or, in the more marked case, it can have a different base joint specification from that of the other selected fingers. The metacarpal joint of the thumb connects the thumb to the hand and is its base joint, so in curved, flat, and closed handshapes when the base joint is specified for the other selected fingers, the default thumb setting is [opposed]. For bent and open handshapes, when the base joint is not flexed in the selected fingers, the default thumb setting is [unopposed] (8).

(8) *Redundant specification ([opposed]/[unopposed]) for the thumb as a selected finger*

    a. open, bent → [unopposed]

    b. curved, flat, closed → [opposed]

Given the representation for the articulator branch in (3), the thumb's behavior in handshape contours can also be explained. The possibilities for thumb position in handshape contours are given in (9), and example signs for each type are given in figure 3.9.

(9) *Possibilities for thumb position in handshape contours (from Brentari 1990b)*

    a. Thumbs may change redundantly with other selected fingers (e.g., WANT, BEAR).

    b. Thumbs may remain constant if other selected fingers change (e.g., RUN, BUG, SEPARATE, HA-HA-HA).

    c. Thumbs may change even if other selected fingers remain unchanged (e.g., TWENTY-ONE, SHOOT-A-GUN).

Figure 3.9
Examples illustrating the possible thumb positions in ASL signs: WANT (thumb is redundant) (top left); SEPARATE (thumb is stable while selected fingers change) (top right); and SHOOT-A-GUN (thumb changes while other selected fingers remain stable) (bottom)

(9a) is the simple case where the thumb behaves like the other selected fingers. (9b) describes a heterogeneous set of exceptional cases. In RUN and BUG, it is only the thumb (of all of the selected fingers) that achieves contact with the body; when this occurs, the thumb can be analyzed as being blocked from participating in the handshape contour. In SEPARATE and HA-HA-HA, the thumb is specified as nonselected and extended.[6] The cases described in (9c) are exceptional, too, but for a different reason. In these forms the thumb structure is present, and [one] is specified at $fingers_0$; it is only a nonbranching $fingers_0$ handshape with a [one] specification that allows the thumb to undergo a handshape contour independently of the other selected fingers. Only the three structures

shown in (10) allow independent thumb aperture change.[7] The generalization can be expressed as a constraint, (11), which states that only when
fingers₁ is otherwise nonbranching can the thumb behave independently
of other selected fingers.

(10) *Structures that allow independent thumb movement (In all three
      cases, the nonselected fingers are [flexed].)*

    a. *'L' handshape*   b. *'3' handshape*

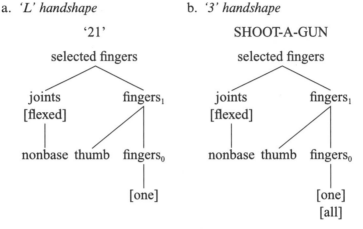

    c. *'A' handshape*

        CIGARETTE-LIGHTER

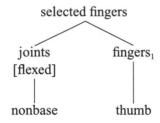

(11) *Constraint on independent thumb behavior*

    The thumb may behave independently from other selected fingers
    only in cases where the fingers₁ node is otherwise nonbranching.

    A final type of thumb behavior explained by the Prosodic Model is the
type of contact that occurs between the thumb and the other selected
fingers. If the base joint is selected (i.e., in flat handshapes), pad contact
is predicted (e.g., GROW, INFORM, WET, DEFLATE), because the
nonbase joint is not flexed. If the nonbase joint is selected (i.e., all

joints, or only the nonbase joints: closed and bent handshapes, respectively), "restrained" contact is predicted, whereby the thumb "restrains" the other selected fingers before release (e.g., UNDERSTAND (open), MILK (closed)).

To sum up this discussion of thumb behavior: These analyses establish the thumb node as a sister to the fingers$_0$ node. The thumb behaves in predictable ways, except in the cases shown in (10), captured as a constraint in (11).

3.4 Handshape Inventories, Redundancy, and Markedness

In this section I address the concept of markedness in handshapes, basing markedness on patterns of distribution and on formal and physical simplicity. Battison (1978), Sandler (1996b), Brentari et al. (1996), and I (Brentari 1990c) have proposed markedness criteria for handshape, based on factors such as acquisition and substitution errors contained in children's signing (McIntire 1977; Sieklecki and Bonvillian 1993; Marentette 1996), use on the nondominant hand (Battison 1978), participation in handshape contours (Brentari 1990c), number of errors in aphasic signing (Whittemore 1986), ease of articulation (Mandel 1981), and frequency of occurrence crosslinguistically (Woodward 1985, 1987).

Handshape markedness criteria

	More marked	Less marked
As 'arm' handshape	no	yes
Acquisition	acquired late	acquired early
Ease of articulation	harder	easier
Use on H$_2$	no	yes
Participation in handshape contours	no	yes
Frequency crosslinguistically	less frequent	more frequent
Substitution errors	omitted	substituted
In children's signing		
In aphasic signing		

The structural properties on which these markedness criteria for handshapes are based can be traced to joint configuration and selected fingers structures. Let us now consider them in terms of the structure in (3). This system straightforwardly expresses markedness by representing relatively more marked handshapes with more complex structures; the more complex the combined structure of joints and selected fingers is, the more marked the handshape is. The unmarked set of handshapes that can appear on H_2 (i.e., 'B', 'A', 'S', 'C', 'O', '1', '5') is thus accounted for. Given the structure proposed in (3), these handshapes are represented as shown in (12).

(12) *Handshapes that may appear on H_2*

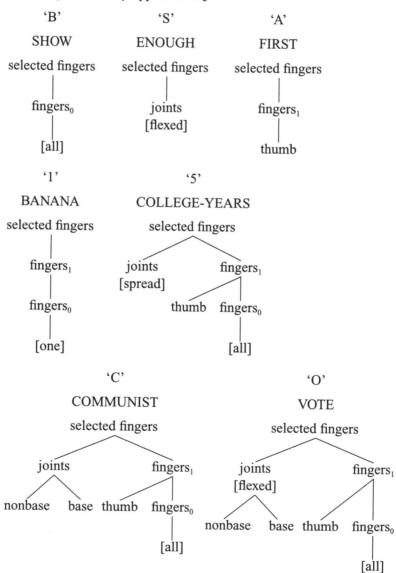

According to Battistella's (1990) general markedness criteria, unmarked structures are simpler, and the [all] and [one] finger structures proposed in the Prosodic Model are simpler, as are the open joint structures. Again according to Battistella, unmarked structures have a greater proliferation of subtypes, and the same two Prosodic Model finger structures—[all] and [one]—have the full range of joint specifications, whereas other sets of fingers have only a subset of these. As noted earlier, this is particularly true of thumb specification. Finally, as will become clear, these unmarked structures have the widest distribution in all the parts of the native ASL lexicon, including the core lexemes, the fingerspelled alphabet, and the classifier predicate forms.

3.5 Place of Articulation

In this section I will describe the *place* branch of structure, following many (but not all) proposals made regarding place structure by van der Hulst (1993). The entire structure of this branch is given in (13). Under this system, the signing space has phonologically distinct specifications for planes and places of articulation. These places of articulation are not simply convenient cataloguing devices, but also are referred to by the phonological grammar. For example, in chapter 6 the y-plane will be utilized in analyzing the fact that in a certain class of signs H_2 may be deleted just in case the plane of articulation is the y-plane.

(13) *The place branch of structure*

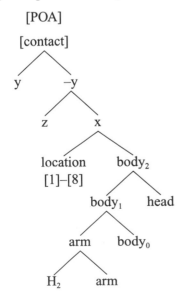

The general principles that guide the feature organization of the place branch are as follows. First, as stated earlier, the place and articulator branches of structure play very similar roles in the structure of signs. Like the articulator branch, the place branch has a large number of internal distinctions that achieve lexical contrast in forms, and it can be established as an autosegmental tier because of its stability and its ability to carry morphological status. To understand the concept of stability of place, consider the structural change in a sign when it is used as the first stem of a compound, such as THINK ^ SELF 'decide for oneself'. The handshape changes, in this case only partially, but the place remains the same (see figure 1.14). To understand the morphological status of place, consider its use in the referential loci for person and spatial agreement (Padden 1983; Engberg-Pederson 1993).

The second guiding principle for analyzing the place branch of structure as I do here, unrelated to the first, is that the places of articulation on the body and the planes of articulation in neutral space are separate subtypes of place of articulation. Also, following Uyechi (1995), I assume here that when signs are produced in space and on the body, this three-dimensional space should be thought of as potentially containing at least three different types of units of analysis: (1) points in a line, (2) lines in a plane, and (3) planes in a three-dimensional space.

A place of articulation is specified for the *plane* in which it is located: an *x-plane*, defined by all of the points in the plane that is perpendicular to the x dimension (i.e., a set of frontal planes) and the body plane, which has a range of further specifications; a *y-plane*, defined by all of the points in the plane that is perpendicular to the y dimension (i.e., a set of horizontal planes); and a *z-plane*, defined by all of the points in the plane that is perpendicular to the z dimension (i.e., a set of midsagittal planes).[8] *x, y,* and *z* are the labels given to the planes of articulation in neutral space. The three dimensions in space and the three planes of articulation are shown in figure 3.10. Examples of signs in each of the planes are shown in figure 3.11. The x-plane in neutral space is often used as a "calendar plane" in signs such as EVERY-MONDAY and EVERY-OTHER-MONDAY (Engberg-Pederson 1993); it is also used in a wide variety of signs, such as MIRROR and JAIL, articulated in neutral space, as well as in signs articulated with respect to the body. The y-plane is the one most commonly used for one-handed signs in neutral space. The z-plane is the one most commonly used for two-handed symmetrical signs.

The x-plane can be one of the planes of neutral space, in which case it functions as just described; however, it is also the plane that corresponds

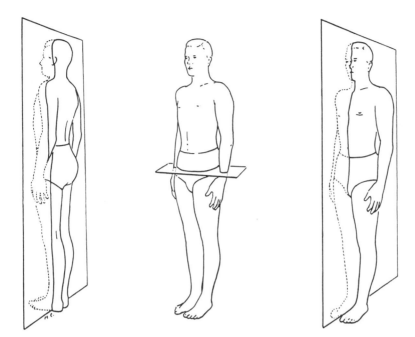

Figure 3.10
The contrastive planes of articulation in ASL based on three-dimensional space:
(left) the frontal or ventral plane (the x-plane); (middle) the horizontal or transverse plane (the y-plane); and (right) the midsagittal plane (the z-plane) (from
Luttgens and Hamilton 1997, 38; by permission)

to the plane of the body, as Uyechi (1995) has noted. When the x-plane
is the plane of the body, it no longer has a smooth surface; instead, it is
abstracted from an ideal x-plane to accommodate the contours of the
body. For those signs articulated with respect to the body, the x-plane has
additional specifications; only this so-called body plane has such a map of
distinctive places of articulation. In the system, there are four major body
regions (head, arm, body, and H_2), each of which also has eight place
distinctions [1]–[8].[9]

This system of representing place has many advantages over previous
proposals. First, it captures the generalization that the maximum number of
oppositions achieved within each of the major body regions is eight (14).

(14) *Principles governing the number of major body region distinctions*

    a. There are four major body regions.

    b. Each region has eight place distinctions.

Figure 3.11
Example signs illustrating the three planes of articulation. One-handed signs (top—left to right): YOUR (x-plane); SIT (y-plane); and THROW (z-plane). Two-handed signs (bottom—left to right): SUNDAY (x-plane); LOCAL (y-plane); and BICYCLE (z-plane)

Second, in a broad transcription only the major body regions need be mentioned. Third, the system makes crosslinguistic predictions about place of articulation. For example, the major body regions and the number of distinctions within each would be expected to be relatively stable crosslinguistically, but the specific definitions of these locations would not.[10]

For ASL, the places of opposition on the head are [1] top of the head (e.g., HAT); [2] forehead (e.g., PERPLEXED); [3] eye (e.g., ONION); [4] cheek/nose (e.g., FLOWER); [5] upper lip (e.g., THIEF); [6] mouth (e.g., SAY-NOTHING); [7] chin (e.g., FRUSTRATED); [8] under the chin (e.g., FULL). Those on the body are [1] neck (e.g., BROKE); [2] shoulder (e.g., RESPONSIBILITY); [3] clavicle (e.g., PERSONALITY); [4] torso-top (e.g., HEART); [5] torso-mid (e.g., SORRY); [6] torso-bottom (e.g., GUT-FEELING); [7] waist (e.g., RUSSIA); [8] hips (e.g., NAVY). Those on the arm are [1] upper arm (e.g., SCOTCH); [2] elbow front (e.g., DRUGS); [3] elbow back (e.g., POOR); [4] forearm back (e.g,. STAGE); [5] forearm front (e.g., BRIDGE); [6] forearm ulnar (e.g., BASKET); [7] wrist back (e.g., SLAVE); [8] wrist front (e.g., DOCTOR). Places on the hand (they are the same for H_1 and H_2) are listed in section 3.6, where they specify one-half of the underlying orientation relation; they are places in type 3 two-handed signs, as well. In addition, since [ipsi] and [contra] are contrastive settings on the body (LEATHER vs. PITTSBURGH), the body can be specified for [ipsi] or [contra] on the $body_2$ node. Polymorphemic forms also routinely exploit a contrast between [ipsi] and [contra] in spatial agreement and pronominals, as well as in classifier forms.

The plane of articulation is the plane toward which a designated hand-part faces. In the representation of two-handed signs, most of which occur in neutral space, the plane of articulation also expresses structural distinctions that affect whether a specific form is or is not able to undergo Weak Drop (H_2 deletion). Because of this representation of place features within the inherent features branch of structure, we can generalize across the behavior of this class of features in core lexemes. Only one plane of articulation is allowed in core lexemes; in classifier forms two planes may be specified. It is important to identify the plane of articulation for several reasons beyond the one of simply specifying where a sign occurs. Movements are made either within the plane of articulation or perpendicular to it, based on the movement features specified; movements and their interaction with planes of articulation are discussed in chapter 4. The plane of articulation also specifies one-half of the underlying orientation relation, described in section 3.6.

3.6 The Orientation Relation

Orientation has a different type of phonological representation than articulator or place. Stokoe (1960) did not acknowledge orientation as a basic parameter of signs; but because it carries lexical contrast, Battison (1978) added it. Even though it is true that orientation carries lexical contrast, this contrast need not be expressed by a set of features as are the internal distinctions of the articulator(s) and place. Instead, underlying orientation in core lexemes can be analyzed in relational terms. Both the HM and the VP Models have argued that underlying orientation should be expressed as a set of relations between planes of articulation on the hand and the place of articulation on the body or the planes of articulation in signing space. The two models have worked out the problem of underlying orientation in different ways. In the HM Model the relation of a handpart to a plane in neutral space is called "orientation," and the relation of a handpart to a place on the body is called "facing." As this model's representation of FALSE in (15) shows, the radial side of the hand (RAFI) is facing the nose (facing), and the base of the hand is oriented toward the horizontal plane (orientation).

(15) *Representation of FALSE (HM Model; orientation features are circled)*

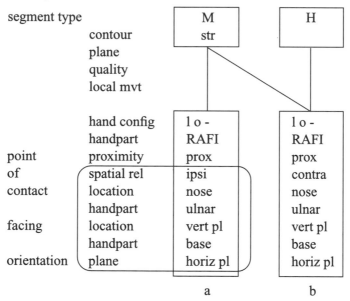

The VP Model conceives of underlying orientation as the set of relations between (1) the hand and its six-sided hand prism (HP), (2) the HP and its six-sided local signing space (LSS), and (3) the six-sided LSS and global signing space (GSS). (The model also includes a relation between GSS and discourse signing space, which is not addressed here.) After stipulating the palm of the hand as 'front' and the tips of the fingers as 'top', expressing orientation of the HP within LSS is possible. The 'front' (palm) of the HP faces the contralateral plane of LSS, and the 'tips' are oriented toward the horizontal plane. This method of expressing orientation also does not constrain the variation in orientation.

The Prosodic Model offers two ways of expressing the multitude of orientation relations in the HM and VP Models. First, underlying orientation is expressed by a single two-part relation, rather than by several relations, and the base of the hand is not used as a handpart, since the base of the hand can be held in one position while other parts assume different positions; for example, the palm can be up or down (e.g., CHILDREN vs. THING vs. WAY). One element of the orientation relation is handpart, specified at the H_1 node, and the other is plane of articulation (x, y, or z); see (16). Second, movement of the hand can be perpendicular to the plane of articulation or within it, given what defines a [direction] or [tracing] path feature, respectively.

(16) *Orientation as a two-place relation*

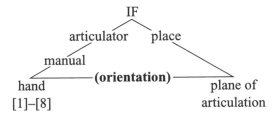

Battison (1978) described the eight places of articulation only as places of contact on H_2, but in fact, they are equally important for specifying underlying orientation of the hand.[11] Examples are given in the following table:

Hand places

	H_2 (passive POA; has a role as a POA)	H_1 (part of active articulator; has a role as part of the orientation relation)
[1] Palm of hand	LEARN	MY
[2] Finger fronts	DISMISS	LABEL
[3] Back of palm	TOUCH	LOVE-SOMETHING
[4] Back of fingers	EASY	CHERISH
[5] Radial side of selected fingers	WOOD	OLD
[6] Ulnar side of selected fingers	TICKET	BROKE (i.e., "no money")
[7] Tip of selected fingers/thumb	TOP	COMPLAIN
[8] Heel of hand	CHEESE	SLIP

When orientation is viewed in this way, as a two-part relation, the hand-parts specified above can capture the minimal contrast between such signs as CHERISH and OLD. In both signs the chin is the point of articulation, 'S' is the underlying handshape, and there is a handshape change to the 'S'. The only difference is that for CHERISH the *back of the fingers* is the handpart specified under the hand node, whereas for OLD the handpart is *radial*. This account also captures underlying orientation by using parts of the hand that are independently motivated as being phonologically significant for H_2. Handpart is placed within the articulator branch to recognize that one part of the hand is phonologically significant to articulate a given sign correctly.

3.7   Nonterminal Features

Certain features occupy nonterminal nodes in the structure. As noted earlier, [stacked] and [spread] are treated in this way. [Alternating] is analyzed as a feature rather than an inferred relationship, because the phonological operation of Weak Drop (Padden and Perlmutter 1987) or Phonological Deletion (Battison 1978) must refer to it; an alternating two-handed sign may not surface as one-handed. Because of its effect of blocking this optional operation, [alternating] is specified at the H_2 node. [Symmetrical] expresses that analogous parts of the hand are oriented toward each other. This is something additional about orientation, which cannot be captured by the orientation relation alone. Because [symmetrical] describes orientation between the two hands in a two-handed sign, it is expressed at the articulator node, which dominates H_1 and H_2. The handpart features [1]–[8] are also located at the H_1 node. [Contact] is specified only once, and is located at the place node in most signs or at the articulator node in some two-handed signs discussed in chapter 7; it can also be located at the inherent features node itself in a few motherese variants, such as SLEEP. How [contact] is realized in the output is predictable from the type of path features specified in the prosodic branch of structure.

3.8   Conclusion

The most important aspects of the structure of the inherent features tree are the major division of inherent features into place and articulator features and the fundamental generalizations that can be captured by placing the inherent features together: their one-to-many relationship with prosodic features, their complex hierarchical structure and ability to express a large number of paradigmatic contrasts, their relationship of mutual exclusivity with the prosodic features. Not every detail of this structure is an innovation of the Prosodic Model, but the model does bring together for the first time structural analyses that provide a cohesive and comprehensive account of the surface facts of ASL.

Chapter 4
Prosodic Features

4.1 Introduction to Movement Types

In this chapter I present a specific organization for the prosodic features—the features that spell out the inventory of all underlying types of movement. Prosodic features may change during the production of core ASL lexemes; that is, they are realized sequentially in time. All well-formed monomorphemic signs have some type of movement. The guiding insights of the Prosodic Model come from placing the inherent and prosodic features on separate branches, as argued and justified in chapter 1, and from placing all movement features on the prosodic branch.

In sign language studies the term *movement* has been used in various ways: as a label for segments (e.g., in the HM, HT, μ Models), as a label for any dynamic aspect of the sign stream (e.g., transitional movements and word-internal movements), and as a label for only those dynamic aspects of signs that are word-internal (handshape change, orientation change, path movement, setting change, and trilled movement). For this reason, and because it is important to be consistent and clear about this family of concepts, I list in (1) the definitions I will use here. Some differences between simple and complex movements were mentioned in chapter 1; these distinctions, plus a few others, are included. The feature geometry of the prosodic branch of structure is given in (2).

(1) *Definitions in the Prosodic Model related to* path *and* movement

    a. *Path movements* are articulated by the elbow or shoulder joints, resulting in a discrete change of place of articulation in the sign space on the body or in the external space in front of the signer (e.g., LOOK).

b. *Path features* are dominated by the path node in the prosodic branch of structure, specifying the shape or direction of a movement, or an arm pivot (e.g., SORRY, LOOK, DAY).

c. *Local movements* are articulated by the wrist or finger joints, resulting in a change of handshape or orientation of the hands, or a trilled movement (e.g., UNDERSTAND, DIE, COLOR).

d. *Simple movements* involve a single local or path movement (e.g., LOOK, UNDERSTAND, DIE).

e. *Complex movements* involve two or more co-occurring path or local movements (e.g., POOR, BETTER, MEETING, OLD).

f. *Lexical movements* are specifications in underlying representation for a lexeme or affix (e.g., all of the examples in (a)–(e)).

g. *Transitional movements* are phrase-level epenthetic movements (e.g., between MOTHER and GIVE).

(2) *The prosodic features branch of structure*

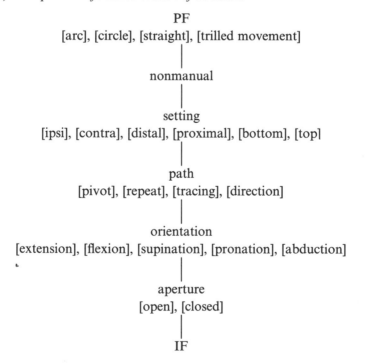

PF
[arc], [circle], [straight], [trilled movement]

nonmanual

setting
[ipsi], [contra], [distal], [proximal], [bottom], [top]

path
[pivot], [repeat], [tracing], [direction]

orientation
[extension], [flexion], [supination], [pronation], [abduction]

aperture
[open], [closed]

IF

It has been proposed that ASL has no movement features—that is, that all movements are the result of interpolation between points of stasis

(Stack 1988; Uyechi 1995). For example, all arc movements, seen for example in HAPPEN, BREAK, and the [multiple] affix, are analyzed in these "movementless" models as having an orientation change and a location change. The Prosodic Model supports an opposing view, which is that path features are needed in ASL grammar. Regarding their realization by specific joints, ASL movements fall into two classes of simple movements. Certain movements can be specified at the prosodic features node as abstract shapes, which can be realized by the shoulder, elbow, or wrist; for example, TELL has a [straight] feature that can be realized by any of these joints.[1] Other movements are invariably realized by the same joints specified by the input features; for example, UNDERSTAND invariably has an aperture change, and DIE invariably has an orientation change. The latter type of movement can be enhanced or reduced by spreading to an adjacent joint. Some signs have both an abstract prosodic shape and a specified handshape change (e.g., TAKE, THROW) or two movements at particular joints (e.g., CAN'T-DO-IT); these are the signs with complex movements.

Arc, straight, and circle are the three abstract shapes that can be specified at the prosodic features node. Straight movements are the only movements that occur in all subcomponents of the lexicon. Straight movements also have the most subtypes and are inserted as epenthetic movements when constraints call for epenthesis; straight movement is therefore taken to be the default movement of ASL, as in the HT Model (Sandler 1989). Not all straight movements need to be specified underlyingly as such at the prosodic features node. A [direction] feature at the path node can only be realized as a straight movement; therefore, in these cases the [straight] feature at the prosodic features node is redundant.[2] Arc movements occur as abstract shapes primarily in affixal or classifier forms; however, a few core forms are specified for such movements. Circle and straight movements occur more frequently as abstract shapes in core lexemes.[3] Examples of movement shapes in core lexemes, affixes, and classifier predicates are given in (3). As mentioned in chapter 1, these basic shapes are distributed in two-movement (disyllabic) sequences in much the same way that tones are combined in tonal melodies in such languages as Venda (Cassimjee 1983). The relevant examples from chapter 1 are reproduced in the table that follows (3); see figure 1.26 for examples of a 'circle + straight' two-movement sequence realized by the orientation node (e.g., LOCK), the aperture node (e.g., APPOINT-MENT), and the path node (e.g., WHEN).

(3) *Abstract prosodic movements in the native lexicon*[4]

   a. *Circle movements*

      i. In core stems: YEAR, TRAVEL-AROUND, WHEN (1st movement)

      ii. In bound affixes: [apportionative] aspect

      iii. In classifier forms: move-in-a-circle

   b. *Straight movements*

      i. In core stems: BLACK, SHAVE, GIRL

      ii. In bound affixes: [iterative] aspect

      iii. In classifier forms: move-from-point 'a'-to-point 'b'-on-a-straight-path

   c. *Arc movements*

      i. In core stems: RAINBOW

      ii. In bound affixes: [multiple] aspect (sometimes referred to as plural; Askins and Perlmutter 1995)

      iii. In classifier forms: seated-audience-arranged-in-an-arc

Abstract movement types and their expression

	Path (location Δ)	Handshape Δ	Orientation Δ
1-movement types			
straight: from [▷]	TELL	WAKE-UP	OPEN
straight: to [▷⏐]	SIT	SAY-NO	CLOSE
tracing [—]	BLACK	****	LONG
circle [O]	YEAR	BEAUTY	ALL
2-movement sequences			
repeat	MILITARY	MELON	BETRAY
repeat: 90° '7'	DETROIT	REMOVE	****
repeat: 90° 'X'	CANCEL	****	HOSPITAL
repeat: set.$_i$ set.$_j$	CHILDREN	NAVY	GO/RETURN HERE
repeat: 180° (bidirectional)	JUMP	WHITE (race)	COOK
alternating	BICYCLE	JESUS	COMPETITION
[O], [—]	WHEN	APPOINTMENT	LOCK

Only the abstract shapes themselves—arc, circle, and straight—are represented at the prosodic features node. Other movement features, such as [alternating], [direction], [tracing], and [repeat], appear elsewhere in the representation.

4.2 Movement Migration: Proximalization and Distalization

As shown in chapter 1, prosodic features are phonetically realized by a set of default joints that execute handshape changes (i.e., finger joints), orientation changes (i.e., wrist), path features (i.e., elbow), and setting changes (i.e., shoulder). It is well known, however, that a sign is often executed by more than the one set of joints specified by its underlying prosodic features, or by a set of joints other than those that execute the movement in the default case. The representation developed in this chapter can explain this phonetic variability. Recall the theory of phonetic enhancement (Stevens and Keyser 1989; Stevens, Keyser, and Kawasaki 1986) that has been proposed for spoken languages. According to this theory, three features—[sonorant], [continuant], and [coronal]—are primary. Secondary features such as [voice], [strident], and [nasal] may enhance the primary features in specific ways. The articulators used by the primary and enhancing features (e.g., [voice] to enhance [sonorant]) are not the same; what is important is the strengthening of perceptual salience of [sonorant] by [voice].

Considering how the perceptual salience of ASL movements can be likewise strengthened or weakened has motivated my use of Enhancement Theory in the Prosodic Model. As an initial hypothesis, the prosodic class nodes are arranged according to physiological adjacency, placing shoulders at one end of a range of possible joints used to articulate a movement and finger joints at the other end.

(4) *Arrangement of class nodes of the prosodic branch from most distal to most proximal joints*

aperture Δ < orientation Δ < path < setting Δ

What often happens in the phonetic realization of a sign is that the movement migrates from the default joint of its particular movement type to a more proximal joint or to a more distal one. One example is HARD (figure 4.1), a sign specified in the input for [direction], indicating that it involves a movement toward a point. [Direction] is realized by the elbow

Figure 4.1
The citation form of HARD (left), which contains an elbow movement, and the distalized form of HARD (right), which contains a wrist movement

Figure 4.2
The citation form of UNDERSTAND (left), which has an aperture change, and a proximalized form of UNDERSTAND (right), which contains a path movement

in the default case, but it can be articulated by the wrist. This operation is called phonetic reduction, or *distalization*. Another example is UNDER-STAND (figure 4.2), a sign specified in the input for an aperture change, which is often realized with an accompanying path movement. This is called phonetic enhancement, or *proximalization*. Movements migrate because of physiological factors, social considerations, or interactions between signers and perceivers. The signing of persons who have Parkinson's disease is often characterized by distalized movements (Brentari and

Poizner 1994), and emerging evidence suggests that young children's sign movements are often proximalized (Conlin et al. 1998).

A local movement (i.e., a handshape change or orientation change) can spread easily to a path movement (i.e., a setting change or path feature) or vice versa. In the Prosodic Model this type of spreading can be straightforwardly handled by the addition of an association line to the adjacent prosodic features node, plus translation statements that instruct the joints how to realize the movement, which may vary in a language-particular way. The translation statements listed in the following table are illustrative. Articulating a full set of these statements will require considering the degrees of freedom of the joints and the particular movement shapes involved. This is a topic relating to the phonetics-phonology interface that goes beyond the scope of this book.

Examples of movement translation statements

	Aperture	Orientation Δ	Path
Type I	opening handshape Δ	wrist flexion	direction away from the signer; e.g., SEND
Type II	closing handshape Δ	wrist extension	direction toward the signer; e.g., TAKE

These effects are phonetically implemented in the cases described here, and they can be blocked by grammatical specifications, such as have been described for tense markers in ASL (see Jacobowitz and Stokoe 1988). The point is that the Prosodic Model represents such movement migrations as natural operations due to production or perceptual considerations. The HT and DP Models put path and local movement at different places in the representation, making such variation less transparent in those models than in the Prosodic Model.

The Prosodic Model also captures the fact that in many affixal operations, local movements and path movements in stems are effected identically. Two examples follow. First, in the exhaustive aspect the movement of the stem is repeated; it does not matter if the movement is a local movement (e.g., HATE [exhaustive] 'to hate every one of them'), a path movement (e.g., GIVE [exhaustive] 'to give to every one of them'), or both (e.g., ADVISE [exhaustive] 'to advise every one of them'). Second, in one form of the intensive aspect, with lengthened holds at the beginning of the stem, it does not matter if the stem is the beginning of a local

movement (e.g., UNDERSTAND [intensive] 'got it!'), a path movement (e.g., TAKE-OFF [intensive] 'outta-here!'), or both (e.g., GRAB-
OPPORTUNITY [intensive]). Sandler (1989, 1993) has used forms like
these to argue that Locations, which bear a strong resemblance to the x-
slots proposed in the DP and Prosodic Models, are segments in ASL;
timing slots and segmental structure will be discussed in chapter 5. These
facts make an argument that goes beyond the justification for segments;
they are evidence for unifying all features involved in these operations
(e.g., aperture, setting, orientation) as a single unit of structure.

4.3   Path Features

Path features are taken to be lines articulated with respect to a plane of
articulation; they are represented at the path node of the prosodic features
branch of structure. All path features specify a movement either within
the plane of articulation or at a 90° angle to the plane of articulation.
Core lexemes are specified with respect to one plane; Wallin (1994) and
I (Brentari 1990c) have argued that classifier predicates may involve a
second plane.

In previous work I have argued for [direction] and [tracing] path
features for ASL (Brentari 1988, 1990c,d). Two other path features are
[pivot], expressed in signs involving the arm, and [repeat], expressed in
disyllabic signs. [Alternating] is a feature used only in two-handed signs
and is represented at the H_2 node, discussed in chapter 7. Phonetic definitions of these features are given in (5), schematic drawings of their realization in figure 4.3, and examples in figure 4.4.

(5) *Definitions of path features*

   a. [direction]: a phonologically specified straight path executed at a
      90° angle to (notated [>|]) or from (notated [|>]) a point in a plane
      of articulation, either from such a point or to such a point (e.g.,
      GIVE, SUBSCRIBE)

   b. [tracing]: a line with an arc, straight, or circle shape articulated
      with respect to a single point within a plane (e.g., RAINBOW,
      BLACK, and SORRY, respectively)

   c. [pivot]: a movement in which the elbow is fixed (e.g., DAY,
      MORNING)

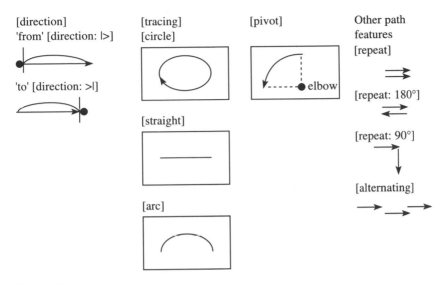

Figure 4.3
The surface realization of path features

  d. [repeat]: a straight movement that is repeated in one of several
     ways: identically, at a 90° angle, at a 180° angle (i.e., bidirectional
     signs)
  e. [alternating] (two-handed signs only): a two-handed movement
     during which the articulators move 180° out of phase with one
     another

In the following sections I argue that path features are needed to make
the grammar as simple as possible: they allow the model to account
for the distribution of movements in the first stem of compounds, the
distribution of contact, and the direction of movement in a class of verb
stems.

4.3.1 The Distribution of Movements in the First Stem of Compounds

There are two groups of signs with identical surface citation forms, which
behave differently in compounds (Brentari 1990d). When occurring as the
first stem of a compound, one group is articulated with the same path
movement that occurs in the citation form (see (6a) and figure 4.5 (top));
another group is articulated without the path movement that occurs in the
citation form (see (6b) and figure 4.5 (bottom)).

Figure 4.4
Example signs illustrating the path features: INFORM [direction] (top left),
SORRY [tracing] (top right), DAY [pivot] (middle left), CHILDREN [repeat]
(middle right), and BICYCLE [alternating] (bottom).

Figure 4.5
The citation form of BLACK (top left) and BLACK as it appears in the first stem of the compound BLACK^NAME (top right); the path movement surfaces in both forms. The citation form of THINK (bottom left) and THINK as it appears in the first stem of the compound THINK^SELF (bottom right); the path movement surfaces only in the citation form.

(6) *Compound forms: inputs and outputs*

    a. *Signs with movement in the first stem*

Citation form	Compound
CALL[5]	NAME^SHINE 'good reputation'
MONEY	MONEY^BEHIND 'savings'
WEDDING	WEDDING^CELEBRATE 'anniversary'
BLACK	BLACK^NAME 'bad reputation'

b. *Signs without movement in the first stem*

Citation form	*Compound*
KNOW	KNOW^THAT
	'know that'
THINK	THINK^SELF
	'decide for oneself'
HEART	HEART^ATTACK
	'heart attack'
WRONG	WRONG^HAPPEN
	'unexpected'
TIME	TIME^SAME
	'simultaneous'

The signs in (6a) are analyzed as having an underlying [tracing] or [direction] feature; the signs in (6b) are analyzed as having no underlying path feature, and as instead containing an epenthetic movement to contact in the citation form. The epenthetic movement is expressed as a [direction] feature. The differing behavior of signs in the first stem of compounds is thereby explained: when an underlying path feature is present, it is preserved in compounds; when no path feature is present in the underlying representation, the first stem will appear as a place of articulation + contact without a path feature.

4.3.2   Predictability of Contact: The Difference between [Direction] and [Tracing] Features

Path features are also needed in the representation to account for the distribution of [contact]. As just shown, signs such as NAME and CALL contain an underlying path feature, and signs such as THINK and KNOW contain no underlying path feature. Like THINK and KNOW, the signs in (7a) contain no path feature; the initial movement to contact is a result of an epenthetic movement. Signs with a path feature can be further distinguished on the basis of how contact is realized. The signs in (7b) and (7c) both retain their path in movement when used as the first stem of a compound (e.g., MONEY^BEHIND 'savings', BLACK^NAME 'bad reputation', READ^CHECK 'proofread'), yet the signs in (7b) realize contact at the beginning or end of the movement, whereas the signs in (7c) realize contact either throughout the entire movement or as a brushing contact during the middle of the movement.

(7) *Distribution of the feature [contact] in three groups of signs*

   a. *No path feature in input;* ∅

     THINK
     HEART
     KNOW
     TIME
     SICK

   b. *Path feature [direction] in input; values [|>] or [>|]*

     MONEY [>|]
     HIT [>|]
     CALL [>|]
     WEDDING [>|]
     ADMIT [|>]

   c. *Path feature [tracing] in input; values [circle] or [straight]*

     WHAT'S-UP [straight]
     BLACK [straight]
     READ [straight]
     SORRY [circle]

The difference between the forms in (7b) and (7c) is analyzed as follows. Even though the path in both sets of forms has a straight shape, the signs in (7b) are specified for the feature [direction], and the signs in (7c) are specified for the feature [tracing]. This is a logical consequence of the definition of these features given in (5). Movements specified for [direction] are realized at a 90° angle with respect to a plane; therefore, in such signs contact occurs at the point when the movement meets the plane. Movements specified for [tracing] are realized within a plane; therefore, in such signs contact occurs throughout the entire movement.

(8) *The relationship between [contact] and path features*

   a. Signs whose representation contains a [direction] feature realize [contact] either at the beginning of the path movement (in a [direction: |>] from a point) or at the end of the path movement (in a [direction: >|] to a point).

   b. Signs whose representation contains a [tracing] feature realize [contact] throughout the path movement in the citation form or, optionally in surface forms, in the middle of the path movement.

To summarize: This account allows contact to be specified at the place node, as described in chapter 3, and allows its surface realization to be predicted from the type of path feature (8). The account explains the differences between surface forms by means of differences in their input structures (having an input path feature or not; having a [direction] or [tracing] input feature).

Using these features, the Prosodic Model can distinguish between signs that look similar or identical on the surface, but behave differently in different phonological contexts. In the HM and HT Models the input contains Movement segments everywhere any kind of movement occurs in the output; such analyses do not differentiate signs with underlying path features from those with epenthetic word-internal movements. The VP Model and Stack's (1988) model offer the opposite but equally incorrect analysis. No input has path features; therefore, all of the signs in (7) are treated alike, and the relevant distinctions go unaccounted for.

One outstanding problem for this analysis is raised by signs with a [circle] tracing, such as FACE, which appears in the compound FACE^STRONG 'resemblance', and YEAR, which appears in the compound NEXT^YEAR 'next year'. As Uyechi (1995, 117) points out, such signs sometimes do lose their [circle] feature in compounds and in forms involving numeral incorporation; she uses this fact as an argument against path features. At this point there is no clear explanation for why circular paths more readily delete in the first stem of compounds. Even in the VP Model, circular movements are not predictable; they must be specified by a "movement function" (Δ). The only aspect of structure distinguishing (for example) THINK, with no underlying path, and FACE, with an underlying circle, is this movement function, since FACE must be prevented from having an epenthetic movement inserted and must surface with a circular path rather than a straight movement to contact. Because of the contrastive nature the movement function serves in these cases, the need to posit it actually supports, rather than obviates, the need for path features.

I reinforce the case for path features with arguments presented by Sandler (1996a) concerning path features in Israeli Sign Language. Sandler argues that movement features are a necessary part of the phonological grammar of sign languages because (1) they are contrastive; (2) they form a phonetically coherent set; (3) they form a class that is referred to in a blocking constraint and other morphophonological processes; (4) they constitute underspecified morphemes; and (5) they are required of well-formed signs. Only the third argument concerning morphophonological interaction will be highlighted here. In a pair of forms from Israeli Sign Language with identical syntactic properties, the ability to allow multiple affixation is based on phonological grounds. CONVINCE contains small circles in the movement, and INFLUENCE contains only a straight movement to contact; as in ASL, in Israeli Sign Language the [multiple] affix is expressed as a horizontal arc in front of the signer. In Israeli Sign Language those signs that are argued to contain a particular movement shape, such as [circle] in the sign CONVINCE, block multiple affixation. Only signs with a straight movement, which is argued to be inserted as a default movement when none is present in the input form, allow multiple affixation.

4.3.3   The Feature [Direction] and ASL Verb Stems

Besides being useful in predicting contact, [direction] serves an important function in the morphology. In this section I summarize earlier findings (Brentari 1988, 1990c) regarding a class of ASL verb forms that have a [direction] feature.

Like most languages, ASL has a class of predicates that can subcategorize for only one syntactic argument, a subject (e.g., SIT, SORRY, RUN), and other classes of predicates that can subcategorize for more than one argument. For example, READ, RESPECT, ADMIT, and ADOPT subcategorize for a subject and an object. GIVE is the typical verb that can subcategorize for three syntactic arguments in many languages, including ASL; see Padden 1983 for an analysis of these signs. In addition to and independent from these syntactic arguments, some ASL verb stems that subcategorize for two syntactic arguments include a [direction] feature, encoding a type of transitivity relation that Jackendoff (1987) has called a *subordinate conceptual function*. The subordinate conceptual function captures transfer events that occur on a level of structure other than syntactic structure.

Briefly, the difference between the *primary conceptual function* and a *subordinate conceptual function* is this. The primary conceptual function is a means of encoding the transfer of energy; it is concerned with notions of agentivity and transitivity among the syntactic arguments of a verb. In the sentences 'I bought it' and 'I sold it' the subject is the volitional agent and the object is the patient; therefore, in both sentences the primary conceptual function is the same.[6] The subordinate conceptual function is a means of encoding the transfer of a theme. In the same sentences, 'I bought it' and 'I sold it', the themes—the money and the object—move in opposite directions; therefore, the two sentences express different subordinate conceptual functions. It is the movement that themes undergo— the subordinate conceptual function—that is important for the ASL analysis presented here.[7]

In languages like Batsbi (a split-ergative language of the northeastern Caucasus Mountains) the subordinate conceptual structure is overtly marked in the morphology by varying the case assignment of the subject noun phrase. (Regarding Batsbi, see DeLancey 1981; the glosses in (9) are from Comrie 1978.)

(9) *Case assignment used to encode the subordinate conceptual level*

   a. txo   naizdrax   kxitra
      we (abs)   to-ground fell
      'We fell to the ground.' (unintentionally; not our fault)

   b. a-txo   naizdrax   kxitra
      we (erg)   to-ground fell
      'We fell to the ground.' (intentionally; through our own
      carelessness)

In (9a) an external force may have caused the subject to fall (i.e., the subject is acted upon). In (9b) there is no external force acting on the subject (i.e., the subject is also the agent). The analogy between Batsbi and ASL is not perfect since in ASL the subordinate conceptual function is expressed in the verbal morphology whereas in Batsbi it is expressed on nouns, yet it is clear that the case assignment in Batsbi encodes subordinate conceptual function.

Languages also often use an alternative form of a verb to encode this function; one of these is the Algonquian language Fox (discussed in Comrie 1981). The verb forms in (10)—direct and inverse—encode the directionality of the two events.

(10) *Different verb morphology used to encode the subordinate conceptual level*

   a. ne -waapam-aa -wa
      1sg see-direct   3
      'I see him.'

   b. ne -waapam-ek -wa
      1sg see-inverse 3
      'He sees me.'

Like the ASL stems discussed in the following paragraphs, the direct and inverse forms in Fox encode the subordinate conceptual function in the verb; however, in Fox this function is expressed in affixal morphology, not as a part of the phonological shape of the stem. Direct forms of Fox verbs, like ASL verbs with typical transfer relations between a subject and object (e.g., TELL in (13c)), encode transfer of the theme (e.g., what is told) from the subject to the object. Inverse forms of Fox verbs, like ASL verbs with atypical (or backward) transfer relations (e.g., SUBSCRIBE in (13b)), encode transfer of the theme (e.g., the periodical) from the object to the subject.

In order to express the subordinate conceptual function, a large class of transitive ASL verbs contains a [direction] feature, which corresponds to the transfer relation in the stem. Those ASL verbs with typical directionality are analyzed as having a [direction: |>] feature; those with atypical directionality are analyzed as having a [direction: >|] feature. The process of encoding transfer relations in the phonological structure of ASL verbs can be expressed as follows:

(11) *Direction-of-Transfer Principle*

  a. Direction expressed by path movement

   When the sign expresses transfer of a theme away from the
   subject, the path moves away from the spatial locus associated
   with the signer (in the default case) or away from the overtly
   marked subject spatial locus. When the sign expresses transfer
   of a theme toward the subject, the path moves toward the spatial
   locus associated with the signer (in the default case) or toward
   the overtly marked subject locus.

  b. Direction expressed by orientation[8]

   When orientation is relevant to expressing the transfer of a
   theme, the back of the hand is oriented toward the signer (in
   the default case) or toward the overtly specified subject locus.

In addition to this directionality encoded in the verb, some ASL verbs allow one or both of the subject and object arguments to be affixed to the verb as spatial loci. This typology of verbs is shown in (12), with example sentences in (13).

(12) *Typology of ASL verbs with a [direction] feature*

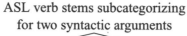

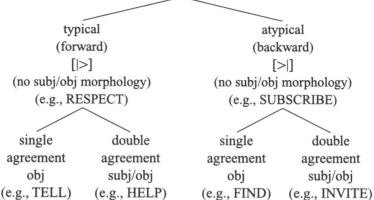

(13) *Example sentences*

a. $INDEX_3$ $_0RESPECT_{-0}$ MY MOTHER.

'She/He respects my mother.' (typical directionality, no agreement)

b. $\overline{}^{\,t}\overline{}$ G-Q MAGAZINE $INDEX_3$ $_{-0}SUBSCRIBE_0$.

'He/She subscribes to *GQ* magazine.' (atypical directionality, no agreement)

c. J-O-H-N $INDEX_3$ $_0TELL_4$ M-A-R-Y $INDEX_4$.

'John told Mary.' (typical directionality, object agreement)

d. M-A-R-Y $INDEX_3$ $_3HELP_4$ J-O-H-N $INDEX_4$.

'Mary helps John.' (typical directionality, subject and object agreement)

e. $\overline{}^{\,t}\overline{}$ BOOK $INDEX_d$, $INDEX_3$ $_dFIND_0$ YESTERDAY.

'He found the book yesterday.' (atypical directionality, object agreement)

f. $\overline{}^{\,t}\overline{}$ M-A-R-Y $INDEX_3$ $_4INVITE_3$ J-O-H-N $INDEX_4$ PARTY.

'Mary invited John to the party.' (atypical directionality, subject and object agreement)

The agreement loci in the atypical class of verbs are in reverse order (i.e., 'object, subject' rather than 'subject, object') even though the subject and object noun phrases occur in their usual sentential positions (e.g., (13f)). These forms show that the verb stem structures of ASL include both a semantic and a syntactic component; the forms in (13a) and (13b) demonstrate that path features play a semantic role, even if [direction] is not a morpheme, but a phonological feature with a partially semantic motivation.

Askins and Perlmutter (1995) and Meir (1995) have built on this analysis in different ways. Askins and Perlmutter observe that in ASL forms with a [direction] feature, but no underlying orientation, the [direction] feature spreads to orientation. A verb such as SEND, whose underlying palm orientation changes according to its agreement morphology, is analyzed as having no underlying orientation. [Direction] spreads from the path node to the basic orientation of the hand. A verb such as INFORM, whose orientation does not change according to its agreement morphology, is analyzed as having an underlying orientation specification. [Direction] is blocked from spreading, and the orientation is the same for all directions of movement and orders of reference loci. Analyzing forms in Israeli Sign Language, Meir (1995) argues that facing (i.e., fingertip) orientation, rather than palm orientation, is the structural feature of orientation that changes in some agreement forms; she further argues that the Direction-of-Transfer Principle for Israeli Sign Language must refer to the grammatical object.

Both analyses confirm the original claims made in Brentari 1988 and add to it by emphasizing the importance of underlying orientation in an analysis of directional verbs. The Prosodic Model can accommodate the new findings. First, regarding orientation in ASL: Recall from chapter 3 that orientation is expressed as a handpart-to-place relation (14).

(14) *The representation of inherent orientation*

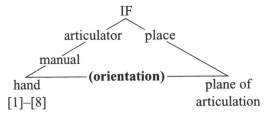

For some stems, orientation is specified in the input (e.g., Askins and Perlmutter's INFORM case); for others, orientation is filled in by the

Direction-of-Transfer Principle (e.g., Askins and Perlmutter's SEND case). Because of Askins and Perlmutter's findings, the Direction-of-Transfer Principle is split into two parts: one for the realization of path movements and one for the realization of orientation. Second, regarding facing and an object reference: The representation of agreement in chapter 3, plus the revised Direction-of-Transfer Principle, can handle the Israeli Sign Language cases that are comparable to the ASL cases.[9] Since the Prosodic Model represents orientation as a relation between a handpart and a place of articulation, if the base of the hand or back of the hand is oriented toward the subject, the orientation specification and articulator specification can achieve the necessary result; there is no need for the Direction-of-Transfer Principle to refer to the grammatical object or to facing features.

The Prosodic Model representations of $_1INFORM_2$, $_1BAWL-OUT_2$, and $_1ADVISE_2$ are given in (15). These examples show explicitly how the model accommodates Meir's (1995) findings and makes more precise those of Askins and Perlmutter (1995).

(15) *The expression of [direction] as orientation in three directional signs (features oriented toward the signer or subject are circled)*[10]

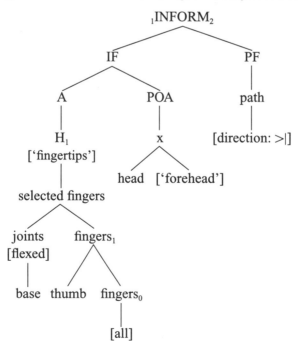

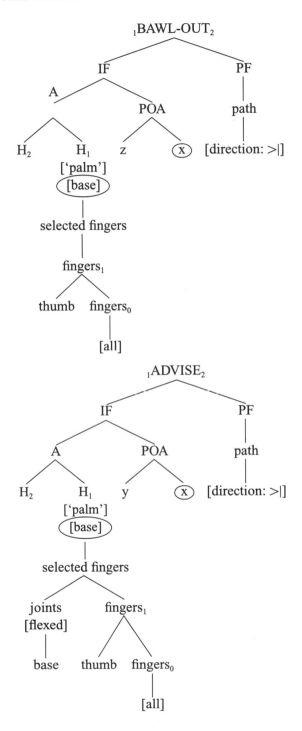

Of these three signs, INFORM is the only one that expresses the [direction] feature only at the path node of the verb. The other two express [direction] on the path movement and on the inherent orientation. ADVISE and BAWL-OUT cannot be described as having no inherent orientation; rather, they have no inherent orientation specification for a ventral (i.e., an x-) plane. The orientation of ADVISE is toward a transverse (i.e., a horizontal or y-) plane; the orientation of BAWL-OUT is toward a midsagittal (i.e., a z-) plane. Therefore, [direction] can spread in ADVISE and BAWL-OUT as Atkins and Perlmutter (1995) have noted, not because they have no inherent feature specification, but because they have no x-plane specification.[11] This allows us to say that an agreement affix is a point specified within a frontal plane, one associated either with the signer or with some nonfirst person, and that [direction] is realized at a 90° angle to this frontal plane. These example representations also show that the Prosodic Model accounts for palm and facing orientation in these cases: by combining the inherent specification for orientation with (11b) of the Direction-of-Transfer Principle, the model achieves the correct surface forms for ADVISE and BAWL-OUT. (11b) is therefore spelled out with respect to redundancies in the system as in (16).

(16) *Direction expressed by orientation*

When orientation is relevant to the expression of the transfer of a theme, the back or base of the hand is oriented toward the signer (in the default case) or toward the overtly specified subject locus.

a. When the stem has an inherent orientation involving a y- or z-plane, the handpart oriented toward the signer or subject is the base of the hand.

b. When the stem has an inherent orientation involving an x-plane, the handpart oriented toward the signer or subject is the back of the hand.

It is also noteworthy that the fingertips are not the part of the hand consistently facing the object argument in such cases. In BAWL-OUT it is the fingertips; in other ASL signs, such as HIT and MAKE-CONTACT-WITH-A-PERSON, it is the back of the fingers. The descriptive generalization is not captured by fingertip orientation, but by the orientation of the back or base of the hand. Thus, we see how the proposal that inherent orientation is a relation and the analysis using a [direction] feature allow the semantic component of verb stems to be integrated into an analysis of agreement.

4.4 Setting Changes

A *setting change* is the movement between two values in a plane in which the articulator can move. Setting features are realized as movements articulated by the shoulder, in the default case. As described in chapter 3, the plane of articulation is the place specification. Within a given plane, one way for an input to specify a movement is to include two points of reference; each type of plane has two possible sets of setting features. The planes are repeated in figure 4.6, and possible settings that can be specified in each plane are given in figure 4.7. Example signs are given in (17).

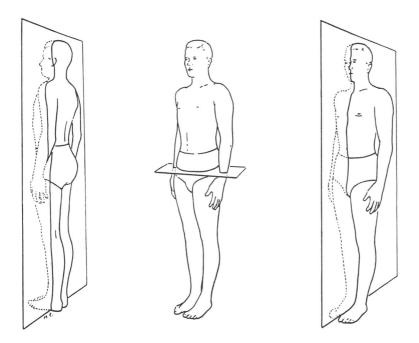

Figure 4.6
The contrastive planes of articulation in ASL based on three-dimensional space: (left) the frontal or ventral plane (the x-plane); (middle) the horizontal or transverse plane (the y-plane); and (right) the midsagittal plane (the z-plane) (from Luttgens and Hamilton 1997, 38; by permission)

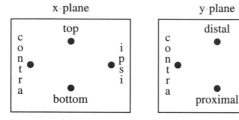
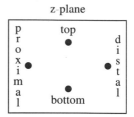

Figure 4.7
Possible setting specifications in each dimension

(17) *Example signs illustrating the use of setting specification in the core lexicon*

　　a. *x- (frontal or ventral) plane*

　　　　BODY [top], [bottom] (torso)
　　　　BACKGROUND [top], [bottom] (H_2)
　　　　MEMBER [contra], [ipsi] (torso)
　　　　FLOWER [contra], [ipsi] (cheek)

　　b. *y- (horizontal or transverse) plane*

　　　　POSTPONE [proximal], [distal]
　　　　CHILDREN [contra], [ipsi]

　　c. *z- (midsagittal) plane*[12]

　　　　ANALYZE [top], [bottom]

There are two ways to disambiguate setting changes from other types of path movements (although these will not determine the source of a movement in all cases). First, if the form in question can undergo metathesis, then it has a setting change, not a path movement. Second, the shape of the output form can make the distinction. I will discuss each of these in turn.

Metathesis applies to a subset of forms containing two points of contact within the same place of articulation (e.g., one of the vertical slices indicated by the eight specifications on the head, body, arm, or H_2). Widely discussed in the literature (Liddell and Johnson 1989; Brentari 1990c,d; Uyechi 1995), metathesis is an optional operation whereby the place of articulation of the preceding sign determines which of the two settings will occur first in a sign with a setting change. When a preceding sign ends in a place of articulation located below the [bottom] setting of DEAF, or on the [ipsi] side of FLOWER, CONGRESS, and MEMBER, these settings occur first; otherwise, [top] and [contra] are the default values for the first setting (18).

(18) *Ordering of settings in the default case*

When no setting order is indicated in the input, the following default settings are used: [contra] will occur before [ipsi], and [top] will occur before [bottom].

The two points of contact in this set of signs must be semi-independent in order for the first one to be seen as assimilating to the place of articulation of the preceding sign. Analyzing these structures as having a path feature makes metathesis more difficult to express; therefore, metathesis provides justification for treating some signs as having a setting change.

Expressing the operation of metathesis via the Prosodic Model allows us to formulate it with the minimum amount of structure, state its distribution and effects more precisely, and more accurately identify the class of signs that undergo it. It is possible to express the structures that most readily allow and disallow metathesis using the feature structures proposed thus far. Metathesis is not as pervasive as once thought (Lucas 1995). Only signs identified as having a setting change—and only a subset of these—undergo metathesis; signs with other types of movements may not undergo it. This is a problem for models of phonology that specify all path movements as setting changes (van der Hulst 1993); metathesis would be expected to be much more widespread if this were the correct representation of all movement.

The operation of metathesis also provides an argument for treating the straight movements to places as epenthetic. In spoken languages metathesis typically involves minimal amounts of structure. If the straight movements are a part of the input, metathesis must necessarily involve not just the settings, but the straight movements as well, which would mean that whole syllables are metathesized, not single features.

Signs most likely to undergo metathesis have the following two structural properties:

(19) *Structural description of signs most likely to undergo metathesis*

a. x dimension setting change (i.e., [top], [bottom])

b. a place of articulation on the body (rather than in neutral space)

As shown in (20), a form with both structural properties is more likely to undergo metathesis than a form with just one; a form having neither may not undergo metathesis under any conditions.

(20) *Structures involving metathesis expressed in the Prosodic Model*

    a. *Metathesis blocked (e.g., THING, CHILDREN, RESTROOM)*

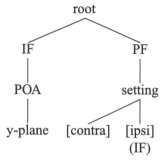

    b. *Metathesis allowed (e.g., DEAF, BODY, ADULT, HEAD)*

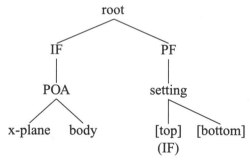

    c. *Metathesis allowed (e.g., MEMBER, FLOWER, BACHELOR, SENATE)*

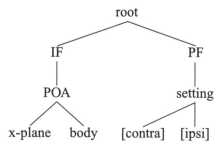

Another property that distinguishes movements originating from a path movement from those originating from a setting change is the shape of

Figure 4.8
Two variants of WE: one is realized with an [arc] path feature (left); the other is realized with a setting change and two short directional movements to contact (right).

the output form. Signs identifiable in this way have alternative pronunciations (e.g., WE, DEAF, FLOWER). The variant with two settings has two straight movements to contact and no orientation change during the intervening movement; the variant with the arc-shaped path feature has a smooth arc between the starting and ending points and an orientation change accompanying the path movement. The two forms of WE are shown in figure 4.8. These setting forms can be seen as having been reanalyzed by the phonology. First, they undergo a smoothing of the transitional movement and second straight movement; second, the transitional movement is reinterpreted by the grammar as a path movement; third, the epenthetic movements are deleted; fourth, an orientation change may optionally be added.

The Prosodic Model account of settings allows setting changes to be manipulated in the input structure to metathesis and in compounds, and it provides a way of inserting epenthetic movements to ensure a well-formed output when such forms occur as single words.

4.5 Orientation Changes

Orientation changes are movements articulated by the wrist joint. As discussed in chapter 1, the fundamental standing position (Luttgens and Hamilton 1997) is taken as basic; this means that the unmarked orientation of the two hands is toward the midsagittal plane (Crasborn 1995).

Unlike the finger joints, which have just two types of movement that can be seen as antagonists to one another (i.e., flexion and extension), the wrist joint can physically execute three kinds of movement: rotation, the surface result of which is that the hand moves either from a supine to a prone position (e.g., BET, HAPPEN, REBEL) or vice versa (e.g., DEAD, COOK); flexion or extension (e.g., YES and GIVE-UP, respectively); and adduction or abduction, or side-to-side movement (e.g., INSULT).

There is lexical contrast among the prosodic features of orientation. The representations for example signs are given in (21), and the signs are shown in figure 4.9. The inherent orientation can be specified in either of two timing positions, to be proposed in chapter 5. The input orientation is specified as a two-part relation in the inherent features branch of structure, as described in chapter 3.

(21) *Possible contrastive prosodic orientation features*

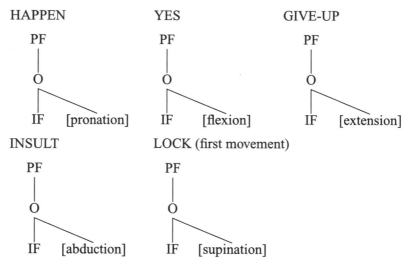

Thus far in my research, I have found that if an orientation change and a handshape change occur in a sign as a complex movement, the linear order of the inherent features need not be the same for both. This is shown in the representations given in (22) for STEAL and GRAB-OPPORTUNITY. The branching prosodic nodes will be aligned using timing units argued for in chapter 5, but the inherent features can be ordered on the prosodic tier differently.

Figure 4.9
Example signs illustrating the possible orientation specifications in ASL: HAPPEN [pronation] (top left), LOCK [supination] (top right), YES [flexion] (middle left), GIVE-UP [extension] (middle right), INSULT [abduction] (bottom)

(22) *Representations of signs with orientation change and aperture change*

STEAL

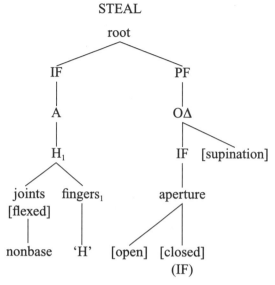

GRAB-OPPORTUNITY

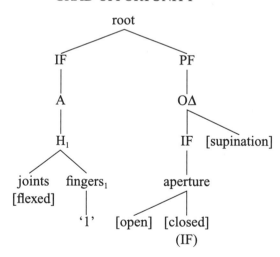

4.6 Handshape Changes

The representation of the fingers node proposed in chapter 3 is specific
enough to allow the aperture node of the prosodic features branch to

specify simply open or closed variants of handshapes in the contrastive inventory. Given this more detailed specification of the contrastive handshapes, we now have the means to integrate handshape changes into the grammar in a straightforward way, a way that has consequences for the segmental and syllable structures of the language. This analysis incorporates the insights of previous research, yet handles the forms more economically. The generalizations to be captured are these:

Descriptive generalizations concerning handshape change
1. There are two types of handshape changes: handshape contours, which are open or closed variants of the same underlying handshape, and handshape contrasts, which specify two contrastive handshapes (Perlmutter 1992).
2. Handshape contrasts are allowed in a more restricted set of contexts than handshape contours.
3. Of the two handshapes in a handshape contour, one of them is underlying and one is redundant; the redundant one is either an open or a closed variant of the underlying one (Stokoe 1960; Friedman 1976, 1977; Mandel 1981; Sandler 1989; Brentari 1990b).
4. Whether the redundant handshape in a handshape contour is the first or the second of the two handshapes is not systematic (Corina 1993).
5. Whether the redundant handshape in a handshape contour is the open or the closed variant is not systematic (Corina, 1993).

Various accounts have been proposed for handshape changes (Sandler 1989; Brentari 1990b,c; Perlmutter 1992; Corina 1993), but they have all failed in one way or another. In the HT Model, for example, Sandler proposed a Handshape Sequence Constraint that identified the domain of handshape contours as the morpheme and stated that the first handshape should be predictable from the second: "In monomorphemic signs, the initial and final handshapes are specified for the same selected fingers, and the first shape may be [+closed] if the second shape is [+open]. Otherwise, the first shape is [+open]" (Sandler 1989, 72). One weakness of this account of handshape change is that the contour cannot in fact be predicted from the second handshape, given Sandler's (1989) description of open and closed handshapes: if an open handshape is in second position, a flat (e.g., INFORM), a fully closed (e.g., ASK), or a bent (e.g., EJACULATE) handshape may be in first position. Another weakness is that this account does not address disyllabic, monomorphemic signs in ASL containing a handshape contrast (e.g., CURRICULUM, PROJECT,

BACKGROUND, BOARD-OF-TRUSTEES, CODE-OF-ETHICS). As a result, Perlmutter (1992) and I (Brentari 1990b,c) independently concluded that there may be only one contrastive handshape per syllable. I will revise this account below, since it has become clear that handshape contrasts may occur within a single syllable in certain contexts (i.e., in fingerspelled loan signs), and that in the native lexicon the constraint on underlying handshapes holds for the prosodic word unit rather than the syllable.

In earlier work (Brentari 1990b) I stated the constraint in terms of a restriction on the number of handshapes that are neither open nor closed in a word, but this account also fails because it does not explain why asymmetries like those described by Corina (1993) exist.[13] Corina points out that, of the two handshapes in a contour, one is more phonologically salient, since it is the one that appears in the affixes, but this handshape is systematically neither the first nor the second, neither the open nor the closed handshape. For example, in HATE [multiple] the first, closed handshape appears in the affix, whereas in ASK [multiple] the second, open handshape appears there (see figure 4.10). The choice of handshape in such affixes is used here as a diagnostic for determining which of the two handshapes in a contour is the inherent one.

Besides these observations about affixes, Corina (1993) provides other evidence that one of the handshapes in a handshape contour is underlying. Some compound forms allow a specific type of reduction in the first

 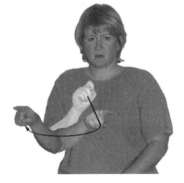

Figure 4.10
The signs HATE [multiple] (left) and ASK [multiple] (right) illustrate that the handshapes in a handshape contour are predictable neither from order (1st or 2nd) nor from aperture specification (open or closed). In HATE the first, closed handshape appears in the [multiple] affix; in ASK the second, open handshape appears.

stem, in which only one of the two handshapes in a handshape contour appears.[14] For example, when MILK, which has the handshape contour '5' → 'S', appears in the compound MILKSHAKE, only the 'S' appears in the surface form. When MALE, which has the handshape contour open → closed, flat 'B', appears in the compound MAN, only the closed, flat 'B' appears in the surface form. The handshape that surfaces in the compound is taken to be underlying.

The Prosodic Model can account for these facts as follows. First, for a given language the allophonic pairs of handshapes that occur in its handshape contour environments are listed. Second, for one-handed core lexemes, one underlying handshape is specified, on the hand branch of the inherent features branch of structure. This is the one that appears in the affix and in the reduced first stem of compounds. The redundant handshape then can be predicted from the underlying handshape and its predictable opposing value at the aperture node. Handshape contour is not predicted by temporal order, since phonologically contrastive ordering of handshapes in such environments does occur (see figure 4.11).

What is required for this analysis to work are the elements of the model proposed thus far, plus the following specifications for each of the underlying joint specifications: whether it is [open] or [closed], and what its predictable allophone is in the handshape contour environment. The two handshapes in a pair are a natural combination (the joints of each pair are the same and the combination follows the principle of ease of articulation for movements of the fingers); the similarity between the two

Figure 4.11
The signs $_2$SHUT-UP (2sg. imperative form; left) and $_0$SEND$_{-0}$ (right) illustrate that temporal order of handshape can be contrastive.

handshapes can therefore be said to be phonetically grounded in the sense of Archangeli and Pulleyblank 1994 (see also Ann 1996). For ASL, the joint classifications given earlier are listed in the following table, each with its underlying value (either [open] or [closed]) and its predictable opposing value in a handshape contour; all handshape contours include one open and one closed handshape. Handshapes with a [flexed] feature are interpreted by the system as [closed] in handshape contour environments; handshapes without a [flexed] feature are interpreted by the system as [open].

Underlying aperture settings for the handshape with five extended fingers

Handshape label	Joints specified	Input value (read from IF)	Redundant value	Sign example
open	none	[open]	[closed]	THROW
curved	base & nonbase	[open]	[closed]	ENVISION
curved [flexed]	base & nonbase	[closed]	[open]	BITE
flat	base	[open]	[closed]	SUN
flat [flexed]	base	[closed]	[open]	INFORM
bent [flexed]	nonbase	[closed]	[open]	WANT
closed [flexed]	all	[closed]	[open]	MILK

The fully open and fully closed handshapes are the least structurally marked, as shown in chapter 3. Fully open handshapes have no joints branch, and fully closed handshapes have an empty joints branch and a [flexed] feature; neither type has a joints branch with any daughters.[15]

This analysis handles several problems related to handshape changes. First, it allows us to better account for phonetic variation of redundant handshapes. By allowing both the fully open and the fully closed handshapes to have status as underlying handshapes, we can account for the fact that in forms containing an underlying 'S' (i.e., [closed]), the redundant [open] value is a partially assimilated curved handshape in the predictable [open] alternant; it is not a fully open handshape. This assimilation phenomenon is especially apparent when the form has a trilled movement. An example is MILK, where the first handshape is a predictable [open] 'S'; all the joints are already slightly flexed—they are not a fully open '5'. Likewise, even in a canonical handshape contour like the one in INFORM, the fact that the [open] alternant of a flat [flexed] 'B' is slightly flexed at the base joint is accounted for, since it is specified for this joint underlyingly.

Second, the analysis transparently expresses that the two handshapes of any contour are allophones in the traditional sense used in analyses of spoken languages. They are phonetically similar, because they are specified for the same joints, and they are predictable within the system in a given environment. This means, of course, that the contour pairs in different sign languages may differ; this is expected if allophonic families of handshapes in sign languages behave like allophonic families of sounds in spoken languages.

Third, the structure proposed in chapter 3 plus this account of aperture change can handle two sets of forms that have consistently been problematic for accounts of handshape change: the curved forms and the bent forms. Recall from chapter 3 that curved and flat handshapes have one variant that is specified for the feature [flexed] and another that is not, and that all bent handshapes are [flexed] (i.e., closed). It might seem counterintuitive to count bent handshapes as closed; however, this is the distribution they exhibit in handshape contours, as shown by WANT, PERPLEXED, ANGRY, and CRUEL, which change from an open to a bent '5' or '1'. In this account the difference in a noncontour environment between the handshape in the fingerspelled letter 'X', where there is no contact between the thumb and selected finger, and the handshape in WRITE, where there is contact between the thumb and selected finger, is not handled by the aperture node. Instead, the fingers$_1$ structure handles this contrast. In the fingerspelled letter 'X' the index finger is selected, but the thumb is not; therefore, the thumb is redundantly closed around the other nonselected fingers. In WRITE, however, the thumb is selected and opposed; therefore, there is contact between the thumb and other selected fingers, as in all the other [closed] handshape variants. Because the system specifies bent handshapes as [flexed], and therefore [closed], these facts are predictable.

Fourth, the proposed representation allows for the inherent handshape of an input structure to be ordered either first or second.

Finally, this account also provides a way of expanding the notion of handshape contrasts, defined in Perlmutter 1992, 1993 only in terms of selected fingers. Here we can see that a change in the joint specifications or a change in fingers—selected or nonselected—can constitute a handshape contrast.

With respect to the lexicalization of fingerspelled borrowings, a topic taken up at greater length in chapters 5 and 6, changes in joints or fingers in fingerspelled letters are handshape contrasts given the definition proposed in Brentari 1990b and Perlmutter 1992; these are also better illuminated by the Prosodic Model than by previous proposals. Like lexical signs, fingerspelled letters can be classified according to their joint specifications, including the presence or absence of the feature [flexed] (see appendix A), and their redundant [open] or [closed] aperture setting. Many partially assimilated fingerspelled forms contain pairs of flexed and nonflexed fingerspelled letters (e.g., O-K, B-A-C-K, C-A-R). This achieves a well-formed handshape contour even while violating the constraint on changes in selected fingers that holds in the (native) core component of the lexicon. In the representation of a form, such as O-K, with two sets of selected fingers, the H_1 node branches to two selected fingers nodes, SF_i and SF_j. The majority of stable handshape contrasts in fingerspelled loan signs either have joint specifications that conform to the pairs of joint specifications found in handshape contours, or have an orientation change or an inserted movement. The proposed account makes it possible to represent changes in joint specification or selected fingers in fingerspelled forms, even though these are prohibited in the core ASL lexicon, and to predict what kinds of fingerspelled forms are likely to be lexicalized as two-letter combinations. The constraint is formulated as MAXIMIZE APERTURE CHANGE (MAXAP Δ; (23)).[16] (I use the notion of a syllable peak here even though I do not give evidence for it until chapter 6; for now, consider the syllable peak to be the most proximal movement specified in an input.)

(23) *MAXIMIZE APERTURE CHANGE (MAXAP Δ)*

Handshape changes that occupy syllable peaks contain alternating [open] and [closed] aperture specifications.

It is important for a phonological grammar of ASL to be able to represent such changes, because only then can it account for the systematic weakening of constraints in the peripheral subcomponents of the lexicon that are not violable in core lexemes. At the same time, it captures the systematicity among different subcomponents of the lexicon.

4.7 An Articulator-Free Feature: [Trilled Movement]

Properties of signs that have been called *trilled movement* (TM) and *secondary movement* have been described in a wide range of theoretical frameworks.[17,18] TMs are produced at a variety of articulatory sites (at the mouth, at sites normally discussed as part of the handshape parameter (i.e., the hand and wrist), and at sites discussed as part of the movement or location parameter of sign); furthermore, they do not spread. These two properties have been discussed for the spoken language features by Halle (1995); in Halle's terms, TM can be analyzed as an "articulator-free" feature. As stated in (24), the place where TM appears in surface forms is largely predictable.

(24) *Principle of [TM] association*

In the absence of any lexical stipulation to the contrary, a [TM] feature associates predictably to the lowest branching class node of the prosodic features tree.

The predictable association of [TM] is used as evidence for the sonority ranking of prosodic features, discussed in chapter 6.

Figure 4.12 provides a descriptive list of TM types, with their single-movement counterparts and example signs. The list is basically the one compiled by Liddell and Johnson (1989), with the addition of 'tremor' (Wilbur 1987), 'tongue wagging' (TW; Davies 1983), 'pivoting' (Uyechi 1995), and 'closing' (the opposite of 'releasing').

'Circling' is produced by repeated small circling movements of the entire hand, accompanied by movement of the wrist, elbow, or shoulder. 'Tremor' is produced by repeated achievement of a single place of articulation and, like 'circling', is accompanied by movement of the wrist, elbow, or shoulder. In these cases the [TM] feature finds no branching class node to associate to, and it instead associates to the empty prosodic features branch. 'Rubbing',[19] 'hooking', 'flattening', 'wiggling', 'releasing', and 'closing'[20] are produced by repeated changes between two aperture specifications of handshape, accompanied by movement of the base and nonbase finger joints. 'Nodding', 'twisting', and 'pivoting' are produced by rapid changes between two orientation specifications, accompanied by movement of the wrist joint. 'Tongue wagging' is produced by rapid changes between two positions of the tongue, either up and down or side to side.

Of the nonmanual movements, only 'tongue wagging' has been included in the list of TMs, because it involves an uncountable number of repetitions.[21] Many nonmanual behaviors consist of opening or closing the mouth once in various ways (e.g., 'op', 'pa', 'thp'), making them more similar to single handshape or orientation changes. For others, the mouth

Joint(s)	Single movements		Trilled movements		Type of movement
	Ex. sign	Illus.	Ex. sign	Illus.	
elbow or shoulder	YEAR		COFFEE		P:'circling'
elbow or shoulder	***	∅	ELECTRI-CITY		POA:'tremor'
thumb	MELT		SOIL		HS:'rubbing'
mid &end finger joints	PERPLEXED		WHO		HS:'hooking'
knuckle	WAKE-UP		WHAT-TO-DO		HS:'flattening'
	***		TYPE		HS:'wiggling'
mid &end finger joints& knuckle	UNDER-STAND		ELEVEN		HS:'releasing'
	TAKE		MILK		HS:'closing'
wrist	WELL		COOL		O:'nodding'
	OPEN		FISH		O:'twisting'
	DAY		WHERE		O:'pivoting'
nonmanual	***	∅	FAR-IN-FUTURE		NM:'tongue wag'

Figure 4.12
Types of trilled movement, their single-movement counterparts, and example signs. Reprinted from *Lingua*, 98, D. Brentari, Trilled movement: Phonetic realization and formal representation, 43–71, 1996, with kind permission of Elsevier Science-NL, Sara Burgerhartstraat 25, 1055 KV Amsterdam, The Netherlands.

maintains a single posture throughout an entire sign (e.g., 'mm', 'th', 'sh'). Besides fitting the definition for TMs, 'tongue wagging' can be substituted for 'wiggling' as an allomorph in certain derived forms and therefore patterns morphophonemically with other TMs. 'Tongue-wagging' always constitutes a separate morpheme where it occurs in ASL.

Phonetically, TMs can always be classified according to their articulatory site (i.e., the tongue or the joints). Phonologically, TMs can be classified according to the prosodic class node they involve: handshape aperture Δ (TM:HS), orientation Δ (TM:O), setting Δ (TM:S), nonmanual Δ (TM:NM), place (TM:POA), or path (TM:P). Matching phonetic to phonological categories, however, is not always straightforward; I will give a few examples of the difficulties and explain how they have been handled here. For example, Liddell and Johnson (1989) consider 'wiggling' simply a kind of nonpath TM, but Corina (1990a), Johnson (1994), and Uyechi (1995) argue that it is a TM:HS. Here I adopt the latter view, because the set {TM:HS} is a proper subset of the set {TM:nonpath (i.e., local movement)} and because, both phonologically and phonetically, 'wiggling' behaves as a type of handshape change—specifically as a type of aperture modification, with each finger flexing at the base joint individually. [Spread] fingers takes 'wiggling' as its 'closing' TM; [−spread] fingers takes 'closing' in the same environment.

A second problem of matching phonetic to phonological categories concerns output forms such as WHERE and DAY. Each of these signs has two variants; in figure 4.12 only the phonetic forms for WHERE and DAY articulated at the wrist—a local movement—are included. There is a phonological difference between the input structures of the two signs. DAY contains a [pivot] path feature articulated by the arm in the x-plane. (In the variant of DAY with orientation change shown in figure 4.12, distalization of movement has occurred.) In contrast, WHERE (as well as TOILET and TREE) has no path feature; instead, it associates the TM directly to the otherwise empty prosodic features branch. The [TM] in WHERE has not distalized. Both path TMs (TM:Ps; e.g., DAY, DRIVE 'incessantly') and nonpath TMs (TM:POA; e.g., WHERE, TOILET) may contain rapidly repeated elbow or wrist movement, but this phonetic fact does not help us disambiguate their respective phonological source. I have taken the position that if the sign has no singly executed counterpart in its morphological paradigm (e.g., WHERE, TOILET), the movement is described simply as TM:POA and called 'tremor'.[22] If the sign has a singly executed form in its morphological paradigm (e.g., DAY, DRIVE, READ), it is analyzed as having a path feature (TM:P) in the input.

The distribution of the various types of TM in monomorphemic, core lexemes is presented in the following table. The column headed *TM association* lists the phonological parameters to which the [TM] feature associates; the row labeled *Syllable nuclei* lists the syllable nuclei of the forms in question. (Syllable nuclei are discussed in chapter 6; for now, consider the syllable nucleus to be the most proximal movement specified in an input or the highest-ranking prosodic feature in the feature tree.) "***" in a cell indicates that I could find no sign to fill it after consulting a number of native ASL informants. When more than one ASL form is used for one English word, the signs are given as SIGN(1) and SIGN(2). The type of TM is given in parentheses with each ASL form.

Distribution of TM in monomorphemic core lexemes

TM Association	Syllable nucleus			
	Path	Aperture	Orientation	POA
P	TRAVEL-AROUND (circling)	***	***	WHO(1) (circling)
				ROMANTIC (circling)
HS	FINGERSPELL (wiggling)	***	***	TYPE (wiggling)
	SNOW (wiggling)			COLOR (wiggling)
	GOSSIP (flattening)			MILK (closing)
	WEIRD (hooking)			ORANGE (closing)
	VARIOUS (flattening)			WHO(2) (hooking)
	DREAM (hooking)			FLIRT (wiggling)
O	FISH (twisting)	***	***	TREE (twisting)
	DENMARK (pivoting)			
POA	MEASLES (tremor)	***	***	ELECTRICITY (tremor)
				TOILET (tremor)

Figure 4.13
A [trilled movement] ([TM]) feature can co-occur in core lexemes with no other path or local movement (e.g., COLOR (left)) or with a path movement (e.g., FINGERSPELL (right)).

The pattern of distribution is illustrated with 'wiggling' in figure 4.13; the representations for the forms shown in the figure are given in (25). Being a TM:HS, 'wiggling' is associated to the aperture node of the prosodic features branch. It can occur in a sign with a path (e.g., FINGER-SPELL, SNOW, WAIT, PLAY-PIANO) or in a sign with no other prosodic features (e.g., COLOR, CANDLE, GERMANY, DIRTY).

(25) *Representations for COLOR and FINGERSPELL*

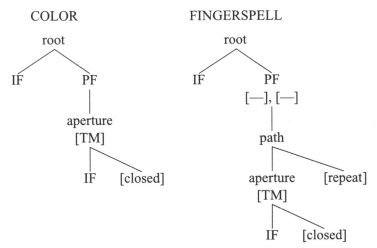

The following table shows the distribution of TM in polymorphemic forms. It is arranged like the previous table, with the same notations. The relevant TM is given in parentheses for each form.

Distribution of TM in polymorphemic forms

TM Association	Syllable nucleus				
	P	HS	NM	O	POA
P	GIVE 'to each in a select group continuously' (circling)	INHALE 'all up' (circling)	***	FALL & TUMBLE TO GROUND (circling)	'fill in circles with a pencil' (circling)
HS	SAY-NO 'to each in a select group' (flattening) RUN-OUT-OF 'gradually' (1) (wiggling)	EXPAND 'gradually' (1) (wiggling)	***	ROLL-OVER-LAUGHING (hooking)	GERMANY (wiggling) MISCHIEVOUS (hooking)
NM	UPRIGHT-BEING 'goes forward slowly' (tongue wagging)	EXPAND 'gradually' (2) (tongue wagging)	***	DIE 'gradually' (tongue wagging)	WATCH 'prolonged' (tongue wagging) STARE-AT 'prolonged' (tongue wagging)
O	SIGN 'awkwardly' (twisting) UPRIGHT-BEING 'goes forward awkwardly' (twisting)	***	***	***	VEHICLE 'continues to run after it is turned off' (twisting)
POA	PUT 'in each place' (tremor)	***	***	***	SEND-MORSE-CODE (tremor)

Signs listed in the second row of the table—SAY-NO 'to each in a select group' ([internal apportionative] aspect), EXPAND 'gradually' ([protractive] aspect), ROLL-OVER-LAUGHING, and MISCHIEVOUS— are illustrated in figure 4.14 and represented in (26).[23] All of the [TM] features are associated to the aperture node; they can occur in signs with a path (e.g., SAY-NO [internal apportionative]), a handshape change (e.g., EXPAND [protractive]), an orientation change (e.g., ROLL-OVER-

LAUGHING), or no prosodic features other than those of the aperture node (e.g., MISCHIEVOUS).

(26) *Representations of [TM] distribution in polymorphemic forms (only prosodic features are shown)*

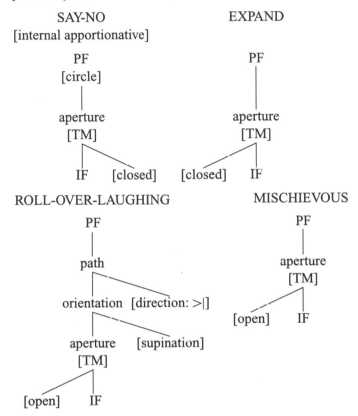

As the tables show, the range of syllable nuclei is more restricted in monomorphemic forms than in polymorphemic forms. In monomorphemic forms, TMs co-occur only with paths or with POAs. In polymorphemic forms, TMs also co-occur with syllable nuclei consisting of single handshape changes and single orientation changes. In polymorphemic forms in which [TM] functions as an affix, the syllable nucleus of the stem is maintained whenever possible; this leads to the greater variation in the types of [TM]+syllable nucleus combinations that occur in these forms.

Figure 4.14
A [trilled movement] ([TM]) feature can co-occur in polymorphemic forms with a
path movement (e.g., SAY-NO 'to each in a select group' [internal apportionative]
(top left)), with a handshape change (e.g., EXPAND 'gradually' [protractive] (top
right)), or with an orientation change (e.g., ROLL-OVER-LAUGHING (bottom
left) and MISCHIEVOUS (bottom right)).

Note also that [TM] can be associated to nonmanual behaviors in polymorphemic forms, but not in monomorphemic forms. In verbs, 'tongue
wagging' and its allomorph 'wiggling' carry the aspectual meaning 'gradually' [protractive] (e.g., EXPAND 'gradually', DEFLATE 'gradually',
RUN-OUT-OF 'gradually'); in adjectives and adverbs, 'tongue wagging'
and 'wiggling' have an intensive meaning (e.g., 'very' FINE; 'very' FAR-
INTO-FUTURE).

4.8 Nonmanual Prosodic Features

Just as there are nonmanual inherent features, so there are nonmanual prosodic features. The timing of prosodic nonmanual behaviors typically depends on the manual component of signs (Liddell 1984a);[24] in any event, in outputs of forms containing both, manual and nonmanual prosodic features are co-temporal, like the other prosodic features discussed in this chapter. For example, in the sign FINALLY, which has the accompanying nonmanual component 'pa', realized as opening of the mouth, the opening of the mouth is synchronized with the beginning and end of the movement of the manual component. Nonmanual behaviors that consist of single postures (e.g., 'mm') or trilled nonmanual movements (e.g., 'tongue wagging') also have predictable temporal properties based on the manual tier.

A node for nonmanual prosodic features is included on the prosodic features branch to account for a type of assimilation that occurs from the manual to the nonmanual component of signs. There are certain ASL forms, such as STUNNED 'dumbstruck' (accompanied by an jaw-drop nonmanual) and VANISH (accompanied by a closing-mouth nonmanual 'thp'), in which the nonmanual behavior expresses the same type of movement as is expressed in the manual component. JAW-DROP is a two-handed sign, articulated by bent 'V' handshapes; H_2 is located at the chin, and H_1 drops down and opens the space between the two hands. This opening of the space between the two hands is copied by the mouth opening. Likewise, in VANISH an open '8' handshape closes to an 'S' handshape, and the simultaneous nonmanual is an inward movement of the tongue accompanied by a closing of the lips. This type of assimilation from the manual to the nonmanual branch is another form of phonetic enhancement. An especially clear example of nonmanual phonetic enhancement of a movement occurs in four variants of the sign PERPLEXED (figure 4.15). The citation form contains only an aperture change. One variant is produced by extending the wrist while flexing the joints of the index finger, thereby adding an orientation change to the handshape change; another variant is produced by rotating the elbow, thereby adding a path movement to the form; yet another variant is produced by moving the head (i.e., by adding a nonmanual component). Such body-enhanced movements are more proximal than any other type of movement in sign; that is, they are articulated by the head or torso

Figure 4.15
Four surface variants of PERPLEXED: citation form (top left), form enhanced
by wrist movement (top right), form enhanced by path movement (bottom left),
and form enhanced by nonmanual, body movement (bottom right)

itself, rather than by an extremity, the arm. A further treatment of nonmanual features is left for future research.

4.9 Conclusion

Prosodic features are realized over time, sequentially; inherent features
are realized simultaneously. All phonological parameters of ASL have
inherent features and prosodic features, and the prosodic features potentially bear a many-to-one relation to the inherent features. This fundamental division contributes to our understanding of many of the phonological
problems presented in the last two chapters.

In this chapter I have proposed a specific prosodic features branch of structure that is based on phonetic and phonological evidence. I have also proposed modifications to the analysis of handshape change, orientation change, path features, and setting changes by more finely specifying the input structure in the inherent features branch of structure, thereby limiting the amount and type of work that the features dominated by the prosodic features branch of structure must perform.

Chapter 5

Timing Units

5.1 Definition of Timing Units in the Prosodic Model

The general questions to be answered about segmentation are these: Are segments necessary? If so, how many and what types of basic timing units on the skeletal tier are needed to capture generalizations about sequences within ASL words? Are sequential timing units the primary way by which signed words are processed, or are they secondary to other units of processing and encoding? In this chapter I investigate the segment, defined as in (1).

(1) *Definition of the segment*

The segment is the minimum concatenative unit referred to by the grammar.

A host of segmental units—both static units (also called *hold segments* or *location segments*) and dynamic units (also called *movement segments* or *paths*)—have been proposed for sign. Since these segmental units have not always been isomorphic with timing units, I summarize the proposals in the table that follows. One detail to keep in mind is that in these proposals, all features are dominated by one type of timing unit or another; in the Prosodic Model, only prosodic features participate in the operations described in this chapter.

Proposals regarding segments, and their relation to timing units

Model	Timing units	Segmental units	Timing units/ segments
HM	segmental	H/L: static articulatory postures	1:1
HT		Ms: transitional period	2:1
DP	segmental	Xs: static articulatory postures	1:1
VP			
μ	moras	Ps: nonpath	0:1 or 1:1
		Ms: path	1:1

Among them, the five models listed in the table take three approaches to handling segments. In the first approach, taken by the HM and HT Models, holds and movements have separate segmental labels. In the HM Model, Hold segments (Hs) are instrumentally defined as steady states having a duration equal to or greater than .1 second. In the HT Model, Location segments (Ls) are particular places that have been achieved; however, in this model only setting is relevant for establishing Ls, since only this aspect of Location typically changes in monomorphemic signs. Note that the Ms in these models largely represent periods of transition between two static elements. I say "largely" rather than "entirely" since both models have features that are exclusively used to specify the shape of paths. The fact that the HT Model reduced the number of these features to [±arc] (Sandler 1989, 127) inspired the developers of the VP Model and the DP Model (as well as Stack (1988)) to create a phonology that eliminated path features and movement segments altogether.

In the second approach, taken by the VP and DP Models, there is only one type of segment: the static units. Movements are encoded by additional features that assist the grammar in predicting the most efficient way to get from one static posture to another. The third approach, taken by the μ Model, is a very different proposal for segmental structure based on a different set of observations about sign well-formedness. The μ Model captures the fact that in order for a sign to be well formed, it must contain some type of movement (either a path or a local movement); therefore, the phonology must contain a unit that expresses this well-formedness condition. Since this well-formedness condition is explicitly sensitive to dynamic elements in the sign stream, and since duration of stasis is argued to be predictable, segmental units of stasis need not be specified. The term *mora* is used for the timing units in the μ Model, yet it makes use of Positions (Ps) and Movement segments (Ms) as well; these units are similar to the HT Model's Ls and Ms, but since many of the features dominated by P and M segments have not been spelled out (see Perlmutter 1990, 1992, 1993), it is difficult to make a detailed comparison. The fact that the μ Model formally recognizes and encodes two types of timing units, the moraic units and the P/M units, is one important difference between the μ Model and the other segmental models.

Under the Prosodic Model, a timing unit that corresponds to the terminal nodes of the prosodic branch of the feature tree is a necessary unit of the phonological grammar of ASL. There are four arguments for taking this position. First, minimal timing units are required in morphophonemic alternation. New evidence for this claim comes from an analysis of a previously undescribed aspect category in ASL. Second, timing units are referred to in purely phonological operations; the evidence for this comes from a revision of the phrase-final lengthening rule proposed by Perlmutter (1992). Third, for many morphemes it is necessary to know whether their phonological input contains timing units as well as features or features alone. This partially determines whether the surface form is realized sequentially or simultaneously (i.e., as a prefix or suffix, or as a parafix). Fourth, as demonstrated in chapter 1, timing units are indispensable to explaining the co-temporal coordination of movements within signs and the lack of such coordination in the transitional movements between signs.

In addition to supporting the need for segmental structure, I will argue for a particular proposal: namely, that signs have a two-slot segmental structure (i.e., a beginning and end), rather than a three-slot structure (i.e., a beginning, middle, and end). The segments proposed here are similar to those proposed for the DP Model (van der Hulst 1993) and by Stack (1988) and Wilbur and Petersen (1997). Although movements play a central role in the phonological structure of ASL, the evidence presented thus far indicates that they behave as prosodic units, rather than as segments. My proposal differs from those of Stack (1988) and van der Hulst (1993) in that the Prosodic Model contains path features. The arguments for including path features in a phonological representation of ASL were made in chapter 4 and are summarized here. Essentially, path features are needed not merely to make structural descriptions more accurate, but to explain the systematicity in surface forms that undergo phonological operations.

Arguments for path features

1. Path features are needed to disambiguate identical citation forms since they behave differently in the first stem of a compound (recall the contrast between THINK and CALL).

2. Proper specification of path features makes it possible to predict contact with the body or with H_2 in path movements. That is, a [direction] feature predicts contact at one or the other end of a path; a [tracing] feature predicts contact throughout the path.

3. The feature [direction] plays an important role in agreement morphology and in thematic relations within the verb phrase.

5.2 Three Segment Slots or Two?

A model like the HT or HM Model that considers movement to be a segment is considered a "three-slot" model, because it allows for a movement to be sandwiched between two nonmovements in monomorphemic lexical items. In order for a segmental account of movement to hold up, however, there should be at least one feature that is common to all movements, much as [sonorant] captures possible syllable nuclei in many spoken languages. In ASL there is no such feature. Moreover, movements cannot always be represented in terms of one feature, as vowels are in spoken languages; rather, they are often represented in terms of two features. With movements, it is only when a path feature such as [tracing], [direction], or [pivot] is present that a one-to-one temporal relationship exists between the number of movement features and the number of movement segments. Yet all word-internal movements are important for the phonology—path movements and local movements of all types. To understand the problem better, consider the forms in (2) and figure 5.1.

(2) *Types of movements and their feature specifications*

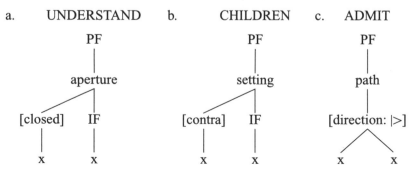

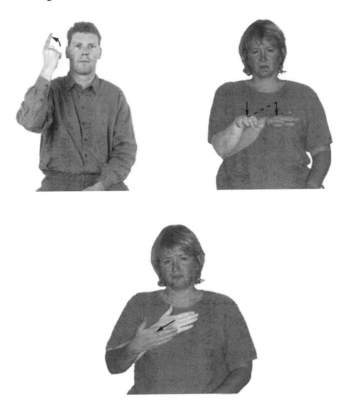

Figure 5.1
Signs illustrating three types of single, word-internal movements in ASL.
UNDERSTAND (top left) has an aperture change; CHILDREN (top right) has a
setting change; and ADMIT (bottom) has a path feature.

Only in the sign ADMIT can we associate the movement to a single
feature specification: in this case, [direction: |>]. In the other two signs,
the movement arises from the inherent features plus an additional specification: a handshape change in UNDERSTAND, a setting change in
CHILDREN.

This issue is relevant to a representation of movement, and it has
been resolved in different ways. The HM and HT Models treat all three
movements in (2) alike by assigning them a movement segment, regardless of whether they are based on one feature or two. The DP Model, the
VP Model, and Stack (1988) treat all three cases alike as well; they represent none of them with a movement feature or segment, instead using a

sign such as CHILDREN (i.e., the one with a setting change) as a kind of prototype for the others, taking changes in place of articulation to be the best example of how movements are represented. The μ Model makes use of movement segments, but only for forms like ADMIT. On the basis of the distribution of handshape changes with respect to movement changes in nonderived forms, the μ Model takes the difference between UNDERSTAND/CHILDREN and ADMIT to be that UNDERSTAND/CHILDREN have a geminate P segment and ADMIT has an M segment.

Like the μ Model, the Prosodic Model holds that all movements count for grammatical well-formedness, yet there are differences in the structure of these types of movement that must be represented. The correct representation must allow all phonological movements to be represented the same way when the first specification of a local movement or path movement is affected in the same way by a phonological or morphological operation, yet it must also keep track of which features give rise to the movements. The Prosodic Model has two advantages over the μ Model: it eliminates movement segments from the structure altogether, allowing the grammar to be more economical, and it allows all movements to have two abstract timing units so that phonological operations can refer to the beginnings and ends of all of them.

The kernel of the Prosodic Model's proposal is this. First, what are called movement segments in the HM and HT Models can be eliminated, because they are not based uniformly on distinctive features, and because, as Perlmutter (1992) has convincingly shown, local movements (i.e., handshape and orientation changes) and path movements (i.e., path features and setting changes) do not need to be ordered with respect to one another in core lexemes. There are no nonderived forms consisting of a handshape change followed by a path movement, or a path movement followed by a handshape change. To paraphrase what Perlmutter (1992) has found, the timing of word-internal path movements with respect to local movements is predictable in stems; a single local movement will align itself with a single path movement. Perlmutter (1992) lists five kinds of well-formed strings of segments in stems, using Positions and Movements;[1] the strings of segments in the μ Model and their equivalents in the Prosodic Model are listed in the table that follows.

Segment sequences in the μ Model and the Prosodic Model

	μ Model's segment string	Prosodic Model's feature description	Prosodic Model's segment string
IMPROVE, CHILDREN	PMP	setting change	2 slots
SICK, SIT	MP	[direction: >|]	2 slots
TAKE-OFF, TELL	PM	[direction: |>]	2 slots
SORRY, FLY	M	[shape: circle] [direction]	2 slots
GERMANY, DIE, UNDERSTAND	P	[TM] orientation change handshape contour	2 slots

Instead of Positions and Movements, the Prosodic Model establishes two abstract timing units in all cases of phonological movement to capture the uniform behavior of all movements in certain morphophonemic operations. In structures that contain a path feature, the two segments are arbitrarily assigned a beginning point and an ending point derived from the path; contact is realized in predictable ways as described in chapter 4. In structures that do not contain a path feature, but rather a setting change, orientation change, or aperture change, one segment is assigned the features of the inherent features branch of structure, and the other segment is assigned the prosodic feature.

The Prosodic Model allows features on any given autosegmental tier to be ordered. The importance of ordering is shown by the minimal pairs TAKE/ DROP (figure 5.2) and SHUT-UP (2sg imperative)/SEND (figure 4.11). This ordering can take place on any of the prosodic structure class nodes. To accomplish the alignment and temporal coordination of features located at different prosodic class nodes, the Prosodic Model employs x-slots. X-slots are defined as minimal, concatenative units of timing, which are systematically constructed at the terminal nodes of the prosodic branch of structure based on prosodic features present in the input of a sign.

X-slots are generated as described in (3).

(3) *The construction of x-slots on the timing tier*

Path features generate two x-slots; all other prosodic features generate one x-slot. The class node with the highest potential number of x-slots determines the number of x-slots for a particular lexeme.

Because x-slots are derived from their input feature specifications and
their order, segmental units are not needed for the purpose of ordering,
but a mechanism *is* needed for aligning prosodic features with x-slots.
Such a mechanism is the simple Association Convention in (4a) (Goldsmith 1976) or, in Optimality Theory, an ALIGNMENT constraint (4b).

(4) *Association of prosodic features to timing units*

    a. *Association Convention*

       In the absence of any constraint to the contrary, prosodic features
       associate to timing units one to one, left to right.

    b. *ALIGNMENT constraint*

       ALIGN (Prosodic features: x-slots, R → L)^2

Inherent features typically spread throughout an entire prosodic word in
core lexemes. Place and articulator features need no ordering with respect
to one another because all inherent features are realized at the same time.

    Let us now explore some cases of the Association Convention at work.
Consider STEAL and COUGH in (5).^{3}

(5) *Basic alignment of features to x-slots*

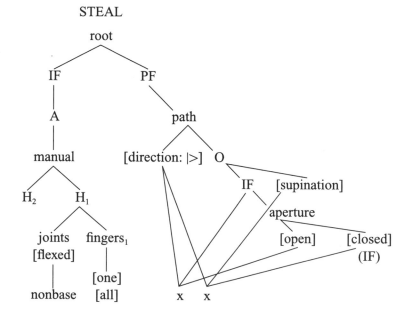

STEAL

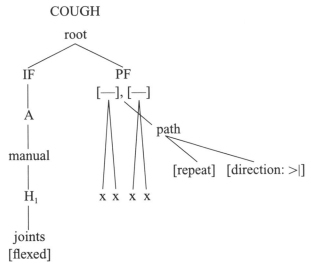

The alignment of prosodic features to x-slots in a sign with one sequential movement is shown for STEAL, and with two sequential movements for COUGH. For STEAL, the path feature [direction: |>] constructs two x-slots on the timing tier. Each of the two [straight (—)] features in COUGH constructs two x-slots as well. Orientation change features and aperture change features are ordered on their tiers with respect to the inherent feature bundle, and on these two tiers, features from the inherent feature bundle contribute to the prosodic structure. In the case of

Figure 5.2
A pair of signs illustrating the importance of order in representing handshape: one-handed forms of TAKE (left) and DROP (right)

orientation, the inherent features contribute a "neutral" or basic orientation, in which the palm is oriented toward the midsagittal plane. In the case of the aperture features, the feature contributed to the prosodic structure is the underlying handshape, a bent 'V', which appears in second position on the aperture tier. This is a [flexed] feature and is interpreted by the aperture node as [closed]. The predictable [open] feature appears first on the aperture tier. For COUGH, the two [straight (—)] features construct four x-slots on the timing tier, and the inherent features are realized on all of them. (In the representations that follow, the prosodic class nodes are shown at an angle to accommodate the segmental tier.)

5.3   Two-Movement Stems

If no more than two x-slots are created by any class node, the output is a one-movement sign. The group of signs containing two sequential movements is much more heterogeneous; as shown in the table that follows, this group can be divided into several subtypes, according to the way that handshapes are distributed across the two movements.

Typology of two-movement signs

Type	# of movements	Distribution of movements		Example sign
I	2 movements	1 contrastive handshape	1 output handshape	CHILDREN
II	2 movements	1 contrastive handshape 2 tokens	3 output handshapes	GOVERNMENT
III	2 movements	1 contrastive handshape 2 tokens	2 output handshapes	DESTROY
IV	2 movements	2 contrastive handshapes	2 output handshapes	BACKGROUND

Type I signs contain one handshape that spreads to all of the timing slots (e.g., CHILDREN, COUGH, MILITARY, LEATHER, PITTS-BURGH, and CANADA). Type II signs contain two path movements and two handshape contours back to back (e.g., REMOVE, JUMP, GOVERNMENT).[4] Type III signs have a handshape contour in the second movement and none in the first (e.g., CURRICULUM, PRO-

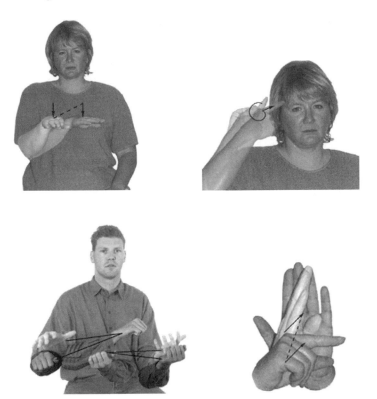

Figure 5.3
Signs illustrating the four types of two-movement signs: CHILDREN (type I) (top left), GOVERNMENT (type II) (top right), DESTROY (type III) (bottom left), and BACKGROUND (type IV) (bottom right)

JECT, DESTROY, EXPENSIVE, INFORM (two-movement form), NOTE-DOWN). Type IV signs have two handshapes and two path movements with one contrastive handshape per movement (e.g., BACK-GROUND, SOCIAL-WORK, NOTRE-DAME, BALL-STATE). The example signs given in the table are pictured in figure 5.3.

The representation of type I signs, exemplified by COUGH in (5), involves straightforward spreading of the inherent features bundle to all four x-slots. The representation of type II signs is exemplified in (6) by GOVERNMENT.

(6) *Feature-to-segment alignment in type II two-movement signs*

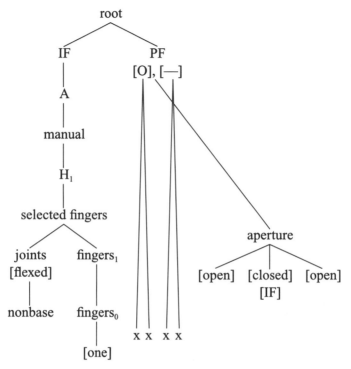

GOVERNMENT

Segment Deletion (OCP) and Association Convention (ALIGN)

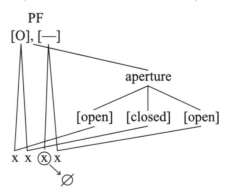

In GOVERNMENT there are two path movements, each with a hand-shape change. The two movements could potentially create four x-slots, but the output form with all four x-slots violates the Obligatory Contour Principle (OCP) (McCarthy 1986).

(7) *The Obligatory Contour Principle*

Adjacent identical feature specifications are prohibited.

Since the output setting at the end of the first movement would be identical to the output setting at the beginning of the second movement, one of them is deleted. The OCP therefore has the appearance of a segment deletion operation. The output contains three x-slots, to which the three aperture settings associate one to one.

The representation of type III signs is exemplified by DESTROY in (8). Four x-slots are created in the same way as for the type II sign GOVERNMENT but again one does not surface because of a potential OCP violation. DESTROY has just one handshape change, however, and here we see the directionality of the Association Convention at work. The aperture change occurs in the second rather than the first movement. The leftmost aperture specification spreads leftward, as shown in (8), in the same way that tones spread to unassociated tone-bearing units (Goldsmith 1976).

(8) *Feature-to-segment alignment in type III two-movement forms*

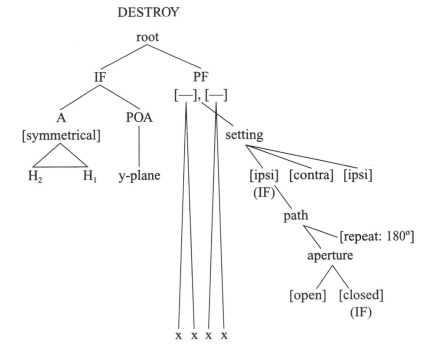

Segment Deletion (OCP), Association Convention (ALIGN), and Spreading

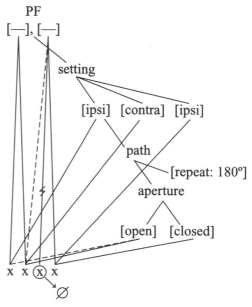

The representation of type IV signs is exemplified by BACKGROUND in (9). In this type, handshapes are distributed to path movements differently. This sign includes 'B' and 'G' of the manual alphabet; the change from one contrastive handshape, 'B', to the other, 'G', occurs during the transitional movement between the two short straight movements. There are no forms that do not involve fingerspelled letters that have handshape changes that occur this way; in other words, handshape changes generally occur during movements specified in the input, not between them. The analysis of these forms follows some aspects of the analyses in Brentari 1990d and Perlmutter 1992. Core lexemes obey a Selected Fingers Constraint, which limits the number of contrastive handshapes to one.

When a form violates this constraint, and when—as in BACK-GROUND—no other movements are present in the input, two straight movements are inserted as a way of making the output more well formed. This type of movement epenthesis is also used in arbitrary name signs (Supalla 1992), which also have no path features. It is not used in all fingerspelled borrowings; for example, CURRICULUM and PROJECT, which have path features in their inputs, do not employ it. (As discussed earlier, epenthetic movements are used in at least two other ways in ASL: to ensure a minimal word, and when the input contains setting specifications.)

Association, epenthesis, and spreading proceed as shown in (9) in type IV forms. First, two segments are constructed and the two handshapes and settings are associated via the Association Convention. Second, the epenthetic direction features are inserted, resulting in the insertion of two straight movements and the creation of accompanying x-slots; the predictable contact behavior associated with them as spelled out in chapter 4 is also realized. Third, the handshapes and settings spread leftward to the inserted movements. The conventions of autosegmental association allow for material dominated by lower nodes—here, aperture—to be subsumed by the association line to the setting node.

(9) *Feature-to-segment alignment in type IV two-movement forms*

BACKGROUND

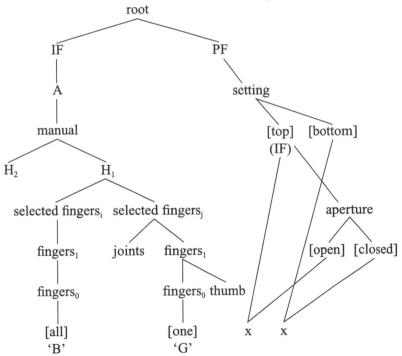

Movement epenthesis and spreading

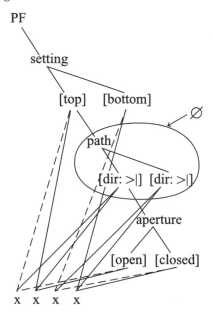

These operations of alignment at one stage and movement epenthesis and spreading at another stage provide the only evidence I have found thus far of the need for operations to refer to two different structures. The ALIGNMENT Constraint or Association Convention refers to a structure without the inserted movements. Epenthesis and the spread of handshape and setting to unassociated segments refer to the structure that contains the handshape-to-segment association via ALIGNMENT. This case is therefore evidence that an intermediate level of representation is needed in ASL phonology.

To summarize: I have argued for a two-slot account of segmental structure, demonstrating that two undifferentiated timing units (i.e., x's) better capture the facts about movements in sign than do the segmental analyses of other models (e.g., the HT, HM, and μ Models, which have both movement segments and path features). The Prosodic Model renders movement segments unnecessary for specifying placement of [contact] and for ordering local and path movements with respect to one another, using distinctions among the path features themselves (i.e., [tracing] and [direction]) to do the work instead. Eliminating movement segments does not diminish the status of movements in general; rather, it assigns them their higher prosodic role, which will be explored further in chapter 6. By using the version of the Association Convention proposed here, the Prosodic Model also explains the systematicity in alignment of prosodic features to segments in a large number of signs.

Although spoken language segments and sign language segments have overlapping uses, the grammatical functions of spoken and sign language segments are not identical. Like spoken language timing slots, the proposed x-slots coordinate feature material, are abstract in nature, and are based on feature specifications. However, x-units in sign and spoken language bear different relations to the features in the feature tree: the former are established by the terminal nodes of the prosodic features branch of the feature tree, whereas the latter occupy the dominant, root node of the tree.

5.4 Phonological Operations Involving Timing Units: Phrase-Final Lengthening

Forms that provide evidence for timing units from a purely phonological operation are those that have undergone phrase-final lengthening. This type of phrase-final, or prepausal, lengthening operation was first proposed by Sandler (1989, 143) and later reanalyzed as Mora Insertion by Perlmutter (1992).[5]

(10) *Mora Insertion as proposed by Perlmutter (1992)*

$$\sigma \qquad \sigma$$
$$| \quad \rightarrow \quad \wedge$$
$$\mu \qquad \mu \;\; \mu$$

Consider the following forms in the context of phrase-final lengthening:

(11) *Mora Insertion in signs based on three types of prosodic features*

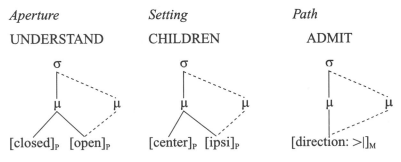

Aperture	*Setting*	*Path*
UNDERSTAND	CHILDREN	ADMIT

[closed]$_P$ [open]$_P$ [center]$_P$ [ipsi]$_P$ [direction: $>|]_M$

UNDERSTAND works just as Perlmutter's account predicts it should; the second handshape or the second setting lengthens. Perlmutter used such examples to argue against the need for static units in the grammar. However, cases with a single path feature (e.g., ADMIT) or with a setting change (e.g., CHILDREN) present challenges to Perlmutter's account. Perlmutter did not address cases that do not end in a P segment—M or PM signs—but not all signs do end in a P in the μ Model; all features that would give rise to P segments create lengthening in the same way. Cases such as ADMIT (a PM sign) or FLY (an M sign) present a problem for the μ Model because a sign with such a [direction] feature in the input does not have a feature specification at the beginning or the end of the movement; however, in phrase-final position even signs with a [direction: |>] feature exhibit a short hold at the end. The moraic units that Perlmutter proposed cannot handle the fact that, in cases where no static element is present at the end of the input containing a [direction] feature, the output in phrase-final position has a static element of predictable length—a short hold—that must be accessed by the phrase-final lengthening operation. Given what has been said about Ps in the μ Model, ADMIT might have a P at the beginning of the movement (because of the contact), but not at the end, so the inserted mora should lengthen the movement, yet it does not. The case illustrated by CHILDREN presents a different challenge. Only the second instance of the [ipsilateral] setting, which occurs at the end of the second inserted movement, is lengthened, not the whole movement to which the setting is associated. The setting specification fails to provide units at the beginning and end of the movement; hence, phrase-final lengthening applies incorrectly here as well.

The Prosodic Model provides a way of treating the second handshape specification in UNDERSTAND, the end of the path movement in ADMIT, and the place of contact in CHILDREN identically for the purposes of phrase-final lengthening. What emerges from these surface facts is the need for path movements to have segmental structure supplied to them, so that the final point can be lengthened. Using the x-slots of the Prosodic Model, phrase-final lengthening can be stated as in (12) and represented as in (13). The class nodes for organizing features and for the x-slots are important for achieving the correct result. Path features produce two x-slots each; the aperture features produce only one. The inserted timing unit at the end of a phrase appropriately lengthens only that timing unit at the end of the sign. This analysis is more like that of Sandler (1989); the differences between them lie in the fact that the Prosodic Model is a two-slot account rather than a three-slot account, and that the timing units are undifferentiated x-slots rather than Locations and Movements.

(12) *Phrase-final lengthening*

A copy of the phrase-final x-slot is inserted phrase-finally.

(13) *Prosodic Model representation of phrase-final lengthening*

UNDERSTAND

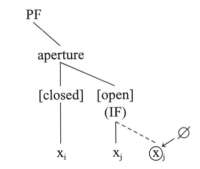

CHILDREN

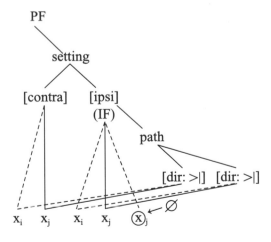

ADMIT

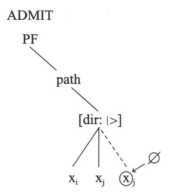

5.5   A Morphophonemic Operation Using Timing Units: A Linearly Ordered Affix in ASL—[Delayed Completive]

We have seen that phrase-final lengthening needs x-units to encode the endpoint of a structure, even when that endpoint is not an input feature. Let us now turn to a case of morphophonemic alternation that requires access to the x-unit at the initial point of a structure, even when that initial point is not specified in the input. This aspectual class, which has not previously been discussed in the literature, is called [delayed completive] aspect.[6] It means 'delay the completion of x'. This type of aspect affixation is a productive morphological operation in ASL. Some forms containing this aspect are given in (14); three of these (RUN-OUT-OF, FOCUS, and UNDERSTAND) are illustrated in figure 5.4; and more forms that may take a [delayed completive] aspect are listed in appendix B.

(14) *Possible and impossible [delayed completive] forms*

RUN-OUT-OF [delayed completive]—'wiggling' and/or 'tongue wagging' on handshape
ZOOM-OFF [delayed completive]—'tongue wagging' on handshape
UNDERSTAND [delayed completive]—'tongue wagging' on handshape
DEFLATE [delayed completive]—'tongue wagging' on handshape
ADMIT [delayed completive]—'tongue wagging' on place of articulation
PASS [delayed completive]—'tongue wagging' on place of articulation

FOCUS [delayed completive]—'tongue wagging' on place of
articulation
*THINK [delayed completive]
*KNOW [delayed completive]
*FEEL [delayed completive]
*LIKE [delayed completive]

The [delayed completive] aspect consists of two sequential parts. The
first part is a trilled movement (i.e., [TM]); the second part is a rapid
closing of the mouth (often transcribed as 'op') coinciding with the
beginning and end of the movement of the stem. There are two allo-
morphs of the [delayed completive] aspect resulting from the realization
of [TM]. [TM:HS] 'wiggling' co-occurs with a spread '5' handshape;
[TM:NM] 'tongue wagging' occurs elsewhere.[7] The key point about the
forms in (14) is that the TM does not occur simultaneously nested within
the movement, as it does in the [exhaustive] or [internal apportionative]
forms noted in chapter 4; rather, it occurs solely on the first x-slot. The
TM and path movement are linearly sequenced. RUN-OUT-OF and
ZOOM-OFF contain path movement and handshape change in the stem,
and the TM associates to the first place of articulation and the first
handshape. UNDERSTAND and DEFLATE do not contain a path
movement, and TM occurs only on the first handshape. PASS, ADMIT,
and FOCUS contain only a path movement in the stem, and the TM
occurs only on the first place of articulation.

The conditions on forms that may undergo this aspectual operation are
both semantic and phonological in nature. The semantic condition is that
all of the possible [delayed completive] forms have an explicit or implicit
telic meaning (Vendler 1967). The forms in (15) illustrate this condition.

(15) *Examples illustrating the semantic requirement on [delayed
      completive] prefixation*

      [Delayed completive] forms choose only telic stems as inputs

Telic stems	*Atelic stems*
READ (i.e., 'read through')	*READ
FALL-ASLEEP	*SLEEP

READ ('read through'; i.e., [punctual] aspect) and FALL-ASLEEP allow
[delayed completive] affixation; READ and SLEEP do not. FALL-
ASLEEP and SLEEP are an excellent illustrative pair: they have identical

Figure 5.4
Input stems that allow [delayed completive] aspect: RUN-OUT OF (top), FOCUS
(middle), and UNDERSTAND (bottom)

Figure 5.4 (continued)
Output forms that contain the [delayed completive] prefix.

phonological forms, and the semantic contrast is therefore crucial. Not all input forms that take [delayed completive] aspect are [punctual]; many are simply telic (e.g., UNDERSTAND, PASS, TAKE). However, when a citation form is atelic (e.g., READ, SLEEP), only the [punctual] aspect form—if one exists—is a possible input.

The phonological condition on [delayed completive] affixation is that the input stem must be a one-movement stem without TMs. The forms in (16) illustrate this condition.

(16) *Examples illustrating the phonological condition on [delayed completive] prefixation*

a. *Base stems with TM do not allow [delayed completive] affixation*

Base contains no TM	*Base contains TM*
INSULT [delayed completive]	*MOCK [delayed completive]
FOCUS [delayed completive]	*CONCENTRATE [delayed completive]
ERECT [delayed completive]	*BUILD [delayed completive]
ENVISION [delayed completive]	*DREAM [delayed completive]

b. *Disyllabic stems do not allow [delayed completive] affixation*

Bidirectional stems	*Repeated unidirectional stems*
[repeat: 180°]	[repeat]
*JUMP	*COUGH
*MAKE-A-ROUND-TRIP	

For each semantically related pair in (16a), the member in the left column contains no TM in the input stem and allows [delayed completive] affixation; the member in the right column contains TM in the input stem and disallows [delayed completive] affixation. (16b) contains forms that are bidirectional or contain repeated unidirectional stems; these forms all disallow [delayed completive] affixation even though they satisfy the semantic condition. INSULT, MOCK, and MAKE-A-ROUND-TRIP are pictured in figure 5.5.

The [delayed completive] form bears a relationship to the simple [protractive] form (i.e., 'perform X over a long time') and to the simple [punctual] form but is distinct from both of them. Examples of the relevant forms for the stems RUN-OUT-OF, FOCUS, and UNDERSTAND are described in the table that follows. The differences between the two simple aspect affixes (i.e., [protractive] and [punctual]) and the complex [delayed completive] aspect affix are as follows. The [protractive] form has [TM], but this feature associates to the stem movement, rather than to the first x-slot as it does in the [delayed completive]. The [punctual] aspect has the 'op' nonmanual on the stem movement, but it does not have the [TM] of the [delayed completive]. The [delayed completive] has a [TM] + 'op' sequence.

[Protractive], [punctual], and [delayed completive] forms for three example stems

Example	Stem	[protractive]	[punctual]	[delayed completive]
RUN-OUT-OF	HS Δ, POA Δ, path	'wiggling' on path, HS Δ	'op' on movement	'wiggling' on 1st HS & 1st POA; 'op' on movement
UNDERSTAND	HS Δ	'tongue-wagging' on HS Δ	'op' on HS Δ	'tongue wagging' on first HS; 'op' on stem movement
FOCUS	path, POA Δ	'tongue wagging' on path	'op' on path	'tongue wagging' on first POA; 'op' on stem movement

The TM in the [protractive] forms surfaces associated to the lowest-ranked prosodic feature (i.e., the least sonorous branching prosodic class node), as is commonly seen in stems with TM.

Let us now focus on why x-units are necessary in order to account for TM prefixation. We will consider three signs, each having a different underlying representation: RUN-OUT-OF, UNDERSTAND, and FOCUS. The first argument is that TM associates to both handshape and place-of-articulation features whenever both of them exist in the stem. The TM is prefixed to the stem RUN-OUT-OF, and since this stem contains a handshape change and a path movement, TM associates to both. On the basis of such stems, we can say that TM either accesses both aperture and setting tiers at one time, or accesses one and spreads to the other. UNDERSTAND contains a handshape change only; and here TM associates to the first handshape only. On the basis of this type of sign, we might posit that TM associates to the first aperture feature when one is present and spreads to the place features. This account cannot work for FOCUS, however, because FOCUS has neither a handshape change nor underlying specifications for where the path begins and ends. FOCUS

Figure 5.5
Input stems illustrating the phonological conditions on [delayed completive] affixation by the addition of [TM]: INSULT (top), MOCK (middle), MAKE-A-ROUND-TRIP (bottom).

Figure 5.5 (continued)
Output forms containing the [delayed completive] prefix: INSULT (top) satisfies
the phonological conditions and is well-formed, MOCK (middle) has a [TM]
feature in the stem and, therefore, the output is ill-formed, MAKE-A-ROUND-
TRIP (bottom) has a bidirectional movement in the stem and, therefore, the
output is also ill-formed.

contains only a path feature, and in this type of stem TM associates to the first predictable setting feature. Thus, the second argument for this type of segmental structure is that neither the setting nor the aperture class node can be specified as the phonological docking site of TM in the [delayed completive] forms. TM associates to the first static element (the first segment) shared by all prosodic features. This is the only way to cover all three forms with one unit of analysis.

The P and M segments in the μ Model fail to make the necessary distinction for [delayed completive] affixation. In the μ Model, a sign that contains only an underlying path feature is a nonbranching M Segment. The first setting is therefore not accessible to the morphology, yet it is precisely this static element to which TM associates in FOCUS. This set of problem cases that the [delayed completive] aspect raises for the μ Model is similar to the set of problem cases discussed earlier with respect to the μ Model's analysis of phrase-final lengthening (i.e., ADMIT). In both sets of forms the input structure contains no feature that corresponds to the unit to which the operation needs access; in the phrase-final lengthening case it is the redundant endpoint that is missing, and in the [delayed completive] case it is the redundant starting point.

The static segment proposed by Stack (1988), the HM Model (Liddell 1984a; Liddell and Johnson 1986, 1989), the HT Model (Sandler 1989, 1993b,c), the VP Model (Uyechi 1995), and the DP Model (van der Hulst 1993) does not exhibit the same problems that the μ Model has in expressing [delayed completive] affixation in segmental terms. Rather than defining segments on the basis of [±path], these models define movements as transition, and they establish segments on the basis of static units; any two specifications on an autosegmental tier will result in an M segment.[8] It is this notion of a static unit that is captured in the Prosodic Model as an abstract x-slot. However, the Prosodic Model's account does have three advantages that other x-slot accounts do not. The first advantage comes from grouping all of the prosodic features together, as argued in chapters 3 and 4; this makes the operation of Tier Conflation, necessary in the HT Model, unnecessary in the Prosodic Model. Tier Conflation (first proposed for spoken languages in McCarthy 1986) is an operation that allows local and path movement features in phonological representations to co-occur on the skeletal tier when handshape and place features are located in separate parts of the representation, as they are in the HT Model.[9] The second advantage of the Prosodic Model's account is that it can handle all phonological movements alike in these cases, without losing the distinctions between movements having a path feature as input and those having a set of local movement features as input; distinctions between stems with respect to contact predictability and behavior in compounds are lost in an account without path features. The third advantage comes from including the [TM] feature in the set of prosodic features, and in a sonority hierarchy, discussed in chapter 6. Because no sonority hierarchy is integrated into the HM Model, when a TM associates to a Hold segment, as occurs in all [delayed completive] forms, the segment changes to an M by "brute force." By contrast, in the Prosodic Model, the addition of a [TM] feature to an x-slot simply raises this x-slot to the level of a syllable nucleus.

5.6 Sequential Movements Are Syllables

The syllable (whose hierarchical, internal structure will be discussed in chapter 6) performs a sequencing function and is referred to in prosodic constraints on the length of signed words. Working and formal definitions of the syllable are given in (17) and (18).

(17) *Functional definition of a syllable (criteria for counting the number of syllables in surface forms)*

   a. The number of sequential phonological movements in a string equals the number of syllables in that string. When several shorter dynamic elements co-occur with a single dynamic element of longer duration, the single movement defines the syllable.

   b. If a structure is a well-formed syllable as an independent word, it must be counted as a syllable word-internally.

(18) *Formal definition of a syllable*

   A syllable must contain at least one weight unit.[10]

It is here that the move is made in the Prosodic Model to call sequential movements syllables. The reasons for doing so are these: (1) no sign is well formed without some type of movement; (2) the limit on the length of signs is determined by the number of sequential movements; (3) the timing of handshape changes with respect to path movements in signs such as BACKGROUND, SOCIAL-WORK, and BALL-STATE is based on such a phonological unit. Syllables are not determined by the number of output x-units; a syllable contains minimally one x-unit and maximally two.

(19) *Output relations between segments and syllables*

    a. One segment = one syllable: signs with a [TM] feature on a single place of articulation (e.g., COLOR, GERMANY)

    b. Two segments = one syllable: the most common case (e.g., UNDERSTAND, SIT, THROW) (both simple and complex movements)

    c. Three segments = two syllables: a sequence of two movements to which segment deletion has applied (e.g., PROJECT, CURRICULUM)

    d. Four segments = two syllables: a sequence of two identical movements (e.g., BACKGROUND, NOTE-DOWN)

Internally, syllable units are based on weight units, but once the syllables are generated, syllable units are counted sequentially to handle word-length restrictions. Like most phonological units, sign language syllables are generated from "below" (i.e., smaller, more primitive units), and they are the building blocks of larger, higher-order units (i.e., prosodic words).

5.6.1 Permutations of Ordering in Experimental Conditions

There is experimental evidence showing that syllabic units and x-slots are available to signers when they are presented with a backward signing task (Wilbur and Petersen 1997). Four adult Deaf signers participated in this study. Two-movement forms were used for this task, and the two forms of most interest here are ITALY and CANCEL—forms containing two straight movements and a [repeat: 90°] tracing feature. The schema for ITALY is shown in (20).[11]

(20) *The two-movement form ITALY (citation form)*

    a. *Schematic drawing of movements (from Wilbur and Petersen, 1997)*

b. *Phonological representation in the Prosodic Model*

ITALY

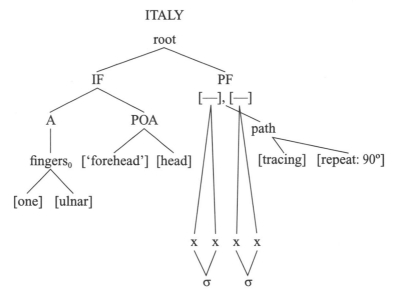

When signers are asked to sign ITALY backward, several outputs are possible, based on the combinatoric possibilities made available by the Prosodic Model syllable and segmental structures presented thus far. Sometimes signers reverse the two movements (i.e., the two syllables) but keep the beginning and ending points of each movement the same. Using the numbering shown in (20) for x-slots, the change is 1234 → 3412. Sometimes, however, signers reverse the segments of the first or both of the movements as well: 1234 → 4321 or 1234 → 4312. These three outputs are given in (21).

(21) *Outputs of reversal (from Wilbur and Petersen 1997; ω = prosodic word, σ = syllable)*

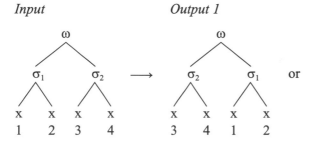

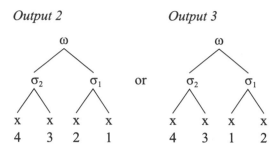

Output 2   *Output 3*

In output 1 only syllables are reversed; in outputs 2 and 3 syllable and segmental structure are reversed. Clearly, segmental units and syllable units are subject to reordering in this task; the task thereby supports the structural claims of the Prosodic Model with external linguistic evidence.

5.6.2   Word Length in Locally Lexicalized Fingerspelled Loan Signs

In this section I present one way that syllables are used in establishing a maximum on word length, using the lexicalization of fingerspelled forms to argue that the longest monomorphemic words in ASL have two movements (i.e., two syllables). (This view has also been argued for in Perlmutter 1992, 1993.) Fingerspelling (the representation of English words in handshapes that depict written letters) serves many purposes in ASL, four of which were described in section 1.2.3. Even if they are not part of the core lexicon, fingerspelled forms are a part of the language and as such should exhibit systematic behavior with respect to constraints proposed for the phonological grammar as a whole.

In this section I will discuss one of the contexts in which fingerspelled forms are used. In specific academic disciplines, such forms are sometimes preferred over coined signs because no single form has achieved consensus among members of the Deaf community or because they refer to a discipline-specific term that may not have been broadly discussed within the Deaf community. Fingerspelled forms of the discipline-specific type undergo a rapid lexicalization process, which I will call *local lexicalization*, whereby a fingerspelled form comes to stand not for each letter in the English word, but for the concept the word conveys; this process fixes the shape of the fingerspelled form for the duration of a single discourse. This process typically occurs over the course of just three productions. When the form appears for the first time, each letter shape is distinctly formed. By the third production, however, these fingerspelled forms conform closely to some of the constraints proposed for well-formed native signs

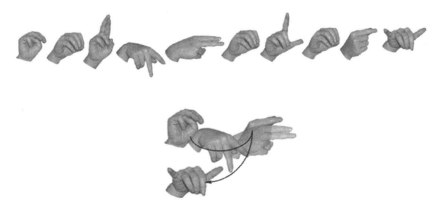

Figure 5.6
The carefully fingerspelled form of M-O-R-P-H-O-L-O-G-Y (top), and the locally lexicalized form (bottom)

and achieve a stable state in which they remain for the rest of the discourse. It is clear from even this limited set of forms that, according to the syllable-counting criteria in (17), many lexicalized fingerspelled loan signs consist of only one syllable since they contain only one sequential movement. This suggests that using changes in selected fingers as an index of number of syllables (Brentari 1990b; Perlmutter 1992, 1993) is not appropriate for these forms.

Some of the forms used for this analysis of word length are given in the table that follows. The formal representation of the lexicalization process is given in (22) for the form M-O-R-P-H-E-M-E; the process is pictured for M-O-R-P-H-O-L-O-G-Y in figure 5.6. These forms are taken from Bienvenu and Colonomos 1987 and from a course videotape for the book *Linguistics of American Sign Language* (Valli and Lucas 1992); Clayton Valli is a prelingually deaf, fluent ASL signer who has produced a videotape that summarizes the written text of the book for linguistics students who are more comfortable with ASL than with English. Each form in the corpus was signed at least three times and as many as twelve times; however, the forms were in transition only during the first three forms and after that they remained the same during each production. There are several phonological operations that can be analyzed during local lexicalization. Those relevant for timing units will be discussed here: how many movements are allowed in such forms, and which elements remain and which are eliminated.

Some of the locally lexicalized fingerspelled forms from the corpus ($\emptyset$ = epenthetic dynamic element; # = word boundary; [XY] = letters that have undergone handshape merger)

# letters	1st/2nd production	3rd production	# syllables
6	S-Y-N-T-A-X	S-Y-$\emptyset$-T-X	2
8	M-O-R-P-H-E-M-E	M-P-H-E	2
9	P-H-O-N-O-L-O-G-Y	P-[HG]-Y	2
10	M-O-R-P-H-O-L-O-G-Y	M-P-[HG]-Y	2
10	L-I-N-G-U-I-S-T-I-C	L-I-N-G-I-C	2

(22) *Local lexicalization of M-O-R-P-H-E-M-E → M-P-H-E*
      *(* = weight unit)*

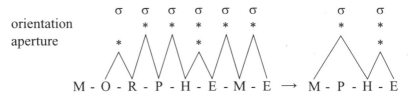

Some constraints involved in the local lexicalization process are as follows:

(23) *Local lexicalization*

    a. 2-MVT (2 movements/word maximum)

    There are at most two movements (i.e., syllables) per prosodic word.

    b. HARMONIZE NUCLEUS (HNUC)

    Local maxima of sonority are chosen as syllable nuclei.

    c. ALIGN constraints

      i. ALIGN(L)

      Align initial handshape of stem with left edge of stem.

      ii. ALIGN(R)

      Align final handshape of word with right edge of word.

    d. MAXIMIZE APERTURE CHANGE (MAXAP Δ)

    Handshape changes that occupy syllable nuclei maximize aperture change, alternating between [open] and [closed] aperture settings.

I will discuss further details of the local lexicalization process in chapter 6, including the constraints involving the retention and deletion of hand-shapes in fingerspelled forms. Here I address only the first constraint in (23). The 2-MVT constraint on phonological words is enforced in all the forms analyzed. Movements are chosen as syllable nuclei on the basis of how sonorous the movement transition from one letter to the next is; the more proximal the movement, the more likely it will be retained. In fin-gerspelled forms the aperture changes and orientation changes are the two types that exist, so whenever an orientation change occurs between two letters, it serves as a syllable nucleus. It is also clear from the examples given in the table that handshapes depicting some letters are retained and the handshapes depicting others are eliminated. The constraints ALIGN(L), ALIGN(R), and MAXAP Δ are enforced; other handshapes undergo handshape merger, which will not be discussed here. Still other handshapes are candidates for elimination.

These forms tell us two things about lexical items. First, words in ASL are maximally disyllabic. Second, syllables are not formed in these lexi-calized fingerspelled words on the basis of the selected finger groups, as the criteria developed elsewhere in the literature suggest (Brentari 1990b; Perlmutter 1992, 1993); rather, syllables are constructed on the basis of orientation changes or well-formed aperture changes.

5.7 Conclusion

In this chapter I have argued for two units relevant to the ordering of phonological material in ASL forms: the x-slot and the syllable.

The Prosodic Model analysis supports a two-slot segmental account of one-movement forms, using the argument that path movements and nonpath movements need not be ordered with respect to one another. I presented evidence that timing units coordinate the prosodic features of the beginnings and ends of movements and that these segments must be accessed both by purely phonological and by morphophonological opera-tions in ASL. This access is necessary even when the beginnings and ends of those movements do not correspond to distinctive features. Movements in this account are handled by a higher-order unit of structure; namely, they are handled as prosodic units, to be discussed in depth in chapter 6.

The syllable is relevant in language reordering tasks such as backward signing. It is also the unit relevant for expressing restrictions on word length in ASL.

Chapter 6
Complexity, Sonority, and Weight in ASL Syllables

6.1   Complexity in Inherent and Prosodic Branches of Structure

The analyses of feature organization in chapters 3 and 4 and of segmental structure in chapter 5 have laid the foundation for the topic covered in this chapter. Having separated inherent features from prosodic features in those chapters, I can now show that the prosodic features branch of structure is the part of structure upon which syllables and higher-order prosodic structure are built.

In this chapter I focus on the internal, hierarchical structure of the prosodic features branch of the input. Phonological complexity within the prosodic features branch of structure differs from complexity within the inherent features branch of structure. I will claim that the type of complexity within the prosodic features branch is properly called *visual sonority*; to demonstrate this, I will show how the phonological grammar of ASL makes use of visual sonority in well-formedness conditions and phonological processes. I will then build upon this notion of sonority to show how weight units are constructed and how the grammar uses them to determine "heavy" syllables, which contain complex movements, and "light" syllables, which contain simple movements.

In this section I define *visual sonority* and argue that it is a special instance of a larger category of "complexity" as defined in Dependency Phonology (Anderson and Ewen 1987; Dresher and van der Hulst 1994). I begin by repeating in (1) the differences in complexity discussed in chapter 2. Structures that have daughters are more complex than those that do not (1a), and structures with branching daughters are more complex than those with nonbranching daughters (1b).

(1) *Designations of relatively simple and relatively complex structures in Dependency Phonology (Dresher and van der Hulst 1994)*

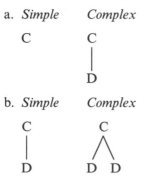

a. *Simple   Complex*

    C   C
                |
                D

b. *Simple   Complex*

    C   C
    | /\
    D   D D

The Prosodic Model as developed thus far exhibits two types of branching structures; both contribute to the overall complexity of the input. The type of complexity found in the inherent features branch of structure is well demonstrated by the hand node of the articulator branch. The terminal features dominated by the hand node are all realized at the same instant, as explained in chapter 3, and the markedness of a handshape is determined by its degree of complexity (i.e., the number of branches the structure has). For example, the handshape 'open 5' is less marked than the handshape 'flat 5' because fully open handshapes have no joint specification and are therefore less complex.

The second type of complexity is found in the prosodic features branch of structure, which dominates all of the movement features. As explained in chapter 4, the nodes on this branch may split into two ordered specifications for a single feature, which are realized sequentially in time. For example, as shown in figure 6.1, UNDERSTAND has an aperture change, SIT has a [direction] feature, and THROW has both an aperture change and a [direction] feature.

Both types of branching add complexity to the feature tree. Let me illustrate this with two brief examples using the general markedness criteria of Battistella (1990) and certain criteria for handshape markedness.

General markedness criteria (Battistella 1990)

	More marked	Less marked
Appears in positions of neutralization		yes
Exhibits more complex phonological structure	yes	
Has more phonological subtypes		yes

Sign-specific markedness criteria applied to handshape

	More marked	Less marked
Acquisition	acquired late	acquired early
Ease of articulation	harder	easier
Use on H_2	no	yes
Participation in handshape contours	no	yes
Frequency crosslinguistically	less frequent	more frequent
Errors in children's signing	omitted	substituted
Errors in aphasic signing	omitted	substituted

Figure 6.1
UNDERSTAND (top left) contains a simple aperture change; SIT (top right)
contains a path movement; THROW (bottom) contains both a path movement
and an aperture change.

These markedness criteria apply to both inherent and prosodic features. Besides frequently replacing marked handshapes with unmarked ones when they make signing errors, children and aphasics replace complex movements (e.g., those with both an aperture change and a path feature) with forms containing a simple movement (i.e., a movement with just one branching prosodic class node). An example of substituting a less marked handshape for a more marked handshape comes from a posterior left hemisphere aphasic subject, EN, who substituted an [all] handshape (i.e., a '5' as in WHITE) for a [one], [mid] handshape (i.e., an '8' as in LIKE) (Brentari, Poizner, and Kegl 1995). An example of substituting a simple movement for a complex movement comes from a 26-month-old Deaf child of Deaf parents. The citation form of WOLF contains both a [direction] feature and an aperture change, but the child's form contained only the [direction] feature. Such substitution errors have been noted in the acquisition of Finnish Sign Language as well (Takkinen 1994). These errors can be seen as the omission of features that make a form more complex (Marentette 1996). Given this, we can say that errors favor less marked structures, regardless of whether the complexity arises from a branching inherent or prosodic structure.

6.2 Prosodic Complexity as Visual Sonority

Although the inherent and prosodic features branches share certain aspects of complexity, branching prosodic class nodes exhibit complexity of a special kind. The number and type of co-occurring branches in a prosodic structure determine its *visual sonority*. The term *sonority* is relevant for the type of complexity represented by branching prosodic features because, even though its phonetic manifestation is very different from that of its spoken language counterpart, this type of complexity functions in the phonological grammar of sign languages in a way that is functionally analogous to sonority in spoken languages, both phonetically and phonologically.

Phonetically, sonority can be thought of as a notion of multidimensional salience (Ohala and Kawasaki 1984; Ohala 1990). One articulatory phonetic correlate of sonority in spoken languages is the relative openness of the oral cavity of the vocal tract; thus, an [a] is more sonorous than an [i]. This contributes to perceptibility of a speech sound. The degree of openness of the vocal tract corresponds to the size of the cavity within which the glottal pulse can resonate, and the amount of resonation is correlated with amplitude of the sound (the subjective equivalent is loudness), making a sound more perceptible at greater distances (MacNeilage,

Hanson, and Krones 1970; see also Davis and MacNeilage 1995). A corresponding articulatory phonetic correlate of visual sonority in sign is the relative proximity of the joint articulating a sign's movement to the midline of the body. The more proximal the joint, the greater the degree of excursion possible in the movement; such movements are consequently more visible at greater distances. A single movement articulated by the elbow is therefore more sonorous than one articulated by the wrist. Despite completely different phonetic bases, both auditory and visual sonority are those properties of a linguistic signal that enhance perceptual salience; this is shown in (2).

(2) *Definition of sonority in spoken and sign languages*

    a. Spoken language: The degree of sonority is correlated with the relative openness of the oral cavity of the vocal tract; the more open the vocal tract is, the greater the degree of sonority.

      i. Articulatory correlate: degree of openness of the vocal tract during phonation

      ii. Perceptual consequence: greater audibility

    b. Sign language: The degree of sonority is correlated with the proximity to the body of the joint articulating the sign gesture to the body; the more proximal the joint articulating the movement is to the midline of the body, the greater the degree of sonority.

      i. Articulatory correlate: proximity to the midline of the body of the joint involved in producing a movement

      ii. Perceptual consequence: greater visibility

The nature of the articulators in speech and sign causes the representations of sonority in the phonology to be different. In spoken languages sonority can be measured on the basis of a single timing unit; in sign this is not possible. Only after seeing the degree of excursion from one timing unit to another can we measure this property. The following sonority hierarchy and the corresponding photos in figure 6.2 illustrate this.

Greater sonority ←————————————————→ Lesser sonority			
DAY	FALSE	PAY	PERPLEXED
(elbow)	(wrist)	(base joint)	(nonbase joint)

All four signs include an articulatory posture of an extended hand and arm and a [one] handshape. DAY involves rotating the elbow; FALSE, flexing the wrist; PAY, flexing the base joint of the fingers (i.e., the

Figure 6.2
Signs representing points on the visual sonority hierarchy, from greatest to least
sonority (left to right): DAY, FALSE, PAY, and PERPLEXED

knuckle joint); PERPLEXED, flexing only the distal joint of the finger.
As a result, DAY has the highest degree of sonority of these four sign
movements, and PERPLEXED has the least.

The sonority hierarchy for sign based on proximity of joints to the body is
given in the table that follows. It is encoded in feature trees by placing feature
nodes with a higher sonority value higher on the feature tree, and those with
a lower sonority value lower on the feature tree. This hierarchy is intended to
be generally predictive of sonority hierarchies in sign languages crosslinguistically. The question of whether a specific feature in a given sign
language is ranked higher or lower than the value predicted here is left
open. Trilled movement is assigned a sonority value of 1, but since it is
not a single movement, it is not listed here. Since [TM] is an articulator-
free feature, it can occur at any of the prosodic branch class nodes.

Sonority hierarchy for sign and for speech

For single sign movements			For speech (Kenstowicz 1994)	
Features	Joints	Sonority value	Features	Sonority value
setting	shoulder	6	vowels	5
path	elbow	5	glides	4
orientation	wrist	4	liquids	3
aperture	metacarpal	3	nasals	2
	interphalangeal	2	obstruents	1

Figure 6.2 (continued)

What has been presented thus far in this section is a phonetic basis for sign sonority, rather than a phonological one. When an input form contains a particular prosodic feature, a redundancy rule fills in the joint that executes the movement. This redundancy rule is based on the types of signs that make use of these features and on the largest type of movement possible for such features. In the default case, setting features are executed by the shoulder, path features by the elbow, orientation features by the wrist, and aperture features by the finger joints. The default joint associated with a specific prosodic feature determines its *inherent sonority* (3a). However, the joint specification of the input form may be altered for a variety of reasons, so that a different joint may actually execute the movement. The phonetic sonority of the output form is called *derived sonority* (3b).[1]

(3) *Definition of inherent and derived sonority*

  a. Inherent sonority is the sonority value based on the input features and default joints assigned them.

  b. Derived sonority is the sonority value based on the joint used in the output form to articulate a sign.

The difference between inherent and derived sonority is illustrated in (4) and figure 6.3. All three signs in (4) have elbow rotation in the output, and as a result they all have the same derived sonority. However, only WILLING has an inherent sonority value of 5. PERPLEXED and FALSE have inherent sonority values of 2 and 4, respectively, based on the features in the input; they are produced using the elbow joint as a result of phonetic enhancement (see below).

(4) *Inherent and derived sonority in three forms*

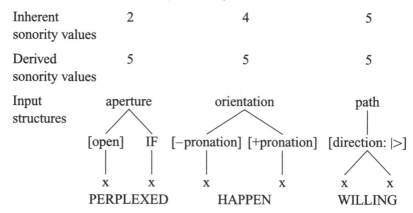

Inherent sonority values	2	4	5
Derived sonority values	5	5	5

Input structures   aperture   orientation   path

[open]   IF   [−pronation]   [+pronation]   [direction: |>]

x   x   x   x   x   x

PERPLEXED   HAPPEN   WILLING

To clarify how derived sonority works in ASL, I will present two systematic examples of its use: in phonetic reduction (distalization) and in phonetic enhancement (proximalization). In analyzing the phonetic production errors of signers with Parkinson's disease, Brentari and Poizner (1994) observed a set of alternations they call distalization of movement (see chapters 1 and 4). When a movement is distalized, the shape of a path movement is maintained, but the movement is transferred to a more distal joint rather than being articulated at a more proximal one. According to this account, the input structures (underlying forms) of the control signers and those with Parkinson's disease are the same, but because the joint that articulates the output movement is more distal in the form produced by the signer with Parkinson's disease, this form has lower derived sonority than the inherent sonority value would predict. Distalized productions of the Parkinsonian signer RH are given in the table that follows; grammatical aspect categories of the forms are indicated in brackets. The citation and distalized forms of HARD are illustrated in figure 6.4 and their respective phonological structures are shown in (5). For the sign HARD, the joint involved in executing the [direction] feature is normally the elbow.

Figure 6.3
Example signs with equal *derived sonority*, but different *inherent sonority*: PER-
PLEXED (top left) has an inherent sonority value of 2; HAPPEN (top right) has
an inherent sonority value of 4; WILLING (bottom) has an inherent sonority
value of 5.

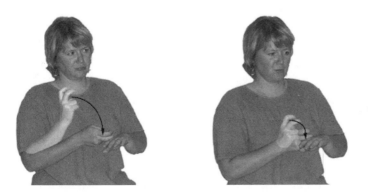

Figure 6.4
The citation form of HARD (left), which has a path movement, and the distalized
form of HARD (right), which has an orientation change

Distalization of movement in forms produced by Parkinsonian signer RH vs. the typical forms produced by a control signer

	Control signer	Parkinsonian signer	
Sign	Joint	Joint	Path
LOOK [exhaustive]	wrist	knuckles	[direction: >|]
LOOK [continuative]	elbow	wrist/elbow	[direction: >|]
CHILDREN	wrist/elbow	knuckles	[direction: >|]
POOR	elbow	wrist	[direction: |>]
BETTER	elbow	knuckles/wrist	[shape: straight]
HARD	elbow	wrist	[direction: >|]

(5) *Representations of control and distalized forms of HARD*

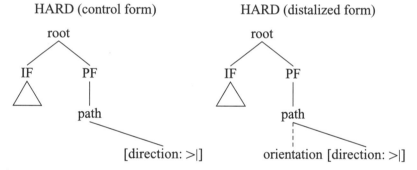

In both RH's and the control signer's productions, the input is the same, a [direction: >|] feature with predictable contact at the end of the movement; however, RH used the wrist to execute the movement. In each case where a Parkinsonian signer distalizes a sign, path features such as [direction] or [tracing] features are translated into distalized counterparts, based on the underlying orientation and on the prosodic features specified.

Another example of how derived sonority works comes from forms discussed by Corina (1990b) that contain an additional movement, articulated by a joint more proximal than the input feature's default joint. This can be seen as a type of phonetic enhancement (Stevens and Keyser 1989; Stevens, Keyser, and Kawasaki 1986) of an underlying specification. In forms containing only a handshape executed by the nonbase joints (i.e., the most distal joints of the fingers), the sonority value is 2. Take PER-PLEXED as an example. There are three possible ways to increase the

Figure 6.5
Four surface realizations of the sign PERPLEXED: the citation form with an aperture change alone (top left); a form with wrist movement enhancement (top right); a form with elbow movement enhancement (bottom left); and a form with enhancement due to body movement (bottom right)

surface sonority of this sign; these are illustrated in figure 6.5 and ranked with respect to sonority in the diagram that follows. One way is to retract the wrist while flexing the joints of the index finger, thereby adding an orientation change to the handshape change; another is to rotate the elbow, thereby adding a path movement to the form; a third is to add a movement of the head.

Lower derived sonority ⟵——————————————⟶ Higher derived sonority

PERPLEXED(1)	PERPLEXED(2)	PERPLEXED(3)	PERPLEXED(4)
(citation form)	(with wrist enhancement)	(with elbow enhancement)	(with nonmanual enhancement)

PERPLEXED(2)–(4) enhance the inherent sonority value of the input form.[2] PERPLEXED(4) is very interesting, because of the use of the body itself as an articulator; the head movement's ability to enhance the perceptual salience of the sign in a manner parallel to that of wrist and elbow movement in PERPLEXED(2) and PERPLEXED(3) is unmistakable. The movements of the body may have a prosodic role in the sign stream, as proposed by Boyes-Braem (1995). Such movements are indeed more proximal in some sense than any other type of movement in sign; that is, they are articulated by the head or torso itself, rather than by an extremity such as the arm. Since a thorough treatment of such forms is not possible here, I leave PERPLEXED(4) unanalyzed in the Prosodic Model, only noting that it reveals another way that sonority value can be enhanced. The forms STUNNED (accompanied by a 'jaw-drop' nonmanual) and VANISH (accompanied by a 'thp' nonmanual) also exhibit nonmanual enhancement of manual articulatory gestures. I know of no contemporary forms in ASL that utilize a body branch of structure for lexical contrast, but Frishberg (1975) cites forms from 1918 that involve such movements. I leave this area for further research.

To sum up: I have shown that the features dominated by the prosodic features branch of structure have a special type of complexity known as visual sonority, analogous in function to sonority in spoken languages. I have also demonstrated two measurements of visual sonority: inherent and derived. Inherent sonority involves assigning a sonority value to a form on the basis of the distinctive features in its input structure. Derived sonority involves assigning sonority to a form on the basis of its surface output, which may include redundant movements inserted to enhance the form's sonority.

6.3   Grammatical Uses of Visual Sonority in Syllables

In order to make the case that sonority plays a phonological role in sign, it is necessary to show how the grammar uses it to determine when a structure is well formed. Bound morphemes in ASL can consist of solely a handshape (e.g., classifier forms), a location (e.g., in the system of reference), or a movement (e.g., grammatical aspect), but unbound morphemes (i.e., stems) must have all three. In some conceivable sign language a signed word could consist of a single parameter—a handshape made anywhere with any type of movement, a single location marked with any handshape and any type of movement, or a single movement made anywhere with any handshape—but no such sign language has yet been found. It is also conceivable that movements, in particular, could not be a necessary part of the underlying structure of signed words, and that the movements made to get from one location to another could be external to the system (Hayes 1993). However, the preceding chapters have presented empirical evidence that all movements do not behave equally; for example, setting changes trigger the insertion of straight, epenthetic movements to contact in some cases whereas path features do not, and [tracing] and [direction] features realize contact in different ways. Moreover, all well-formed signs have a movement—a fact often noted in almost every framework.[3] In the Prosodic Model, this well-formedness condition is expressed as in (6). It can be formulated in Optimality Theory in a constraint that captures the minimum and maximum length on core, prosodic words, stating that words consist of at least one but not more than two syllables; it incorporates the 2-MVT constraint from chapter 5.

(6) *Prosodic well-formedness condition on movement ($PWD = 1 \leq 2\sigma$)*

Core lexemes consist of at least one and not more than two syllables, where a syllable is defined as consisting of one sequential movement.

In spoken languages such well-formedness conditions are common, and they refer to the syllable in part because they address the degree of sonority or the sonority contour required by a language-particular grammar. For example, in Iraqi and Cairene Arabic an epenthetic vowel is inserted into a string containing a consonant or consonants that are otherwise unsyllabifiable, so that all consonants are parsed (i.e., so that none are deleted; e.g., /giltlha/ → [giltilha]). Another type of prosodic well-formedness condition addresses the notion of the minimum word. For example, in many spoken languages prosodic word units must be binary feet (a constraint called FOOT BINARITY (FTBIN) in Prince and Smolensky 1993. A word must consist of either one bimoraic "heavy" syllable or two monomoraic "light" syllables. The mora in spoken languages is an abstract unit measured most frequently in terms of length but also involving complexity (see Perlmutter 1995 for an overview of the use of the mora in spoken languages). One language in which FTBIN holds is

English; as a result, [tæ] is an ill-formed word in English; but [tæp] and [tuʷ] are well-formed words.

In the Prosodic Model, transitional movements are not represented in the input, and lexical movements are all represented in the prosodic features branch of structure. As illustrated in (7), simple movements are those with one branching prosodic class node; complex movements are those with more than one. These types of movement correspond exactly to the simple (1a) and complex (1b) structures defined in Dependency Phonology.

(7) *Prosodic Model representations of different types of movement*

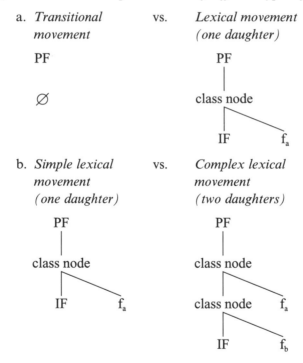

The well-formedness condition on movement (6) can be seen as being related to visual sonority, in the following way. As discussed in section 6.3.1 (recall also section 4.3.1), there is a set of signs that do not have a movement in their input; an epenthetic movement must be inserted in these signs. The existence of these signs and the operation of movement epenthesis are collective evidence that signs must conform to (6) or they will be ungrammatical and fail to surface; this is one place where visual sonority plays a role in the grammar. Movement epenthesis in ASL, FTBIN, and vowel epenthesis in Iraqi and Cairene Arabic ensure that outputs conform to the prosodic well-formedness conditions of the language in question.

In spoken languages sonority also plays a role in identifying syllable nuclei (Zec 1988; Prince and Smolensky 1993; Dell and Elmedlaoui 1985; Guerssel 1986). The feature with the highest degree of sonority in a local domain is chosen as the nucleus. If there is a sonority hierarchy in sign, then movements of higher sonority values should be preferred over movements of lower sonority when choosing syllable nuclei. In section 6.3.2, where local lexicalization of fingerspelled forms is discussed, we will see that this is indeed the case in ASL.

By way of background, several sonority hierarchies that have been proposed in the literature for sign are given in table 6.1; all of these proposals conform to the one on page 218 when simple movements are considered. Static articulators play no role in the sonority hierarchy, which is one reason why these features are grouped together as inherent features.

6.3.1 The Minimal Syllable

I now make the move of calling the minimal word, which consists of a single, simple, sequential movement, a *minimal syllable*. The arguments for doing so are (1) the functional similarity between movements and sonorous sounds in spoken languages, and (2) the role that movement plays in determining the minimal word.

Recall from section 4.3.1 (also see Brentari 1990c,d) that the input for certain forms (e.g., THINK, KNOW, MY, and signs for body parts) includes an epenthetic path ([direction: >||]) movement, which provides the necessary sonority to allow the inputs to surface as well-formed outputs. These movements have been analyzed as epenthetic since they are entirely predictable: movement is present when the forms appear as single words, but not when they appear as the first stem of a compound. These forms contrast with another set of forms that exhibit movement both when used as single words and when used as the first stem of a compound. These sets of forms are exemplified in (8a) and (8b), respectively, and illustrated in figure 6.6.

Table 6.1
Visual sonority hierarchy proposals. (The bold line indicates the threshold of sonority to the right of which a word is ill formed.)

higher sonority ←   → lower sonority

	P+TM P+HSΔ P	HSΔ	short P	Loc+TM	plain L L+contact
Sandler 1993c (segments)					
Brentari 1993 (class nodes)	P	full HSΔ partial HSΔ OΔ		TM	static articulators
Corina 1990b (class nodes)	P	full HSΔ full OΔ	POAΔ		partial HSΔ partial OΔ
Blevins 1993 (articulators)	P	nonstatic articulators			static articulators
Perlmutter 1992	P	moraic positions			nonmoraic positions
van der Hulst 1993	path movements	local movements			no movements
	DYNAMIC ARTICULATORS				STATIC ARTICULATORS

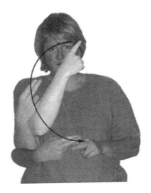

Figure 6.6
A compound whose first stem exhibits no movement—THINK^SELF (left)—
and a compound whose first stem exhibits movement—BLACK^NAME (right).
Both THINK and BLACK have movement in their citation forms.

(8) *Contrasting input forms as evidenced by the presence or absence of*
movement in compound forms

   a. *Forms with movement in single words, but not in the first stem of a*
      compound

Single word	In compounds
THINK	THINK^SELF 'decide for oneself'
	THINK^TOUCH 'obsessed'
	THINK^HOLD 'memorize'
	THINK^FREEZE 'shocked'
KNOW	KNOW^THAT 'be aware of something'
HEART	HEART^ATTACK 'heart attack'
WRONG	WRONG^HAPPEN 'unexpected'
TIME	TIME^SAME 'simultaneous'

   b. *Forms with movement both in single words and in the first stem of*
      compounds

Single word	In compounds
SLEEP	SLEEP^SUNRISE 'oversleep'
BLACK	BLACK^NAME 'bad reputation'
THRILL	THRILL^INFORM 'news'
CALL/NAME[4]	NAME^SHINE 'good reputation'
MONEY	MONEY^BEHIND 'savings'

On the basis of such a distribution of movement, the input structure for the stems in (8a) and (8b) are posited to be the ones in (9a) and (9b), respectively. When (8a) stems appear as single words, movement epenthesis occurs as shown.

(9) *Structure of forms with and without input movements*

    a. *Input structure of THINK and movement epenthesis*

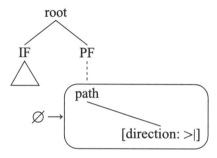

    b. *Input structure of BLACK*

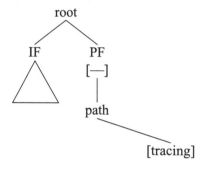

6.3.2 Syllable Construction in Lexicalized Fingerspelled Forms

Sonority also plays a role in ASL grammar in the construction of syllables in fingerspelled forms.[5] As noted in chapter 5, fingerspelled forms of the discipline-specific type go through a rapid *local lexicalization* process, whereby a fingerspelled form comes to stand not for each letter in the English word, but for the concept the word conveys; this process fixes the shape of the fingerspelled form for the duration of a given discourse. This operation typically occurs over the course of just three productions. When the form appears for the first time, each letter shape is distinctly formed; this is used as evidence that the input structure for these forms contains all of the fingerspelled letters of the English word (the same is not true for other nonnative forms, such as initialized signs, abbreviated signs, and arbitrary name signs, discussed in chapter 8). By the third production, lexicalized fingerspelled forms conform closely to constraints proposed for other well-formed native signs, and they have achieved a stable state in which they will remain for the rest of the discourse. A subset of the forms used for this analysis is shown in the following table; the corpus comes from the ASL tapes accompanying Valli and Lucas 1992 and Bienvenu and Colonomos 1987.

Some of the locally lexicalized fingerspelled forms from the corpus ($\varnothing$ = epenthetic dynamic element; # = word boundary; [XY] = letters that have undergone handshape merger)

# letters	1st/2nd production	3rd production	# syllables
6	S-Y-N-T-A-X	S-Y-$\varnothing$-T-X	2
8	C-U-P-B-O-A-R-D	C-P-[wig]-D	2
8	L-O-C-A-T-I-O-N	[LI]-O-$\varnothing$-C-N	2
8	M-O-R-P-H-E-M-E	M-P-H-E	2
9	P-H-O-N-O-L-O-G-Y	P-[HG]-Y	2
10	M-O-R-P-H-O-L-O-G-Y	M-P-[HG]-Y	2
10	L-I-N-G-U-I-S-T-I-C	L-I-N-G-I-C	2
5	C-H-I-L-D	[CII]-I-L-D	1

Local lexicalization can be seen as an operation that exerts a set of constraints on such forms.

(10) *Local lexicalization*

   a. HARMONIZE NUCLEUS (HNUC)

      Local maxima of sonority are chosen as syllable nuclei.

   b. PROSODIC WORD = $1 \leq 2\sigma$ (PWD = $1 \leq 2\sigma$)

      Core lexemes consist of at least one syllable and not more than two.

   c. 2-HANDSHAPES (2-HS)

      Core lexemes consist of at most two handshapes.

   d. SELECTED FINGERS (SF)

      i. Core lexemes consist of at most one contrastive handshape.

      ii. Aperture changes affect only selected fingers.

  e. MAXIMIZE APERTURE CHANGE (MAXAP Δ)

  Handshape changes that occupy syllable nuclei maximize
  aperture change, alternating between [open] and [closed] aperture
  settings.

  f. PARSE HANDSHAPE (PARSE-HS)

  All handshapes in the input must be present in the output.

  g. ALIGN(L)

  Align initial handshape of stem with left edge of stem.

  h. ALIGN(R)

  Align final handshape of word with right edge of word.

These constraints are cast within the framework of Optimality Theory;
they are ranked with respect to one another[6] and are violable when a
higher-ranked constraint must be satisfied. PWD = $1 \leq 2\sigma$ was explained
in the text preceding (6), and MAXAP Δ was explained in section 4.6.
There are several constraints on handshape that can be explained as a
group. Universal PARSE constraints (McCarthy and Prince 1995) require
that a structure present in the input should have a corresponding structure
in the output. The relevant formulation of this universal constraint in this
ASL context is PARSE HS, which requires that all of the handshapes in the
input of a lexicalized fingerspelled form be present in the output as well.
This constraint conflicts with the 2-HS constraint; therefore, some letters
will be eliminated. Exactly which letters are eliminated is in part due to
MAXAP Δ, which requires that handshapes alternate between open and
closed forms, and the ALIGNMENT constraints ALIGN(L) and ALIGN(R),
which require that the first handshape in a lexicalized fingerspelled form
be the first handshape in the spelling of the English word and that the
last handshape in a lexicalized fingerspelled form be the last handshape in
the spelling of the English word. Finally, in all locally lexicalized fingerspelled forms, the SELECTED FINGERS constraint is violated.

   The most important constraint for this analysis is HNUC, which generally chooses from among the available handshape changes and orientation changes in the input form those movements that are the best possible
syllable nuclei and that conform most closely to the other constraints
in (10). These are either orientation or aperture features since, except for
the letter 'Z', there are no path movements either in the production of

fingerspelled letters or in transitions between fingerspelled letters. Orientation changes are always chosen over aperture changes when they are available, thereby demonstrating their higher-ranked sonority status and the role that sonority plays in the lexicalization. The carefully fingerspelled and locally lexicalized forms of P-H-O-N-O-L-O-G-Y, M-O-R-P-H-O-L-O-G-Y, M-O-R-P-H-E-M-E, and C-H-I-L-D are illustrated in (11)–(14) and explained in detail below. The sonority values listed in section 6.2 are given both for the carefully fingerspelled forms and for the locally lexicalized forms (* = weight unit, discussed in section 6.4).

(11) *Local lexicalization of P-H-O-N-O-L-O-G-Y → P-[HG]-Y*

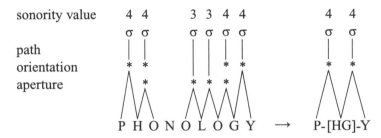

(12) *Local lexicalization of M-O-R-P-H-O-L-O-G-Y → M-P-[HG]-Y*

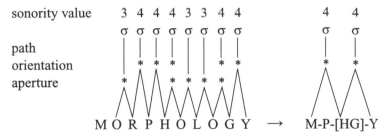

(13) *Local lexicalization of M-O-R-P-H-E-M-E → M-P-H-E*

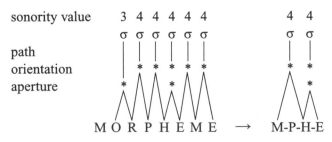

(14) *Local lexicalization of C-H-I-L-D → [CH]-I-L-D*

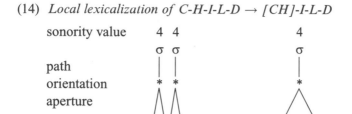

I will highlight one aspect of the local lexicalization for each of these forms. The movements in the output form P-[HG]-Y are orientation changes; this satisfies HNᴜᴄ. There are three orientation changes in the input of P-H-O-N-O-L-O-G-Y, and only two in the locally lexicalized output form P-[HG]-Y, thereby conforming to PWᴅ = 1≤2σ. The two that are retained are the ones allowing the first and last letter to be retained as well, thereby conforming to Aʟɪɢɴ(L) and Aʟɪɢɴ(R). P, H, and G are very similar in handshape. They are all [open] and [one]; the addition of the thumb in G and the [all] feature in H are smoothly integrated into the sequence. The locally lexicalized form of M-O-R-P-H-O-L-O-G-Y is similar to that of P-H-O-N-O-L-O-G-Y, except that the initial M is added to satisfy Aʟɪɢɴ(L). The orientation change from M to P is a wrist flexion (i.e., wrist nod), and the orientation change from P to H is a change from [prone] to the "default" position facing the midsagittal plane. These two orientation changes are integrated into one movement. The locally lexicalized form of M-O-R-P-H-E-M-E, M-P-H-E, demonstrates the same operation at work in the M→P→H sequence. It also satisfies Aʟɪɢɴ(L) and Aʟɪɢɴ(R) by choosing the orientation changes that allow M and E to remain in the output. The locally lexicalized form for C-H-I-L-D is monosyllabic rather than disyllabic. At this point I have no explanation for why the local lexicalization of C-H-I-L-D, with five input letters, is monosyllabic, and the local lexicalization of S-Y-N-T-A-X, with six input letters, is disyllabic. No letters of C-H-I-L-D are deleted, but all are smoothly integrated into the orientation change that occurs between H and I. In the locally lexicalized form [CH]-I-L-D, the orientation of the initial C has regressively assimilated to that of the H, and the two handshapes have merged; that is, the index and middle fingers are straight and the ring and pinkie fingers are curved. This type of handshape merger takes place to satisfy Pᴀʀsᴇ HS and will be discussed in more detail shortly.

In chapter 3 I argued for a division between joint specifications and selected fingers (i.e., handshape contrasts), which simplified the analysis of aperture changes (i.e., handshape contours) in core lexemes. Extracting the joint specifications from the fingers specification is helpful here as well. The letters of the ASL manual alphabet can be grouped according to the joint specifications for each letter—[flexed] or nonflexed—and then assigned a corresponding aperture setting. (A chart of the manual alphabet is given in figure 1.8.) The classification of the letters according to aperture setting is given in the following table; recall that the distinctive joint specifications are fully open, bent, curved, flat, and fully closed. A [flexed] joint specification becomes a [closed] aperture setting; a joint structure without a [flexed] feature becomes an [open] aperture setting (15).

Aperture setting of each letter of the ASL manual alphabet

Nonflexed		[Flexed]	
B	C	A	D (unspecified)
G	D (specified)	E	F (specified)
H	F (unspecified)	M	N
I	J	O	S
K	L	T	X
P	Q		
R	U		
V	W		
Y	Z		

(15) *Redundancy rule: joint specification → aperture setting*

   [flexed] → [closed]
   ∅ → [open]

Sequences of letters that do not conform to MaxAp Δ are the most likely to be deleted in the locally lexicalized form; for example, E-M in the E-M-E sequence of M-O-R-P-H-E-M-E, and the N in the N-T sequence in S-Y-N-T-A-X.

There are also *routinized sequences* for handshapes frequently used in locally lexicalized forms. Two such sequences appear in the corpus: I-O-N and I-N-G. I-O-N becomes [IO]; I and O are articulated together as a result of merger. The change from O to N is not a licit aperture change,

Figure 6.7
The sequence I-O-N in careful fingerspelling (left) and as a routinized sequence
(right), including the epenthetic 'C' inserted to ensure a well-formed syllable

but by inserting a C between this combined [IO] handshape and N, a well-
formed aperture change is ensured (figure 6.7).

Given the division of handshape features into fingers and joint features, we can focus on the way that the maximum number of handshapes
are incorporated into the output. Whenever possible, features of adjacent
handshapes are accommodated by handshape merger, as in the [CH]
combination in C-H-I-L-D and the [IO] of the routinized sequence for
I-O-N. The nonselected fingers of H curve to express the C; and since I
and O are articulated by different selected fingers, they can be expressed
simultaneously.

These forms confirm proposals made in earlier chapters and provide
important evidence for the use of visual sonority in the lexicalization of
forms. First, the effects of HNUC are seen in the choice of wrist movements over handshape movements in the lexicalized forms. Second, the
effects of ALIGNMENT constraints are obvious in the choice of letters
retained in the locally lexicalized forms and in the way they align with the
movements. Third, syllables are not constructed in these lexicalized fingerspelled words on the basis of the selected finger groups, as we might
expect from the criteria developed elsewhere in the literature (Brentari
1990b; Perlmutter 1992, 1993); rather, they are constructed on the basis
of the sonority value of the dynamic units of the form. The SELECTED
FINGERS constraint is violated in all of these forms, but the number and
types of violations can be described systematically; that is, the violations
are not random. Fourth, evidence from local lexicalization strengthens
the argument made in chapter 3 for separating the fingers specification
from the joint specification. This separation allows us to assign fingerspelled letters to [open] and [closed] aperture settings on the basis of their
[flexed] or nonflexed joint specifications, thereby allowing changes in
fingerspelled letters to be seen as licit or illicit aperture change. Sequences
of letters that do not alternate between [open] and [closed] aperture spec-

ifications are the most likely to be deleted from the lexicalized form. Because of these behaviors, I conclude that local lexicalization reveals the several operations involved in syllabification and word formation. Because of the way these operations function in the grammar, the term *syllable* is considered appropriate for the two units of locally lexicalized forms based on sequential movements. They invoke sonority, they are submorphemic, they are sublexical, and they are inherently units of prosody.

6.4 Subsyllabic Units of Prosodic Analysis

I will now use the basic unit of the syllable, corresponding to sequential, phonological movements, as a reference point for examining subsyllabic structure. The analysis will show that there is a grammatical difference between simple and complex movements, and that the former have one weight unit and the latter have two. The analysis assumes that the division of features into inherent and prosodic features is correct, and that the analysis of the prosodic features branch of structure with respect to visual sonority and its role in the grammar is correct.

Several observations led me to investigate the nature of subsyllabic structure. First, using *A Dictionary of American Sign Language on Linguistic Principles* (*DASL*; Stokoe, Casterline, and Croneberg 1965) as a corpus of signs, one finds an asymmetry between the number of signs that contain simple movements (i.e., those with one branching class node) and the number that contain complex movements (i.e., those with more than one branching class node).

(16) *Definition of simple and complex movements*

    a. Simple movement: a movement involving a single local or path movement (e.g., SIT, LOOK, UNDERSTAND, DIE)

    b. Complex movement: a movement involving more than one co-occurring local or path movement (e.g., THROW, POOR, BETTER, MEETING, OLD)

Of the signs in *DASL*, 82% contain simple movements; only 18% contain complex movements. This is an unexpected asymmetry, and it tells us something both about the ASL lexicon and about complex movements: namely, complex movements are not the preferred form for an ASL lexical item.

The second observation that led to the following analysis of subsyllabic structure is that there appears to be grammatical pressure on certain complex morphological forms to reduce the number of simultaneously occurring movements. The third observation is that certain derived nominals of two separate types allow only forms with simple movements to be possible input forms.

In this section I discuss the third observation, showing that the difference between simple and complex movements determines which ASL forms are appropriate inputs for reduplicative nominals. McCarthy and Prince (1994) and Shaw (1992, 1994) have convincingly shown that, in spoken languages, the prosodic material present in the reduplicant in reduplicated forms is an indicator of the unmarked syllable structure. To take one example, in Nootka only the onset+nucleus portion of the stem is reduplicated in the following forms (Shaw 1992):

Unmarked structures in Nootka reduplication

Stem	Reduplicated form	Meaning
/c'awa/	/c'a-c'awa-čiɬ/	'naming one'
/ʔu/	/ʔu-ʔu-'iɬh/	'hunting it'
/wa:s/	/wa:-wa:s-čiɬ/	'naming where ...'
/ta:kʷa/	/ta:-ta:kʷa-'i:h/	'hunting only that'
/čims/	/či-čims-čiɬ/	'naming a bear'
/čims/	/či-čims-'iɬh/	'hunting bear'

The first work on noun-verb pairs in ASL (Supalla and Newport 1978) contains an analysis of such pairs; Supalla and Newport specifically describe them as (1) related in meaning and (2) containing a verb that expresses the activity performed with or on the object named by the noun.[7] The structural alternation between the noun and the verb is that the movement of the verb is repeated once in the unidirectional forms, and in the bidirectional forms it is repeated twice.[8] This operation can be analyzed as suffixal because, in bidirectional forms, the first of the two sequential movements is copied after the entire base is produced (e.g., IRON, PIANO). An additional part of this structural description, not previously mentioned, is that both the reduplicant and the base of the reduplicated form are simple movements in all forms discussed by Supalla and Newport. I am aware of no reduplicated forms that contain complex movements using their definition. All of the forms that undergo reduplication of the stem to produce the noun form contain one and only one branching prosodic feature. Example noun-verb pairs are given in (17);

Figure 6.8
The noun-verb pair CLOSE-WINDOW (left) and WINDOW (right); the nominal
doubles the movement of the input stem and exhibits a shorter, more restrained
manner of movement.

the verb form comes first in each pair, and the noun second. An example
pair is pictured in figure 6.8; the full list from Supalla and Newport 1978
appears in appendix C.

(17) *Noun-verb pairs (from Supalla and Newport 1978)*

    a. *Reduplicated movement*

        SIT/CHAIR
        GO-BY-PLANE/AIRPLANE
        GO-BY-BOAT/BOAT
        GO-BY-ROCKET/ROCKET
        HIT-WITH-HAMMER/HAMMER
        GO-BY-FLYING-SAUCER/FLYING-SAUCER
        CLOSE-WINDOW/WINDOW

    b. *Reduplicated aperture change*

        SNAP-PHOTOGRAPH/CAMERA
        FLICK-LIGHTER/LIGHTER
        THUMP-MELON/MELON
        STAPLE/STAPLER
        SQUEEZE-PLIERS/PLIERS
        TAKE-PILL/PILL

    c. *Reduplicated orientation change*

        STRIKE-MATCH/MATCH

Most of the forms in (17) contain a simple path movement and no hand-shape change; a few contain a simple handshape change and no path movement (e.g., SNAP-PHOTOGRAPH) (verb) vs. CAMERA (noun)) or a simple orientation change (e.g., STRIKE-MATCH (verb) vs. MATCH (noun)). There are also two other sets of forms that undergo reduplication, which pattern with the noun-verb reduplication forms. Those in (18) are noun-verb pairs, but they do not conform to the semantic restriction outlined by Supalla and Newport (1978); that is, the verbs do not express an activity performed with or on the object named by the noun. The forms in (19) are noun forms that have no corresponding verb. However, both of these sets of reduplicated forms are almost exclusively made up of base forms containing simple movements.[9]

(18) *Forms that do not meet Supalla and Newport's (1978) semantic*
      criteria, but nonetheless undergo reduplication to form a nominal

      SUPPORT/SUPPORT
      OWE/DEBT
      CALL/NAME
      APPLY/APPLICATION
      ASSIST/ASSISTANT

(19) *Reduplicated noun forms without corresponding verbs*

      CHURCH
      COLD
      COUGH
      DOCTOR
      CUP
      NURSE

An analysis of reduplication has been expressed in segmental terms in the HT Model, as shown in (20), as well as in the HM Model (Liddell and Johnson 1986).

(20) *Reduplication in the HT Model (Sandler 1989) (lowercase letters*
      represent entire feature matrices)

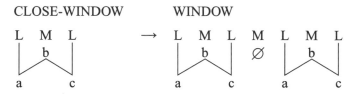

The problem that arises from such analyses is that there is no uniform class of segmental sequences that can pick out the forms eligible for reduplication. In addition to LML (the sequence of CLOSE-WINDOW in (20)), the forms that undergo reduplication can consist of other segment sequences: M segments (e.g., the pair AIRPLANE and FLY), or a single handshape change (e.g., STAPLER and STAPLE), which are represented in earlier versions of the HT Model (Sandler 1989) as single Ls. This problem arises because the unit of analysis is the segment, and because the account ignores the number of subsyllabic movements. It is in the prosodic features branch of structure that the true structural generalization can be found.

The Prosodic Model alternative to a segmental analysis uses a subsyllabic unit, called a *weight unit*, to capture the simple versus complex movement distinction. Each branching prosodic feature constitutes a weight unit, as shown in (21). The representation using simultaneous weight units to capture this generalization is given in (22).

(21) *Construction of a weight unit: A weight unit is constructed for every prosodic feature*

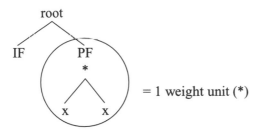

(22) *Input and output representations using simultaneous weight units*

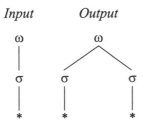

Additional evidence for the usefulness of weight units in derivational operations in ASL comes from nominals not formed by reduplication (see Padden and Perlmutter 1987). These are called *activity nouns*, because

Figure 6.9
The verb READ (left) and the activity nominal READING (right), formed by the
addition of [TM]

all well-formed structures of this type are derived from verbs of "activity"
(Vendler 1967). In each form a [TM] feature associates to the stem's
movement. Like reduplicated nominals, all of these forms have an input
stem with a single, simple movement. This distinction is formally quanti-
fied in the Prosodic Model using weight units. Examples are listed in (23)
and pictured in figure 6.9; the representation of activity nominalization is
shown in (24). The derived nouns in (23b) are ungrammatical either
because the verb is a stative verb rather than an activity verb (23bi) or
because the activity verb contains a complex movement (23bii).

(23) *Activity noun formation in ASL*

   a. *Examples of verbs and their corresponding activity nouns*

        READ   READING
        RAP   RAPPING
        CHAT   CHATTING
        DRIVE   DRIVING
        DRAW   DRAWING
        WRITE   WRITING
        SHOP   SHOPPING
        RUN   RUNNING
        WALK   WALKING
        ACT   ACTING

  b. *Examples of verbs from which no activity noun is derived*

   i. *Stative verbs*

SIT	*SITTING
SMILE	*SMILING
STAND	*STANDING
WANT	*WANTING
DESIRE	*DESIRING
LOVE	*LOVING
LIKE	*LIKING

  ii. *Activity verbs with a complex movement*

ENVISION	*ENVISIONING
DREAM	*DREAMING
TAKE	*TAKING
GRAB	*GRABBING

(24) *The input and output representations of activity nominalization*

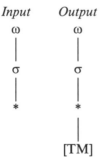

| *Input* | *Output* |

6.5 Weight Units and Their Interaction with Syntactic Constituents

One further argument for the importance of weight units in the phonological grammar of ASL comes from a relationship between sentence-final position and "heavy" phonological structures. The descriptive generalization is that the greater the number of weight units in a verb form, the more strongly it will gravitate to sentence-final position. This type of interaction is described by Zec and Inkelas (1990, 373) for topicalization in Serbo-Croatian and by Ross (1967) for heavy NP shift in English. The examples in (25) exhibit this principle in ASL. The form of GIVE in (25a) contains one weight unit because it contains one prosodic feature (i.e., the [direction] feature). In this case either word order is possible. The form in (25b) contains two weight units because it contains the [direction] feature and the [TM] feature indicating the [habitual] aspect. In these forms placing the verb in nonfinal position is acceptable, but not preferred. The form in (25c) contains three weight units because it contains the [direction] feature and the [TM] and [arc] features, which express the [exhaustive] aspect. In this case the verb must appear in sentence-final position.

(25) *Influence of weight units on word order*

    a. $_1$GIVE$_2$ BOOK.   'I give you the book.'

        $\overline{\text{BOOK}}^{\text{t}}$ $_1$GIVE$_2$.   'As for the book, I give [it] to you.'

    b. ?$_1$GIVE$_2$ [habitual] BOOK.   'I give books to you all the time.'

    c. $\overline{\text{BOOK}}^{\text{t}}$ $_1$GIVE$_2$ [habitual].   'As for the books, I give [them] to you all the time.'

        *GIVE [exhaustive] BOOK.   'I give a book to each and every one of you.'

        $\overline{\text{BOOK}}^{\text{t}}$ GIVE [exhaustive].   'As for the books, I give [them] to each and every one of you.'

The asymmetrical realization of the "verb sandwich" construction in ASL, described by Fischer and Janis (1990), is a similar phenomenon. In this construction two instances of the verb appear, one before and one after an object. The first instance is a simple form; the second is typically a morphologically complex form.

(26) *"Verb sandwich" constructions*

    a. Schema for verb sandwich constructions (from Fischer and Janis 1990)
SUBJECT VERB (OBJECTS) (ADJUNCTS) VERB + LOTS-OF-INFLECTION

    b. SALLY THERE HMM TYPE T-E-R-M PAPER TYPE [unrealized inceptive]...
'Sally was just about to start writing her term paper ...'

    c. S-H-E LISTEN R-A-D-I-O LISTEN [continuous]...
'She was continuously listening to the radio ...'

The fact that morphologically complex forms gravitate to sentence-final position in these two environments supports the arguments made thus far in this chapter that ASL exhibits a grammatical sensitivity to the number of component parts of movements.

To conclude: The claim that there is a grammatical distinction between simple and complex movements has been supported by three arguments. First, the asymmetry in the distribution of simple and complex movements in the *DASL* corpus is significant (82% vs. 18%, respectively); it suggests that simple movements are preferred in the ASL lexicon. Second, derived reduplicated and activity nominals both select simple movement forms as inputs and reject inputs with complex movements. Third, the number of subcomponents of movements can influence sentential word order; that is, the greater the number of subcomponents, the more likely that the word will appear sentence-finally.

6.6 Conclusion

In this chapter I have investigated the internal structure of sign movements, represented in the Prosodic Model by the prosodic features branch of structure. First, I proposed a sonority hierarchy within the prosodic features branch, based on the proximity of the joint in question to the midline of the body. Features in the input structure provide the information to determine the *inherent sonority* of the input form. In the output, joints other than the default joints may execute the input features' movement; the sonority value of the output is the *derived sonority* of the form. Second, I showed that purely phonological operations, such as syllable formation in locally lexicalized forms, use this sonority hierarchy to construct syllable nuclei; thereby demonstrating the usefulness of the sonority hierarchy in the phonological grammar. Third, I used weight units (sublexical components of movement) to explain morphophonological operations that are sensitive to the number of movement components in a form (the operations that derive reduplicative nouns and activity nouns) and to show why the complex verb in a "verb sandwich" construction is attracted to sentence-final position. That heavy forms are attracted to sentence-final position is true generally in ASL and is not specific to the "verb sandwich" construction.

I would like to directly address the question of applying the term *mora* to the weight unit I have proposed in this chapter. Perlmutter (1992, 1993) proposed that moras in ASL are units of duration; in contrast, I have used the term *mora* in previous work to capture the type of distinctions among phenomena involving movement complexity (Brentari 1993). More recently Perlmutter (1995) has examined the notion of the mora for spoken languages; he concludes that it is primarily a unit of weight, but that in spoken languages at least, the surface effect of increasing weight is to increase duration. I completely agree with this characterization as it applies to moras in spoken languages, but I believe that it is not accurate as it applies to the sign language facts; I use the term *mora* neither for the weight units described in this chapter nor for the duration phenomena described in chapter 5, precisely because the two types of grammatical work are distinct in sign. Just as there are systematic patterns of phonological distribution for duration phenomena (i.e., phrase-final position lengthens holds, and protractive aspect lengthens the holds of a certain class of verbs), so there are systematic patterns of phonological distribution for weight phenomena (i.e., asymmetrical make-up of the lexicon and the phonological shape of the base in reduplicated derived nouns and in derived activity nouns). To call units of duration "moras," as Perlmutter has done, only accounts for duration phenomena and fails to incorporate complexity; to call units of complexity "moras" misses the phenomena related to duration. For this reason, I refer to the subcomponents of movement as "weight units" to avoid confusion.

Chapter 7

The Structure of Two-Handed Signs

7.1   The Importance of Two-Handed Signs in a General Description of Sign Language Phonology

Two-handed signs are so intriguing to phonologists who are interested in sign languages because they provide such a clear case of a phonetic difference between signed and spoken languages, and because this difference can offer clues to the correct underlying representation of signs more generally.[1] The phonetic difference lies in the fact that spoken languages do not have two identical articulators of any sort that could behave in the way that the two hands behave in sign. The important clues come from the fact that the hands are not independent articulators in two-handed signs. Instead, one hand is the *dominant hand*, called H_1, the one that is used for fingerspelling and to articulate one-handed signs in most cases. The other hand, called the *nondominant hand* or H_2, is severely restricted in the kinds of handshapes and movements it can exhibit. Also, in two-handed signs the hands engage in certain behaviors that verify other aspects of the representation proposed thus far. Two questions regarding H_2 have generated considerable debate: Does H_2 need to be represented in all two-handed signs? If so, are different representations required for different types of two-handed signs, or can one basic representation handle them all?

   How H_2 is restricted, and how those restrictions shed light on what phonological structure works best for two-handed signs, is the subject of this chapter. I present an analysis of two-handed signs, which expands on the systematic expression of the place of articulation, the types of orientation, and the types of contact that can occur in one-handed signs. I provide a formal structure for expressing the restrictions on H_2 according to the model developed in chapters 3–6. Specifically, the features of

H_2 are grouped together in the feature tree and are dominated by their own class node, called H_2. My analysis will show that H_2 behaves as a weak branch of prosodic structure; specifically, it behaves as a word-level appendix.

To explain the phonological role(s) of H_2, the notion of a secondary articulator has been proposed in the HT Model (Sandler 1993c), that of a feature in the μ Model (Perlmutter 1991), that of a coda in earlier versions of the Prosodic Model (Brentari 1990c; Brentari and Goldsmith 1993), and that of a weak branch of prosodic structure in the DP Model (van der Hulst 1996). The assumption is that the goal is to achieve the simplest representation of H_2 and one that expresses the broadest range of empirical facts. In section 7.2 I present general facts about the way H_2 is restricted across different types of signs and outline the major points made in previous proposals for representing H_2. In section 7.3, using evidence from synchronic variation and diachronic change, I present several arguments that support a single basic feature representation for all types of two-handed signs. In section 7.4 I propose a specific structure and thereby resolve the challenges raised in section 7.3. In section 7.5 I present evidence from the optional phonological operation of Weak Drop, which bears on issues of phonological economy. In section 7.6 I explain how this feature structure is linked to and limited by its prosodic role as a word-level appendix. I discuss various formal proposals for representing the behavior of H_2 and compare them with the Prosodic Model account.

At the outset of this analysis, it is worth considering why a linguistic analysis of H_2 is needed at all, since it has been suggested from time to time that the behavior of H_2 is simply an extension of the physiological notion of hemispheric dominance and since H_1 is most often the physiologically dominant hand—the one used for writing, handling utensils, playing racquet sports and billiards, and so on. The strongest version of the argument is that the asymmetry between the functions of the two hands can be explained in terms of the asymmetrical role of the two hemispheres; a weaker version is that articulatory or perceptual phonetic restrictions are sufficient to explain the asymmetry between the two hands (e.g., see Dotter and Holzinger 1994).

But neither hemispheric asymmetries nor phonetic considerations can completely explain the structure of two-handed signs. A physiological explanation is not sufficient because even for the purposes of nonlinguistic tasks, individuals can develop equal dexterity in both hands; for example,

a pianist can play equally complex pieces with either hand, even simultaneously. Signers are similarly well trained to use either hand for equally
complex signs under certain conditions—poetry and narratives of various
kinds, to name just two instances. Consider (1), a quotation from Clayton
Valli's poem "Snowflake" (Valli 1995).

(1) *Example of both hands' dexterity and coordination in signing ASL
    (Valli 1995)*

    SNOWFLAKE-FALLS ## .... (H_2)
    WHITE BEAUTY INSIDE (H_1)

All of the signs in (1) are one-handed signs, normally signed with H_1, but
in the poem the four signed words have been split. Three "rhyming" signs
are articulated one after the other by H_1; simultaneously, an independent classifier predicate is articulated by H_2.[2] SNOWFLAKE-FALLS,
articulated by H_2, is a classifier form ('F' handshape), moving in a sine-
wave shape diagonally across the signing space. WHITE, BEAUTY, and
INSIDE are articulated in sequence by H_1. Each has a closing '5' handshape; the sign WHITE begins just after the movement of SNOWFLAKE
begins, and the closing movement of INSIDE ends when SNOWFLAKE
reaches final hold. Articulating signs with different movements and handshapes simultaneously with the two hands is physiologically complex and
is never seen in monomorphemic signs (or even in most polymorphemic
signs). It can be done, however, thus demonstrating a high degree of dexterity and coordination on the part of both hands.

A purely phonetic explanation is likewise insufficient. A good example
is provided by the optional rule of Weak Drop (WD), first proposed by
Battison (1974, 1978) as a rule of phonological deletion and later discussed by Padden and Perlmutter (1987).[3] WD is a process whereby H_2
is totally deleted under certain conditions; that is, a two-handed sign
becomes a one-handed sign. Padden and Perlmutter's description of WD
is as follows: The input consists of a nonalternating Type 1 two-handed
sign (i.e., a sign in which the two hands have the same handshape, place
of articulation, and movement), and the output is one-handed. Some signs
that undergo WD as stated are QUIET, BRAVE, SUNDAY, BODY,
GET, and HAPPEN; some signs that may not undergo WD as stated are
*BICYCLE, *COMPETE, *MALAYSIA. The phenomenon of WD can
be explained by the principle of ease of articulation as a way of producing
the sign more simply or with less effort. In the cases where H_2 can delete,
it supplies only redundant information; however, "redundant informa-

Figure 7.1
Examples of type 1 signs that may and may not undergo Weak Drop. QUIET
(top) may optionally be realized as a one-handed sign; WITH (bottom) may not.

tion" must be spelled out, not in phonetic terms, but in phonological
terms. If "totally redundant" means that H_2 can be dropped if it is doing
exactly what H_1 is doing, we are at a loss to explain why only some
nonalternating signs allow WD. WEDDING, WITH, WITHOUT, and
GERMANY do not undergo WD. Even though the structural description
for WD is met in BRAVE, GET, QUIET, WITH, and GERMANY (i.e.,
all are two-handed and nonalternating), BRAVE, GET, and QUIET may
undergo WD, but WITH and GERMANY may not (see figure 7.1).[4] A
distinction such as the one between BRAVE and GERMANY can only
be explained by examining different possibilities for the formal representation of these signs. An arbitrary, grammatical definition of complexity and redundancy is required, not simply a definition that refers to
physiological or phonetic complexity.

Figure 7.2
Examples of the three types of two-handed signs (Battison 1978): SINCE is a type
1 sign (top left); SIT is a type 2 sign (top right); TOUCH is a type 3 sign (bottom).

7.2   Alternative Accounts of H_2

H_2 is known to be restricted in various ways in two-handed signs. The
first observations about two-handed signs can be traced to Stokoe (1960),
but Battison (1978) was the first to study two-handed signs at length.
In his discussion of "motor acts while signing," Battison (1978, 28–30)
proposes three types of two-handed signs, which are repeated here from
chapter 1 and illustrated in figure 7.2. In type 1 signs both hands are
active and perform identical motor acts (e.g., SINCE). The hands may
or may not contact each other, they may or may not contact the body,
and they may carry out either a synchronous (e.g., RESTRAINED-
FEELINGS) or an alternating (e.g, WHICH, JESUS) pattern of movement. In type 2 signs one hand is active and one hand is passive, but both

hands are specified for the same handshape (e.g., SIT). In type 3 signs one hand is active and one hand is passive, and the two hands have different handshapes (e.g., TOUCH). (Battison also proposed a fourth type, type C, for compounds that combine two or more of the above categories.) Inquiring into the amount of independent information contributed by each hand in two-handed signs, Battison concluded that this amount was highest in type 3 signs, lowest in type 1 signs, and intermediate in type 2 signs. In other words, type 1 signs exhibit the most redundancy, and type 3 the least. Battison then proposed the Symmetry and Dominance Conditions on monomorphemic forms, both of which have been much discussed in the literature and are worth reproducing here.

The *Symmetry Condition* (Battison 1978, 33–34) states that if both hands move independently during the articulation of a sign, then both hands must be specified for the same location, the same handshape, and the same movement, and the orientation specifications for the two hands must be either symmetrical or identical. "Same location" can refer to either the same major place bilaterally on the body (e.g., BRAVE) or, more accurately, on the same side of the body (e.g., SINCE). *Symmetrical orientation* can be defined as an orientation in which identical parts of the two hands have mirror orientation with respect to the plane that separates them (e.g., WITH); these are called "mirror signs" by van der Hulst (1995). *Identical orientation* can be defined as an orientation of both hands that is identical with respect to the body, but not with respect to the two hands (e.g., RIGHT/CORRECT). Signs that exhibit identical but not symmetrical orientation are called "shadow signs" by van der Hulst (1996).

The *Dominance Condition* (Battison 1978, 34) is inversely related to the Symmetry Condition and states that if the hands do not have the same specification for handshape in a two-handed sign, then one hand must be passive (i.e., not moving) while the other articulates the movement; also, H_2 is restricted to a small set of handshapes ('B', 'A', 'S', 'C', 'O', '1', '5').

The Symmetry and Dominance Conditions have survived the test of close scrutiny and reinvestigation surprisingly well, but they left many areas unexplored and later investigators have worked to refine, extend, and formalize them. In the first steps toward a formal transcription system for sign (Stokoe 1960; Stokoe, Casterline, and Croneberg 1965), and later in the HM Model, little attempt was made to build these restrictions into the representation. Both hands were represented as independent articulators; as a result, all physiologically possible combinations of movements and handshapes on the two hands appeared to be equally plausible in monomorphemic forms because they were equally simple and straightforward to depict. The HM Model representations for type 1–3 signs are given in (2). (To what extent the limitations on H_2 should be encoded in the phonological representation is a question revisited at the end of the chapter.)

(2) *HM Model representations for type 1–3 signs*

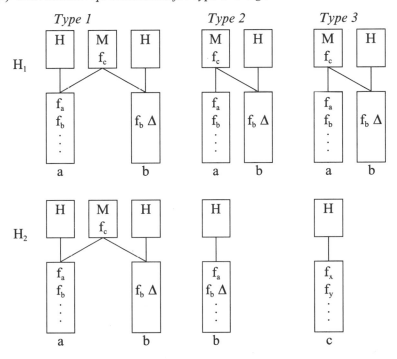

In the HT Model, the representations for H_2 in type 1 signs and type 3 signs are quite distinct. For type 1 signs the HT Model uses the term *double-dez*, borrowed from Stokoe (1960), and for type 3 signs it uses the term 'H_2-place'. Sandler (1989, 1993a) argues that the differences between double-dez and H_2-place signs are best handled by two different representations because " … in double-dez signs, both hands act as articulators, while in H_2-place signs H_1 articulates while H_2 functions as a location, or more precisely, as a specification of the place feature class in the Location matrix" (1989, 97). These two representations restrict double-dez and H_2-place signs in different ways, as shown in (3). For example, double-dez signs must copy everything from the LML template; also, H_2-place signs may specify only a place feature and one of the two possible handshapes (i.e., no movement is allowed on H_2). More recent work specifically on H_2 within the HT Model (Sandler 1993a; van der Hulst and Sandler 1994) has added further support for this position by arguing that double-dez and H_2-place signs behave differently with respect to WD.

(3) *HT Model representations for type 1–3 signs*

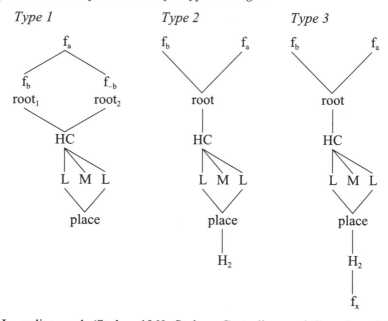

In earlier work (Stokoe 1960; Stokoe, Casterline, and Croneberg 1965; Liddell and Johnson 1989), H_2 was always represented as a separate unit of structure. The HT Model account is simpler. By treating H_2 as a place in the representation of H_2-place signs, this model claims there is no root node or class node that corresponds to H_2; in such signs, H_2 is a feature. This leads to the claim that H_2 need only sometimes be represented as a separate unit of structure—namely, in type 1 signs. Perlmutter (1991) has pushed the attempt to reduce the representation of H_2 to a set of features to a greater extreme, claiming that in no case should H_2 be treated as a separate unit of structure.

An alternative to the HT Model account of H_2 was first proposed in Brentari 1990c and Brentari and Goldsmith 1993. We have argued that by representing H_2-place signs and double-dez signs with distinct structures, the HT Model fails to capture a wide range of facts about H_2 in categories of signs that do not fall cleanly into the two categories of type 1 and type 3 signs (for example, the entire class of type 2 signs, for which the HT Model uses a type 3 representation). In Brentari and Goldsmith 1993, we argue that H_2 behaves rather like a syllable coda or a word-level appendix in many spoken languages—that is to say, as a specific type of weak branch of prosodic structure. This argument is supported by van der Hulst's (1996) more general analysis of H_2 as a weak branch of prosodic structure. Briefly, the arguments made in these accounts are as follows.

First, like weak branches of prosodic structure in many spoken languages, H_2 can demonstrate only a small subset of independent contrasts demonstrated by a given sign as a whole. (For work on spoken languages demonstrating this point, see for example Goldsmith 1990, Prince 1984, Itô 1986, Wiltshire 1992.) Building on work by Battison (1978), these analyses show that the handshapes 'B' and '1' (in all their realizations using available aperture and thumb specifications) are the only handshapes licensed by H_2, where *licensed* can be defined as the ability to be specified independently (Itô 1986; Goldsmith 1990).

Second, Goldsmith and I argue that the forms that are not H_2-place signs or double-dez signs are sufficiently numerous that they cannot be ignored; moreover, they exhibit certain types of redundancies that need to be explained and straightforwardly represented. We argue that the correct representation should severely restrict the features of place, handshape, orientation, and movement expressed independently by H_2, but still allow features from H_1 to assimilate to H_2.

The DP Model analysis of H_2 is very similar to the one presented in this book (van der Hulst 1996; van der Hulst and Sandler 1994).

The approaches to H_2 mentioned thus far are compared schematically in the following table and are characterized as "H_2 always," "H_2 sometimes," and "H_2 never" (a characterization first expressed in van der Hulst 1996). Although the approaches differ in ways that I will describe later in the chapter, the table makes it clear that the "H_2 always" and "H_2 never" approaches both treat H_2 in a uniform way. Only the HT Model account proposes different analyses of H_2 for different types of two-handed signs.

Possible approaches to phonological representations of H_2

Sandler 1993	van der Hulst 1996 Brentari 1990c	Perlmutter 1991
H_2 sometimes	H_2 always	H_2 never
treat H_2 as a structural unit only in type 1	treat H_2 as a partially independent unit of prosodic structure	treat H_2 as a set of features
treat H_2 differently in types 1 and 2	always treat H_2 the same in the phonology	

7.3   Arguments Supporting a Single Structure for Two-Handed Signs

In this section I present evidence that the systematic behavior exhibited by type 1, type 2, and type 3 signs is most efficiently represented by one fundamental structure with three variants. The argument is that a great deal of systematicity in synchronic dissimilation and assimilation processes is lost if we set up a dichotomy between double-dez and H_2-place signs; putting it the other way around, all the forms discussed here can be viewed as assimilation and dissimilation (rather than feature changes) if we set up one basic H_2 representation. In sections 7.3.4 and 7.3.5 I will demonstrate the same phonological pattern in diachronic change.

7.3.1   Synchronic Evidence from Type 2 Signs

The first set of synchronic forms that does not fit cleanly into either the double-dez or the H_2-place category is the entire class of type 2 signs. In type 2 signs H_2 does not move, but as in type 1 signs, H_1 and H_2 exhibit the same handshape. These forms are rather numerous; examples are given in (4).

(4) *Examples of type 2 signs (signs followed by (*) also have a type 1 form)*

a. *[all] handshape (i.e., '5' or 'B')*

ADD-TO	BEHIND	CATCH-UP-TO
WEEKEND	BETWEEN	DEFEAT
APPOINTMENT	BEFORE	AFTER
MOST	NEXT	PEAR
MAXIMUM	EACH	REDUCE
AVOID	MOST	MINIMUM

b. *Thumb only*

REMEMBER   LETTER

c. *[one] handshape*

DEPEND   RIGHT/CORRECT(*)
THERMOMETER

d. *[one] > [all] handshape (i.e., 'H')*

ABOUT   KNIFE   FUN
SHORT   SOON   TRAIN
EITHER(*)   HARD   NAME
SALT

e. *Other handshapes*

KEEP   THIN   LAST
INSTITUTE(*)   WHISKEY(*)   WORLD(*)

These signs demonstrate clearly that when the two hands exhibit the same handshape, both hands do not have to be in motion and the handshape exhibited by H_2 is a copy of the handshape of H_1. In fact, there are only two choices for H_2 in type 2 or 3 signs: it can be a copy of the H_1 handshape or it can be one of Battison's handshapes ('B', 'A', 'S', 'C', 'O', '1', '5'; see chapter 1 for more details). If one of the goals of a formal representation is to encode restrictions on form, these choices should be apparent from the phonological structure to the greatest extent possible. Although the HT Model builds other types of restrictions into the structures possible for H_2, it fails to account for the type of redundancy in handshape found in type 2 signs, since it represents type 2 signs using a type 3 structure, showing the same handshape specification twice.

7.3.2 Synchronic Evidence from Lexical Exceptions and Morphophonological Operations

Synchronic evidence supporting a single representation for two-handed signs also comes from lexical exceptions and morphophonological operations.

In the two-handed signs HELP, START, and SHOW, H_2 and H_1 have different handshapes and H_2 exhibits movement; they are therefore lexical exceptions to the Symmetry and Dominance Conditions and to the categories double-dez and H_2-place in the HT Model. It is predicted that H_2

should perform as a 'place' in the HT Model account of these signs. By contrast, these forms are not exceptions in the Prosodic Model; instead, they are analyzed as cases of assimilation of movement to H_2.

In forms that have undergone Weak Freeze (Padden and Perlmutter 1987), input forms have a [TM] feature, and the movement of H_2 can be seen as being deleted or failing to appear in the output. The effect of Weak Freeze is that a type 1 sign becomes a type 2 sign under certain casual signing conditions (Brentari 1990c, 1992; Brentari and Goldsmith 1993). Weak Freeze outputs can be accounted for as cases of movement dissimilation or partial deletion using the structure proposed in section 7.4.

Verbs containing aspect morphology also give rise to forms that fall into neither the double-dez nor the H_2-place category. In the [exhaustive] aspect, a complex aspect composed of a smooth arc path and co-occurring short, repeated movements, one part of H_1's movement assimilates to H_2, and therein lies a problem for the HT Model. The path feature should not associate to the place in an H_2-place sign. Moreover, only the [arc] feature of the aspect affix assimilates to H_2; the repeated short straight movements do not. In the Prosodic Model a single path feature can associate to the H_2 structure.

Another aspect affix meaning 'characteristically-X' results in two-handed surface forms with large repeated circular movements. If one assumes that affixes associate to stems, type 1 signs should exhibit 'characteristically' X aspect morphology on both hands (e.g., ANGRY → 'characteristically' ANGRY), since the movement of both hands is part of the stem. Type 2 and type 3 signs should exhibit the affixal movement only on H_1 (e.g., CRUEL → 'characteristically' CRUEL), because a movement of H_2 is not part of the stem. The HT and Prosodic Models make the same predictions for these forms.

The HT Model has proposed a way of handling each of these operations; however, it must treat each one as a separate case with distinct formulations for the structural changes involved. The Prosodic Model representation proposed in sections 7.4 and 7.5 will handle these operations by referring to one structure and adding or deleting association lines.

7.3.3 Psycholinguistic Evidence

There is system-external evidence from two sources that supports treating assimilation of movement and handshape using a single mechanism.

Figure 7.3
The diachronic change in WHISKEY from a type 3 sign (left) to a type 2 sign (right) (from Long 1918)

First, in the sign production errors of individuals with Parkinson's disease, assimilation of H_1 features to H_2 is common, but individuals vary with respect to whether the assimilation occurs in handshape, movement, or both (Brentari and Poizner 1994; Loew, Poizner, and Kegl 1995). Second, there is evidence that Deaf children acquiring Finnish Sign Language as a first language produce errors involving assimilation of handshape and movement (Takkinen 1994).

7.3.4   Diachronic Evidence: Type 3 → Type 2 signs

Two processes of historical change in ASL, discussed here and in section 7.3.5, support the idea of using a single representation for H_2.

Five type 3 forms have diachronically become type 2 signs by allowing one hand H_2 to copy the handshape of the other (a point raised first in Frishberg 1975 and later, in this context, in Brentari 1990c. These signs are RIGHT, WORLD, INSTITUTE, WHISKEY, and EITHER. The source for these forms is Long 1918; the diachronic change in WHISKEY is shown in figure 7.3. The first four signs used to have an [all] or [one] handshape on H_2; now the handshape on H_2 copies the handshape on H_1. EITHER used to have a spread 'H' handshape on H_2 and [one] handshape on H_1; now the handshape on H_1 copies the handshape on H_2.

This diachronic process strengthens the argument that the handshape component of all two-handed signs should be represented by one structure, since in the process, the information dominated by one hand in the old form is lost, and the handshape of the other hand is always the choice for the new form. This operation involves a deletion and reassociation of information already present in the structure, rather than a change in structure, and my account will provide a way to show the relationship between the 1918 forms and the current forms as one of diachronic assimilation.

Furthermore, some of these signs—WORLD, INSTITUTE, RIGHT/ CORRECT, WHISKEY, and EITHER—have undergone further diachronic change and have both a type 1 and a type 2 variant. In the type 1 variant, movement as well as handshape assimilated from H_1 to H_2. In the HT Model, with two representations for double-dez (type 1) and H_2-place (types 2 and 3) signs, the type 1 and type 2 variants of these signs would be represented by completely different structures, despite their strong surface similarity. Even if these are surface variants, H_2s in both type 1 and type 3 signs must have access to the movement features in order to undergo association to or disassociation from them.

7.3.5 Diachronic Evidence: Type 1 → Type 2 Signs

If we observed only diachronic change of the type just described, it would be plausible to posit that type 2 signs are simply a transitional stage from type 3 to type 1 and to employ the HT Model's two representations, thereby accounting for this diachronic process as a fundamental shift in category from H_2-place to double-dez, rather than a case of assimilation. However, another type of diachronic change shows that type 2 signs are not simply a transitional stage, but a structural class of signs that is a well-formed output in its own right, thus strengthening the argument that two-handed signs have one basic structure with two variants.

DEFEAT, REVENGE, and MOST, which were type 1 signs (Long 1918), have undergone a diachronic change to type 2 signs involving the disassociation of H_2 from the sign's movement. (DEFEAT is shown in both the 1918 and current forms in figure 7.4.) REVENGE still has a type 1 variant; DEFEAT and MOST no longer do.[5]

7.4 The Prosodic Model's Structure for H_2

Thus far I have provided evidence supporting a representation for H_2 that has one basic structure, rather than two. I now take up two related questions: What should the single feature structure look like in the phonological representation? and Should it be a part of the structure of all two-handed signs, or just a subset of them?

Figure 7.4
The diachronic change in DEFEAT from a type 1 sign (left) to a type 2 sign
(right) (from Long 1918)

The Prosodic Model structures for type 1, type 2, and type 3 signs
are given in (5).[6] Although fingers (a handshape feature), place, [contact]
(a place feature), [alternating] (a movement feature), and [symmetrical]
(an orientation feature) must be part of an H_2 specification, they could be
scattered throughout the representation at their appropriate class nodes as
described in previous chapters. All of these features are grouped together
as a single unit of structure in the Prosodic Model because the distinctive
and redundant information of H_2 is rendered more identifiable in one
place in the structure.

(5) *Prosodic Model representation of type 1–3 signs*[7]

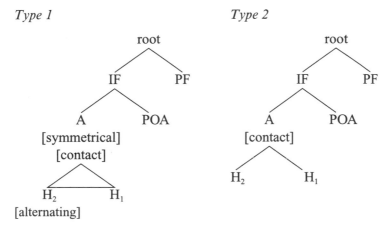

Type 3

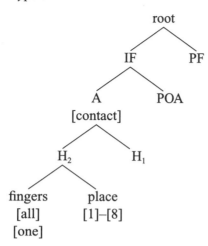

A feature [2-handed] in an input form generates the H_2 branch of structure. The H_2 branch bears the same relation to the H_1 branch in all cases: namely, H_1 is the head of the manual node and H_2 is the dependent branch.[8] The reasons for this are that H_1 structures are more complex than H_2 structures, and that the direction of assimilation is from H_1 to H_2 in most cases. The representation in (5) assumes the following conventions:

1. The system interprets an empty H_2 node as having the same features as H_1.
2. Only when a horizontal line connects H_2 to H_1 does H_2 have access to prosodic features; otherwise, H_2 has access only to other inherent features (i.e., place).

Given these conventions and the structure in (5), it is possible to create hybrid forms of these three types of signs.

The types of synchronic and diachronic operations discussed above can be handled by these structures as follows. To achieve a change from a type 2 to a type 1 sign, an association line between H_1 and H_2 is added to allow access to the prosodic features (6). To achieve Weak Freeze, or to achieve a change from a type 1 to a type 2 sign, the reverse of this operation is used; the association line between H_1 and H_2 is deleted (7), thereby denying H_2 access to the prosodic features.

(6) *Diachronic change: type 2 → type 1 (e.g., WORLD)*

(7) *Diachronic change: type 1 → type 2 (e.g., INTERPRET after Weak Freeze; see also DEFEAT, figure 7.4)*

To achieve assimilation of movement in a type 3 sign, an association line must be drawn from H_2 to H_1 (8), thereby allowing H_2 access to the prosodic features. To achieve assimilation of handshape in a diachronic change from a type 3 to a type 2 sign, the H_2 finger and place specifications must be deleted (9); when there is no H_2 specification for fingers, H_2 copies the H_1 specifications.

(8) *Structure for a moving H_2 in a type 3 sign (e.g., SHOW)*

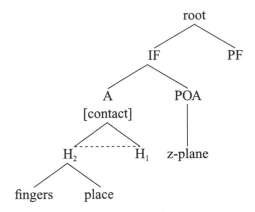

(9) *Diachronic change: type 3 → type 2 (e.g., WHISKEY; see figure 7.3)*

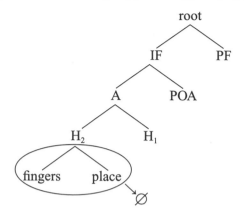

In summary, the Prosodic Model structure proposed here has two major advantages over the HT Model structure. The first is empirical coverage. The Prosodic Model structure can handle signs with two contact features or two places of articulation. There is at least one monomorphemic sign that has both two contacts and two places of articulation: INTERNALIZE (figure 7.5).[9] In this sign H_1 is placed inside a 'C'-shaped H_2, and both hands are located at the chest. Although the number of such "double contact" and "double place" signs is small, these monomorphemic forms are indicative of a widely used structure in polymorphemic forms. If H_2 is not an independent feature structure, then

Figure 7.5
An example sign with two places of articulation and two contacts: INTERNALIZE. One place is the inside of H_2, where H_1 makes contact; the second is the chest, where the articulator (i.e., both hands) makes contact.

these forms violate the prohibition in feature geometry theory according to which there may be only one feature of a given type per branch of structure (Clements 1985; Sagey 1986).

The second advantage is that this model allows a unified analysis of the cases of diachronic and synchronic variation just presented. Both type 1 and type 3 signs can be the diachronic source of type 2 signs, and all of the cases can be seen as simple assimilation and dissimilation phenomena of a sort that ought to be able to be represented by deletion or addition of an association line, rather than by an entirely different structure. In no case is new information added to a form; rather, information available in the input structure is deleted and/or reassociated. Signs that have undergone diachronic change from type 3 to type 2 demonstrate handshape assimilation; type 3 signs with H_2 movement illustrate movement assimilation; and signs that have undergone Weak Freeze or diachronic change from type 1 to type 2 exemplify movement dissimilation. Within a model that proposes a single structure for two-handed signs, these phenomena can be represented as different but related variants of a common phonological structure. Within a model that proposes distinct representations for type 1 and type 3 signs, these cases must be treated as a heterogeneous set of operations, each with a distinct formulation.

7.5   An Optimality-Theoretic Account of Weak Drop

Padden and Perlmutter (1987) state that nonalternating type 1 signs (i.e., those with synchronous movement) may undergo Weak Drop (WD) and that all alternating signs may not undergo WD.[10] Formulating this in terms of output constraints, we might say that alternating WD forms are not well-formed outputs and therefore do not surface. Sandler (1993a) has used this as evidence for distinct double-dez and H_2-place representations, claiming that, in general, double-dez signs should undergo WD when they meet its structural description, and H_2-place signs do not undergo WD. Examples of type 1–3 signs that do and do not allow one-handed forms to surface are given in appendix D.[11] Using the Prosodic Model representation developed thus far, I show in this section that systematic constraints on contact, handshape, orientation, movement, and place features all play a role in determining which WD outputs are well formed, and that type 1, type 2, and type 3 signs may surface as one-handed signs under certain conditions. This analysis strengthens the case for representing all two-handed signs using one flexible structure, rather than representing type 1 and type 3 signs differently.

Definitions for each of the features involved are given in (10). These features were discussed in chapters 3 and 4 in the context of inherent and prosodic feature geometry; more details about their use in specifying two-handed signs are presented here.

(10) *Definitions of features of two-handed signs*

    a. *Path features*

        i.   [alternating] ([alt]): A movement that occurs 180° out of phase. Without a specification for this feature, movements of the two hands are executed in phase (i.e., they are nonalternating).

        ii. [direction: |>]: A movement that occurs "from a point," in which a [contact(p)] feature is realized at the beginning of the movement. All [direction] features are expressed as paths that occur at a 90° angle to a specified plane.

        iii. [tracing]: A path movement that occurs within a plane. In such movements a [contact] feature is realized throughout the entire movement.

    b. *Orientation features*

        [symmetrical] ([sym]): A property of orientation. The two hands of a two-handed sign are oriented toward analogous parts of the hands, in addition to being oriented toward a place of articulation. Without a specification for this feature, both hands are oriented toward a place of articulation alone, just like the single hand in a one-handed sign, and they are said to have an 'identical' orientation.

    c. *Contact features*

        i.   [contact:articulator] ([contact(a)]): Contact that occurs on a branch of structure dominated by the articulator node. In two-handed signs this type of contact occurs between the two hands.

        ii. [contact:place] ([contact(p)]): Contact that occurs on a branch of structure dominated by the place node. This type of contact is found in one-handed signs that have a [direction] path feature.

      iii. [contact:articulator+continuous] ([contact(ac)]): Contact
         between the two hands that is continuous.

  d. *Place*

      i. The place of articulation of the sign itself: x-plane, y-plane,
        z-plane, body, and so on, as described for one-handed signs.

      ii. The eight places of articulation on H_2, as described in
        chapter 4.

  e. *H_2 handshape*

      i. Fingers: Selected fingers—[all], [one].

      ii. Joints: The specified joints of a handshape—base or nonbase.

These features are used by the grammar to group together signs from all three types that may or may not undergo WD. Not all of these features play a role in all three types of signs (e.g., a type 3 sign is never specified for [alternating] or [symmetrical]). As argued in section 3.7, [symmetrical] is located at the articulator node, since it refers to the orientation of H_1 and H_2 toward each other and is not a property of either hand alone. Two kinds of orientation are possible between the two hands: identical and symmetrical. Following distinctions made in Battison's (1978) definitions, symmetrical orientation refers to both H_1-to-H_2 and articulator-to-POA dimensions of orientation, and identical orientation refers only to the articulator-to-POA dimension. For this reason, symmetrical orientation is considered more marked and identical orientation is considered less marked (i.e., redundant) for two-handed signs. Symmetrical signs are assigned the feature [symmetrical]; when a sign has identical orientation, no further specification is needed beyond the representation of inherent orientation as given in chapter 3—the handpart features to a POA. An independent factor is that WD is disallowed in any two-handed sign in which H_2 is synchronically morphemic (see (1b) of appendix D for examples).

An analysis using Optimality Theory in conjunction with the H_2 structure developed thus far can account for all of the WD facts in monomorphemic signs. The presence of an [alternating] or [contact(ac)] feature always makes a sign ineligible for WD. No WD form surfaces for BICYCLE or REQUEST; BICYCLE has an [alternating] feature and REQUEST has a [contact(ac)] feature (see figure 7.6). (By contrast,

Figure 7.6
Examples of signs illustrating nonviolable constraints on Weak Drop. No two-handed sign with an [alternating] feature in the input will surface with a one-handed output (e.g., BICYCLE (top)). No two-handed sign with a [contact(ac)] feature in the input will surface with a one-handed output (e.g., REQUEST (bottom)). The forms on the right are ill-formed.

QUIET (figure 2.2) allows WD. It has [contact(a)], which does not block WD.) These conditions can be expressed as ranked constraints, as in (11). The constraints PARSE[contact(ac)] and PARSE[alternating] are ranked higher than the constraint for WD, formulated here as ELIMINATE REDUNDANCY (ELIMRED). The constraint tableaux for BICYCLE and REQUEST show why the one-handed WD form fails to surface.

(11) *Constraints on WD (First pass)*

    a. ELIMINATE REDUNDANCY (ELIMRED)/Weak Drop (formerly called phonological deletion)

An input sign that is two-handed and whose H_2 has totally redundant feature specifications has a well-formed one-handed output.

b. PARSE[alternating]

When an [alternating] feature appears in the input, it must appear in the output.

c. PARSE[contact(ac)]

When a [contact(ac)] feature appears in the input, it must appear in the output.

Constraint tableau for BICYCLE

/BICYCLE/	PARSE[alt]	ELIMRED
BICYCLE(WD)	*!	
☞ BICYCLE		*

Constraint tableau for REQUEST

/REQUEST/	PARSE[contact(ac)]	ELIMRED
REQUEST(WD)	*!	
☞ REQUEST		*

When [symmetrical] and [contact(a)] both occur in an input form, the one-handed WD output fails to surface as well. To express this notion whereby two constraints of the PARSE family, neither of which is sufficient to block a WD output alone, can do so when they occur together, the Prosodic Model employs the mechanism of Local Constraint Conjunction (Prince and Smolensky 1993; Smolensky 1993; Fukazawa and Miglio, in press). A sign that disallows WD on these grounds is WITH (figure 7.7).

(12) *Local Constraint Conjunction*

Constraints A and B are lower ranked than constraint C ($C \gg A,B$), but this no longer holds when both A and B are violated ($A+B \gg C$).

Figure 7.7
An example sign illustrating the effects of Local Constraint Conjunction of
PARSE[symmetrical] and PARSE[contact(ac)]. The input of WITH has both features
(left); the one-handed output is ungrammatical and does not surface (right).

(13) *Local Constraint Conjunction and WD*

In this analysis, C is ELIMRED; A and B are PARSE constraints
(PARSE[symmetrical] and PARSE[contact(a)]).

a. PARSE[symmetrical]

When a [symmetrical] feature appears in the input, it must
appear in the output.

b. PARSE[contact(a)]

When a [contact(a)] feature appears in the input, it must appear
in the output.

The need for Local Constraint Conjunction becomes apparent if we
consider signs with either a [symmetrical] feature or a [contact(a)] feature,
but not both. Two example signs are pictured in figure 7.8. QUIET has a
[contact(a)] feature, but no [symmetrical] feature, and the one-handed
form is a possible output. SUNDAY has a [symmetrical] feature, but no
[contact(a)] feature; the one-handed form is a possible output for this sign
as well. Together, under Local Constraint Conjunction, PARSE[symmetrical]
and PARSE[contact(a)] outrank ELIMRED, as the tableau for WITH indicates; alone, as the tableaux for QUIET and SUNDAY indicate, neither
does so.

Figure 7.8
Example type 1 signs illustrating the need for Local Constraint Conjunction. The input of QUIET (top left) has a [contact(a)] feature and no [symmetrical] feature; the one-handed WD output (top right) is well formed. The input of SUNDAY (bottom left) has a [symmetrical] feature and no [contact(a)] feature; the one-handed WD output (bottom right) is also well formed.

Constraint tableau for QUIET

/QUIET/	ELIMRED	PARSE[contact(a)]	PARSE[sym]
☞ QUIET(WD)		*	
QUIET	*		

Constraint tableau for SUNDAY

/SUNDAY/	ELIMRED	PARSE[contact(a)]	PARSE[sym]
☞ SUNDAY(WD)			*
SUNDAY	*		

Constraint tableau for WITH

/WITH/	PARSE[contact(a)] PARSE[sym]	ELIMRED	PARSE[contact(a)]	PARSE[sym]
WITH(WD)	*!			
☞ WITH		*		

These constraints also hold for type 2 and type 3 signs, and they explain why a large number of type 2 signs may not surface as one-handed forms (see (14), the example tableau for ABSTRACT, and figure 7.9).

(14) *Type 2 signs whose inability to undergo WD is explained by constraints developed for type 1 signs*

DEPEND[contact(c)]   SOON[contact(c)]
PEAR[sym][contact(a)]   PAPER[sym][contact(a)]
THERMOMETER[contact(c)]   TRAIN[contact(c)]
SCHOOL[sym][contact(a)]   ABSTRACT[sym][contact(a)]
MARRIAGE[sym][contact(a)]

Constraint tableau for ABSTRACT

/ABSTRACT/	PARSE[contact(a)] PARSE[sym]	ELIMRED	PARSE[contact(a)]	PARSE[sym]
ABSTRACT(WD)	*!			
☞ ABSTRACT		*		

Figure 7.9
The input of the type 2 sign ABSTRACT (left) has a [contact(a)] and a [sym-metrical] feature; the one-handed output (right) would therefore violate the Local Constraint Conjunction of PARSE[contact(a)] and PARSE[symmetrical] and does not surface.

There are also type 2 signs that may surface with a one-handed variant (see (15), the example tableau for REMEMBER, and figure 7.10). These signs would not violate any of the constraints ranked higher than ELIMRED.

(15) *Type 2 signs that may undergo WD*

REMEMBER	REDUCE
KNIFE	NAME
THIN	SHORT/BRIEF
LAST	HARD
BETWEEN	BEFORE
NEXT	GAIN-WEIGHT
FUN	

Constraint tableau for REMEMBER

/REMEMBER/	ELIMRED	PARSE[contact(a)]	PARSE[sym]
☞ REMEMBER(WD)		*	
REMEMBER	*		

There are some type 2 signs whose inability to undergo WD cannot be explained by the constraints developed thus far: WHEN, AVOID,

Figure 7.10
The input of the type 2 sign REMEMBER (left) does not have any features whose
omission would create an ill-formed output; therefore, a one-handed output may
surface (right).

MAXIMUM, JAIL. These are signs that involve a PARSE PLACE constraint that allows a one-handed form to surface if the place of articulation is a horizontal plane (a y-plane). This would allow the horizontal
plane to be a "default" plane.

(16) *PARSE PLACE*

> When the input contains a place of articulation that is a z-plane
> (midsagittal) or an x-plane (frontal) plane, it must appear in the
> output.

In sum: The distribution of WD in type 2 signs makes it clear that it is
not sign class that makes a sign eligible for WD, but the well-formedness
constraints that involve H_2 more generally.

There are a number of type 3 signs that allow WD (see (17), the
example tableau for READ, and figure 7.11).

(17) *Type 3 signs that may undergo WD ([all] handshape)*

CUP	WRITE
DANCE	CHECK
ONCE	DEVELOP
LIST	WHAT
READ	FIND
LATER	FALL
MONEY	SUBTRACT

Figure 7.11
The input H_2 of the type 3 sign READ (left) has an open 'B' handshape with a palm H_2-place; therefore, it has a well-formed one-handed output (right).

Constraint tableau for READ

/READ/	PARSE HS/H_2	PARSE PLACE/H_2	ELIMRED
☞ READ(WD)			*
READ			

These signs can be accounted for by taking the open 'B' handshape and the palm contact as the "default" H_2 handshape and place, respectively. The open 'B' handshape was shown in chapter 3 to have no joints branch of structure and one fingers feature ([all]); it is one of the least marked handshapes in ASL overall.

All other type 3 signs—those with other handshapes and/or other places of articulation—are prohibited from undergoing WD (see (18), the example tableau for LOCAL, and figure 7.12; also see appendix D for a more complete set of examples).

(18) *Type 3 signs that may not undergo WD*

    a. PARSE PLACE/H_2 *violations*

        ENGLISH   WARN
        DOLLAR   LEAVE-SCHOOL

Figure 7.12
The input of the type 3 sign LOCAL (left) has a Parse HS/H_2 (joints) and a
Parse Place/H_2 violation; therefore, its one-handed output (right) does not
surface.

b. *Parse HS/H_2 (joints) violations*

SODA-POP   JOIN
GET-ON   GASOLINE
ENOUGH

c. *Parse HS/H_2 (fingers) violations*

BERRY   WORD
MECHANIC   CIGARETTE
CANDLE   BANANA

Constraint tableau for LOCAL

/LOCAL/	Parse HS/H_2	Parse Place/H_2	ElimRed
LOCAL(WD)	*!	*!	
☞ LOCAL			*

The additional constraints needed to account for type 3 signs are given
in (19); these constraints are also ranked higher than ElimRed.

(19) *Additional handshape and H_2-place constraints needed to account for*
     type 3 signs

    a. PARSE HANDSHAPE/H_2 (PARSE HS/H_2)

       When an H_2 handshape feature appears in the input, it must
       appear in the output, except when [all] is the only fingers$_0$ feature.

    b. PARSE PLACE/H_2

       When an H_2 place feature appears in the input, it must appear
       in the output, except when ['palm'] is the H_2 place feature.

Although a few constraints apply to only one type of two-handed sign
(e.g., PARSE[alternating] applies only to type 1 signs and PARSE HS/H_2
applies only to type 3 signs), the ranked constraints as an entire set apply
whenever possible. The systematicity in WD is attributable to the definitions of the features and their relationship to specific structures in the Prosodic Model. Theoretical mechanisms in Optimality Theory and those of
the Prosodic Model explain the WD facts in monomorphemic signs more
comprehensively than do previous accounts. The analysis does not, however, predict which forms will definitely undergo WD; rather, it eliminates
candidates that will not undergo it. Unfortunately, Optimality Theory
cannot account for the optional nature of WD, since for any well-formed
one-handed output, there is also a well-formed two-handed output. Variation in outputs is difficult to express in any known formalism and is beyond
the scope of this analysis.

7.6 Alternative Accounts of H_2 Revisited

Recall from section 7.2 that there are three basic approaches to H_2 representation: "H_2 always," "H_2 sometimes," and "H_2 never." The "H_2
sometimes" account, instantiated by the HT Model, has just been argued
against at length.

It is now necessary to consider the "H_2 never" account, proposed by
Perlmutter (1991). Although Perlmutter considers only place, handshape,
and [alternating] features in discussing H_2, let us assume that this account,
like the Prosodic Model account, requires a set of features that could
be dispersed throughout the representation, rather than collected in one
structural unit as they are here. The "H_2 never" account is tempting, since
it would make the feature tree simpler.

The "H_2 never" proposal rests on the premise that the handshape of H_2
can be predicted from one of the eight handshape places of articulation—
that is, that the entire sign can be accounted for with one handshape

Figure 7.13
Pairs of signs that illustrate that the handshape of H_2 is not always predictable from the place of contact: 4TH-YEAR-IN-COLLEGE (top left) and POPULAR (top right); TRY-ON (bottom left) and PUT-ON-SHOE (bottom right).

specification, that of H_1. This account faces two problems, however. The first is data coverage. Although place of articulation can predict handshape in many cases, it fails to do so in at least two pairs of forms: 4TH-YEAR-IN-COLLEGE vs. POPULAR, and TRY-ON vs. PUT-ON-SHOE (figure 7.13). Both 4TH-YEAR-IN-COLLEGE and POPU-LAR have finger-tip contact, but the former is produced with an open [all] (i.e., '5') handshape, and the latter is produced with a [one] handshape. Both TRY-ON (clothing) and PUT-ON-SHOE have a 'C' H_1 handshape, but they have different H_2 handshapes. In addition, the difficulty pre-sented by signs with two places of articulation or two [contact] features discussed earlier in the chapter (e.g., INTERNALIZE) in the context of the HT Model's representation of H_2 is also a problem for the "H_2 never" approach (Perlmutter 1991). Neither of these approaches can represent these signs without violating the principle of feature geometry that says that there may be only one feature of a given type per branch of structure. Though it is true that these are polymorphemic forms, they are worth mentioning here. The second problem with the "H_2 never" account is that without an H_2 branch of structure that unites all H_2 features under one node, the explanation that WD is possible owing to redundancy of H_2 will be lost.

In sum, in sections 7.2–7.6 I have shown that one basic H_2 structure can (1) capture the relevant processes of assimilation, dissimilation, and deletion while maintaining a formal similarity between similar structures, (2) accommodate a place-of-articulation specification other than H_2 in type 3 signs, (3) accommodate two types of contact, and (4) account for the facts of WD.

7.7 H_2 as a Prosodic Unit

So far I have analyzed only the mechanisms for grouping H_2 features together and stating the substantive feature limitations on H_2. In this section I address the role of H_2 as a prosodic unit. Using evidence from disyllabic forms, I show that H_2 features constitute a word-level appendix, making it possible for more information to be expressed at this level of prosodic structure. In previous work Goldsmith and I argued that H_2 was similar to a syllable coda in spoken languages (Brentari and Goldsmith 1993); however, examination of the distribution pattern of H_2 features in disyllabic signs reveals that constraints on H_2 operate at the level of the phonological word, rather than at the level of the syllable.[12] The descriptive generalizations that change the relevant domain of reference from the syllable to the word are given in (20).

(20) *Distribution facts concerning independent H_2 features*

  a. There are no disyllabic monomorphemic signs that contain two independent H_2 specifications.

  b. There are no compounds formed from two stems that are both type 3 signs with different H_2 specifications.

The forms in (21) illustrate these generalizations: namely, that no prosodic word contains two distinct H_2 specifications. Disyllabic forms with one H_2 specification are given in (21a); compound forms with two redundant H_2 specifications are given in (21b); disyllabic forms in which both stems are type 3 signs but the H_2 specification is the same in both stems, or in which one is redundant and one is distinctive, are given in (21c); and ungrammatical disyllabic forms composed of two type 3 signs, each with a different H_2 specification, are given in (21d).

(21) *Distribution of H_2 in disyllabic signs*

    a. *Disyllabic words and compounds with one H_2 specification*

        BACKGROUND
        HELP
        CURRICULUM
        CHAIR
        BLACK ^ NAME 'bad reputation'

    b. *Polymorphemic forms with two redundant specifications*

        JESUS ^ BOOK 'Bible'
        WORD ^ BOOK 'dictionary'
        TEACHER
        SERVER

    c. *Polymorphemic forms with one distinctive H_2 specification*

        CHECK ^ READ 'proofread'
        MONEY ^ BEHIND 'savings'
        NUDE ^ ZOOM 'streak' (verb)

    d. *Ungrammatical compounds with two distinctive H_2 specifications*

        *WORD ^ HELP
        *CHECK ^ VOTE
        *MONEY ^ ENOUGH

The forms in (21d) are plausible stem combinations for compounds in ASL both morphosyntactically and semantically. WORD ^ HELP (a noun-verb combination, like MALE ^ MARRY 'husband') might mean 'thesaurus'; CHECK ^ VOTE (a verb-verb combination, like READ ^ CHECK 'proofread') might mean 'the act of recounting votes after an election'; and MONEY ^ ENOUGH (a noun-adjective combination, like BOY ^ SAME 'brother') might mean 'well-to-do'. However, none of these is a well-formed ASL compound, and I argue that the reason is that each contains two type 3 stems with different H_2 specifications. The forms in (21c) demonstrate that a compound can be formed from two type 3 stems, but only if they have the same H_2 specification (e.g., CHECK$^\wedge$READ). A prosodic word constraint (22) restricting the number of H_2 specifications per word is therefore enforced.

(22) *H_2 constraint for ASL*

> There may be a maximum of one distinct H_2 specification per prosodic word.

To represent the addition of H_2 information at the level of the prosodic word, I propose the structure in (23). The substantive restrictions on H_2 are still the same as those proposed in Brentari 1990c and Brentari and Goldsmith 1993. Only the handshapes 'B', 'A', 'S', 'C', 'O', '1', and '5' are allowed; for place, H_2 allows only the eight hand places of articulation described in section 3.6 (see also figure 1.26). They are the same places used to specify one half of the underlying orientation relation, as described in chapter 3.

(23) *Word-level appendix structure*

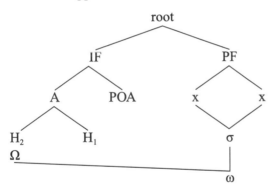

The restriction on handshape can be expressed more specifically using the fingers features [all] versus [one], and the joint specifications. Only the [all] set of fingers allows for an almost full range of joint specifications on H_2 (i.e., open, closed, curved, flat, but not bent); no joint variations on an H_2 [one] handshape are allowed. A further restriction on place of articulation also concerns the [one] handshape. [One] allows only five of the eight possible hand places of articulation; [all] allows all of them.

Under this analysis, all two-handed signs are more complex prosodic units than one-handed signs; but only type 3 signs fill the appendix with distinctive material. As a result, the facts raised by Sandler (1993a) and van der Hulst and Sandler (1994) about the following assimilation in compounds can be explained.[13] When both stems in a compound are two-handed signs, nothing happens. H_2 simply copies what H_1 is doing in both stems, and both redundant H_2 specifications appear in the output (e.g., MONEY^BEHIND 'savings'). When the second stem is a type 1 sign and the first stem is a one-handed sign, two outputs are possible. Either a kind of "Weak Prop" rule may apply, whereby the one-handed sign becomes a type 1 two-handed sign and the H_2 structure is filled with the features of H_1 of the first stem; or the H_2 material of the second stem appears during the articulation of the first stem (e.g., SLEEP^CLOTHES 'pajamas').[14] The latter is the only choice in compounds whose second stem is a type 3 sign and whose first stem is one-handed; the distinctive H_2 material of the second stem appears on the first stem and a type of regressive assimilation takes place (e.g., BLACK^NAME 'bad reputation'). Calling the empty node a word-level appendix strengthens the prediction that prosodic words, including compounds, should be either completely one-handed or completely two-handed.

7.8 Conclusion and Residual Issues

Under the analysis proposed here, all two-handed signs are more complex prosodically than one-handed signs; however, there is an important distinction between complexity resulting from H_2 information and complexity resulting from prosodic feature specifications. When complexity arises from prosodic features, it contributes to the type of complexity described in chapter 5 as visual sonority. This type of complexity is related to the number of joints involved in the production of some phonological movement—handshape change, orientation change, or path movement— and is realized sequentially over time. Branching prosodic class nodes link up with syllable-internal prosodic structure, defined as weight units. In contrast, H_2 specification primarily involves inherent features; it is part of information structure. This type of complexity is realized at a single instant and involves a more complex paradigmatic structure.

A residual issue for feature specification of H_2 is that, even though there are a few cases where the H_2 handshape is not predictable from the H_2 place (e.g., TRY-ON vs. PUT-ON-SHOE), in most cases it *is* predictable. Perlmutter (1991) presents arguments for pursuing this line of investigation. This predictable relationship, even if it is partial rather than absolute, remains an issue for future research; its resolution may ultimately simplify H_2 representation further.

I return now to the question with which the chapter began: to what extent should the restrictions on H_2 be a part of its structure and to what extent should they be expressed by constraints? Even though H_2 does seem to function as an "echo articulator" in some cases and as a "place" in others (Sandler 1993a), the analysis presented here shows that this distinction should not be drawn by placing the features of these two types of signs in different parts of the representation. Instead, I have proposed a structure that is fundamentally the same for all two-handed signs and that allows these two roles to blend and overlap with one another as necessary. An explanation of the differences in behavior regarding WD can be achieved by constraints and their interaction.

To conclude: This analysis shows how the Prosodic Model developed in chapters 3–6 handles one challenging set of signs. The Prosodic Model structure for H_2 employs one basic structure, which allows the synchronic and diachronic operations exhibited by ASL to be represented by the operations of assimilation and dissimilation. H_2 is a dependent branch of prosodic structure, one that operates at the level of the word. Also, the constraint ranking proposed in the analysis of WD makes it clear that complexity and redundancy must be expressed in phonological terms, not simply phonetic terms, and that WD behaves systematically across all three types of two-handed signs.

Chapter 8

Contributions of Sign Language Phonology to Phonological Theory and Cognitive Science

8.1 The Prosodic Model Revisited

This chapter will focus on the most general findings of the Prosodic Model and how they contribute to general questions in phonology and cognitive science. In this section I present fundamental differences and similarities between the Prosodic Model and other models of sign language phonology, thereby reemphasizing my debt to previous work and putting the conclusions from previous chapters into this context. In section 8.2 I use the model to address a general issue in sign language research, the organization of the ASL lexicon; I show how certain global generalizations about ASL can be revealed using the structures and constraints I have argued for in this book. In section 8.3 I address similarities and differences between signed and spoken language in the units used in phonological analyses, such as the syllable, root, node, segment, and weight unit. This discussion of units of analysis leads to section 8.4, where I discuss the biological systems that serve sign languages and specifically the use that sign languages make of the capabilities of the visual system.

First, I would like to make clear the Prosodic Model's innovations with respect to the HT Model and the HM Model.[1] The Prosodic Model differs from both of these in the way that it bundles all movement features —not just path features—into a prosodic branch of structure so that they can more easily interact in phonological operations. The Prosodic Model employs a handshape representation similar to that of the HT Model (and of the model proposed in van der Hulst 1996), except that it considers aperture features to be movement features. Its way of representing orientation is very similar in spirit to that of the HM Model (and of the model proposed in Uyechi 1995); inherent orientation is considered to be relational, between a handpart and a place of articulation. Within the representation of place of articulation, the idea of treating place as a set of planes rather than a set of points appeared first in the HM Model, but was more fully developed by Uyechi (1995). Finally, the two-slot approach to timing slots in ASL is due to Stack (1988) and was developed further by van der Hulst (1993) and Uyechi (1995).

The Prosodic Model's and the HM Model's representations of FALSE are given in (1), showing at a glance the innovations made by the Prosodic Model. The first point to notice is that the Prosodic Model divides the features of the HM Model representation into two branches: those that participate in the movement (i.e., the prosodic features) and those that do not (i.e., the inherent features).

(1) *Comparison of HM Model and Prosodic Model representations of FALSE*

    a. *HM Model representation of FALSE*

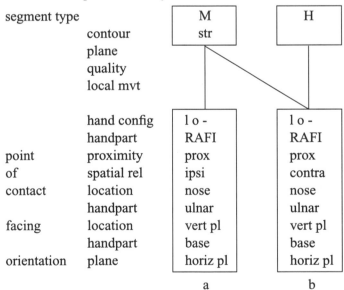

b. *Prosodic Model representation of FALSE*

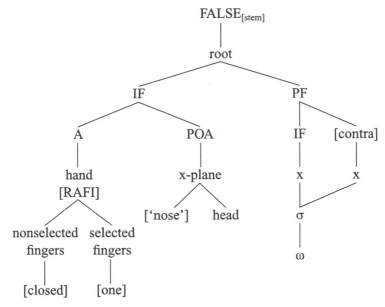

In the HM Model representation of FALSE, the only features that participate in the movement are [ipsi] and [contra]. In the Prosodic Model representation, the feature [contra] is specified in the prosodic branch of structure; the [ipsi] feature is filled in by inherent structure, but it is a redundant feature in this case so it does not appear in the representation. The orientation and facing features [ulnar], [vertical plane (VP)], [base], and [horizontal plane (HP)] of the HM Model representation have been replaced in the Prosodic Model representation by features of the place and hand structures of the inherent features branch, in the following way. As discussed in chapter 3, the body is redundantly an x-plane (a frontal plane). Because of the planar view of place of articulation, specifying the radial side of the hand (RAFI; i.e., one of the eight possible handparts) and the nose (i.e., one of the eight possible horizontal slices of the head region) is all that is necessary to achieve the inherent orientation in the Prosodic Model. The [1o-] handshape feature cluster of the HM Model is specified in the Prosodic Model as a [one] selected fingers$_0$ feature and a [flexed] nonselected fingers feature; the system interprets the absence of a joint specification as a completely open handshape. With respect to other phonological units, the x-slots and the weight units of the Prosodic Model have no structural equivalent in the HM Model, but the typical monosyllabic form has three timing units in the HM Model and two in the Prosodic Model.

Next let us compare the HT Model with the Prosodic Model, using representations of the sign DESTROY (2).

(2) a. *Hand Tier Model: DESTROY*

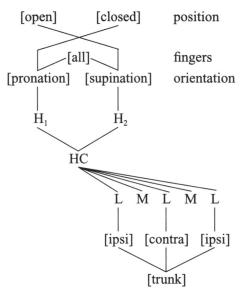

b. *Prosodic Model: DESTROY (output)*

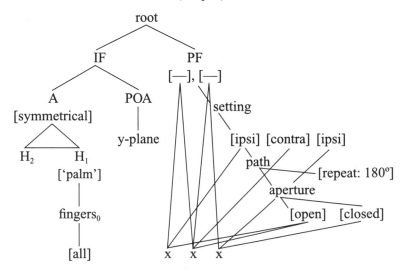

In this instance the differences are more subtle. Both models contain feature geometries, but each organizes the features somewhat differently. In the HT Model, handshape and orientation as a set of features appear as part of the hand configuration tier, setting changes are specified in the Location segment, and path features (and no other movement features) are specified in the Movement segment. Since both models use phonological operations to justify their feature organization, let us look more closely at the kinds of evidence used in each case. With regard to handshape, in the HT Model several convincing arguments support placing handshape on its own tier and considering orientation as being dependent on handshape. Other than placing all features participating in movement on one autosegmental tier, the organization of handshape in the Prosodic Model has much in common with the approach taken by Sandler (1996b). With regard to orientation, the HT Model specifies only absolute features of palm orientation, which are insufficient to capture a range of phenomena concerning verb agreement and the orientation of parts of the hand (Meir 1995; Askins and Perlmutter 1995). In the Prosodic Model inherent orientation is a relation between one of eight handparts and a place of articulation; an analysis using this structure can account for the verb agreement facts discussed in chapter 4.

The rest of the HT feature organization is built around the segments L(ocation) and M(ovement). The HT Model argues for viewing movement as a segment and thus, like the HM Model, has a three-slot timing structure (i.e., static L + dynamic M + static L, or LML); the Prosodic Model has a two-slot timing structure,[2] where movement functions as a higher-order prosodic unit rather than as a segment.[3] There are five timing units in the HT Model representation of DESTROY in (2); in the Prosodic Model representation, there are only three. In the HT Model representation, the features for handshape position must be stipulated to associate to the second and third Ls. In the Prosodic Model, this feature-to-segment linking follows the Association Convention, which states that in the absence of any higher-ranked constraint to the contrary, prosodic features associate to timing slots right to left. The Association Convention, formulated in this way, covers a greater range of cases than does the HT Model's Tier Conflation.

A final difference between the two models (not shown in (2)) concerns the distribution of the feature [contact]. In the Prosodic Model, [contact] is a place feature whose realization is redundant, being based on the type of movement feature specified ([tracing] results in continuous movement or brushing contact at the middle point of the path in casual signing; [direction] results in contact at the beginning or end of the movement). In the HT Model, [contact] must be specified on every segment of every lexeme.

The differences in the three models' representations of two-handed signs are also important (3).

(3) *Comparison of HM, HT, and Prosodic Model representations of two-handed signs (f_a, f_b, f_c stand for comparable handshape, place, and movement features; f_x, f_y stand for comparable distinctive features of H_2)*

    a. *HM Model (cf. Liddell 1990)*

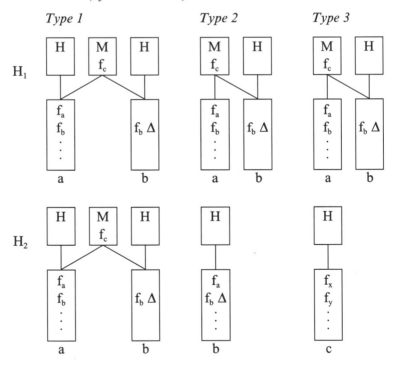

b. *HT Model*

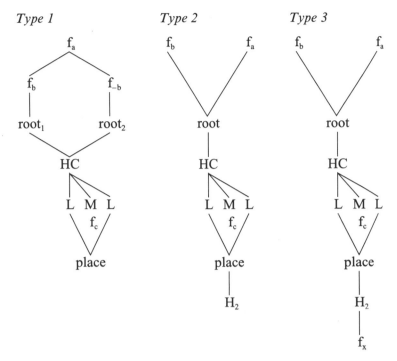

c. *Prosodic Model*

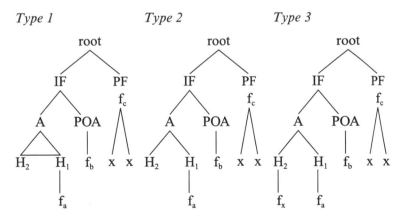

In the HM model, H_2 is an independent articulator and no constraints on H_2 are built into the system; thus, the redundancies inherent in type 1 and type 2 structures are not captured. In the HT Model, the two roles of H_2 as an articulator and as a place are built into the representation as parts of structure. Type 1 and type 3 are different structures, and type 2 is an intermediate structure, which looks more like a type 3 structure than a type 1 structure. In the Prosodic Model, the basic structure is the same for all two-handed signs, but H_2 becomes increasingly complex from type 1 to type 3 signs. The Prosodic Model's account of two-handed signs is more flexible than the HT Model's, yet more constrained than the HM Model's. The Prosodic Model structure has the flexibility needed to show assimilation and dissimilation of features in two-handed signs and created hybrid forms, both synchronically and diachronically, whereas the HT Model forces signs into a relatively more rigid dichotomy between type 1 and type 3 signs.

8.2   Constraints, Inventories, and the Lexicon

Linguists use primarily system-internal evidence and supporting system-external evidence in arguing for or against particular analyses. But each language is situated within a culture, a geographic setting, and a history. The study of language competence can be enhanced by examining the particular problems that signed languages present.

The profile of the Deaf community in the United States has created a situation where a grammar is in place but lexical items are being generated at a rapid rate; therefore, lexical innovation is an important source of grammatical evidence for ASL. ASL is relatively young—approximately two centuries old. Like that of many indigenous sign languages, its birth coincided with a raised national consciousness about the welfare of all citizens; legislative acts that created schools for the Deaf provided settings where a critical mass of Deaf individuals could live together and thrive. Such a setting, maintained over a sufficient number of generations, is necessary for a *langue* to emerge. (See Lane 1984 for a history of the Deaf community in the United States; this sequence of events is currently occurring in Nicaragua—see Kegl, Senghas, and Coppola 1995; Senghas 1995.) Moreover, the cultural profile of the Deaf community in the United States has changed dramatically in a short time. The number of Deaf individuals in the professions of medicine, law, veterinary science, dentistry, business, and research (in the sciences and in the humanities) has increased sharply in recent years, creating a need for specialized ASL vocabulary. There are more and more Deaf teachers in educational settings that serve Deaf children; as they find ways to use ASL to its best advantage as a pedagogical tool, the language also grows and changes (Padden 1995, 1998).

Using a constraint-based approach to explain lexical innovations, it can be shown that lexicalization employs existing well-formedness principles of the language (this type of analysis has been carried out on Japanese; see Itô and Mester 1995a,b). Lexical innovations have long been of socio-linguistic interest, but they are of formal interest as well.[4] The Prosodic Model reveals asymmetries in handshape inventories showing that not all parts of the ASL lexicon are equivalent. I take the position here that the ASL lexicon has both native and nonnative components, and that the native lexicon is not homogeneous but consists of three overlapping parts. Given the history of ASL and the fact that the fingerspelled alphabet and classifier predicates have existed in the language from the beginning, the native lexicon (4) includes (1) the fingerspelled alphabet, (2) the poly-morphemic predicates, often called classifier predicates, and (3) the core lexicon. To be part of the nonnative component, a form must have some evidence of fingerspelling.[5]

(4) *Native lexicon in ASL*

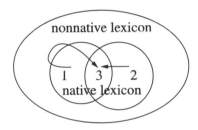

1. *The fingerspelled alphabet:* a set of handshapes, a few of which are also specified for orientation, orientation change, or movement (i.e., ASL names for the orthographic letters, such as 'K', 'P' (orientation), 'J' (orientation change), 'Z' (movement))

2. *Classifier predicates:* polymorphemic system made up of bound roots and a variety of types of affixes (e.g., 2-stooped-upright beings-side by side-facing forward-move forward-carefully-from 'a'-to 'b', 'dock-in-space')

3. *Core lexicon:* a repository of forms that can originate directly from the classifier predicate system or from the fingerspelled alphabet after conforming to a set of "nativization" constraints (e.g., BREAD, TO-FLY, AIRPLANE)

The fingerspelled alphabet (part 1) is a set of names for the English alphabet, consisting primarily of handshapes, a few of which are also specified for orientation or for movement; regarding uses of fingerspelling in ASL, including borrowing words from English, see section 1.2.3. The polymorphemic component (part 2) is made up of bound roots and various types of affixes that can be combined to form classifier predicates (Supalla 1982). These structures remain a productive part of the native lexicon. They lack both person/number inflection and derivational morphology, and instead encode primarily spatial reference (Padden, in press). They do this by allowing affixation of derivational and inflectional morphology of person, number, and aspect, given other semantic or syntactic constraints. Unlike classifier forms, which are root+affix ..., stem+affix ... forms do allow person, number, and aspect morphology and are a part of the core lexicon. Two examples of such stem+affix forms one from Padden and Perlmutter 1987 and one from Padden 1983, are the verb ACT, which has a derived nominal form ACTING (activity nominalization through affixation of a [TM] feature to the stem), and the verb GIVE, which has a number of forms that exhibit person and/or agreement ($_1$GIVE$_3$, $_3$GIVE$_1$ (showing person agreement by a change in the beginning and end points of the sign), or $_1$GIVE$_{3pl}$ (showing affixation of an arc movement to the stem)).

The core lexicon (part 3) is fed both indirectly by the fingerspelling system (fingerspelled forms enter after adhering to the constraints argued for on independent grounds throughout this book; see (5)–(6)) and directly by the classifier predicate system. The indirect way that fingerspelling feeds the core lexicon is the topic of the following sections. An example of direct borrowing from the classifier predicate system involves the sign AIRPLANE. The handshape in AIRPLANE is a productive bound classifier morpheme that can be combined in the polymorphemic part of the lexicon in forms such as 'dock-in-space'; the stem is also the basis for the verb TO-FLY and the derived noun AIRPLANE, which can be placed in the core lexicon because it has undergone nominalization.

(5) *Constraints on all signs in the core lexicon*

    a. HARMONIZE NUCLEUS (HNUC)

    Local maxima of sonority are chosen as syllable nuclei.

    b. MAXIMIZE APERTURE CHANGE (MAXAP Δ)

    Handshape changes that occupy syllable nuclei maximize aperture change, alternating between [open] and [closed] aperture settings.

c. Prosodic Word $= 1 \leq 2\sigma$ (PWD $= 1 \leq 2\sigma$)

Core lexemes consist of at least one syllable and not more than two.

d. 2-Handshapes (2-HS)

Core lexemes consist of at most two handshapes.

e. Selected Fingers (SF)

i. Core lexemes consist of at most one contrastive handshape.

ii. Aperture changes affect only selected fingers.

f. Align(L)

Align initial handshape of stem with left edge of stem.

g. Align(R)

Align final handshape of word with right edge of word.

h. Parse Handshape (Parse HS)

All handshapes in the input must be present in the output.

i. Obligatory Contour Principle (OCP)

Adjacent identical feature specifications are prohibited in core lexemes.

(6) *Constraints on all two-handed signs in the core lexicon*

a. Eliminate Redundancy (ElimRed)

An input sign that is two-handed and whose H_2 has totally redundant feature specifications has a well-formed one-handed output.

b. Parse[alternating] (Parse[alt])

When an [alternating] feature appears in the input, it must appear in the output.

c. Parse[contact(ac)]

When a [contact(ac)] feature appears in the input, it must appear in the output.

d. Parse[contact(a)]

When a [contact(a)] feature appears in the input, it must appear in the output.

e. PARSE[symmetrical] (PARSE[sym])

When a [symmetrical] feature appears in the input, it must appear
in the output.

f. PARSE HANDSHAPE/H₂ (PARSE HS/H₂)

When an H_2 handshape feature appears in the input, it must
appear in the output, except when [all] is the only fingers$_0$ feature.

g. PARSE PLACE/H₂

When an H_2 place feature appears in the input, it must appear in
the output, except when ['palm'] is the H_2 place feature.

Evidence for the autonomy of the three subcomponents of the native
lexicon of ASL comes from examining their handshape inventories.

Correspondence and noncorrespondence in handshape inventories within the
native lexicon of ASL[6]

Correspondence (part 1 = part 2 = part 3)	Noncorrespondence (part 1 has handshapes not present in parts 2 & 3)	Noncorrespondence (part 1 lacks handshapes present in parts 2 & 3)
'B' (open) (curved)	'D'	'B' (bent) (flat)
'H' (open)	'E'	'H' (bent) (curved) (flat)
'1' (open) (bent)	'M'	'1' (flat) (curved)
'A'	'K'/'P' contrast	'horns'
'S'	'G'/'Q' contrast	'7'
	'V'/'K' contrast	'8'
	'U'/'H' contrast	

There is considerable correspondence among these subcomponents, but
there is also noncorrespondence between the handshapes in part 1 (the
fingerspelled alphabet) and those in parts 2 and 3 (the classifier predicates
and core forms). As the table indicates, part 1 has certain handshapes
and handshape contrasts that parts 2 and 3 lack, and part 1 lacks certain
handshapes that parts 2 and 3 have. A word about the handshape contrasts: 'K' and 'P', 'U' and 'H', and 'Q' and 'G' are contrastive by virtue
of a specified orientation in these fingerspelled letters, and 'K' and 'V'
are contrastive by virtue of a feature [stacked], but these pairs of handshapes are not contrastive in the classifier predicate system or in the core
lexicon; they are allophonic, created by an operation that allows the palm

of the hand to be oriented toward the midsagittal z-plane, in the absence of higher-ranking, conflicting constraints.[7]

In the nonnative lexicon (7), three peripheral components or strata can be identified on the basis of their behavior with respect to independently proposed constraints and the typology of nonnative signs described by Padden (in press). Using Optimality Theory, we can see that as we move farther from the core, forms systematically are more "faithful" to their input fingerspelled letters and obey fewer of the constraints that hold for the core lexicon.

(7) *The nonnative lexicon (peripheral lexical strata)*

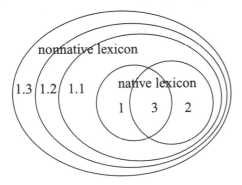

a. Stratum 1.1

Arbitrary name signs, abbreviated signs, initialized signs, $\leq$ 2-letter loan signs
These forms violate the constraint SF.

b. Stratum 1.2

Partially assimilated loan signs, $>$ 3-letter loan signs
These forms violate SF, 2-HS, and MAXAP Δ.

c. Stratum 1.3

Commonly fingerspelled words, sign+fingerspelled compounds
These forms violate SF, 2-HS, MAXAP Δ, and PWD $= 1 \leq 2\sigma$.

As a basis for stratification, I follow Battison (1978) in using one of the nonnative classes of signs that has members in all strata of the nonnative lexicon: *loan signs*. I then use the structural differences that emerge from this set of signs to locate other types of nonnative forms in the established strata. Loan signs are signs that (1) contain fingerspelled letters, (2) occur in a restricted place of articulation (in the so-called neutral space in front of the signer rather than with respect to a specified place on the body), and (3) have a restricted set of movements (i.e., those following the natural transitions between letters). They may contain more than two handshapes. For example, BUT (B-T), WOULD (W-D), WHAT (W-T), JOB (J-B) contain two handshapes, but EASY (E-S-Y) and EARLY (E-R-L-Y) contain more than two. In addition to loan signs, the analysis proposed here will explain other types of nonnative vocabulary. *Arbitrary name signs* are generated by combining the first letter of the person's first (or first and family) English name in a set of restricted places of articulation in combination with a restricted set of movements (a trilled movement, one or two straight movements, or a movement that is the enhanced form of the local movement). In *initialized signs* and *abbreviated signs*, the handshape of the initial letter of the English word is combined with the movement and place of articulation of a native form. As Padden (in press) describes them, initialized signs are often, but not always, members of a semantic field. Two examples are COMPUTATION, with a 'V'/'K' handshape, and the related initialized signs STATISTICS, ALGEBRA, CALCULUS, GEOMETRY, and TRIGONOMETRY; and SCIENCE, with an 'A' handshape, and the related initialized signs BIOLOGY, CHEMISTRY, and EXPERIMENT. This semantic generalization does not apply to abbreviated signs (e.g., 'feedback' (F-B), 'videotape' (V-T), 'withdraw' (W-D)). One important difference between loan signs, on the one hand, and arbitrary name signs, abbreviated signs, and initialized signs, on the other, is that all of the fingerspelled letters of the English word are a part of the underlying form of loan signs but not of the other groups of signs. Finally there are forms in ASL that are simply fingerspelled in their entirety, either alone (e.g., unfamiliar place names and some company names) or in combination with a sign, as in the *sign+fingerspelled compounds* L-E-G+WORK 'legwork', SUN+B-U-R-N 'sunburn').

The movements in these forms are systematically different. The movements and places of articulation in abbreviated and initialized signs are taken from a core form. For example, the abbreviated form 'social work' (S-W) takes its movement and place from HELP; the initialized form BIOLOGY takes its movement and place from SCIENCE. Loan signs (e.g., JOB (J-B), BUT (B-T), SURE (S-R-E)), which employ no movements from a core form, may employ epenthetic straight movements to a point of contact or movements involving phonetic enhancement of the transitions between fingerspelled letters, by adding an appropriate path movement to the local movement articulated by the sequence of handshapes. Arbitrary name signs may employ straight movements to a point of contact, trilled movements for signs with no contact, or enhanced fingerspelled transitions.

Using stable loan signs as a basis for stratification, we can see that more of the constraints in (5) are violated as we move from stratum to stratum. By first understanding how the constraints operate in core forms, we will be able to apply them consistently to these other types of forms. Most ASL words that contain fingerspelled letters are not part of the core component of the lexicon, but certain forms containing remnants of the fingerspelled alphabet are placed there because (1) they contain exclusively fingerspelled letters in input, (2) they conform to all the constraints in (5), and (3) the handshapes of the output conform to the set of handshapes in parts 2 and 3 of the core lexicon. One such form is BREAD, whose constraint tableau is given here.

Constraint tableau for BREAD ('8' [open], [closed]) (nativized form)

/BREAD/	PWD = $1 \leq 2\sigma$	ALIGN(L)	MAXAP Δ	2-HS	ALIGN(R)	SF(a)	SF(b)	FAITH
BREAD	**		**	***		***	*	
BREA⟨D⟩	*		**	**	*	**	*	*
⟨B⟩READ	*	*	**	**		**	*	*
B⟨RE⟩AD				*		**		**
BA					*	*		***
BD						*		***
☞ '8' [o] [cl]								*****

ALIGNMENT and FAITHFULNESS constraints—both of which are common to analyses in Optimality Theory—are important in this analysis. ALIGNMENT constraints match up prosodic categories, such as syllables, with morphological categories, such as stems. In this case ALIGN(L) (5f) matches the first letter of a stem of an English word with the first handshape of the word, and ALIGN(R) (5g) matches the final letter of the English word with the final handshape of the word. FAITHFULNESS constraints guarantee that the shape of the output matches the input to the greatest extent possible. They militate against deletions from the input form—PARSE constraints—or against epenthesis in the output form—FILL constraints. The only FAITHFULNESS constraint used is PARSE HS

(5h), which requires that all handshapes present in the input must also be present in the output.[8] To make the role of FAITHFULNESS in the lexicon clear, I use the term FAITH instead of PARSE HS in the constraint tableaux in this section.

The only constraint that must be crucially ranked in the core form BREAD is FAITH. No other constraint is violated in the output form, '8' [open], [closed];[9] the other forms are less harmonic in the following ways. The first candidate, the fully fingerspelled form BREAD, violates MAXAP Δ (5b) twice with respect to aperture because 'B' and 'R' are both [open] and 'E' and 'A' are both [closed]. It violates 2-HS (5d) three times because it contains five, not three, handshapes. It violates SF(a) (5e) three times because although 'B' and 'E' contain the same selected fingers, 'R', 'A', and 'D' cause three changes in selected finger groups. It violates SF(b) only once, and it does not violate ALIGN(L), ALIGN(R), or FAITH. The second and third candidates, with unparsed first and last letters, incur one violation fewer of 2-HS and SF(a), but they violate ALIGN(R) and ALIGN(L), respectively. Deleting two of the middle handshapes (the fourth candidate) eliminates the violations of MAX-AP and PWD = $1 \leq 2\sigma$ (5c), but the violations of SF and 2-HS remain. The forms with two handshapes (the fifth and sixth candidates) are quite well formed (the sixth, B-D, incurs only one violation of SF(a)); but the actual output fares even better, violating none of the proposed constraints except FAITH (which it violates five times). (Note that the only form that does not violate FAITH is the fully fingerspelled form.)

Next consider loan signs with two handshapes, such as JOB (J-B).

Constraint tableau for 'job' (J-B) (nonnative, stratum 1.1; loan sign)

/JOB/	PWD = $1 \leq 2\sigma$	ALIGN(L)	MAXAP Δ	2-HS	ALIGN-R	FAITH	SF(a)	SF(b)
JOB			*				*	*
☞ J-B						*	*	*

In such forms FAITH is no longer dead last. The actual output violates SF(a) and SF(b). It is equivalent in structure and number of violations to the B-D form of BREAD, except that it has not rid itself of the fingerspelled letters. This form violates FAITH once.

The tableau for EASY, a nonnative form in stratum 1.2, shows FAITH moving up farther in the constraint hierarchy. Violations of 2-HS and SF define this stratum.

Constraint tableau for 'easy' (E-S-Y) (nonnative, stratum 1.2; loan sign)

/EASY/	PWD = 1≤2σ	ALIGN(L)	ALIGN(R)	FAITH	MAXAP Δ	2-HS	SF(a)	SF(b)
EASY	*				**	**	*	
E-Y				**			*	*
☞ E-S-Y				*	*	*	*	*

In stratum 1.3, exemplified here by S-T-O-C-K MARKET, FAITH is ranked above all constraints except ALIGN(L) and ALIGN(R). In this stratum any violation of FAITH is fatal.

Constraint tableau for 'stock' in S-T-O-C-K MARKET (nonnative, stratum 1.3; sign+fingerspelled word)

/STOCK/	ALIGN(L)	ALIGN(R)	FAITH	PWD = 1≤2σ	MAXAP Δ	2-HS	SF(a)	SF(b)
☞ STOCK				**	**	**	*	
S-K			***		**		*	

In the following table we can trace the degree to which loan signs are faithful to the input with respect to the constraints of the core lexicon. It is important to stress that forms can be stable members of these strata.

The ranking of FAITHFULNESS in lexical components of ASL

	Nonnative		
Native	Stratum 1.1	Stratum 1.2	Stratum 1.3
PWD = 1≤2σ	PWD = 1≤2σ	PWD = 1≤2σ	ALIGN(L)
ALIGN(L)	ALIGN(L)	ALIGN(L)	ALIGN(R)
MAXAP Δ	MAXAP Δ	ALIGN(R)	FAITH
2-HS	2-HS	FAITH	MAXAP Δ
ALIGN(R)	ALIGN(R)	2-HS	PWD = 1≤2σ
SF(a)	FAITH	MAXAP Δ	2-HS
SF(b)	SF(a)	SF(a)	SF(a)
FAITH	SF(b)	SF(b)	SF(b)

None of the loan signs discussed so far involve combinations of forms from two subcomponents of the native lexicon; I have discussed only loan signs containing fingerspelled letters. Initialized and abbreviated signs combine movements of core forms with one or two fingerspelled letters, respectively. Padden (in press) discusses some restrictions on these combinations. For example, she notes that if a handshape in a core form retains its status as a classifier, a fingerspelled letter may not be substituted for it. Signs violating these combinatoric restrictions are judged ungrammatical by native ASL signers, and many such forms occur in manually coded English systems. Another constraint on such combinations occurs in the name sign system of ASL (Supalla 1992). Arbitrary name signs use fingerspelled letters, and classifier name signs combine size and shape specifiers with movement roots. Native signers reject as odd or ungrammatical signs that combine the two types. For example, given the inventory of handshapes there should be no name sign containing an 'E' fingerspelled letter and a classifier movement root; thus, substituting 'E' for 'upright-being' as in *'(Evelyn)-moves-forward' instead of 'upright-being-moves-forward' is illegitimate when forming a name sign. Likewise, a name sign combining 'W' (William) with a curved joint specification, as in *'hunched-over-(William)', would be ungrammatical.

The constraints argued for thus far would allow "movement from a core form+one fingerspelled letter" combinations that crucially do not violate the combinatoric restrictions sketched above to be placed in the core lexicon. *Mutatis mutandis*, forms with two fingerspelled handshapes would be members of stratum 1.1 of the nonnative lexicon. The following tableau shows constraint rankings for an initialized form with two handshapes: W-S 'workshop'. The candidate set highlights a crucial ranking between ALIGN(L) and ALIGN(R). Because of the 2-HS constraint, all of these forms allow for two empty handshape slots in the input, in addition to the path movement from the core form. The tableau shows that a two-handshape form incurring one violation of ALIGN(R) is preferred over a form incurring one violation of ALIGN(L). The preferred form chooses the two leftmost handshapes of the two English stems.

Constraint tableau for 'workshop' + GROUP (path) (nonnative, stratum 1.1; abbreviated sign)

'workshop'+GROUP	ALIGN(L)	ALIGN(R)	2-HS	MAXAP Δ	SF(a)
☞ W-S+GROUP		*			*
W-P+GROUP	*				*

Although further research in this area is indicated, this type of analysis makes predictions about what combinations of handshapes and movements will be acceptable as new lexical items are introduced. One prediction is that if a form moves from one peripheral stratum to another, it should move toward the core and should satisfy more, not fewer, of the proposed constraints. Not all forms will move, however, and there are some forms that will remain in stratum 1.3 for principled reasons (Padden 1998).

8.3   Units of Phonological Analysis

In this section I discuss some of the differences between the sign language and spoken language use of the units listed in (8).

(8)   *Units of phonological analysis*

   a. Timing unit (segment): the smallest concatenative unit on the timing tier

   b. Weight unit: a branching class node in the prosodic branch of structure, which adds complexity to syllable nuclei and can be referred to by phonological and morphophonological processes

   c. Syllable: (i) the fundamental parsable prosodic unit; (ii) (in sign language) a sequential, phonological movement

   d. Root node: the node at which the phonological representation interfaces with the morphosyntactic features of the form

   e. Prosodic word: phonological domain consisting of a stem+affixes[10]

The syllable is an important unit in sign and spoken language phonology. Even taking into account all of the important differences described below between timing units and root nodes, and between timing units and weight units, the syllable in sign languages works very much like its spoken language counterpart. Sign syllables have no onset-rime distinction, but the inherent features capture much of the information structure of the content, and the prosodic features capture the prosodic properties. Sign syllables capture weight and duration distinctions and are referred to by higher structures to determine well-formed movement combinations and word length. It is clear from the types of constraints developed in the Prosodic Model, however, that in order to understand the role of the syllable, we need a set of constraints that conspire to create canonical words—that is, core lexemes. Of the constraints listed in section 8.2, only two constrain the syllable; the others constrain lexemes. Disyllabic core forms are crucial in this enterprise, because only by analyzing them can we determine which constraints are word-level constraints and which are syllable-level constraints. To take two examples: only by analyzing disyllabic forms can we see that H_2 is a word-level appendix and not a syllable-level coda or that a single group of selected fingers covers the domain of a word rather than a syllable; and only by observing mono- and polymorphemic disyllabic forms can we see the effects of SELECTED FINGERS in words. To say that all syllables require a movement is circular, because a syllable in ASL is defined by its movement. But to say that all lexemes require a movement captures the fact that all well-formed words have a movement, or are supplied one by the operation of movement epenthesis. The syllable has been argued to be more important than the segment in acquisition (Locke 1993), a claim that is strengthened by the arguments made here in favor of the Prosodic Model. Most core lexemes in ASL contain one sequential movement (i.e., one syllable),[11] and even if the syllable-internal units in spoken and signed languages are not equivalent, it is these types of movements that appear in the babbling of young Deaf children learning sign (Petitto and Marentette 1991; Marentette 1995).

Now let us look at the role of the root node and its relation to timing units. The root node is generally understood to dominate all of the features in a tree. Because vowels and consonants can be captured in phonological structures as temporally discrete units, a root node and a timing slot can be equivalent in a spoken language. However, timing units and root nodes do different kinds of phonological work: timing units handle temporal order and duration and feed higher-order prosodic structure; the root node manages the features in a given domain. Certain assumptions about timing units and root nodes may have their origins in the development of generative phonology. Let us consider three points in this development: segmental representation (Chomsky and Halle 1968 (*SPE*)), autosegmental representation (Clements and Keyser 1983 (C-V phonology)), and moraic phonology (Hayes 1989). In *SPE*, a single feature matrix and a single timing unit were bound together in the theory. In C-V phonology, timing and syllabic information are handled by the timing tier, and timing units can be marked [±syllabic]. In moraic phonology, no content is left in timing units at all; they are abstract timing units, and they exist purely for reasons of syllabification and metrical theory. It is from moraic phonology that the Prosodic Model benefits most. In moraic phonology, timing and content are more radically independent than they are in C-V phonology, and this is true in the Prosodic Model as well. In the Prosodic Model of sign language phonological structure, a root node dominates all the features in a geometry just as it does in spoken language phonological structure, and in this sense the root node in sign languages is the interface with the morphosyntactic features of the form, just as it is in spoken languages. However, the timing units of sign languages are based on feature specifications selected only from the prosodic branch of structure; and instead of being one to one as in spoken languages, the canonical relationship of timing slots to root nodes in sign languages is two to one; a root node and a timing slot are not equivalent (9).

(9) *Canonical relationship between timing units and root nodes in the Prosodic Model*

a.   root node

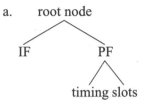

b.   one root node

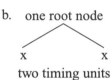

two timing units

In the Prosodic Model, it is not the case that one x-slot is more consonant-like and the other is more vowel-like; an analogy of this sort will not work. It is the inherent features branch of structure, in total, that is consonant-like, and the prosodic features branch of structure, in total, that is vowel-like. But the consonant entity (the inherent tier) and the vowel entity (the prosodic tier) *are realized at the same time* in signed languages, not in a temporally discrete way as they are in spoken languages. In this context it is useful to consider the two-part definition of C(onsonant)-units and V(owel)-units proposed by Clements and Keyser (1983); (1) C- and V-units define functional positions within the syllable (Cs are [+syllabic]; Vs are [−syllabic]); (2) they serve the additional and equally important function of defining the primitive units of timing at the subsyllabic levels of phonological representation. Only the second part of this definition holds for sign languages. One conclusion that might be drawn from this discussion is that the additional roles that timing units might have in spoken language—for example, the role of sonority sequencing within syllables—are a function of the auditory biological substrate to which it is linked and in which it is expressed.

Finally, let us consider the importance of movements as vowels and as weight units. Researchers have noted parallels between vowels in spoken languages and movements in sign languages, given the ways in which these aspects of the signal function in their respective language types (Liddell 1984a; Sandler 1989), but this comparison can be misleading if one does not look beyond the segmental level to the prosodic roles that vowels play in spoken languages and that movements play in sign languages as syllable nuclei (Brentari 1990b,c,d; Perlmutter 1992; Sandler 1993c). In particular, the two language types differ in the way syllable complexity is realized within the syllable (i.e., syllable weight). In spoken languages syllable weight is realized as a durational effect in most cases (e.g., in CVV and C_1VC_2, where C_2 is [+voice]), and it is always realized by the addition of more linear information. In sign languages weight is a function of the complexity of the movement (see chapter 6); it is realized by the number of subcomponents within the sequential movement. These components are realized at the same time and have no lengthening or durational effect. In the Prosodic Model, canonical status is granted to single, simple movements—those with one weight unit. This status is based on the empirical evidence of (1) asymmetry of distribution of simple and complex movements, (2) the ability of simple movements to undergo two types of nominalization (see chapter 6), and (3) the simplification of complex movements by young children. This deeper understanding of movements shows that they are vowel-like, and that single, sequential movements are decomposable in ways that are relevant to the grammar.

8.4   Similarities between the Architecture of the Visual System and the Prosodic Model

Sign language phonology, and the Prosodic Model in particular, speaks to several general questions concerning the role that the systems of audition and vision play in the grammatical models proposed by linguists. Why should phonological representations of spoken languages and sign languages look different? Should the most efficient solution to the problem of designing a language with the best signal-to-meaning ratio in time and space be the same for a spoken language as for a sign language? Although it is clear that many types of vertical processing (e.g., pattern recognition, paradigmatic processing) and horizontal temporal processing (e.g., ordering and sequencing of objects in time, syntagmatic processing) take place in both vision and audition (Bregman 1990), signal transmission and peripheral processing give rise to differences in the inherent strengths built into the designs of the two types of phonological systems. Moreover, as Hirsh and Sherrick (1961) have shown, the threshold for identifying temporal order in audition and in vision is approximately 20 msec, yet important differences are found at the peripheral level of the cochlea and the retina.

Differences between vision and audition

	Vision	Audition
Speed of signal transmission	186,000 miles/sec	1,089 feet/sec
Temporal resolution peripherally	2 msec	25–30 msec
Spatial arrangement information	peripheral	nonperipheral

The difference in speed of transmission between light waves and sound waves is enormous and has consequences for the perception of objects and sounds. Vision can take advantage not only of light waves reflected from the target object but also of light waves reflected from other objects in the environment ("echo" waves); these waves are available simultaneously. This same echo phenomenon in audition is available to the listener much more slowly. Only after the sound waves produced by the sound source have already struck the ear will echoes from other objects in the environment do the same. (In fact, spatial localization is calculated on the difference between the time when the sound waves strike the ear nearer to the source and the time when they strike the ear farther from the source, coupled with differences in volume of the sound reaching the two ears.) The result is that a more three-dimensional or "spatial" image is available more quickly in vision.

The two modalities' manners of peripheral processing differ as well. Although identification of temporal order is roughly the same in both modalities, audition has the advantage in detecting whether two equivalent stimuli are presented simultaneously or sequentially.[12] This is referred to as the threshold of temporal resolution in studies of audition (Kohlrausch, Püschel, and Alphei 1992) and the threshold of flicker fusion in studies of vision (Chase and Jenner 1993). Humans can temporally resolve auditory stimuli when they are separated by an interval of only 2 msec (Green 1971; Kohlrausch, Püschel, and Alphei 1992); the visual system requires a 20 msec interstimulus interval (Chase and Jenner 1993). The visual system has an advantage in processing spatial arrangement of objects. Spatial arrangement of visual stimuli is registered at the most peripheral stage of the visual system, at the retina and lens, whereas spatial arrangement of auditory simuli can be inferred only by temporal and intensity differences of the signal between the two ears.

Although these differences in peripheral processing do not prove that the language systems in sign and speech must be designed differently, it is a curious fact that the type of near minimal pair that is quite common in spoken languages (in which words differ by just one sound—e.g., /sæd/, /mæd/, /læd/, /fæd/ or /mæs/, /mæd/, /mæp/, /mæn/) exists only rarely in sign (CONGRESS vs. CHRISTIAN, 'upright-being-move-forward' vs. ASK). Reversals of the initial and final settings of signs are more common, but these occur within one place of articulation and almost always involve morphologically related forms (DECLINE vs. IMPROVE, BORROW vs. LEND, $_1$GIVE$_2$ vs. $_2$GIVE$_1$, $_1$INFORM$_2$ vs. $_2$INFORM$_1$). This suggests that the peripheral advantages of the two types of systems contribute to the phonological makeup of core lexemes in the two types of languages. The Prosodic Model allows pairs of the sort described by Klima and Bellugi (1979), Stokoe (1960), and Stokoe, Casterline, and Croneberg (1969) (e.g., APPLE vs. ONION, SUMMER vs. UGLY) whereby the relevant contrast is expressed not on one timing unit alone but in the inherent feature geometry that is realized in the entire lexeme. This allows the type of minimal pair shown in (10) to count as such.

(10) *Minimal pairs demonstrable in the Prosodic Model*

   a. *CANDY vs. APPLE*

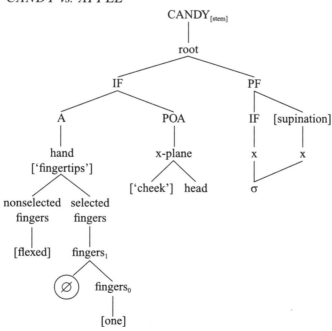

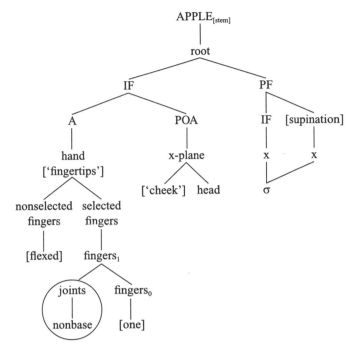

b. *ONION vs. APPLE*

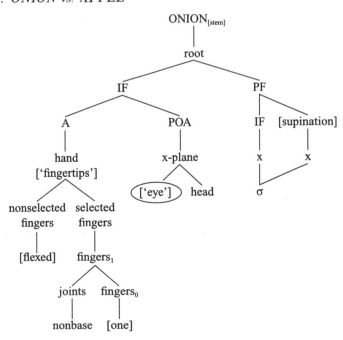

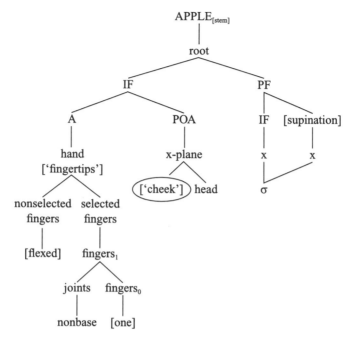

In CANDY and APPLE the minimal contrast involves a joints handshape structure: the presence of a nonbase joint specification versus no joints branch at all.[13] In ONION and APPLE the minimal contrast involves a place feature: ['eye'] versus ['cheek'].

One advantage that work on sign language phonology has over work on spoken language phonology is that a great deal more is known about higher-level processing in vision than is known about higher-level processing in audition. In part, this is due to two somewhat accidental facts about these areas of scientific inquiry. First, work on audition arose in part from work striving to improve the hearing of individuals with hearing loss, and so researchers focused their attention on the peripheral mechanism; work on vision has been engaged in trying to explain normal visual processing. Second, from the anatomical perspective, the visual system is much more accessible for neurophysiological measurements since both in humans and higher-order primates these neural structures are on the surface of the cortex; the auditory cortex, by contrast, is inaccessible from the surface of the brain. Models of sign language phonology can therefore draw upon well-developed research on higher order visual processing more generally in a way that models of spoken language phonology cannot. Although I can only touch upon this type of dialogue here, it is certainly a worthwhile target for future empirical studies.

In this section I will discuss the Prosodic Model in the context of work done in the past twenty years on higher-order vision. Two major claims that have been made about the architecture of the visual system are relevant here: that it is divided into the *magnocellular system* and the *parvocellular system*, and into the object-centered *"what system"* and the spatial-orientation *"where system."*

The first, "lower" division into parvocellular and magnocellular visual subsystems was discovered in cats by Hubel and Wiesel (1959, 1962); the discovery was reinforced by anatomical and physiological work by Livingstone and Hubel (1984, 1987a,b,c, 1988) on higher primates. Anatomical and physiological evidence for these two subsystems of the visual mechanism has also been found in humans (Galaburda and Livingstone 1993). The magnocellular system performs stereopsis and motion detection. The parvocellular system performs tasks that have to do with scrutinizing objects and making fine distinctions of form and color. This anatomical and physiological split takes place quite early in visual processing, and the implication of the magnocellular system in the rapid processing of speech has been documented. Postmortem studies of the brains of severe lifelong dyslexics show that the magnocellular layers of the visual system are less developed in such patients; behavioral studies of living severe dyslexics demonstrate a deficit in performance of rapid processing during visual and auditory tasks (Tallal, Miller, and Fitch 1993). One complication involved in applying these findings is that the only consistent deficit produced by lesion studies of the parvocellular system is in tasks involving color discrimination. It appears that perception of shape, orientation, and location of objects (even static objects) may be handled, at least in part, by the magnocellular system. In considering the role of the parvo- and magnocellular systems with respect to place features, a comment by Livingstone and Hubel is helpful:

The magnocellular system might be primarily concerned with global spatial organization: deciding which visual elements, such as edges and discontinuities, belong to and define individual objects in the scene, as well as determining the overall three-dimensional organization of the scene, the positions of objects in space, and movements of objects. [The parvocellular system] is more important for analyzing the scene in greater and more leisurely detail. (1988, 748)

Work on the second, "higher" division within the visual system—the "what" and "where" systems—was pioneered in primates by Ungerleider and Mishkin (1982); it demonstrates that a ventral (or occipitotemporal) pathway in the visual cortex is specialized for object perception ("what"), and that a dorsal (or occipitoparietal) pathway is specialized for spatial perception ("where"). In rhesus monkeys, lesions in the temporal area produce impaired performance on object discrimination tasks; lesions in the parietal area produce impaired ability to choose a response location based on a visual landmark (Ungerleider and Mishkin 1982). These higher systems interact with the magno- and parvocellular subsystems via complex connections (Milner and Goodale 1995). This picture is complicated, however, by several factors. In both the parvo/magno and temporal/ parietal pathways, information travels both "upstream" to central areas in the brain via the afferent synaptic connections and "downstream" to more peripheral areas via the efferent synaptic connections; this makes the direction of influence difficult to isolate. Recent research has also identified overlap between the systems. Finally, most experimental work on the two higher pathways has involved processing primarily of static locations and orientation of objects in space, rather than processing of movement patterns of objects—for example, the identification of objects by movement patterns such as gait, typical wing movements, or flight pattern.

Even with the complications mentioned above, data collected from signers could be very useful in research on these two visual subsystems, since there are parallels between the visual processing system and the structure of sign language. Returning to the hierarchical feature structure proposed for ASL in the Prosodic Model, we can see these parallels. The diagram in (11) depicts the hypothesized relationships between the phonological role played by the features and the area of the visual system involved in processing their specific type of information.

(11) *Labeling of features according to visual pathways involved*

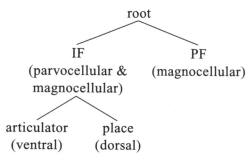

The prosodic features can be thought to fall squarely within the domain of information processed by the magnocellular system; the inherent features, within the domains processed by both systems. The split between inherent and prosodic features is "early"—high in the feature tree—just as the split between the parvo- and magnocellular visual systems is relatively more peripheral than the dorsal/ventral division. Within the inherent features branch of the feature tree, "what" information processed by the ventral system is contained in the details of the articulator node, but the handshape's orientation to the place of articulation is a global activity of the type described by Livingstone and Hubel (1988) and potentially a part of the "where" system. Jeannerod (1994) has studied non-linguistic motor representations and has come to the same conclusion. Place features (locations on the body or within the three-dimensional signing space in front of the signer) can be seen as information processed by both the magno- and parvocellular systems within the dorsal (parietal) system. Although some research has been done on the possible impact of the temporal/parietal visual distinction on the construction of conceptual structure in spoken language (Landau and Jackendoff 1993), clearly more experimental work with signers would bring together data from language—and, in particular, phonology—and vision that could lead to illuminating results in both areas. Of course, parallels between the vision and sign language processing systems must be taken into account along with contributions by the motor system.

8.5 Conclusion

What do these differences mean for sign language grammars and for universal grammar? In chapter 1 I hypothesized that the closer our analyses are to the phonetics, the more apparent the differences are between sign language and spoken language, and that the closer our analyses are to grammatical function, the more apparent the similarities become. The findings presented here support this hypothesis, indicating that the formal role of distinctive features, syllables, and segments as building blocks of a grammar with constraints is the same for signed and spoken languages, but that the substantive definitions in both types of languages—those that are more phonetic and less grammatical—depend on conditions of naturalness in each modality and on specifics about production and processing that grow out of experience with linguistic messages conveyed in each.

Appendix A: The Letters of the ASL Manual Alphabet Labeled [Flexed] or Nonflexed

(Drawings of the handshapes are given in figure 1.8.)

A	[flexed]	M	[flexed]
B	nonflexed	N	[flexed]
C	nonflexed	O	[flexed]
D	selected fingers nonflexed nonselected fingers [flexed]	P	nonflexed
		Q	nonflexed
E	[flexed]	R	nonflexed
F	selected fingers [flexed] nonselected fingers nonflexed	S	[flexed]
		T	[flexed]
G	nonflexed	U	nonflexed
H	nonflexed	V	nonflexed
I	nonflexed	W	nonflexed
J	nonflexed	X	[flexed]
K	nonflexed	Y	nonflexed
L	nonflexed	Z	nonflexed

Appendix B: Verb Forms That Do and Do Not Allow [Delayed Completive] Aspect

Verb forms that allow the [delayed completive] aspect

ADMIT	ADD	ADVANCE
ADVISE	CHANGE	FIND
ARREST	CAPTURE	CHALLENGE
MOVE	ASK	BLOOM
FOCUS	TAKE-UP	CONFESS
BURY	REDUCE	SATISFY
LOSE	MEMORIZE	INSULT
LEAVE	DEFLATE	INHALE
AGREE	ANNOUNCE	MEET
ARRIVE	BEGIN	BET
BREAK	INTERRUPT	ERECT
MISS	PASS	SIT
CALL-BY-TTY	GIVE-BIRTH-TO	LAY-OFF
SHOOT	SPEAK-OUT	WALK-OUT
STEAL	ZOOM-OFF	UNDERSTAND
VANISH	SAY-NO-TO	RUN-OUT-OF
KISS	EMBRACE	BEAT (i.e., 'conquer/overcome')

Some verb forms that do not allow [delayed completive] aspect

ADVERTISE	REQUEST	BUILD
DREAM	COOK	COMPETE
BUTTER	CLEAN	CONCENTRATE
DANCE	MAKE-A-LIST	MEASURE
MOCK	SHARE	TALK
SAY (archaic?)	COMMUTE	JUMP

Appendix C: Forms That Undergo Reduplicative Nominalization

(The verb form is the first one, the noun is second.)

a. Reduplicated movement

SIT/CHAIR
CALL/NAME
HIT-WITH-HAMMER/HAMMER
GO-BY-PLANE/AIRPLANE
GO-BY-BOAT/BOAT
GO-BY-FLYING-SAUCER/FLYING-SAUCER
GO-BY-ROCKET/ROCKET
GO-BY-SHIP/SHIP
GO-BY-TRAIN/TRAIN
GO-TO-BED/BED
PUT-ON-BRACELET/BRACELET
PUT-ON-BACKPACK/BACKPACK
COVER-WITH-BLANKET/BLANKET
PUT-ON-BROOCH/BROOCH
PUT-ON-CLOTHESPIN/CLOTHESPIN
CLIP-FINGERNAILS/CLIPPER
OPEN-DOOR/DOOR
PRESS-DOORBELL/DOORBELL
TURN-DOORKNOB/DOORKNOB
PULL-DRAWER/DRAWER
PUT-ON-COAT/COAT
PUT-ON-EARRING/EARRING
PUT-ON-DRESS/DRESS
PUT-ON-EARPHONES/EARPHONES
PUT-ON-GAS MASK/GAS MASK
PUT-ON-GOGGLES/GOGGLES
CLOSE-GATE/GATE
ADD-GAS-TO-TANK/GAS
SHIFT-GEARS/GEARSHIFT

SHOOT/GUN
HANG-UP/HANGER
SCREW-ON-JAR LID/JAR LID
PLUG-IN/PLUG
PUT-ON-RING/RING
PUT-ON-HAT/HAT
PUT-ON-HEARING-AID/HEARING-AID
ZIP-UP/ZIPPER
PUT-ON-SCARF/SCARF
CUT/SCISSORS
TURN-SCREW/SCREWDRIVER
PUT-ON-SOCK/SOCK
PUT-ON-SUSPENDERS/SUSPENDERS
PUT-ON-TAPE/TAPE
TELEPHONE/TELEPHONE
OPEN-UMBRELLA/UMBRELLA
OPEN-WALLET/WALLET
BLOW-WHISTLE/WHISTLE

b. *Reduplicated aperture change*

SNAP-PHOTOGRAPH/CAMERA
FLICK-LIGHTER/LIGHTER
THUMP-MELON/MELON
STAPLE/STAPLER
SQUEEZE-PLIERS/PLIERS
TAKE-PILL/PILL

c. *Reduplicated orientation change*

STRIKE-MATCH/MATCH

Appendix D: Descriptive Categories of Two-Handed Signs According to Their Ability to Undergo Weak Drop

Examples of type 1 signs that disallow Weak Drop (WD)

a. *[Alternating] type 1 signs*

BICYCLE	COFFEE	TO-SIGN
MALAYSIA	TO-USE-ASL	UNDERSTANDING [characteristic]

b. *Signs in which H_2 is morphemic in the synchronic grammar*

HANG-CLOTHES	CHEERLEADER
LOOK-AT [reciprocal]	CORRESPOND-WITH-EACH-OTHER

c. *Signs with continuous contact*

GERMANY	WRESTLING	COOPERATE
BUTTERFLY	MEASURE	RUN
ASSIMILATE	REQUEST	SUPERVISE
SQUIRREL	FACTORY	

d. *Signs with [symmetrical] and [contact(a)]*

WEDDING	WITH	TALK-TO-SELF
CONTACT	CONFLICT	LINK-UP-WITH
SHOES	JAPAN	WORTHLESS

Examples of type 1 signs that allow WD

a. *Type 1 signs with no contact, identical orientation*

NOTHING   VOMIT   MOCK

b. *Type 1 signs with [symmetrical] orientation and no contact*

BASKETBALL	CHAT	SUNDAY
SUCCESSFUL	TRY	WAIT
DIE	LEAVE	ATTENTION
BREEZE	TEACH	ENCOURAGE
FAMOUS	VAIN	
HAPPEN		

c. Signs with [symmetrical] orientation, [contact(p)]

YOUNG	DEER	HEALTHY/BRAVE
SWEAT	ADDRESS	LIVE
RUSSIA	NUN	MUMPS

d. Signs with identical orientation, [contact(a)]

GET   CONDENSE/SUMMARIZE

Type 2 signs that may undergo WD

FUN	REMEMBER	KNIFE
REDUCE	HARD	THIN
NAME	LAST	SHORT/BRIEF
BETWEEN	NEXT	GAIN-WEIGHT
BEFORE		

Type 2 signs that may not undergo WD explained by restrictions on type 1 signs

DEPEND [contact(c)]	SOON [contact(c)]
TRAIN [contact(c)]	ABSTRACT [sym] [contact(a)]
THERMOMETER [contact(c)]	MARRIAGE [sym] [contact(a)]
SCHOOL [sym] [contact(a)]	PAPER [sym] [contact(a)]

Type 2 signs that may not undergo WD because of PARSE-PLACE

WHEN   MAXIMUM   JAIL
AVOID

Type 3 signs that may undergo WD ([all] handshape)

CUP	WRITE	DEVELOP
DANCE	FIND	MONEY
ONCE	CHECK	WHAT
LATER	SUBTRACT	LIST
READ	FALL	

Type 3 signs that may not undergo WD

*a. Type 3 signs that may not undergo WD explained by restrictions on type 1 signs
(all have a [contact(ac)] feature in the input)*

SHOW	NEW-ORLEANS	MEDICINE
START	HELP	IMPRESS

b. Type 3 signs that may not undergo WD because of PARSE-PLACE

LEAF	AUTUMN	DOCTOR
TRASH	DECLINE	SHEEP
CRACKER	POOR	BASKET

c. *Type 3 signs that may not undergo WD because of P_{ARSE} HS/H_2 (fingers)*

| BERRY | MECHANIC | WORD |
| BANANA | CANDLE | CIGARETTE |

d. *Type 3 signs that may not undergo WD because of P_{ARSE} HS/H_2 (joints)*

SODA-POP	JOIN	GET-ON
BLOW-UP	GROW	ELECTION
PEAR	ENOUGH	GASOLINE

e. *Type 3 signs that may not undergo WD because of $P_{ARSE}\text{-}P_{LACE}/H_2$*

ENGLISH	WARN	DOLLAR
HIDE	LEAVE-SCHOOL	CHOCOLATE
DEFLATE	TOAST	

Notes

Chapter 1

1. I am referring here to a moment in the evolution of language after the move toward using the auditory/aural channel as the primary mode of communication had already been accomplished.

2. See Anderson 1993, Corina and Sandler 1993, Brentari 1995, and van der Hulst and Mills 1996 for interesting overviews of historical and methodological approaches to sign language phonology, and for additional discussion on current themes in sign language phonology and their contribution to phonological theory as a whole.

3. This strategy for discussing spoken language units was also used by Uyechi (1995).

4. These affixes may take the form of prefixes, suffixes, or parafixes that occur as simultaneous layers with the stem.

5. This definition of selected fingers does not always consistently identify them, but it does so in the majority of cases. It does not identify forms in which the thumb contacts the body and does not move, while other fingers do not contact the body and do move (e.g., BUG, FINE [intensive], EJACULATE).

6. As Supalla and Newport point out, both the noun and the verb may be derived from a stem form, not specified as a noun or a verb, which appears as the verb form on the surface.

7. The verb forms on which such loci occur, their distribution, and their phonetic realization vary from one sign language to another.

8. Engberg-Pedersen calls all of these deictic systems "time lines," but each has a different function, and not all are related solely to time itself; this is why I speak of them here as "deictic lines of reference."

9. It is not clear whether this compound is a VA, NA, NV, or VV compound, since NAME (the noun) and CALL (the verb) both come from the same stem, as do SHINE (the verb) and SHINY (the adjective), which even have the same surface forms.

10. The form in figure 1.15 contains nine morphemes, but this may not be the maximum number of morphemes per syllable.

11. Locke (1993) uses the term *prosody* to refer to aspects of language such as stress, rhythm, and intonation. This use of the term can refer to continuously varying aspects of the signal, which may assist young babies in identifying their mothers' voices and can help all listeners in identifying affective states. In work by Halle and Vergnaud (1987) and Hayes (1995), prosody is the set of grammatical properties investigated in metrical theory, such as stress and prominence. These uses of the terms *prosody* and *prosodic* play less of a role in the Prosodic Model, but represent areas into which it can and should be expanded (see Miller 1996).

12. See, however, the analysis of disyllabic forms in chapter 5; an underlying level and a surface level are insufficient to account for these forms.

13. Three-dimensional computer graphic analysis of normal and apraxic subjects' production of the ideomotor gestures from the Boston Diagnostic Aphasia Exam (Goodglass and Caplan 1972), such as carving a turkey, reveals that when normal subjects execute these gestures, joint rotation is systematically coordinated, whereas apraxic subjects' gestures lack this coordination (Poizner et al. 1990).

14. The citation form is the form one might find in a dictionary, or the form elicited when one asks, "What is the sign for 'x'?"

15. It is an interesting fact that in executing the sign for TO-SIGN-Italian Sign Language, -Sign Language of the Netherlands, -German Sign Language, -Langue des signes québecoise, and -ASL, this orientation of the two hands is used. The ASL sign for TO-SIGN-ASL has an alternating, outward directional movement and handshape change with palms oriented toward the midsagittal plane. Not all of these signs use the same handshape (i.e., Italian Sign Language uses a '3' handshape), but the signs for TO-SIGN in Langue des signes québecoise, German Sign Language, Sign Language of the Netherlands, and Italian Sign Language have an alternating circular movement with palms pointed inward.

16. The physiological facts outlined in this section were first discussed by Crasborn (1995).

17. There is one more contact discussed by Liddell and Johnson (1989), known as 'web' (e.g., FOOTBALL, PREGNANT, WRESTLING), but because H_1 contacts the ulnar side of each finger of H_2, 'web' can be treated as a subclass of 'ulnar.'

Chapter 2

1. This is a paraphrase of the following passage: "The lexical entry for *telegraph* must contain just enough information for the rules of English phonology to determine its phonetic form in each context; since the variation is fully determined, the lexical entry must contain no indication of the effect of context on the phonetic form." Despite the subsequent debate about how abstract such representations should be, this remains one of the most explicit statements of what underlying representations ideally ought to include.

In this book the terms *underlying representation* and *input structure* are considered equivalent to *lexical entry*.

2. What is "simple," according to *SPE*, is evaluated by the criteria of "learnability" and "formal simplicity."

3. In the statement, "In our treatment, boundaries are units in a string, on a par in this sense with segments" (*SPE*, 371), only morphological boundaries are at issue. In Lexical Phonology (Kiparsky 1982), boundaries do not behave as phonological elements; instead, they regulate word-building operations. In constraint-based models, both phonological and morphological boundaries are visible (e.g., the phonological word vs. the morphological word).

4. For further discussion of Local Constraint Conjunction, see Smolensky 1993 and Fukazawa and Miglio, in press.

5. In this book I use the older, more familiar terms for these constraint types, even though FAITHFULNESS has been replaced by IDENTITY, PARSE by MAXIMIZE, and FILL by DEPENDENCY (McCarthy and Prince 1995).

6. Within Optimality Theory, an account of cases of opacity has been proposed by McCarthy (1997).

7. The number of syllables is equal to the number of sequential movements.

8. I am grateful to the participants at the University of Trondheim Workshop on Sign Phonology (November 1994)—in particular, Irene Greftegreff, Wendy Sandler, Harry van der Hulst, and Lars Wallin—for helping me to crystallize this discussion.

9. Chinchor (1978) was the first to discuss a syntagmatic definition of the sign syllable.

10. Stack (1988) and Hayes (1993) have argued the position that movements play no role in the phonology.

11. Some readers may think that *sonority* is a spoken language term applied to sign languages inappropriately; it is intended to capture the role that perceptual salience plays in both signed and spoken languages, and is not tied to any particular phonetic realization of that salience.

12. Both CVC and CVV syllables are considered heavy syllables here, even though there are languages that call for an analysis of CVV syllables whereby the two vowels are both part of the nucleus.

13. I am aware that languages differ with respect to heavy-light distinctions, but I want to use the simplest case to make my point.

14. Lowercase letters represent feature bundles.

The movement connecting 'b' to 'c' is inserted by a rule of Movement Epenthesis, which is not relevant here.

15. GO-TO and ASK are a minimal pair in the HM Model, but there are only a handful of such pairs.

16. The Hand Configuration tier includes orientation, whereas handshape in Stokoe's model did not. Battison (1978) was the first to add orientation as a fourth phonological parameter.

17. Perlmutter (1992) does not discuss DANCE; I have extended his analysis to cover forms containing only a movement.

Chapter 3

1. Sandler argues that handshape has the properties of many-to-one association (e.g., two handshapes to one location in the sign UNDERSTAND), stability (e.g., the handshapes in one pronunciation of DON'T-LIKE remain stable, even though the other parts of the sign change), and morphological status (e.g., classifier handshapes are morphemes).

2. Wilbur (1993) uses the term *articulatory tier*, but she includes all of orientation, location, and handshape in the group of features dominated by this node.

3. In the sign EITHER (Long 1918) the H_2 handshape 'V' spreads to H_1.

4. The terms *aperture change, handshape contour,* and *allophonic handshape change* are equivalent and are used interchangeably in this book.

5. The 'animal face' classifier handshape, often cited as problematic for previous analyses of handshapes, can be handled in this system. The selected fingers are specified as having quantity features in a dependency relation, [one] dominating [all], and the point-of-reference feature is [mid]. The pinkie finger and index finger are nonselected fingers and are redundantly specified as [extended]. FRESHMAN and SOPHOMORE are specified with the same feature structure as the '7' and '8' handshapes, respectively, except that the nonselected fingers are open.

6. In the form HA-HA-HA, the extended thumb might also be a remnant of the fingerspelled 'A'.

7. This specific set of cases supports Sandler's (1996b) claim that the extended index finger is (at least one of) the least marked handshape(s). In the Prosodic Model, since [one] forms have a nonselected fingers specification and a feature specified under the $fingers_0$ node, they are not structurally the least marked form as Sandler claims.

8. *X, y,* and *z* are simply convenient labels. In mathematics, planes are defined either in terms of the plane in which two lines intersect (e.g., the x/z-plane, the y/z-plane, the y/x-plane) or by the set of points in the plane perpendicular to a particular line. The frontal, horizontal, and midsagittal planes are defined in the Prosodic Model by the points in the plane perpendicular to the line that refers to that dimension in space.

9. The idea of treating the body and the head as separate articulatory spaces was first discussed in Johnson 1994, and many of the places of articulation are adopted from Liddell and Johnson 1989.

10. For example, one place of articulation not exploited in ASL is the armpit, but this place is used in Langue des signes québecoise in the sign STUDENT.

11. Liddell and Johnson (1989) discuss one more contact, known as 'web' (e.g., FOOTBALL), but because H_1 contacts the radial side of each of the H_2 fingers, 'web' can be treated as a subclass of 'ulnar'.

Chapter 4

1. TELL also has a [direction] feature, which will be discussed later in the chapter.

2. As noted by Uyechi (1995, 127), direction of circular paths is not contrastive in ASL.

3. A large number of signs have an [arc] movement that is the result of the elbow's execution of a straight movement, specified as a [direction] feature (e.g., TELL, GIVE, LOOK-AT, SEE).

4. Recall from chapter 2 that the native lexicon is made up of the core lexemes, the classifier predicates, and the manual alphabet.

5. This form of CALL is used in utterances such as "Call me Diane."

6. In Japanese Sign Language these two verbs are a minimal pair for [direction].

7. English, by the way, does not typically encode the subordinate conceptual function overtly.

8. The back of the hand is either the base of the hand or the back of the hand, depending upon the orientation specification for the particular sign.

9. A reflexive verb form discussed by Meir (1995) has no counterpart in ASL, so I have no comments on this part of her analysis.

10. The representation of aperture changes and the nondominant hand have not yet been discussed, so they are not shown here.

11. When the subject is 2sg, the plane in which the reference locus is specified is a distal x-plane rather than a proximal x-plane. When the subject is 3sg, the possible x-planes in which the reference locus is specified form 60° angles to the x-plane associated with the signer's body:

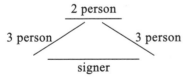

12. I have found no signs articulated in a midsagittal plane that are specified for proximal and distal settings.

13. In Brentari 1990b the constraint is stated as follows: "There may be a maximum of one [−peripheral] handshape per prosodic word."

14. Handshape assimilation from the second stem to the first, a common operation in compounds (Sandler 1989), has not occurred in these forms; rather, one of the handshapes of the handshape contour has been deleted in the first stem.

15. In Brentari 1990b,c I used the feature specification [peripheral] to capture the fact that fully open and fully closed handshapes are unmarked, but the feature geometry proposed here makes this specification unnecessary.

16. This constraint is violated in some fingerspelled loan signs (e.g., E-S-Y 'easy' and E-R-L-Y 'early').

17. This section summarizes the findings presented in Brentari 1996b. I wish to thank Robert E. Johnson, Scott Liddell, David Perlmutter, and Carol Padden for discussions and correspondence concerning the structure of the polymorphemic forms considered in this section.

18. The abbreviation *TM* comes from the term *trilled movement* (Padden and Perlmutter 1987) and from the abbreviation *TIM* (*trilled internal movement*) used in Sandler 1993c.

19. 'Rubbing' is included as a TM involving aperture change because it is produced with repeated changes in handshape from flat to closed, in addition to a thumb position change from opposed to unopposed.

20. There may actually be two types of closing. One would include changes in aperture, in signs such as MILK, where the fingers have the same specification for [spread] throughout the sign; the other would involve changes in the specification for [spread], in signs such as SAND-CRAB and CUT-WITH-SCISSORS.

21. There are other nonmanual signs that include rapidly repeated lip movements, such as one transcribed as 'bi, bi, bi', but the morphological role of these movements is less well understood, and only 'tongue wagging' will be discussed here.

22. This achievement of a target need not involve contact (i.e., touching another articulator); 'tremor' may take place in the neutral space in front of the signer (e.g., TOILET).

23. In the table, prose descriptions of various types of aspectual morphology are given. The labels for grammatical aspects used in Klima and Bellugi 1979 cover only a subset of these forms; it is with caution that I use square brackets as a way of noting the aspectual categories (e.g., [internal apportionative], since differentiating among these aspectual categories is sometimes difficult.

24. See Ebbinghaus and Hessman 1996 for a few exceptions to this claim in German Sign Language.

Chapter 5

1. Position segments in the μ Model and Location segments in the HT Model are considered roughly equivalent.

2. There are forms (e.g., LOCK, APPOINTMENT) that appear to be counter-examples to the right-to-left direction specified in the ALIGNMENT constraint. In these cases, the addition of a handshape change can be seen as a type of phonetic enhancement of the circular path movement; in both of these cases, a variant of these signs without the handshape change in the first movement exists.

3. The H_2 portion of the representations in (5), (6), (8), and (9), not included there, will be explained in chapter 7.

4. The shape of the first movement is not at issue here, so REMOVE (with two straight movements) and GOVERNMENT (with a circle and a straight movement) have been grouped together.

5. I have renamed Perlmutter's rule of Mora Insertion as phrase-final lengthening because even though I agree with the generalization of the facts he discusses, my analysis differs from his on two points. First, Perlmutter claims the environment is word-final, but it is in fact phrase-final; no lengthening occurs phrase-internally in this context (see Brentari 1990c for further discussion). Second, I disagree with Perlmutter about the timing unit needed for this lengthening operation.

6. In Brentari 1996b I called this [protractive/inceptive] aspect, but after discussing these forms with linguists studying Athapaskan languages, I concluded that [delayed completive] describes their use more accurately.

7. Davies (1983) proposes that the tongue wag and the finger wiggle are both structural components of the [protractive] aspect (i.e., the form in which the TM occurs throughout the movement); however, either part is sufficient to carry the relevant meaning.

8. There are still points of divergence among these models in the formulation of static units, but these are not addressed here. Also, the segments in question would have to be accessed after Tier Conflation in the HT Model, as described in Sandler 1993b.

9. It is important to point out here that Tier Conflation alone will not result in the correct surface distribution of handshapes-to-path movements when there is a mismatch in the number of handshape changes and path movements (e.g., DESTROY).

10. Weight units are described in chapter 6.

11. The form of ITALY used in this experiment was the older ASL form articulated at the forehead, not the newer form borrowed into ASL from Italian Sign Language.

Chapter 6

1. The terms *inherent sonority* and *derived sonority* are used differently here than they are in Goldsmith and Larson 1990 or in Goldsmith 1991, where *inherent sonority* refers to the sonority of a given feature (or segment) in isolation, and *derived sonority* refers to the sonority of a feature or segment within its local domain.

2. I do not, as Corina (1990b) does, claim that the form without phonetic enhancement, PERPLEXED(1), is ungrammatical; rather, I note that the enhanced forms are more commonly seen.

3. An exception can be found in Edmondson 1990, 1993.

4. The input form for the noun and the verb is taken to be the same here, following Supalla and Newport 1978 and Brentari 1990c,d.

5. This is a summary of one section of Brentari 1994.

6. I will postpone arguments for the ranking of these constraints until chapter 8, since they require introducing material extraneous to this discussion.

7. It is quite possible that there is a morphological/semantic component to the analysis of these forms as well. It is probably no accident that the forms that undergo nominalizing reduplication are all of a single semantic class; namely, each form has a specific handshape representing either a size and shape specifier or an instrument classifier, both of which contain detailed information about the object involved in the event.

8. Many other alternations involving movement repetition have been called reduplication (e.g., Uyechi 1995), but reduplication is defined here as an operation involving a single copy of a portion of the base, as it is defined in spoken languages. Other types of movement repetition—for example, in activity nouns and some grammatical aspect forms that involve many (often an uncountable number of) repetitions—are analyzed as using a [TM] feature.

9. Two possible counterexamples that belong in the set of signs in (18) are LEARNING (derived from LEARN) and ACQUISITION (derived from GET); both of these signs appear in some ASL dialects.

Chapter 7

1. I would like to thank the students at the Linguistic Society of America Summer Institute at the University of New Mexico, 1995, and participants in the sign language workshop at the annual meeting of the German Linguistic Society, Göttingen, 1995, for their helpful discussion of these issues. An earlier version of this chapter appeared as Brentari 1996a.

2. The term *rhyming* is used to describe the relationship between WHITE, BEAUTY, and INSIDE, because all features of these signs are the same except for place of articulation. In particular, the handshape and handshape changes are the same in all three signs.

3. Battison (1974) and Padden and Perlmutter (1987) consider WD to be a unified phenomenon, and this is also the position taken here.

4. Of course, when one hand is occupied, all signs can be made one-handed. The phenomenon analyzed here is one-handed variants of two-handed signs that are considered fully grammatical under normal signing conditions.

5. Both DEFEAT and REVENGE have also undergone additional restructuring of movement.

6. The relation between H_1 and H_2 in the structure proposed here bears similarities to the relation in the structures proposed by Ahn (1990), Wilbur (1993), and van der Hulst (1996).

7. These are representations of maximal structures. For example, not all type 1 signs are specified [symmetrical]; when no orientation feature is present in two-handed signs, the orientation is 'identical'.

8. Labeling this relation between H_1 and H_2 as "head-dependent asymmetry" was first proposed in van der Hulst 1996.

9. Thanks to Lorna Rozelle for pointing this sign out to me.

10. Since Padden and Perlmutter (1987) address only [alternating], not [contact], the analysis here does not contradict their findings, but instead extends them in a particular direction.

11. There is a great deal of dialectal and even idiolectal variation regarding which signs have acceptable Weak Drop outputs. In this section I discuss forms that have a high degree of acceptance among the native signers I have surveyed.

12. Van der Hulst (1996) analyzes H_2 as a weak prosodic branch of structure, making no further claim about whether this weak branch is of the syllable or of the prosodic word.

13. The account proposed in van der Hulst 1996 is quite similar to the one proposed here.

14. This is an optional operation. Often the one-handed sign in the first-stem position remains one-handed.

Chapter 8

1. The HM and the HT Models are the only ones discussed here because my goal is to clarify the insights of the Prosodic Model with respect to the two models that are most widely used.

2. Van der Hulst (1993) and Wilbur and Petersen (1997) also propose a two-slot timing structure.

3. Perlmutter (1992) treats movement as a higher-order prosodic unit as well; but see chapter 6 for relevant points of similarity and difference between the Prosodic Model and the model proposed by Perlmutter.

4. Only native signers or Deaf individuals who have been signing since 2–4 years of age should be consulted as linguistic informants. This is absolutely necessary when lexical innovation data are gathered.

5. There are other types of forms that undergo nativization, such as nonmanual elements and forms form other sign languages, but those types of borrowings are not addressed here.

6. Open, bent, flat, and curved joint specifications for handshape are analyzed in chapter 3; these are merely descriptive labels here.

7. Given the Prosodic Model's view that in the fundamental signing position the hands are oriented toward the midsagittal plane, this operation is quite natural.

8. In current versions of Optimality Theory, FAITHFULNESS is a family of constraints called IDENTITY (McCarthy and Prince 1995), but here I use the older, more familiar term FAITHFULNESS.

9. Two explanatory remarks about this well-formed candidate are in order. First, the movement realized in the output form is a trilled movement—namely, flattening. Second, '8' is a conventionalized, shorthand way of notating a handshape with the middle finger selected and nonselected fingers open. The handshape change [open], [closed] with this set of selected fingers indicates an output form that rapidly changes from having all of the fingers extended (just like 'B') to one

where the middle finger is flattened. The extended index finger approximates the 'D'. This handshape change within the form became a handshape merger in which the [extended] nonselected fingers result in the 'B' and 'D' of 'bread' and the selected finger [mid] rapidly opens and closes.

10. This definition purposely leaves aside classifier predicates, which combine movement roots and affixes (Supalla 1982).

11. There is a set of derived signs that do not contain a movement (e.g., STARE).

12. The term *equivalent* means that the respective visual and auditory stimuli are processed by the magnocellular subsystem (i.e., the "fast" subsystem, discussed in subsequent paragraphs) in both vision and audition.

13. This type of minimal pair can also be expressed in the HT Model and in recent revisions of the HM Model.

References

Aarons, D., B. J. Bahan, J. Kegl, and C. Neidle. 1992. Clausal structure and a tier for grammatical marking in American Sign Language. *Nordic Journal of Linguistics* 15(2), 103–142.

Aarons, D., B. J. Bahan, J. Kegl, and C. Neidle. 1995. Lexical tense markers in American Sign Language. In Emmorey and Reilly 1995.

Ahn, S.-H. 1990. A structured-tiers model for ASL phonology. In Lucas 1990.

Anderson, J., and C. J. Ewen 1987. *Principles of Dependency Phonology*. Cambridge: Cambridge University Press.

Anderson, S. 1993. Expression and its relation to modality. In Coulter 1993.

Ann, J. 1992. Physiological constraints in Taiwan Sign Language handshape-change. *Nordic Journal of Linguistics* 15(2), 143–157.

Ann, J. 1996. On the relation between ease of articulation and frequency of occurrence of handshape in two sign languages. *Lingua* 98, 19–41.

Archangeli, D., and D. Pulleyblank. 1994. *Grounded Phonology*. Cambridge, Mass: MIT Press.

Askins, D., and D. Perlmutter. 1995. Allomorphy explained through phonological representation: Person and number inflection of American Sign Language. Paper presented at the annual meeting of the German Linguistic Society, Göttingen.

Bahan, B. 1996. *Non-manual realization of agreement in American Sign Language*. Doctoral dissertation, Boston University, Boston, Mass.

Bagemihl, B. 1991. Syllable structure in Bella Coola. *Linguistic Inquiry* 22, 589–646.

Battistella, E. L. 1990. *Markedness: The evaluative superstructure of language*. Albany, N.Y.: SUNY Press.

Battison, R. 1974. Phonological deletion in American Sign Language. *Sign Language Studies* 5, 1–19.

Battison, R. 1978. *Lexical borrowing in American Sign Language*. Silver Spring, Md.: Linstok Press.

Bienvenu, M. J., and B. Colonomos. 1987. *Introduction to American Deaf culture*. Vol. 2, *Values*. Burtonsville, Md.: Sign Media Inc.

Blevins, J. 1993. The nature of constraints on the nondominant hand in ASL. In Coulter 1993.

Bloomfield, L. 1933. *Language*. New York: Henry Holt.

Bos, H. 1990. Person and location marking in Sign Language of the Netherlands: Some implications of a spatially expressed syntactic system. In Prillwitz and Vollhabor 1990.

Bos, H., and T. Schermer, eds. 1995. *Sign language research 1994*. Hamburg: Signum Verlag.

Bosch, A. 1991. Phonotactics at the level of the phonological word. Doctoral dissertation, University of Chicago, Chicago, Ill.

Boyes-Braem, P. 1981. Distinctive features of the handshapes of American Sign Language. Doctoral dissertation, University of California, Berkeley.

Boyes-Braem, P. 1990. *Einführung in die Gebärdensprache und ihre Erforschung* [Introduction to sign language and sign language research]. Hamburg: Signum Verlag.

Boyes-Braem, P. 1995. The use of "Mundbilder" as prosodic cues in Swiss German Sign Language. Paper presented at the Linguistic Society of America Summer Institute, Albuquerque, N.M.

Bregman, A. S. 1990. *Auditory scene analysis*. Cambridge, Mass.: MIT Press.

Brentari, D. 1988. Backwards verbs in ASL: Agreement re-opened. In *CLS 24*. Vol. 2, *Parasession on Agreement in Grammatical Theory*. Chicago Linguistic Society, University of Chicago, Chicago, Ill.

Brentari, D. 1990a. Co-extensive moras in American Sign Language syllable structure. Paper presented at the annual meeting of the Linguistic Society of America, Chicago, Ill.

Brentari, D. 1990b. Licensing in ASL handshape. In Lucas 1990.

Brentari, D. 1990c. Theoretical foundations of American Sign Language phonology. Doctoral dissertation, University of Chicago, Chicago, Ill. [Published 1993 by University of Chicago Occasional Papers in Linguistics, Chicago, Ill.]

Brentari, D. 1990d. Underspecification in American Sign Language phonology. In *Proceedings of the 16th Annual Meeting of the Berkeley Linguistics Society*. Berkeley Linguistics Society, University of California, Berkeley.

Brentari, D. 1992: Phonological representation in American Sign Language. *Language* 68, 359–374.

Brentari, D. 1993. Establishing a sonority hierarchy in American Sign Language: The use of simultaneous structure in phonology. *Phonology* 10, 281–306.

Brentari, D. 1994. Prosodic constraints in American Sign Language. In *Proceedings of the 20th Annual Meeting of the Berkeley Linguistics Society*. Berkeley Linguistics Society, University of California, Berkeley. [Reprinted in Bos and Schermer 1995.]

Brentari, D. 1995. Sign language phonology: ASL. In Goldsmith 1995.

Brentari, D. 1996a. Eine prosodische Beschreibung zweihändiger Gebärden in ASL [A prosodic analysis of two-handed signs in ASL]. *Das Zeichen* 37, 372–386.

Brentari, D. 1996b. Trilled movement: Phonetic realization and formal representation. *Lingua* 98, 43–71.

Brentari, D. In press. Relations between core and periphery in American Sign Language phonology. In *Proceedings from WECOL 1996*. California State University, Fresno.

Brentari, D., and J. Goldsmith. 1993. Secondary licensing and the nondominant hand in ASL phonology. In Coulter 1993.

Brentari, D., and H. Poizner. 1994. A phonological analysis of a Deaf Parkinsonian signer. *Language and Cognitive Processes* 9(1), 69–99.

Brentari, D., H. Poizner, and J. Kegl. 1995. Aphasic and Parkinsonian signing: Differences in phonological disruption. *Brain and Language* 48, 69–105.

Brentari, D., H. van der Hulst, E. van der Klooij, and W. Sandler. 1996. [One] over [all]; [All] over [one]: A dependency phonology analysis of handshape in sign languages. Ms., University of California, Davis, University of Leiden, and Haifa University.

Browman, C. P., and L. Goldstein. 1989. Articulatory gestures as phonological units. *Phonology* 6, 201–251.

Cassimjee, F. 1983. An autosegmental analysis of Venda phonology. *Studies in the Linguistic Sciences* 13(1), 43–72.

Chamberlain, C., J. P. Morford, and R. I. Mayberry, eds. 1998. Language acquisition by eye. Mahwah, N.J.: Lawrence Erlbaum.

Chase, C., and A. R. Jenner. 1993. Magnocellular visual deficits affect temporal processing of dyslexics. In Tallal, Galaburda, Llinás, and von Euler 1993.

Chinchor, N. 1978. The syllable in ASL. Paper presented at the Sign Language Symposium, MIT, Cambridge, Mass.

Chomsky, N. 1957. *Syntactic structures*. The Hague: Mouton.

Chomsky, N., and M. Halle. 1968. *The sound pattern of English*. New York: Harper and Row.

Christdas, P. 1988. The phonology and morphology of Tamil. Doctoral dissertation, Cornell University, Ithaca, N.Y.

Clements, G. N. 1985. The geometry of phonological features. *Phonology Yearbook* 2, 225–252.

Clements, G. N. 1990. The role of the sonority cycle in core syllabification. In J. Kingson and M. Beckman, eds., *Between the grammar and the physics of speech: Papers in laboratory phonology 1*. New York: Cambridge University Press.

Clements, G. N. 1991. Vowel height assimilation in Bantu languages. In *Proceedings of the 17th Annual Meeting of the Berkeley Linguistics Society: Special Session on African Language Structures*. Berkeley Linguistics Society, University of California, Berkeley.

Clements, G. N., and S. J. Keyser. 1983. *CV phonology: A generative theory of the syllable*. Cambridge, Mass.: MIT Press.

Comrie, B. 1978. Ergativity. In W. Lehman, ed., *Syntactic typology*. Austin: University of Texas Press.

Comrie, B. 1981. *Language universals and linguistic typology*. Chicago: University of Chicago Press.

Conlin, K. E., G. R. Mirus, C. Mauk, and R. Meier. 1998. Acquisition of first signs: Place, handshape and movement. In Chamberlain, Morford, and Mayberry 1998.

Corina, D. 1990a. Handshape assimilation in hierarchical phonological representations. In Lucas 1990.

Corina, D. 1990b. Reassessing the role of sonority in syllable structure: Evidence from a visual-gestural language. In Ziolkowski, Noske, and Deaton 1990.

Corina, D. 1993. To branch or not to branch: Underspecification in ASL handshape contours. In Coulter 1993.

Corina, D., H. Poizner, U. Bellugi, T. Feinberg, D. Dowd, and L. O'Grady-Batch. 1992. Dissociation between linguistic and non-linguistic gestural systems: A case for compositionality. *Brain and Language* 43, 414–447.

Corina, D., and W. Sandler. 1993. On the nature of phonological structure in sign language. *Phonology* 10(2), 165–207.

Coulter, G. 1982. On the nature of ASL as a monosyllabic language. Paper presented at the annual meeting of the Linguistic Society of America, San Diego, Calif.

Coulter, G., ed. 1993. *Phonetics and phonology*. Vol. 3, *Current issues in ASL phonology*. San Diego, Calif.: Academic Press.

Crasborn, O. 1995. Articulatory symmetry in two-handed signs. M.A. thesis, University of Nijmegen.

Crasborn, O., and E. van der Kooij. 1997. Relative orientation in sign language phonology. In J. Coerts and H. de Hoop, eds., *Linguistics in the Netherlands 1997*, 37–48. Amsterdam: John Benjamins.

Damasio, A. R. 1994. *Descartes' error: Emotion, reason, and the human brain*. New York: G. P. Putnam.

Damasio, H., and A. R. Damasio. 1980. The anatomical basis of conduction aphasia. *Brain* 103, 337–350.

Davies, S. 1983. The tongue is quicker than the eye: Nonmanual behaviors in ASL. In W. Stokoe and V. Volterra, eds., *Proceedings of the Third International Symposium on Sign Language Research*. Silver Spring, Md.: Linstok Press.

Davis, B. L., and P. MacNeilage. 1995. The articulatory basis of babbling. *Journal of Speech and Hearing Research* 48, 1199–1211.

Davis, S. 1990. The onset as a constituent of the syllable: Evidence from Italian. In Ziolkowsi, Noske, and Deaton 1990.

Davis, S. 1991. Coronals and the phonotactics of non-adjacent consonants. In Paradis and Prunet 1991.

DeLancey, S. 1981. An interpretation of split ergativity and related patterns. *Language* 57, 626–656.

Dell, F., and M. Elmedlaoui. 1985. Syllabic consonants and syllabification in Imdlawn Tashlhiyt Berber. *Journal of African Language and Linguistics* 7, 769–773.

Desouvrey, L.-H. 1994, Les classes de verbes en langue des signes québecoise. M.A. thesis, Université du Québec à Montréal.

Docherty, G. J., and D. R. Ladd, eds. 1992. *Gesture, segment, prosody: Papers in laboratory phonology II.* New York: Cambridge University Press.

Dotter, F., and D. Holzinger. 1994. Typologie und Gebärdensprache. Ms., University of Klagenfurt.

Dresher, E., and H. van der Hulst. 1994. Head-dependent asymmetries in phonology. Ms., University of Toronto and Leiden University.

Ebbinghaus, H., and J. Hessman. 1996. Signs and words: Accounting for spoken language elements in German Sign Language. In W. Edmondson and R. Wilbur, eds., *International review of sign linguistics I.* Hillsdale, N.J.: Lawrence Erlbaum.

Edmondson, W. 1990. Segments in signed languages: Do they exist and does it matter? In W. Edmondson, ed., *SLR '87: Papers from the 4th International Symposium on Sign Language Research.* Hamburg: Signum Verlag.

Edmondson, W. 1993. Segments, morphemes, syllables and signs. Paper presented at the Workshop on Sign Language Phonology and Morphology, Amsterdam and Leiden.

Emmorey, K., and J. Reilly, eds. 1995. *Language, gesture, and space.* Hillsdale, N.J.: Lawrence Erlbaum.

Engberg-Pederson, E. 1993. *Space in Danish Sign Language.* Hamburg: Signum Verlag.

Firth, J. R. 1957. Sounds and prosodies. In *Papers in linguistics, 1934–1957.* Oxford: Oxford University Press.

Fischer, S. 1996. The role of agreement and auxiliaries in sign language. *Lingua* 98, 103–110.

Fischer, S., and W. Janis. 1990. Verb sandwiches in American Sign Language. In Prillwitz and Vollhaber 1990.

Fischer, S., and P. Siple, eds. 1990. *Theoretical issues in sign language research, vol. 2.* Chicago: University of Chicago Press.

Friedman, L. 1976. Phonology of a soundless language: Phonological structure of American Sign Language. Doctoral dissertation, University of California, Berkeley.

Friedman, L. 1977. Formational properties of American Sign Language. In L. Friedman, ed., *On the other hand: New perspectives in American Sign Language.* New York: Academic Press.

Frishberg, N. 1975. Arbitrariness and iconicity. *Language* 51, 696–719.

Fukazawa, H., and V. Miglio. In press. Restricting conjunction to constraint families. In *Proceedings from WECOL 1996*. California State University, Fresno.

Galaburda, A., and M. Livingstone. 1993. Evidence for a magnocellular defect in developmental dyslexia. In Tallal, Galaburda, Llinás, and von Euler 1993.

Goldsmith, J. 1976. Autosegmental phonology. Doctoral dissertation, MIT, Cambridge, Mass. [Published 1979, Garland Press, New York.]

Goldsmith, J. 1989. Licensing, inalterability, and harmonic rule application. In *CLS 25*. Vol. 1, *The General Session*. Chicago Linguistic Society, University of Chicago, Chicago, Ill.

Goldsmith, J. 1990. *Autosegmental and metrical phonology: A new synthesis*. Oxford: Blackwell.

Goldsmith, J. 1991. Phonology as an intelligent system. In D. J. Napoli and J. Kegl, eds., *Bridges between psychology and linguistics: A Swarthmore festschrift for Lila Gleitman*. Hillsdale, N.J.: Lawrence Erlbaum.

Goldsmith, J. 1992a. Local modeling in phonology. In S. Davis, ed., *Connectionism: Theory and practice*. Oxford: Oxford University Press.

Goldsmith, J. 1992b. Tone and accent in Llogoori. In D. Brentari, G. Larson, and L. MacLeod, eds., *The joy of syntax*. Amsterdam: John Benjamins.

Goldsmith, J. 1993a. Harmonic phonology. In Goldsmith 1993b.

Goldsmith, J., ed. 1993b. *The last phonological rule*. Chicago: University of Chicago Press.

Goldsmith, J., ed. 1995. *A handbook of phonological theory*. Oxford: Blackwell.

Goldsmith, J. 1996. Tone in Mituku: How a floating tone nailed down an intermediate level. In J. Durand and B. Laks, eds., *Current trends in phonology: Models and methods*, CNRS, Université de Paris-X, and University of Salford Publications, University of Salford.

Goldsmith, J., and G. Larson. 1990. Local modeling and syllabification. In Ziolkowski, Noske, and Deaton 1990.

Goodglass, H., and E. Kaplan. 1972. *The assessment of aphasia and related disorders*. Chicago: Lea and Febiger.

Green, D. M. 1971. Temporal auditory acuity. *Psychological Review* 78, 540–551.

Greftegreff, I. 1993. Distinctive features in NTS [Norwegian Sign Language] handshapes. Paper presented at the Workshop on Sign Language Phonology and Morphology, Amsterdam and Leiden.

Guerssel, M. 1986. Glides in Berber and syllabicity. *Linguistic Inquiry* 17, 1–12.

Halle, M. 1959. *The sound pattern of Russian*. The Hague: Mouton.

Halle, M. 1986. On distinctive features and their articulatory implementation. *Natural Language & Linguistic Theory* 1, 91–105.

Halle, M. 1995. Feature geometry and feature spreading. *Linguistic Inquiry* 26, 1–46.

Halle, M., and J.-R. Vergnaud. 1987. *An essay on stress*. Cambridge, Mass.: MIT Press.

Harris, J. 1983. *Syllable structure and stress in Spanish*. Cambridge, Mass.: MIT Press.

Haugen, E. 1949. Phoneme or prosodeme. *Language* 25, 278–282.

Hayes, B. 1981. A metrical theory of stress rules. Doctoral dissertation, MIT, Cambridge, Mass. [Published 1985, Garland Press, New York.]

Hayes, B. 1989. Compensatory lengthening in moraic phonology. *Linguistic Inquiry* 20, 253–306.

Hayes, B. 1993. Against movement. In Coulter 1993.

Hayes, B. 1995. *Metrical theory*. Chicago: University of Chicago Press.

Hirsh, I. J., and C. E. Sherrick. 1961. Perceived order in different sense modalities. *Journal of Experimental Psychology* 62, 423–432.

Hockett, C. 1954. Two models of grammatical description. *Word* 10, 210–231.

Hoek, K. van. 1992. Conceptual spaces and pronominal reference in American Sign Language. *Nordic Journal of Linguistics* 15(2), 183–199.

Hooper, J. 1972. The syllable in phonological theory. *Language* 48, 525–540.

Hubel, D. H., and T. N. Wiesel. 1959. Receptive fields of single neurones in the cat's striate cortex. *Journal of Physiology* (London) 148, 574–591.

Hubel, D. H., and T. N. Wiesel. 1962. Receptive fields, binocular interaction and functional architecture in the cat's visual cortex. *Journal of Physiology* (London) 160, 106–154.

Hulst, H. van der. 1993. Units in the analysis of signs. *Phonology* 10(2), 209–241.

Hulst, H. van der. 1995. The composition of handshapes. In *Working papers in linguistics 23*. Department of Linguistics, University of Trondheim, Dragvoll.

Hulst, H. van der. 1996. On the other hand. *Lingua* 98, 121–143.

Hulst, H. van der, and A. Mills. 1996. Issues in sign linguistics: Phonetics, phonology and morpho-syntax. *Lingua* 98, 3–17.

Hulst, H. van der, and W. Sandler. 1994. Phonological theories meet sign language: Two theories of the two hands. In C. Dyck, ed., *Toronto working papers in linguistics*. The Linguistics Graduate Course Union, Department of Linguistics, University of Toronto.

Hulst, H. van der, and N. Smith, eds. 1982. *The structure of phonological representation*. 2 vols. Dordrecht: Foris.

Humphries, T. C., C. Padden, and T. J. O'Rourke. 1994. *A basic course in American Sign Language*. Silver Spring, Md.: T. J. Publishers.

Hyman, L. 1985. *A theory of phonological weight*. Dordrecht: Foris.

Itô, J. 1986. Syllable theory in prosodic phonology. Doctoral dissertation, University of Massachusetts, Amherst. [Published 1989, Garland Press, New York.]

Itô, J., and A. Mester. 1995a. Japanese phonology. In Goldsmith 1995.

Itô, J., and A. Mester. 1995b. The core-periphery structure of the lexicon and constraints on reranking. In *University of Massachusetts occasional papers 18: Papers in Optimality Theory*. Graduate Linguistic Student Association, University of Massachusetts, Amherst.

Jackendoff, R. 1987. The status of thematic relations in linguistic theory. *Linguistic Inquiry* 18, 369–411.

Jacobowitz, E. L., and W. Stokoe. 1988. Signs of tense in ASL verbs. *Sign Language Studies* 60, 331–340.

Jakobson, R. 1968 [1941]. *Child language, aphasia and phonological universals*. The Hague: Mouton.

Jakobson, R. 1984 [1939]. The zero sign. In. L. R. Waugh and M. Halle, eds., *Russian and slavic grammar studies 1931–1981*. The Hague: Mouton.

Jakobson, R., G. Fant, and M. Halle. 1951 [reprinted 1972]. *Preliminaries to speech analysis*. Cambridge, Mass.: MIT Press.

Jakobson, R., and M. Halle. 1956 [reprinted 1971]. *Fundamentals of language*. The Hague: Mouton.

Jeannerod, M. 1994. The representing brain: Neural correlates of motor intention and imagery. *Behavioral and Brain Sciences* 17, 182–245.

Johnson, R. E. 1986. Metathesis in American Sign Language. Paper presented at the Theoretical Issues in Sign Language Research I Conference, Rochester, N.Y.

Johnson, R. E. 1990. Distinctive features for handshape in American Sign Language. Paper presented at the Theoretical Issues in Sign Language Research III Conference, Boston, Mass.

Johnson, R. E. 1993. Lexical movement segments: Evidence from lexicalized fingerspelling. Paper presented at the Workshop on Sign Language Phonology and Morphology, Amsterdam and Leiden.

Johnson, R. E. 1994. Handshape features in American Sign Language. Ms., Gallaudet University, Washington, D.C.

Johnson, R. E., and S. Liddell. 1984. Structural diversity in the American Sign Language lexicon. In *CLS 20*. Vol. 1, *The General Session*. Chicago Linguistic Society, University of Chicago, Chicago, Ill.

Kager, R. 1989. *A metrical theory of stressing and destressing in English and Dutch*. Dordrecht: Foris.

Kegl, J. 1985. Locative relations in American Sign Language word formation, syntax, and discourse. Doctoral dissertation, MIT, Cambridge, Mass.

Kegl, J., A. Senghas, and M. E. V. Coppola. 1995. Creation through contact: Sign language emergence and sign language in Nicaragua. In M. de Graff, ed., *Comparative grammatical change: The intersection of language acquisition, creole genesis, and diachronic syntax*. Cambridge, Mass.: MIT Press.

Kenstowicz, M. 1994. *Phonology in generative grammar*. Oxford: Blackwell.

Kimura, D. 1993. *Neuromotor mechanisms in human communication.* Oxford: Oxford University Press.

Kiparsky, P. 1979. Metrical structure assignment is cyclic. *Linguistic Inquiry* 10, 421–442.

Kiparsky, P. 1982. Lexical phonology and morphology. In I. S. Yang, ed., *Linguistics in the morning calm.* Seoul: Hanshin.

Klima, E., and U. Bellugi. 1979. *The signs of language.* Cambridge, Mass.: Harvard University Press.

Kohlrausch, A., D. Püschel, and H. Alphei. 1992. Temporal resolution and modulation analysis in models of the auditory system. In M. E. H. Schouten, ed., *The auditory processes of speech: From sounds to words.* Berlin: Mouton de Gruyter.

LaCharité, D. 1993. On the need for negative constraints and repair: Constraint mutation in Setswana. *The Linguistic Review* 6, 257–278.

LaCharité, D., and C. Paradis. 1993. Introduction. *The Canadian Journal of Linguistics* 38(2), 127–153.

Landau, B., and R. Jackendoff. 1993. "What" and "where" in spatial language and spatial cognition. *Behavioral and Brain Sciences* 16, 217–265.

Lane, H. 1984. *When the mind hears.* New York: Random House.

Levins, J. 1985. A metrical theory of syllabicity. Doctoral dissertation, MIT, Cambridge, Mass.

Liddell, S. 1984a. THINK and BELIEVE: Sequentiality in American Sign Language. *Language* 60, 372–392.

Liddell, S. 1984b. Unrealized-inceptive aspect in American Sign Language: Feature insertion in syllabic frames. In *CLS 20.* Vol. 1, *The General Session.* Chicago Linguistic Society, University of Chicago, Chicago, Ill.

Liddell, S. 1990a. Four functions of a locus: Re-examining the structure of space in ASL. In Lucas 1990.

Liddell, S. 1990b. Structures for representing handshape and local movement at the phonemic level. In Fischer and Siple 1990.

Liddell, S. 1993. Holds and positions: Comparing two models of segmentation in ASL. In Coulter 1993.

Liddell, S. 1995. Real, surrogate, and token space. In Emmorey and Reilly 1995.

Liddell, S., and R. E. Johnson. 1983. American Sign Language: The phonological base. Ms., Gallaudet University, Washington, D.C.

Liddell, S., and R. E. Johnson. 1986. American Sign Language compound formation processes, lexicalization, and phonological remnants. *Natural Language & Linguistic Theory* 4, 445–513.

Lieberman, P., E. Kako, J. Friedman, G. Tajchman, L. S. Feldman, and E. B. Jiminez. 1992. Speech production, syntax comprehension, and cognitive deficits in Parkinson's disease. Ms., Brown University, Providence. R.I.

Livingstone, M., and D. Hubel. 1984. Anatomy and physiology of a color system in the primate visual cortex. *Journal of Neuroscience* 4, 309–356.

Livingstone, M., and D. Hubel. 1987a. Connections between layer 4b of area 17 and thick cytochrome oxidase stripes of area 18 in the squirrel monkey. *Journal of Neuroscience* 7, 3371–3377.

Livingstone, M., and D. Hubel. 1987b. Psychophysical evidence for separate channels for the perception of form, color, movement and depth. *Journal of Neuroscience* 7, 3416–3468.

Livingstone, M., and D. Hubel. 1987c. Segregation of form, color, and stereopsis in primate area 18. *Journal of Neuroscience* 7, 3378–3415.

Livingstone, M., and D. Hubel. 1988. Segregation of form, color, movement and depth: Anatomy, physiology, and perception. *Science* 240, 740–749.

Locke, J. 1993. *The child's path to spoken language.* Cambridge, Mass.: Harvard University Press.

Loew, R., H. Poizner, and J. Kegl. 1995. Flattening of distinctions in a Parkinsonian signer. *Aphasiology* 9(4), 381–396.

Lombardi, L. 1990. The non-linear order of the affricate. *Natural Language & Linguistic Theory* 8, 375–426.

Long, J. S. 1918 [reprinted 1963]. *The sign language: a manual of signs.* Washington, D.C.: Gallaudet University Press.

Lucas, C., ed. 1990. *Sign language research: Theoretical issues.* Washington, D.C.: Gallaudet University Press.

Lucas, C. 1995. Sociolinguistic variation in ASL: The case of DEAF. In Bos and Schermer 1995.

Luttgens, K., and N. Hamilton. 1997. *Kinesiology: Scientific basis of human motion.* 9th ed. Dubuque, Iowa: Brown and Benchmark.

MacNeilage, P., R. Hanson, and R. Krones. 1970. Control of the jaw in relation to stress in English. *Journal of the Acoustic Society of America* 48, 120 (abstract).

Mandel, M. A. 1981. Phonotactics and morphophonology in American Sign Language. Doctoral dissertation, University of California, Berkeley.

Marentette, P. 1995. It's in her hands: A case study of the emergence of phonology in American Sign Language. Doctoral dissertation, McGill University, Montreal.

Marentette, P. 1996. The emergence of phonology in American Sign Language: A case study. Paper presented at the Theoretical Issues in Sign Language Research Conference, Montreal.

Mattingly, I., and A. Liberman. 1988. Specialized perceiving systems for speech and other biologically significant sounds. In G. Edelman, W. Enar Gall, and W. Maxwell Cowen, eds., *Auditory function: Neurobiological bases of hearing.* New York: Wiley.

McCarthy, J. 1986. OCP effects: Gemination and antigemination. *Linguistic Inquiry* 17, 207–263.

McCarthy, J. 1997. Sympathy and phonological theory. Paper presented at the Hopkins Optimality Theory Workshop/Maryland Mayfest '97, Baltimore, Md.

McCarthy, J., and A. Prince. 1986. Prosodic Morphology. Ms., University of Massachusetts, Amherst, and Rutgers University, New Brunswick, N.J.

McCarthy, J., and A. Prince. 1993a. Generalized alignment. Ms., University of Massachusetts, Amherst, and Rutgers University, New Brunswick, N.J.

McCarthy, J., and A. Prince. 1993b. Prosodic Morphology II: Constraint interaction and satisfaction. Ms., University of Massachusetts, Amherst, and Rutgers University, New Brunswick, N.J.

McCarthy, J., and A. Prince. 1994. Emergence of the unmarked: Optimality in Prosodic Morphology. In *NELS 24*. Graduate Linguistic Student Association, University of Massachusetts, Amherst.

McCarthy, J., and A. Prince. 1995. Faithfulness and reduplicative identity. In *University of Massachusetts occasional papers 18: Papers in Optimality Theory*. Graduate Linguistic Student Association, University of Massachusetts, Amherst.

McDonald, B. 1982. Aspects of the American Sign Language predicate system. Doctoral dissertation, University of Buffalo, Buffalo, N.Y.

McIntire, M. 1977. The acquisition of American Sign Language hand configurations. *Sign Language Studies* 16, 247–266.

Meier, R., and R. Willerman. 1995. Pre-linguistic gesture in deaf and hearing infants. In Emmorey and Reilly 1995.

Meir, I. 1995. Syntactic-semantic interaction in Israeli Sign Language verbs: The case of backwards verbs. In Bos and Schermer 1995.

Mester, A. 1994. The quantitative trochee in Latin. *Natural Language & Linguistic Theory* 12, 1–61.

Miller, C. 1996. Phonologie de la langue des signes québecoise: Structure simultanée et axe temporel. Doctoral dissertation, Université du Québec à Montreal.

Milner, A. D., and M. A. Goodale. 1995. *The visual brain in action*. New York: Oxford University Press.

Mohanan, K. P. 1986. *Lexical phonology*. Dordrecht: Reidel.

Moravcsik, E., and J. Wirth. 1986. Markedness: An overview. In F. Eckman, E. Moravcsik, and J. Wirth, eds., *Markedness*. New York: Plenum Press.

Nadeau, M. 1993. Y a-t-il un ordre des signes en LSQ? In C. Dubuisson and M. Nadeau, eds., *Études sur la langue des signes québecoise*. Montreal: Les Presses de l'Université de Montréal.

Nespor, M., and I. Vogel. 1986. *Prosodic phonology*. Dordrecht: Foris.

Ohala, J. 1990. Alternatives to the sonority hierarchy for explaining segmental sequential constraints. In Ziolkowski, Noske, and Deaton 1990.

Ohala, J., and H. Kawasaki. 1984. Phonetics and prosodic phonology. *Phonology Yearbook* 1, 113–127.

Padden, C. 1983. Interaction of morphology and syntax in American Sign Language. Doctoral dissertation, University of California, San Diego. [Published 1988, Garland Press, New York.]

Padden, C. 1990. The relation between space and grammar in ASL verb morphology. In Lucas 1990.

Padden, C. 1995. Foreign words borrowed into sign languages. Paper presented at the Linguistic Society of America Summer Institute, Albuquerque, N.M.

Padden, C. 1998. American Sign Language and reading ability in Deaf children. In Chamberlain, Morford, and Mayberry 1998.

Padden, C. In press. The ASL lexicon. *International Review of Sign Linguistics.*

Padden, C., and D. Perlmutter. 1987. American Sign Language and the architecture of phonological theory. *Natural Language & Linguistic Theory* 5, 335–375.

Paradis, C. 1988. On constraints and repair strategies. *The Linguistic Review* 6, 71–97.

Paradis, C. 1989. On coronal transparency. *Phonology* 6, 317–349.

Paradis, C., and J.-F. Prunet, eds. 1991. *Phonetics and phonology.* Vol. 2, *On the special status of coronals.* San Diego, Calif.: Academic Press.

Perkell, J. S., and D. H. Klatt, eds. 1986. *Invariance and variability in speech processes.* Hillsdale, N.J.: Lawrence Erlbaum.

Perlmutter, D. 1990. On the segmental representation of transitional and bidirectional movements in ASL phonology. In Fischer and Siple 1990.

Perlmutter, D. 1991a. Prosodic vs. segmental structure: A moraic theory of American Sign Language syllable structure. Ms., University of California, San Diego.

Perlmutter, D. 1991b. Representing the non-dominant hand. Presentation at the Linguistic Society of America Summer Institute, Santa Cruz, Calif.

Perlmutter. D. 1992. Sonority and syllable structure in American Sign Language. *Linguistic Inquiry* 23, 407–442.

Perlmutter, D. 1993. Why ASL syllable structure is like that of oral language. Paper presented at the Worskhop on Sign Language Morphology and Phonology, Amsterdam and Leiden.

Perlmutter, D. 1995. The mora in phonological theory. In Goldsmith 1995.

Petitto, L. 1987. On the autonomy of language and gesture: Evidence from the acquisition of personal pronouns in American Sign Language. *Cognition* 27, 1–52.

Petitto, L. A., and P. Marentette. 1991. Babbling in the manual mode: Evidence for the ontogeny of language. *Science* 251, 1493–1496.

Pizzuto, E. 1987. Aspetti morfo-syntattici. In Volterra 1987.

Poizner, H., E. Klima, and U. Bellugi. 1987. *What the hands reveal about the brain.* Cambridge, Mass.: MIT Press.

Poizner, H. 1990. Language and motor disorders in deaf signers. In G. E. Hammond, ed., *Cerebral control of speech and limb movement*. Amsterdam: North-Holland.

Poizner, H., L. Mack, M. Verfaillie, L. Rothi, and K. M. Heilman. 1990. Three-dimensional computergraphic analysis of apraxia: Neural representations of learned movements. *Brain* 111, 282–307.

Prillwitz, S., R. Leven, H. Zienert, T. Hanke, and J. Henning. 1989. *Hamburg notation system for sign language: An introduction*. Hamburg: Signum Verlag.

Prillwitz, S., and T. Vollhabor, eds. 1990. *Current trends in European sign language research*. Hamburg: Signum Verlag.

Prince, A. 1983. Relating to the grid. *Linguistic Inquiry* 14, 19–100.

Prince, A. 1984. Phonology with tiers. In M. Aronoff and R. Oehrle, eds., *Language sound structure*. Cambridge, Mass.: MIT Press.

Prince, A., and P. Smolensky. 1993. Optimality Theory. Technical Report 2, Rutgers University Center for Cognitive Science, Rutgers University, New Brunswick, N.J.

Reilly, J., M. McIntire, and U. Bellugi. 1990. The acquisition of conditionals in American Sign Language development: Facial expression. *Applied Psycholinguistics* 11, 369–392.

Ross. J. R. 1967. Constraints on variables in syntax. Doctoral dissertation, MIT, Cambridge, Mass. [Distributed by Indiana University Linguistics Club, Bloomington.]

Sagey, E. 1986. The representation of features and relations in nonlinear phonology. Doctoral dissertation, MIT, Cambridge, Mass. [Published 1990, Garland Press, New York.]

Sainburg, R., M. F. Ghilardi, H. Poizner, and C. Ghez. 1995. Control of limb dynamic in normal subjects and patients without proprioception. *Journal of Neurophysiology* 73(2), 820–835.

Sandler, W. 1986. The spreading hand autosegment of American Sign Language. *Sign Language Studies* 50, 1–28.

Sandler, W. 1987a. Assimilation and feature hierarchy in American Sign Language. In *CLS 23*. Vol. 2, *Parasession on Autosegmental and Metrical Phonology*. Chicago Linguistic Society, University of Chicago, Chicago, Ill.

Sandler, W. 1987b. Sequentiality and simultaneity in American Sign Language phonology. Doctoral dissertation, University of Texas, Austin.

Sandler, W. 1989. *Phonological representation of the sign*. Dordrecht: Foris.

Sandler, W. 1990. Temporal aspect and ASL phonology. In Fischer and Siple 1990.

Sandler, W. 1993a. Hand in hand: The roles of the nondominant hand in sign language phonology. *The Linguistic Review* 10, 337–390.

Sandler, W. 1993b. Linearization of phonological tiers in ASL. In Coulter 1993.

Sandler, W. 1993c. A sonority cycle in American Sign Language. *Phonology* 10(2), 243–279.

Sandler, W. 1995. Markedness in the handshapes of sign language: A componential analysis. In H. van der Hulst and J. van de Weyer, eds., *Leiden in last: HIL phonology papers I.* The Hague: Holland Academic Graphics.

Sandler, W. 1996a. Phonological features and feature classes: The case of movements in sign language. *Lingua* 98, 197–220.

Sandler, W. 1996b. Representing handshapes. *International Review of Sign Language Linguistics* 1, 115–158.

Schick, B. 1990. Classifier predicates in American Sign Language. *International Journal of Sign Language Linguistics* 1, 15–40.

Scobbie, J. M. 1991. Attribute value phonology. Doctoral dissertation, University of Edinburgh.

Scobbie, J. M. 1993. Constraint violation and conflict from the perspective of declarative phonology. *The Canadian Journal of Linguistics* 38(2), 155–167.

Selkirk, E. 1982. The syllable. In van der Hulst and Smith 1982.

Selkirk, E. 1984. *Phonology and syntax: The relation between sound and structure.* Cambridge, Mass.: MIT Press.

Selkirk, E., and K. Tateishi. 1988. Constraints on minor phrase formation in Japanese. In *CLS 24.* Vol. 1, *The General Session.* Chicago Linguistic Society, University of Chicago, Chicago, Ill.

Senghas, A. 1995. Children's contribution to the birth of Nicaraguan Sign Language. Doctoral dissertation, MIT, Cambridge, Mass.

Shaw, P. 1992. Nuclear vs. non-nuclear moras. Ms., Linguistics Department, University of British Columbia, Vancouver. [Presented at the Berkeley Phonology Workshop series.]

Shaw, P. 1994. The prosodic constituency of minor syllables. In E. Duncan, D. Farkas, and P. Spaelti, eds., The Proceedings of the Twelfth West Coast Conference on Formal Linguistics, 117–132. Stanford, Calif.: CSLI Publications. [Distributed by Cambridge University Press.]

Sieklecki, T., and J. D. Bonvillian. 1993. Development of American Sign Language phonology in young children of Deaf parents: Acquisition of handshape. Ms., University of Virginia, Charlottesville.

Smith, W. 1990. Evidence for auxiliaries in Taiwanese Sign Language. In Fischer and Siple 1990.

Smolensky, P. 1993. Harmony, markedness, and phonological activity. Paper presented at the Rutgers Optimality Workshop, Rutgers University, New Brunswick, N.J.

Stack, K. 1988. Tiers and syllable structure: Evidence from phonotactics. M.A. thesis, University of California, Los Angeles.

Steriade, D. 1982. Greek prosodies and the nature of syllabification. Doctoral dissertation, MIT, Cambridge, Mass. [Published 1990, Garland Press, New York.]

Steriade, D. 1990. Moras and other slots. In *Formal Linguistics Society of Midamerica 1*. Linguistics Department, University of Wisconsin, Madison.

Stevens, K., and S. J. Keyser. 1989. Primary features and their enhancement in consonants. *Language* 65, 81–106.

Stevens, K., S. J. Keyser, and H. Kawasaki. 1986. Toward a phonetic and phonological theory of redundant features. In Perkell and Klatt 1986.

Stokoe, W. 1960. Sign language structure: An outline of the visual communication systems of the American Deaf. *Studies in Linguistics, Occasional Papers 8*. [Available from Linstok Press, Silver Spring, Md.]

Stokoe, W., D. Casterline, and C. Croneberg. 1965. *A dictionary of American Sign Language on linguistic principles*. Silver Spring, Md.: Linstok Press.

Supalla, S. 1992. *The book of name signs*. San Diego, Calif.: Dawn Sign Press.

Supalla, T. 1982. Structure and acquisition of verbs of motion and location in American Sign Language. Doctoral dissertation, University of California, San Diego.

Supalla, T. 1985. The classifier system of American Sign Language. In C. Craig, ed., *Noun classification: Proceedings of a symposium on categorization and noun classification*. Philadelphia: Benjamin Publishing.

Supalla, T. 1990. Serial verbs of motion in ASL. In Fischer and Siple 1990.

Supalla, T., and E. Newport. 1978. How many seats in a chair? The derivation of nouns and verbs in American Sign Language. In P. Siple, ed., *Understanding language through sign language research*. New York: Academic Press.

Svaib, T. 1992. Compound nouns in American Sign Language: Which way are they headed? Paper presented at the 4th International Conference on Theoretical Issues in Sign Language Research, San Diego, Calif.

Takkinen, R. 1994. Sign articulation of a deaf boy at the age of 2–3 years and 6–8 years. In I. Ahlgren, B. Bergman, and M. Brennan, eds., *Perspectives on sign language usage*. Durham, England: The International Sign Linguistics Association.

Tallal, P., A. Galaburda, R. Llinás, and C. von Euler, eds. 1993. *Temporal information processing in the nervous system*. New York: New York Academy of Sciences.

Tallal, P., S. Miller, and R. H. Fitch. 1993. Neurobiological basis of speech: A case for the preeminence of temporal processing. In Tallal, Galaburda, Llinás, and von Euler 1993.

Trubetzkoy, N. 1939. *Grundzüge der Phonologie*. Göttingen: Vandenhoeck and Ruprecht. [English translation *Principles of phonology* published 1969, University of California Press, Berkeley.]

Ungerleider, L., and M. Mishkin. 1982. Two cortical visual systems. In D. J. Ingle, M. A. Goodale, and R. J. W. Mansfield, eds., *Analysis of visual behavior.* Cambridge, Mass.: MIT Press.

Uyechi, L. 1994. Local and global signing space in American Sign Language. In *NELS 24*. Graduate Linguistic Student Association, University of Massachusetts, Amherst.

Uyechi, L. 1995. The geometry of visual phonology. Doctoral dissertation, Stanford University, Stanford, Calif. [Published 1996 by CSLI Publications, Stanford, Calif.]

Valli, C. 1990. Snowflake. In *Poetry in motion.* Burtonville, Md.: Sign Media, Inc.

Valli, C., and C. Lucas. 1992. *Linguistics of American Sign Language: An introduction.* Washington, D.C.: Gallaudet University Press.

Vendler, Z. 1967. Verbs and times. In *Linguistics in philosophy.* Ithaca, N.Y.: Cornell University Press.

Vennemann, T. 1972. On the theory of syllabic phonology. *Linguistische Berichte* 18, 1–18.

Volterra, V., ed. 1987. *La lingua italiana dei segni.* Bologna: Il Mulino.

Wallin, L. 1994. Polysynthetic signs in Swedish Sign Language. Doctoral dissertation, University of Stockholm.

Whittemore, G. 1986. The production of ASL signs. Doctoral dissertation, University of Texas, Austin.

Wilbur, R. B. 1987. *American Sign Language: Linguistic and applied dimensions.* 2nd ed. Boston: Little, Brown.

Wilbur, R. B. 1990. Why syllables? What the notion means for ASL research. In Fischer and Siple 1990.

Wilbur, R. B. 1993. Syllables and segments: Hold the movement and move the holds! In Coulter 1993.

Wilbur, R., E. Klima, and U. Bellugi. 1983. Roots: The search for origins of signs in ASL. In *CLS 19*. Chicago Linguistic Society, University of Chicago, Chicago, Ill.

Wilbur, R. B., and L. Petersen. 1997. Backwards signing and ASL syllable structure. *Language and Speech* 40, 63–90.

Wiltshire, C. 1992. Syllabification and rule application in harmonic phonology. Doctoral dissertation, University of Chicago. [Published 1993 by University of Chicago Occasional Papers in Linguistics, Chicago, Ill.]

Woodward, J. 1985. Universal constraints on two-finger adjacency and choice. *Sign Language Studies* 46, 53–72.

Woodward, J. 1987. Universal constraints across sign languages: One-finger contact handshapes. *Sign Language Studies* 57, 375–383.

Zec, D. 1988. Sonority constraints on prosodic structure. Doctoral dissertation, Stanford University, Stanford, Calif.

Zec, D., and S. Inkelas. 1990. Prosodically constrained syntax. In S. Inkelas and D. Zec, eds., *The phonology-syntax connection*. Chicago: University of Chicago Press.

Ziolkowski, M., M. Noske, and K. Deaton, eds. 1990. *CLS 26*. Vol. 2, *Parasession on the Syllable in Phonetics and Phonology*. Chicago Linguistic Society, University of Chicago, Chicago, Ill.

Index of Illustrated Signs

ABSTRACT (two-handed and one-handed forms), 273
ADMIT, 181
APPOINTMENT, 48
ASK, 106, 160

BACKGROUND, 187
BICYCLE, 122, 268
BLACK (citation form), 139
BLACK^NAME, 139, 229

'characteristically', 57
CHILDREN, 97, 181, 187
CIGAR, 111
CLOSE-WINDOW, 13, 239
COLOR, 169

DAY, 103, 138, 218
DEAF, 43
DEFEAT (1918 form and modern form), 261
DESTROY, 187
DRIVE-TO, 16, 18
DROP, 66, 185

ENVISION, 108
EXPAND, 172

FALSE, 27, 218
FEW, 111
FILM (verb 'to film'), 108
FINGERSPELL, 169
FOCUS, 198–99
4th-YEAR-IN-COLLEGE, 278

$_2$GIVE$_0$ #SORRY, 73
$_2$GIVE$_1$, SORRY, 49
GIVE-UP, 157
GOVERNMENT, 187

HAPPEN, 157, 221
HARD (distalized and citation forms), 134, 221
HATE, 106, 160
HELP, 16

I-O-N (fingerspelled form and routinized sequence), 236
*Impossible sign, 9
INFORM, 138
INSULT, 44, 157, 202–3
INTERNALIZE, 264
-ish, 57

K, 111
KISS, 108
KNOW-NOTHING, 109

LOCAL, 122
  two-handed and one-handed forms, 276
LOCK, 48, 157

MAKE-A-ROUND-TRIP, 202–3
Manual alphabet of ASL, 12
MISCHIEVOUS, 172
MOCK, 202–3
MORPHOLOGY (fingerspelled and locally lexicalized forms), 209

Open handshapes, 104

PAY, 219
PERPLEXED, 219, 221
  four surface realizations of, 174 223
Polymorphemic form, 21
POPULAR, 278
PUT-ON-SHOE, 102, 278

QUIET, 57
  one-handed form, 60, 250
  two handed form, 271
  two-handed form, 60, 250
  with WD output, 271
QUIET ['characteristically'], 57
  one-handed form, 60
QUIET ['characteristically']-ish, 57
QUIET-ish, 57
QUIET-ish ['characteristically'], 57

READ, 14, 242
  two-handed and one-handed forms, 275
READING, 14, 242
REBEL, 44, 103
REMEMBER, 8
  two-handed and one-handed forms, 274
REQUEST, 17, 268
ROLL-OVER-LAUGHING, 172
RUN-OUT OF, 198–99

SALAD, 111
SATURDAY, 109
SAY-NO, 172
SEE, 111
SELF, 20, 99
SEND, 66
$_0$SEND$_{-0}$, 161
SEPARATE, 115
SHOOT-A-GUN, 115
SHUT-UP (2nd person imperative), 66, 161
SINCE, 8, 251
SIT, 5, 122, 216, 251
SORRY, 138
SUNDAY, 108, 122, 271
  with WD output, 271

TAKE, 66, 185
  citation and reduced forms, 31
THING, 97
THINK
  citation form, 20, 99, 139
THINK ˆSELF, 20, 99, 139, 229
THROW, 6, 122, 216
TOUCH, 8, 251
TRY-ON, 102, 278

UNDERSTAND, 5, 181, 198–99, 216
  citation and proximalized form, 134

WANT, 109, 115
WE
  disyllabic form, 62
  with path feature, 155
  with setting change, 155

WHEN, 48
WHISKEY (1918 form and modern form),
  259
WILLING, 221
WINDOW, 13, 239
WITH
  *one-handed form, 250, 270
  two-handed form, 250, 270

YES, 44, 157
YOUR, 122

General Index

'1', 9, 163, 255
2-HANDSHAPES (2-HS), 232, 300
2MVT CONSTRAINT, 211, 225
4TH-YEAR-IN-COLLEGE, 278
'5', 9, 105, 112, 161–63, 197, 214–15, 249
'7', 112
'8', 112, 173, 215

'A', 9, 298, 300
Aarons, D., 19
Abbreviated sign, 231, 298
Abduction, 156
ABSTRACT, 272
Accent language, 80
ACT, 294
ACTING, 294
Active fingers. *See* Selected fingers
Activity noun, 241–43, 294
Abduction, 156
ADMIT, 141, 143, 181–82, 194, 197, 204
ADOPT, 143
ADULT, 154
ADVISE, 135, 148–50
Affix, 58, 100, 105, 131, 135, 196–205
Affricate, 65
AFTERNOON, 103
Agentivity, 143
Ahn, S.-H., 34, 40, 64, 88
AIRPLANE, 241, 294
ALGEBRA, 298
Algonquian, 144–45
ALIGN, 190, 300
ALIGN (L), 211, 232, 234, 301–2
ALIGN (R), 211, 232, 234, 301–2
ALIGNMENT, 54–55, 184, 192, 236, 299–300
[All], 96, 100, 112, 119, 215, 234, 267, 275, 278, 281
Allophone, 70, 85, 100, 105, 109, 161, 163, 296
Alphei, 307

Alternation, 196–205
[Alternating], 126, 133, 136–37, 261–63, 267, 277
ANALYZE, 152
Anderson, J., 3, 28, 63, 67, 90, 95, 213
ANGRY, 163, 258
Ann, J., 102–4, 106, 162
Aperture, 106, 136, 161, 186, 219, 236
change in, 66, 88, 131, 134, 163, 173, 183, 185, 189, 211, 214, 233, 235
and constraints, 232, 300
and feature geometry, 131–32, 158, 163, 191, 201, 204
in Moraic Model (μ Model), 88
and one-handed signs, 5
as "position," 42
reduplicated change, 239
and spreading, 189
and thumb, 116
Aperture features, 69, 194
Aperture specification, 165, 255
Aphasics, 215
APPLE, 308, 310
APPOINTMENT, 131
Arbitrary name sign, 190, 231, 298, 302
[Arc], 244, 258
Arc movement, 62, 105, 131, 155, 258
Archangeli, D., 162
Arm, 136, 167, 217, 224
as articulator, 102
and contrast, 102
and feature geometry, 97–98
and metathesis, 152
as passive articulator, 98
and places of opposition, 123
and spreading, 25
Articulation, 197
Articulator, 91, 133, 137, 148, 217, 224, 247
and feature geometry, 64, 120, 184, 214, 267, 313
and handpart, 126

Articulator (*cont.*)
    and movement, 151
    and stasis, 227
    and [trilled movement], 164
Articulator features, 97–98
Articulatory planes, 91. *See also* Visual
    Phonology Model (VP)
ASK, 105–6, 159, 308
Askins, 147–48, 150
Assimilation, and direction, 101
Association Convention, 63, 65, 184–86,
    189–92, 193, 289
Asymmetry, 67, 78, 96
    and hands, 248
    and handshape inventories, 293
    and movement, 245, 306
    and verb, 244
Atelic activities, 14
Atelic meaning, 200
Autosegmental phonology, 3, 23, 56, 65
Autosegmental representation, 304
AVOID, 273–74

'B', 9, 161–62, 190, 255, 275, 300
Babble, 71
BACHELOR, 154
B-A-C-K, 164
BACKGROUND, 62, 152, 160, 187, 190,
    205–6
Backward signing, 206–8
Bagemihl, B., 74
Bahan, B., 100
BALL-STATE, 187, 205
Bantu, 80
[Base], 287. *See also* Visual Phonology
    Model (VP)
Base finger joints, 165
Base joint, 162, 167, 217
BASKET, 123
BAT, 14
Batsbi, 144
BATTING, 14
Battison, R., 5, 7, 9, 83, 96, 101, 117, 123,
    125–26, 249, 251, 257, 267, 297
Battistella, E. L., 69, 119, 214
BAWL-OUT, 148–50
BEAR, 114
BEAUTY, 249
Bella Coola, 74
Bellugi, U., 2, 16, 19–20, 58, 94, 308
BET, 156
BETTER, 130
BICYCLE, 7, 249, 267–69
Bidirectionality, 238
Bienvenu, M. J., 94, 209, 231
Bimoraic syllable. *See* Syllable

Binarity, 67. *See also* Dependency
    Phonology
    in the Dependency Phonology Model, 89–
    90
Binary feet, 225
BIOLOGY, 298
BLACK, 132, 136, 139, 141
BLACK^NAME, 140, 282
Bloomfield, L., 83, 85
BLOW-BY-EYES, 29
BOARD-OF-TRUSTEES, 62, 160
BODY, 152, 154, 249
Body, 123
    as articulator, 224
    and contact, 180
    and major body regions, 121–22
    and metathesis, 152
    and place of articulation, 121
    places of opposition, 122
    and prosodic role, 224
    and sign space, 129
    and two-handed sign, 252
Bonvillian, J., 117
BORROW, 308
Bos, H., 15
Bosch, A., 71
[Bottom], 152–53
BOY^SAME, 280
Boyes-Braem, P., 15, 102, 105, 110, 224
Brain, 2, 310–12
    and damage, 2
Branch. *See* Feature geometry
BRAVE, 249–50, 252
BREAD, 11, 299–300
BREAK, 131
Bregman, A. S., 306
Brentari, D., 4, 7, 14, 17, 19–20, 22, 26, 28–
    29, 51, 64, 75, 77, 80, 96, 101–2, 112,
    114, 117, 134–35, 136–37, 143, 147, 152,
    159–60, 160, 164, 190, 209, 211, 215,
    220, 227, 236, 246, 248, 255, 258–59,
    279, 281, 306
BRIDGE, 123
[Broad], 110
BROKE, 122
BUG, 114–15
BUT, 298

'C', 9, 278
Cairene Arabic, 225, 227
CALCULUS, 298
Calendar plane. *See* Grammar
CALL, 139–41, 180
CAMERA, 240
CAN'T-DO-IT, 131
CANADA, 186

CANCEL, 206
CANDLE, 169
CANDY, 310
C-A-R, 164
Cassimjee, F., 131
Casterline, D., 70, 83, 237, 252–53, 254, 308
Chase, C., 307
*CHECK^READ, 281
*CHECK^VOTE, 280
['cheek'], 310
CHEMISTRY, 298
Chereme, 86
Cheremic Model, 83
CHERISH, 45, 126
Chest, 85
C-H-I-L-D, 233–34
CHILDREN, 96, 125, 152, 154, 181–82, 186, 194
Children
  and signing, 117, 135, 215, 259, 292, 304, 306
  and speech, 109
Chin, 45, 126, 173
Chinchor, 84
Chinese, 10
Chomsky, N., 53, 55
Christdas, P., 71
CHRISTIAN, 308
CIGAR, 110
[Circle], 142–43
Circle+straight movement, 72, 131
Circling, 165
Circular movement, 32, 57, 143, 258
  and feature geometry, 131–33
  and predictability, 142
Classifier forms, 81–82, 131
  and place of articulation, 123
Classifier forms. See Classifier predicates
Classifier name sign, 302
Classifier predicate, 21, 107, 119, 249, 293–94, 296
  and fingerspelling, 294
  and plane of articulation, 136
Clements, G. N., 53, 63–64, 76, 79, 95, 265, 304–5
[Closed], 51, 69, 161–64, 186, 235–36, 300
CLOSE-WINDOW, 11, 241
Closing, 165
Cochlea, 307
CODE-OF-ETHICS, 160
Cognitive science, 284
Colonomos, B., 94, 209, 231
COLOR, 130, 169, 206
Color, 311
COMPETE, 249

Complex movement, 130, 156, 237–43
  definition of, 237
Complex syllable, 79–80
Complexity, 68. See also Dependency Phonology
  definition of, 28
  and Dependency Phonology Model, 89–90
  and inherent features, 213
  and prosodic features, 213–24
Compound, 18–21, 120, 142, 155, 180, 227, 229
  and assimilation, 98
  and handshape, 161
  and movement, 137–40
  and nondominant hand (H₂) restrictions, 282
  and two-handed signs, 252
COMPUTATION, 298
Comrie, B., 144
CONGRESS, 51, 62, 153, 308
Conlin, K. E., 135
Consonant, 225
  and feature geometry, 304
  and syllabic structure, 78
[Consonantal], 69, 95
Constraints, 9–10, 164. See also Local Constraint Conjunction; Sonority Sequencing Constraint
  ALIGN (L), 211, 232, 234, 301–2
  ALIGN (R), 211, 234, 301–2
  and boundaries, 54
  and classifier predicates, 21
  and complexity, 22
  and derivation, 55
  ELIMINATE REDUNDANCY (ELIMRED), 268–69, 270, 273, 276
  and feature geometry, 56
  and fingerspelling, 208
  and grammar, 53
  and handshape, 106, 160
  2-HANDSHAPES (2-HS), 232, 300
  HARMONIZE NUCLEUS (HNUC), 232–33, 234, 236
  and lexical innovation, 293
  list of, 294–96
  and loan signs, 299–303
  and local lexicalization, 231
  MAXIMIZE APERTURE CHANGE (MAXAP Δ), 164, 211, 232, 235, 300
  and movement, 70
  on nondominant hand (H₂), 291–92
  and nonnative lexicon, 297–303
  OBLIGATORY CONTOUR PRINCIPLE (OCP), 189–90
  and Optimality Theory, 54
  and other constraint-based theories, 55–68

Constraints (*cont.*)
  and output, 61
  PARSE, 55, 268–69, 270, 277
  PARSE HANDSHAPE (PARSE HS), 232, 234,
    299–300
  PARSE PLACE/H$_2$, 274
  and prosodic word, 70, 281
  PROSODIC WORD = 1 ≤ 2σ (PWD = 1 ≤ 2σ),
    232, 234, 304
  and selected fingers, 164
  SELECTED FINGERS (SF), 232, 236, 304
  and spoken language, 110
  and structure preservation, 58
  and syllable, 70, 205, 303–4
  and thumb, 116–17
  and two-handed sign, 277
  and Weak Drop, 265
  and word length, 225
  as universals, 54
[Contact], 51, 126, 140–41, 192, 261–63,
    266–67, 270, 289–90
Contact, 75, 104, 137, 194, 225, 247
  and body, 115
  with body, 180
  and feature geometry, 98, 142, 264
  and fingerspelling, 298
  finger tip, 278
  in Hold-Movement Theory, 85
  and metathesis, 152–53
  and movement, 290
  and nondominant hand (H$_2$), 46
  and path feature, 51
  and predictability, 140, 192
  and segment, 183
  and setting, 62
  and setting change, 155
  and sonority, 222
  and thumb, 114
  and two-handed signs, 251, 265–67
[Continuative] aspect, 65, 69, 133
Continuous movement, 290
Contour tone, 62
[Contralateral], 26, 49, 51, 123, 152–53, 287
Contrast, 69, 96, 100, 112, 120, 123, 224.
    See also Handshape contrasts
  and compounds, 142
  and handshape, 101, 190
  and inherent and prosodic features, 93
  and nondominant hand (H$_2$), 280
  and prosodic features, 156
  and prosodies, 24
Contrastive features, 45, 69, 85–86, 102,
    105–8, 159, 182, 310, 313
  and timing units, 211
  and tone, 24
CONVINCE, 143
COOK, 156

Coppola, M. E. V., 292
Core syllable, 79
Corina, D., 2, 7, 75, 77, 88, 105, 159–60,
    167, 222
[Coronal], 69, 133
COUGH, 185–87
Coulter, G., 6, 70
Crasborn, O., 43, 45, 155
Croneberg, C., 70, 83, 237, 252–53, 254, 308
[Crossed], 110
CRUEL, 163, 258
CURRICULUM, 159, 186, 190, 206

'D', 300
Damasio, A. R., 2
Damasio, H., 2
DANCE, 88
Danish, 10
Danish Sign Language, 15, 100
DARK, 103
Davies, S., 100, 165
Davis, B. L., 216–17
Davis, S., 79, 110
DAY, 102–3, 130, 136, 167, 217–18
DEAD, 156
DEAF, 42, 62, 98, 153–55
Deaf community
  and fingerspelling, 10
  Nicaragua, 292
  U.S., 1, 208, 292
Deaton, K., 71
Declarative Phonology, 55
DECLINE, 308
Default joint, 25
Default plane, 274
Default position, 234
DEFEAT, 260
DEFLATE, 116, 172, 197
Deitic sequence. *See* Grammar
DeLancey, S., 144
[Delayed campletive] aspect, 196–205
Dell, F., 75–76, 227
Dependency Phonology, 3, 28, 67–68, 95–
    96, 112
  and feature geometry, 63–66
Dependency Phonology Model (DP), 89–
    90, 97–98, 135–36, 178–179, 181–82,
    204, 213, 248. *See also* Binarity;
    Complexity; Head-dependent
    asymmetry
  and nondominant hand (H$_2$), 255
  and well-formedness, 226
Derived sonority, 219–24, 245
Desouvrey, L-H., 15
DESTROY, 187, 189, 288–89
Dez, 83. *See also* Handshape
Diachronic change, 52, 54, 248, 256

Diachronic operations, and feature
    geometry, 262–63
DIE, 130–131
[Digitated], 110
DINOSAUR, 103
diphthong, 65
[Direction], 18, 33, 51, 125, 131, 134, 136,
    140–41, 142–51, 145, 147, 180, 185, 192,
    194, 214–15, 220, 222, 225, 244, 266, 290
Direction-of-Transfer Principle, 145, 147–
    48, 150
DIRTY, 169
Discourse Signing Space, 91, 124. *See also*
    Visual Phonology Model (VP)
[Distal], 152
Distal joint, 69, 75, 133, 220
    definition of, 30
Distalization, 30–33, 133–35, 167, 220–24
    definition of, 134
    and physiology, 31–33
Distinctive features. *See* Contrastive
    features
[Distributed] aspect, 69
Disyllabic forms, 6, 62, 131, 136, 279–80,
    304
    and movement, 46–48
    and prosodic features, 25
DOCTOR, 112, 123
Dominance Condition, 252–53, 257
Dominant hand (H$_1$), 9–10, 96, 102, 164,
    173, 247, 250, 278
    and features geometry, 94, 101–3, 267
    and opposition, 123
    and type 2 signs, 258
    and type 3 signs, 258
    and Weak Drop, 249
Dotter, F., 248
Double contact sign, 264–65
Double place sign, 264–65
Double-dez sign, 253–55, 256, 260, 265
Downstep, 61–62
Dresher, E., 3, 28, 63, 67, 90, 95, 213
DRIVE, 167
DRIVE-TO, 16, 18
DROP, 65–67
DRUGS, 123
Duration, 23
[durative] aspect, 58
Dutch Sign Language, 10
Dynamic movement, 129
Dynamic units, 6, 177–80, 236

'E', 300
Ear, 307
    inner, 2
EARLY, 298

EASY, 298, 300
EITHER, 259–60
EJACULATE, 159
Elbow, 30–31, 69, 75, 103, 133, 136, 217,
    219–20, 223–24
    and circling, 165
    and distalization, 133–34
    and movement, 131
    and path movement, 4, 129
    and tremor, 165
    rotation of, 219
ELIMINATE REDUNDANCY (ELIMRED), 268–69,
    270, 273, 276
Elmedlaoui, M., 75–76, 227
Engberg-Pederson, E., 4, 15–16, 100, 120
English, 80, 85, 96, 109, 112, 209, 225–26,
    230, 232, 243, 293–94, 299, 302
Enhancement Theory, 69, 133
ENVISION, 109
Epenthesis, 74
Epenthetic movement, 63, 130–131, 140,
    142, 153, 155, 190–92, 225–30, 298, 304
EVERY-MONDAY, 120
EVERY-OTHER-MONDAY, 120
Ewen, C. J., 3, 28, 63, 67, 90, 95, 213
[Exhaustive] aspect, 135, 197, 244, 258
EXPAND, 170, 172
EXPENSIVE, 187
EXPERIMENT, 298
[Extended], 51, 104, 113
[Extension], 51, 97
Extension, 156
    and joints, 106–7
['Eye'], 100
Eye gaze, 100
    and feature geometry, 98

'F', 249
FACE, 142
FACE^STRONG, 142
Facing, 124, 148, 287
    in Hold-Movement Theory, 85
    orientation of, 147, 150
FAITH, 300–1
FAITHFULNESS, 54–55, 299–300
FALL-ASLEEP, 197, 200
FALSE, 27, 84, 88, 92, 124, 217, 219, 286–
    87
FALSE STATEMENT, 84
Fant, G., 23, 85
FAR-INTO-FUTURE, 172
Feature geometry, 3, 88, 93–96, 137
    and alternative models, 35, 39–42
    and articulator, 64
    and articulatory structure, 95
    and assimilation, 95

Feature geometry (*cont.*)
and complexity, 213–24
and constraint-based theories, 56
and contact, 142
and Dependency Phonology, 63–66
and Dependency Phonology Model, 89
and differences among models, 286–92
and dominant hand (H_1), 94, 101–3
and fingers, 158–59
and hand, 101–6, 103
and handshape change, 158–64
and handshape inventories, 117–19
handshape vs. orientation, 35
and head-dependent asymmetry, 96
and inherent and prosodic features, 64
and inherent features, 22, 26–28, 183–85
and joints, 104, 106–10
and manual behavior, 100–12
and markedness, 117–19
and nondominant hand (H_2), 94, 101, 247–48, 255, 279, 281–82
and nonmanual behavior, 100–12
and nonmanual prosodic features, 173
and nonselected fingers, 102–6
and nonterminal features, 126
and ordering, 65–66
and orientation, 97–98, 123–26
and orientation change, 156–58
and phonological operations, 95
and physiology, 95, 133–34
and place of articulation, 94, 119–23
and prosodic features, 22, 25–28, 129–76, 183–85
prosodic vs. inherent features, 22, 25–28
and redundancy, 117–19
and selected fingers, 102–6
and spoken language, 64, 95
and thumb, 113–17
and timing units, 179–82, 304–5
and [trilled movement], 165–72
and two-handed signs, 256–65, 277–82
and type 1 signs, 261–65
and type 2 signs, 261–65
and type 3 signs, 261–65
and x-slots, 183–93
FEEL, 113
FEW, 110
FILL, 55, 299
FILM, 107–10
FINALLY, 173
FIND, 104, 146
FINE, 172
Finger features, 236-37
Finger joints, 30, 75, 133, 219
and local movement, 4–5
and movement, 130, 156

Finger specifications, and feature geometry, 263
Finger wiggling, 100
Fingers, 103, 281. *See also individual finger names*; Nonselected fingers; Selected fingers.
articulation of, 161
back of, 126, 150
and feature geometry, 158–59, 261–65
radial side of, 92
restrictions on, 7
specification, 236
tips of, 124
Fingers$_0$, 115
and thumb, 113
Fingers$_1$, 110–12, 116
and thumb, 113
separation from joints, 104–5
FINGERSPELL, 169
Fingerspelling, 7, 10–11, 81, 110, 119, 160, 163–64, 190, 208–11, 227, 230–37
and constraints, 55
and core lexicon, 293
in two-handed sign, 247
Finnish Sign Language, 215, 259
Firth, J. R., 23
Fischer, S., 15
Fitch, R. H., 311
Flattening, 165
[Flexed], 51, 104, 107, 110, 113–14, 162–64, 186, 235–36, 287
[Flexion], 51, 97
Flexion, 156, 167
and joints, 106–7
FLOWER, 51, 62, 122, 152–55
FLY, 194, 241, 294
FOCUS, 196–197, 200–2, 204
FOOT BINARITY (FTBIN), 225–27
Forearm, 30, 45
as articulator, 102–3
Forehead, 5, 85
Fox, 144–45
French, 10
French Sign Language, 10
Friedman, L., 159
Frishberg, N., 224, 259
Frontal plane, 31–32, 120–21, 150, 152, 167, 287
FRUSTRATED, 122
Fukazawa, 269
FULL, 122
Fundamental signing position, 31
Fundamental standing position, 155

'G', 190, 234, 296
Galaburda, A., 311

Generative phonology, 304
GEOMETRY, 298
German, 10
GERMANY, 88, 169, 206, 250
Gesture, 1–2, 75
  and physiology, 95
Gesture. *See also* Movement; *individual*
  types of movement
GET, 249–50
GIRL, 132
GIVE, 14, 58, 130, 135–36, 143, 243–44,
  294, 308
GIVE [[durative] multiple], 58
GIVE [[multiple] iterative], 58
GIVE [durative], 58
GIVE [iterative], 58
GIVE [multiple], 58
GIVE-UP, 156
GIVING, 14
Global Signing Space, 91, 124. *See also*
  Visual Phonology Model (VP)
GO-TO, 17
Goldsmith, J., 3, 22–23, 53–56, 61, 75–76,
  78–80, 184, 189, 248, 255, 258, 279, 281
Goodale, 312
GOVERNMENT, 72, 186–89
GRAB-OPPORTUNITY, 156
Grammar
  and complexity, 250
  and compound, 18–21
  and constraints, 53
  and deitic lines of reference, 15
  and distalization, 220
  and disyllabic forms, 63
  economy of, 53
  and epenthetic movement, 226–27
  and feature geometry, 179, 213–24
  and fingerspelling, 230–37
  and handshape change, 159, 164
  and lexical innovation, 292–94
  and movement, 135, 237–46, 238
  and movement segments, 182
  and path features, 137–51
  and phonology, 1–2
  and redundancy, 250
  and segment, 177–78
  and segmental structure, 26–27
  and sonority, 213–37, 216
  and static units, 194
  and syllable, 71–72
  and Weak Drop, 250, 267
Green, D. M., 307
Greftegreff, I., 110
GROW, 116
GUT-FEELING, 123

'H', 110, 112, 234, 259, 296
H$_2$-place, 252–55
H$_2$-place signs, 256, 258, 260, 265
HA-HA-HA, 114–115
[Habitual] aspect, 244
Halle, M., 23, 53, 64, 70, 85, 165
Hamilton, N., 31, 155
Hand, 69. *See also* Dominant hand (H$_1$);
  nondominant hand (H$_2$)
  as articulator, 247
  as independent articulator, 253
  and symmetry, 248
  back of, 96, 145, 148, 150
  base of, 92, 148, 150
  and contact, 251
  and contrast, 103
  and extension, 217
  and feature geometry, 97–98
  handpart-to-place relation, 147–48
  index side, 112
  and orientation, 45–46, 286
  and orientation change, 155
  and orientation of parts, 289
  and phonetics, 248
  radial side, 112, 124, 126, 287
  and spreading, 25
  and Trilled Movement (TM), 165
  ulnar side, 92
Hand prism, 91–92, 124. *See also* Visual
  Phonology Model (VP)
Handshape, 62, 75, 131, 135, 190–92, 214,
  257. *See also individual types*
  and abbreviated signs, 298
  and allophones, 105
  and aperture change, 167
  as articulator, 98
  and assimilation, 162, 265
  bent, 107, 114, 117, 159, 163, 173, 186
  change and feature geometry, 158–64
  change and Trilled Movement (TM), 170
  change in, 33, 65, 130, 133, 140, 162–63,
    167, 173, 181–182, 189–190, 197, 201,
    223, 241
    and default joints, 30
    and timing, 30
  closed, 5, 105, 107, 114, 117, 159–62
  closed and constraints, 232
  and constraints, 106, 232, 236, 299
  and contrast, 101, 102, 103, 106
  curved, 107, 114, 163
  and differences among models, 285
  and Dominance Condition, 252
  and feature geometry, 45, 66–67, 94, 100–
    1, 204, 263, 289, 310
  features, 236–37

Handshape (*cont.*)
  and finger selection, 112
  and finger wiggling, 100
  and fingerspelling, 211, 293
  and fingerspelling constraints, 299
  flat, 107, 114, 116, 159, 161, 163
  and H$_2$-place signs, 254
  in Hand Tier Model (HT), 86
  in Hold-Movement Theory, 85
  'horns', 112
  and initialized signs, 298
  and joint configuration, 117–18
  and licensing, 255
  and loan signs, 298
  and location, 224
  and markedness, 69
  and merger, 211, 234, 236
  in Moraic Model (μ Model), 88
  and morpheme, 224
  and movement, 129, 224
  and nondominant hand (H$_2$), 281
  and nondominant hand (H$_2$) restrictions,
    21
  open, 103, 105–6, 107, 114, 159–60, 162,
    275, 278, 287
  open and constraints, 232
  open and flat, 110
  and orientation change, 156
  partially closed, 7
  partially open, 7
  and path movement, 205
  and predictability, 101, 105, 110, 161–63
  and reduction in, 160–61
  at rest, 103
  and restriction, 281
  and routinized sequences, 235–36
  and selected fingers, 117–18
  separation of handshape and aperture, 51
  and stability, 164
  and static units, 194
  and syllable, 80
  and synchronic forms, 256
  and timing, 25
  and timing slots, 186
  and tongue wagging, 100
  transitional change in, 29
  and two-handed signs, 252, 259–60
  and type 3 signs, 252
  types of, 9
  and Visual Phonology Model (VP), 91
  word-internal change in, 29
Handshape change duration/movement
    duration ratio (HSΔ/Mov ratio), 28–30
Handshape contour, 88, 105, 108, 159–60,
    163, 186

Handshape contrast, 88, 159, 163, 296–97
Handshape features, and nondominant
    hand (H$_2$), 277–79
Handshape inventories, 296–97
  and feature geometry, 117–19
Handshape Sequence Constraint, 159
Hand Tier Model (HT), 35, 45, 72, 86–88,
    94, 96, 131, 135, 159, 179, 181–82, 192,
    204, 240, 248, 253–255, 257, 260, 264,
    285–92
  and movement, 129, 142, 289
  and nondominant hand (H$_2$), 277
  and segment, 178
  and 3-slot structure, 180
Hanson, R., 216–17
HAPPEN, 45, 131, 156, 249
HARD, 133, 220
Harmonic Phonology, 3, 55, 57, 61, 67, 79.
    See also Prominence
Harris, J., 65
HAT, 122
HATE, 105–106, 135, 160
Haugen, E., 23
Hayes, B., 64, 71, 78–79, 225, 304
HEAD, 154
Head, 173, 224
  and metathesis, 152
  movement of, 223
  as passive articulator, 98
  places of opposition on, 122
Head-dependent asymmetry, 67, 89–90. *See
    also* Dependency Phonology
HEART, 122, 140–41
HELP, 16–18, 146, 257, 298
[High], 65, 96
High tone, 62
Hirsh, I. J., 306
HIT, 141, 150
HNUC, 232–33, 234, 236
Hockett, C., 83
Hoek, K. van, 98
Hold, 194, 249
Hold Deletion, 84
Hold segment, 87. *See also* Static units
Hold-Movement Model (HM), 83–84, 87,
    92, 96, 123–24, 181–82, 192, 204–5, 240,
    252–53, 285–92
  and movement, 129, 142
  and segment, 178
  and 3-slot structure, 180
Holzinger, D., 248
Hooking, 165
Hooper, J., 71
[Horizontal plane], 287
Horizontal temporal processing, 306–7

Hubel, D. H., 311, 313
Hulst, H. van der, 3, 28, 34, 50, 63–64, 67–68, 71, 88, 90, 95, 97–98, 101–2, 105, 119, 153, 179, 204, 213, 248, 252, 254–55, 282, 285–86
Hyman, L., 64, 79

'I', 112
IF, 66–67
Ill-formedness, 235–36
  and handshape, 47
IMPROVE, 308
INDEX, 146
Index finger, 104, 110, 163, 223, 234
Index finger joint, and nonmanual phonetic enhancement, 173
Indexical pointing, 100
INFLUENCE, 143
INFORM, 116, 147–50, 159, 162, 187, 308
Information-bearing capacity, 78
I-N-G, 235
Inherent features, 93–127
  [1]–[8], 46, 50, 121–23, 125
  [2-handed], 49, 242
  [all], 49, 96, 100, 112, 119, 215, 234, 267, 275, 278, 281
  [contact], 49, 126, 140–41
  [contralateral], 49, 50, 123, 152–54
  [crossed], 49, 110
  definition of, 22, 93
  different from prosodic features, 237–46
  [extended], 49, 51, 104, 113
  and feature geometry, 64, 86, 183–85, 286–92, 305, 308–11
  [flexed], 49, 51, 104, 107, 110, 113–114, 162–164, 186, 235–236, 287
  [ipsilateral], 49, 50, 123, 152–54
  list of, 49–50
  and many-to-one relationship with prosodic features, 93
  and markedness, 215
  [mid], 49, 112
  and movement, 181, 237–46
  [one], 49, 95–96, 112, 115, 119, 215, 217, 234, 267, 278, 281, 287
  [opposed], 49, 113–114
  and ordering, 184
  and orientation, 185
  vs. prosodic features, 48–51, 126–27
  and segment, 183
  [spread], 49, 95, 110, 126, 167
  and spreading, 184, 187
  [stacked], 49, 110, 126, 296
  and static articulators, 227
  and syllable, 303

[symmetrical], 50, 126, 261–63, 266–67, 269–70
  and timing units, 177
  [ulnar], 112, 287
  [unopposed], 49, 114
  and visual pathways, 312–13
Inherent sonority, 219–24, 245
Initialized sign, 231, 298
Inkelas, S., 80, 243
Input, 61, 133, 155, 164, 168, 194, 200, 204, 219
  and aperture change, 134
  and complexity, 214
  and constraints, 55, 232
  and distalization, 220
  and epenthetic path, 227
  and features geometry, 262
  and fingerspelling constraints, 299
  and handshape, 100
  and loan signs, 301
  and local movement feature, 205
  and metathesis, 153
  and movement, 151, 190, 226, 242
  and nominals, 238–43
  as orientation, 147
  and path features, 190, 205
  and phrase-final lengthening, 196
  and prosodic features, 213–46
  and setting specification, 191
  and sonority, 245
  and surface forms, 142
  and timing units, 179
  and tone, 62
  and [trilled movement], 258
  and Trilled Movement (TM), 167
  and Weak Drop, 269
  and Weak Freeze, 158
  and x-slots, 184
Input-output correspondence, 61
INSIDE, 249
INSTITUTE, 259–60
INSULT, 43, 45, 156, 200
Intensifiers, 172
[Intensive] aspect, 136
[Internal apportionative] aspect, 197
INTERNALIZE, 264, 278
INVITE, 146
I-O-N, 235
[Ipsilateral], 26, 49, 51, 123, 152–53, 194, 287
Iraqi, 225, 227
Israeli Sign Language, 142, 147–48
Italian, 10, 80
Italian Sign Language, 15
ITALY, 206–7
[iterative] aspect, 58
Itô, J., 15, 23, 71, 74, 76, 78, 82, 255, 293

Jackendoff, R., 143, 313
Jacobowitz, E. L., 19, 135
JAIL, 120, 274
Jakobson, R., 23, 70, 85
Japanese, 3, 10, 82, 293
Japanese Sign Language, 15
Jaw-drop, nonmanual, 173, 224
Jeannerod, M., 313
Jenner, A. R., 307
JESUS, 251
JOB, 298
Johnson, R. E., 19, 34, 40, 45, 62, 71, 83, 88, 102, 110, 152, 165, 167, 204, 240
Joint articulation, and sonority, 217
Joint features, 236–37
Joint specification, 107, 161, 163–64, 219, 235–36, 281,
    and open handshape, 214
Joints, 105, 135. *See also* Distal joint; Proximal joint
    and enhancement, 32–33
    and extension, 106–7
    and feature geometry, 104, 106–10, 218
    [flexed], 106–7
    and flexing movements, 32
    and flexion, 106–7
    and handshape, 51, 117–18
    list of, 32
    and movement, 131
    nonflexed, 236
    and orientation, 43
    and predictability, 163
    proximal, 218
    and reduction, 32–33
    and redundancy, 219
    and sonority, 28
    separate from selected fingers, 113
    and spreading, 25
    and timing, 30
    and two-handed signs, 267
JUMP, 186

'K', 110, 296, 298
Kawasaki, H., 3, 69, 76, 133, 216, 222
Kegl, J., 17, 21, 29, 215, 259, 292
Kenstowicz, M., 56, 75
Keyser, S. J., 3, 69, 134, 222, 304–5
Kimura, D., 2
Kiparsky, P., 55–56
KISS, 107, 109
Klima, E., 2, 16, 19–20, 58, 94, 308
KNOW, 75, 140–41, 227
KNOW-NOTHING, 107–8
Knuckle joint, 218
Knuckles, and local movement, 4–5
Kohlrausch, A., 307

Kooij, van der, E., 45
Krones, R., 216–17

[Labial], 95
LaCharité, D., 55
Landau, B., 313
Language, and deficits, 2
Language acquisition, 54, 215
Language breakdown, 54
Language competence, 292–93
Language encoding, 177
Language games, 94
Language perception, 224
Language processing, 2, 27–28, 177
Language production, 2, 208–9, 230–31
Langue, 292
Langue des signes québécoise, 15
Larson, G., 75, 79
LEATHER, 51, 123, 186
L-E-G+WORK, 298
LEND, 308
Lens, 307
Letter, and joint specification, 235
Lexeme, 82, 97, 106, 112, 119, 123, 131, 168, 182, 235, 290, 303, 308
    and feature geometry, 65
    and handshape, 161
    and movement, 43, 304
    and orientation, 96
    and place of articulation, 123
    and place of articulation, 136
    and Selected Fingers Constraint, 190
    and x-slots, 183
Lexical movement, 130
Lexical Phonology, 54–58
Lexical rules, 56–58, 60
Lexicon
    ambiguity in, 45
    and complex movement, 70, 237
    components of, 293
    and constraints on, 285, 292–303
    and exceptions, 257–58
    and fingerspelled letters, 164
    and fingerspelling, 208
    innovation in, 11, 292–94, 302
    and movement, 131, 237
    and native component, 81–83, 160, 164, 294–97
    and nonnative component, 81–83, 297–303
    and number of syllables, 70
    and redundancy, 53
    and syllable, 211
Lexicon. *See also* Local lexicalization
Liddell, S., 14–15, 19–20, 34, 40, 45, 62, 71, 83, 102, 152, 165, 167, 173, 204, 240, 306

Liberman, A., 2
Lieberman, P., 2
Light waves, 307
LIKE, 215
Livingstone, M., 311, 313
Llogoori, 80
Loan signs, 209, 297–99, 301
LOCAL, 275
Local Constraint Conjunction, 54–55, 269–70
Local lexicalization, 11, 208–11, 227, 230–37, 245
Local movement, 7, 14, 135, 178, 180, 182
  coordinate with path movement, 30
  definition of, 130
  and feature geometry, 204
  as input, 205
  and one-handed signs, 4–5
Local Signing Space, 91–92, 124. *See also* Visual Phonology Model (VP)
Location. *See also individual body parts*; Planes; Place of articulation
  change in, 131
    and timing, 28–30
  and feature geometry, 94
  in Hand Tier Model (HT), 86 (*See also* Hand Tier Model)
  in Hold-Movement Theory (HM), 85
  and monomorphemic forms, 5–6
  and morpheme, 224
  and timing, 25
  and two-handed signs, 252
  and Visual Phonology Model (VP), 91
LOCK, 72, 131
Locke, J., 304
Loew, R., 259
Lombardi, L., 65
Long, J. S., 260
LOOK, 129–130
LOVE-SOMETHING, 45
[Low], 96
Low tone (L), 61–62
Lucas, C., 153, 209, 231
Luttgens, K., 31, 155

'M', 104, 112, 114
MacNeilage, P., 216–17
Magnocellular system, 311
Major body place. *See* Place of articulation
Major body position. *See* Setting
MAKE-A-ROUND-TRIP, 200
MAKE-CONTACT-WITH-A-PERSON, 150
MALAYSIA, 249
MALE, 161

MALE^MARRY, 280
MAN, 161
Mandel, M. A., 5, 7. 42, 117, 159
Marentette, P., 71, 117, 215, 304
Markedness, 103, 106, 214–15, 267, 275
  definition of, 69–70
  and features geometry, 117–19
  and handshape, 162
  and syllable, 74
MATCH, 240
Mattingly, I., 2
MAXIMZE APERTURE CHANGE (MAXAP Δ), 164, 211, 232, 235, 300
MAXIMUM, 274
McCarthy, J., 3, 23, 54–55, 61, 70, 189, 204, 232, 238
McDonald, B., 21
McIntire, M., 2, 117
MEETING, 130
Meier, R., 71
Meir, I., 17, 147–148
MELT, 110
MEMBER, 62, 152–154
Merger, 211
Mester, A., 3, 82, 293
Metathesis, 152–54
Metrical structure, 72, 78
  and syllable, 80–81
Metrical theory, 304
[Mid], 112
Middle finger, 112, 234
Midsagittal plane, 31–32, 120, 150, 152, 186, 234, 297
  and orientation, 155
Miglio, V., 269
MILITARY, 186
MILK, 161–162
MILKSHAKE, 161
Miller, C., 311
Mills, A., 97–98
Milner, A. D., 312
Minimal pair, 85
Minimal syllable, 227–30
Minimal word, 55, 74–75, 225, 227–30
MIRROR, 120
Mirror signs, 252
MISCHIEVOUS, 170–71
Mishkin, M., 311–12
MISS, 29
Mituku, 61
MOCK, 112, 200
Mohanan, K. P., 56
Mon Khmer, 23
MONEY, 139, 141
MONEY^BEHIND, 140, 282

*MONEY^ENOUGH, 280
Monomorphemic forms, 4–11, 42, 72, 81,
    98, 180, 249, 252–53
  and feature geometry, 264–65
  and Hand Tier Model (HT), 178
  and handshape, 159
  and movement, 75, 129
  and nonmanual behaviors, 172
  and syllable nuclei, 171
  and Trilled Movement (TM), 168, 171
  and two movements, 208
  and WEAK DROP, 267–77
Monosyllabicity, 6
Mora, 55–56, 88–89, 178–79
  definition of, 28, 79
  and feature geometry, 64
  and syllable, 71
  and weight unit, 245–46
Mora Insertion, 88, 193–94
Mora. See also Syllable
Moraic Model (μ Model), 72, 88–89, 178,
    182, 192, 194, 204, 248
  and features, 88
  and movement, 129
Moraic phonology, 304
Moraic unit, 194
Moravcsik, E., 69
MORNING, 103, 136
M-O-R-P-H-E-M-E, 209, 233–35
Morpheme, 7, 53, 56, 110, 147, 179, 224
  and handshape contour, 159
  tongue wagging, 167
M-O-R-P-H-O-L-O-G-Y, 209, 233–34
Morphology, 196, 294
  and agreement, 147
  and assigning of class, 18
  and boundaries, 53
  'characteristically' X, 58–60
  and fingerspelling, 10
  and movement, 182, 238
  and place, 98
  and place of articulation, 120
  and setting, 204
  and tense, 19
  and timing units, 179
  and two-handed sign, 258
  and verbs, 144
Morphophonological operations, 183, 196–
    205; 257–258
Morphosyntactic features, 305
MOST, 260
MOTHER, 130
Mouth, 165–66
  and feature geometry, 98
  and prosodic features, 173–4
  and Trilled Movement (TM), 165

Movement. See also Handshape change;
    Oneintation change; Spreading;
    individual body parts; individual types of
    movement
  and abbreviated signs, 298
  and abduction, 32
  abduction/adduction, 43
  and adduction, 32
  and assimilation, 258–59, 263, 265
  and asymmetry, 306
  asynchronous, 7, 9
  complexity of, 306
  and contact, 140
  definitions of, 129
  and dissimilation, 258, 265
  and disyllabic forms, 46–48
  and extension, 32
  and extension/ flexion, 43
  and feature geometry, 94, 100, 237–46,
    286–92
  and finger joints, 156
  and fingerspelling, 298–99
  and flexion, 32
  and H$_2$-place signs, 254
  and handshape, 258–59
  in Hand Tier Model (HT), 86
  in Hold-Movement Model (HM), 84
  in Hold-Movement Theory, 85
  and initialized signs, 298
  inserted, 164
  and joints, 131
  and language acquisition, 304
  and loan signs, 298
  and minimal syllable, 227
  and monomorphemic forms, 75
  and mora, 194
  and morpheme, 224
  and nondominant hand (H$_2$), 101, 257
  and one-handed signs, 3–4
  and orientation
  and partial deletion, 258
  as path movement only, 34–35
  and physiology, 36–40
  and place of articulation, 123, 125
  and predictability, 227
  and prone/supine rotation, 43
  as prosodic unit, 88, 179, 289
  and prosodic word, 211
  and redundancy, 6–7
  and reduplication, 58–60, 239
  rotation, 45
  and segments, 180–93, 192–93, 289
  side-to-side, 45
  and sonority, 211, 217, 222, 226
  and syllable, 72–73, 80–81, 303–4
  syllable-internal, 30

as syllable nuclei, 306
and symmetry, 237
and synchronic assimilation, 256
and synchronic dissimilation, 256
synchronous, 7
as tone, 24
as transition
and two-handed signs, 252–253, 257
vertical, 45
in Visual Phonology Model (VP), 91
as vowel, 305
and weight units, 237–46, 305–6
and well-formedness, 205
Movement features, 4
and Dependency Phonology Model (DP), 90
and differences among models, 285–92
and distalization, 25, 30–33
and disyllabic forms, 25
and feature geometry, 25–51
and many-to-one relation between prosodic and inherent features, 25, 34–46
and nondominant hand (H$_2$), 260
and prosodic-to-inherent features, 25
and proximilization, 25, 30–33
relation to movement segment, 180
and timing, 25, 28–30
Movement migration, 25, 30–33, 133–136
Movement roots, 81–82
Movement (Ms). See Hand Tier Model (HT)
Movement segment(s)
and grammar, 182
relation to movement features, 180–86
Movement units. See Dynamic units
[Multiple], 105, 131, 143, 160
MY, 227

'N', 104, 112, 114
Nadeau, M., 15
NAME, 140
Name signs, 298
[Nasal], 23, 69, 95, 133
Narrative, 249
NAVY, 51, 123
Nespor, M., 23
Neurology, 2, 16, 71
Neutral space, 5–6
defined, 5
Newport, E., 11, 18, 238–40
NEXT^YEAR, 142
NO, 11
Nodding, 165
Node. See Feature geometry
Nominals, 11–15, 238. See also Activity noun
Nominalization, 81, 294, 306

Nonbase finger joints, 165, 222
Nonbase joint specification, 310
Nondominant hand (H$_2$), 9, 96, 119, 136, 152, 173, 180, 250, 274
and assimilation, 282
as coda, 22, 248, 255, 279
and compounds, 280
and contact, 46
as echo articulator, 283
as feature, 248, 254
and feature geometry, 94, 101, 125, 247, 254, 255, 267, 279, 281–82
and handshape, 118
and Hold-Movement Model, The (HM), 253
as independent articulator, 291
and opposition, 123
and predictability, 282–83
as prosodic unit, 272–82
as secondary articulator, 248
restrictions on, 10, 247–48, 277–78, 283
and two-handed signs, 267
and type 3 signs, 265
as weak branch of prosodic structure, 248
and Weak Drop, 249–50
as word-level appendix, 304
Nonmanual behavior, and Trilled Movement (TM), 167
Nonselected fingers, 236
and contact, 104
and feature geometry, 102–6
and predictability, 104
Nootka, 238
Nose, 92, 124, 287
Noske, M., 71
NOTE-DOWN, 187, 206
NOTRE-DAME, 187
Noun, 144, 147. See also Activity noun; Nominalization; Nominal
activity, 13
reduplicated, 11–13
Noun phrase, 100
Noun-verb pairs, 18, 238–40
NP shift, 243
NURSE, 112

'O', 9
Object, 143, 145, 147, 244
Obligatory Contour Principle (OCP), 189–90
Ohala, J., 75–76, 216
O-K, 164
OLD, 45, 126, 130
Old Czech, 23
[One], 95–96, 112, 115, 119, 215, 217, 234, 267, 278, 281, 287

One-handed signs, 4–7, 30, 60, 249, 265, 270
  and [alternating], 126
  and derivation, 58
  and movement, 58
  and place of articulation, 120, 274
  and prosodic units, 281–82
  and Weak Drop, 269
ONION, 122, 308, 310
Onset, 78–79, 90
Opacity, 61
[Open], 51, 69, 161–62, 164, 234–36, 300
OPPORTUNITY, 136
[Opposed], 113–14
Optimality Theory, 3, 54–55, 58, 61, 70,
  184, 225, 232, 265–77, 297, 299
Ordering, 206–8
Orientation, 92, 97–98, 136, 148, 150, 219,
  222, 281
  and [symmetrical], 126
  change and Trilled Movement (TM), 170
  change in, 80, 92, 96, 131, 133, 155–58,
    164–65, 167, 173, 183, 185, 211, 223, 234
    and constraints, 232–33
    and default joints, 30
    as movement, 129
    and timing, 28–30
  and contrast, 102, 126
  definition of, 51
  and direction, 145
  and feature geometry, 33, 45, 100, 123–26,
    131–32, 156–58
  and fingerspelling, 294
  of hands, 130
  in Hold-Movement Model (HM), 85
  identical, 252, 267
  and inherent features, 51, 286
  and inherent vs. prosodic features, 43–46
  and lexeme, 97
  neutral, 186
  and nondominant hand (H$_2$), 101
  and physiology, 43–44
  and place of articulation, 123–24
  and plane of articulation, 123
  and prosodic features, 51
  reduplicated change, 239
  as relation between handpart and place of
    articulation, 289
  specification of, 148
  symmetrical, 252, 267
  and timing, 25
  and two-handed signs, 265–67
  and verbs, 147
  and Visual Phonology Model (VP), 91–92
Orientation specifications, and two-handed
  signs, 252
Oscillation. See Trilled movement (TM)

Output, 126, 173, 194, 205
  and backward signing, 207–8
  and constraints, 55, 232, 265
  and distalization, 220
  and epenthetic path, 227
  and fingerspelling constraints, 299
  and local lexicalization, 234
  and movement, 142
  and nondominant hand (H$_2$) restrictions
  and one-handed sign, 249
  and setting change, 155
  and sonority, 245
  and Weak Drop, 269
  and Weak Freeze, 258
  and well-formedness, 58, 227
  and x-slots, 186, 189
OVERNIGHT, 102

'P', 110, 234, 296
Padden, C., 7, 11, 13, 17, 55–58, 120, 126,
  143, 241, 249, 258, 265, 292, 294, 297–
  98, 301–2, 303
Palm, 96
  and contact, 275
  orientation of, 32, 45, 124–25, 147, 150,
    186, 289, 296
Paradis, C., 55, 78, 110
Parameters, 1, 224–25. See also Handshape;
  Location; Movement; Orientation
  in Battison, 96
  and many-to-one relation between inherent
    and prosodic features, 34–46
Parkinson's disease, 29, 103, 134, 220, 222, 259
PARSE, 55, 232, 268–69, 270, 277
PARSE HANDSHAPE (PARSE HS), 232, 234, 299–
  300
PARSE PLACE/H$_2$, 274
Parvocellular system, 311
PASS, 197, 200
[±Path], 204. See also Hold Movement
  Model
Path features, 51, 126, 133, 135, 180, 183,
  194, 204, 215, 219, 225, 258, 285
  and contrast, 142
  and default joints, 30
  definition of, 130, 136–37
  and feature geometry, 136–37
  and grammar, 137–51
  as input, 190, 205
  and other models, 178
  relation to segments, 179–80
  and Trilled Movement (TM), 167
  and two-handed signs, 265–66
Path movement, 7, 16–17, 129, 135, 137,
  141, 145, 148, 155, 173, 180, 182, 197,
  223, 240

coordinated with local movement, 30
definition of, 129
and distalization, 220
and feature geometry, 33, 204
and fingerspelling, 298–99
and one-handed signs, 4–5
and predictability, 182
and segments, 194
as setting change, 153
and syllables, 80
and timing, 28–30
and Trilled Movement (TM), 170
Path shape, 4
PAY, 217
Peripheral components, vs. native
    components, 3
Peripheral processing, 306–7
Perlmutter, D., 4, 7, 13–14, 55–58, 72, 75–
    76, 101, 105–6, 126, 147–48, 150, 159–
    60, 163–64, 179, 182, 190, 193–94, 208–
    9, 211, 225, 236, 241, 245–46, 249, 254,
    258, 265, 277, 294, 282, 294, 306
PERPLEXED, 122, 163, 173, 218–19, 222–
    24
PERSONALITY, 122
Petersen, L., 179, 206
Petitto, L. A., 2, 71, 304
Phoneme, 83, 85
Phonetic enhancement, 3, 133, 173, 220, 222
Phonetics, 70–71, 95, 110, 113, 136, 220–24,
    313
  and articulation, 2
  and asymmetry, 248
  difference between signed and spoken
      language, 163, 247
  and hand, 248
  and handshape, 162
  and perception, 2
  and phonology, 135
  vs. phonology, 69
  and prosodic features, 133
  and sonority, 216–24
  and syllable, 6–7
  and Trilled Movement (TM), 167
  and two-handed signs, 248–50
Phonological boundaries, 53
Phonological Deletion, 126
Phonological rules, 56–58
Phonological word, 53, 279
P-H-O-N-O-L-O-G-Y, 233–34
Phrase-final lengthening, 179, 204
Phrase-final position, 80
Physiology
  and distalization, 31–33
  and dominant hand (H$_1$), 248–49
  and feature geometry, 95, 133–34

of hand, 104–5
and joints, 106–7
and movement types, 36–40
and nondominant hand (H$_2$), 248–49
and orientation, 43–44
and proximilization, 31–33
and sonority, 216
and spoken language, 305
and study of audition, 310–11
and study of vision, 310–11
and two-handed signs, 253
and Visual Phonology Model (VP), 90–
    91
Pinkie finger, 110, 112, 234
PITTSBURGH, 51, 123, 186
[Pivot], 136, 167, 180
Pivoting, 165
Pizzuto, E., 15
Place
  and feature geometry, 110–1, 120, 204,
      261–65
  handpart-to-place relation, 147–48
  in Hand Tier Model (HT), 258
  of opposition, 122–23
  as set of planes, 286
  and stability, 98
  and Trilled Movement (TM), 167
Place features, 97–98
  and feature geometry, 184
  and H$_2$-place signs, 254
  and nondominant hand (H$_2$), 277–79
  and visual processing, 311, 313
Place harmony, 42
[Place of articulation], 85
Place of articulation, 33, 68, 85, 110, 124,
    277, 308
  and abbreviated signs, 298
  changes in, 182
  and contact, 125, 140, 152
  and feature geometry, 45, 94, 119–23, 264
  and fingerspelling, 298
  and initialized signs, 298
  and loan signs, 298
  and morphological status, 120
  and one-handed signs, 5–6, 274
  and orientation, 125, 286
  as plane, 287
  and stability, 120
  and two-handed signs, 247, 265, 267
Place of articulation features, 201
  [1]–[8], 46, 50, 121–23, 126
  [contact], 51, 126, 140–41, 192, 261–63,
      266–67, 270
  [contralateral], 26, 49, 51, 123, 152–53, 287
  [ipsilateral], 26, 49, 51, 123, 152–53, 194,
      287

Place specifications, 263
Plane of articulation, 119–23, 124
  and movement, 141
  and path features, 136
  and setting change, 151
PLAY-PIANO, 169
Poetry, 10, 94, 249
Poizner, H., 2, 16, 28–30, 135, 215, 220, 259
Polish, 23
Polymorphemic forms, 15–18, 249, 304
  and classifier predicates, 21
  compounds, 18–21
  and grammatical aspect, 19–21
  and native lexicon, 294
  and nonmanual behaviors, 172
  and syllable nuclei, 171
  and Trilled Movement (TM), 170–71
Polymorphemic verbs. See Classifier
  predicates
POOR, 123, 130
POPULAR, 278
Position. See Aperture
Postlexical component, 56–58, 60
POSTPONE, 152
Prague School, 70
Primary conceptual function, 143–44
Prince, A., 3, 23, 54–55, 61, 70–71, 74–76,
  78–79, 225, 227, 232, 238, 269
PRINT, 104
PROJECT, 159, 186–87, 190, 206
Prominence, 67
Prominence. See also Harmonic Phonology
[Pronation], 51, 97
[Prone], 234
Pronominals, 123
Prosodeme, 23
Prosodic, definition of, 23
Prosodic features, 205
  [abduction], 50
  [alternating], 50, 126, 133, 136–37, 261–63,
    267, 277
  [arc], 50, 244
  [bottom], 50, 152–153
  [circle], 50, 142–143
  [closed], 50, 51, 69, 161–164, 186, 235–236,
    300
  and complexity, 213–24
  [contralateral], 49, 50, 123, 152–54
  definition of, 22, 24-28, 129
  difference from inherent features, 174–75,
    237–46
  [direction], 18, 33, 50, 51, 125, 131, 134,
    136, 140–41, 142–51, 180, 185, 192, 194,
    214–15, 220, 222, 225, 244, 266, 290
  [distal], 50, 152
  [extension], 50, 51, 97

  and feature geometry, 64, 129–76, 183–85,
    213–46, 226, 286–92, 305
  [flexion], 50, 51, 97
  vs. inherent features, 48–51, 126–27
  [ipsilateral], 49, 50, 123, 152–54
  list of, 50
  and many-to-one relationship with inherent
    features, 93
  and markedness, 215
  and movement, 226, 237–46
  nonmanual, 173–75
  nonmanual and assimilation, 173
  nonmanual and predictability, 173
  [open], 50, 51, 69, 161–62, 164, 234–36, 300
  and phonetics, 133
  [pivot], 50, 136, 167, 180
  [pronation], 50, 51, 97
  [proximal], 50, 152
  [repeat], 50, 133, 136–37, 206
  and segments, 183
  and sonority, 165, 213–37
  [straight], 50, 131, 185–86
  and subsyllabic movement, 241
  [supination], 50, 51, 97
  and syllable, 303
  and timing units, 177–211
  [top], 50, 152–53
  [tracing], 33, 50, 51, 125, 133, 136, 140–41,
    142, 180, 192, 222, 225, 266, 290
  [trilled movement], 50, 64, 201, 205, 218,
    242, 244, 258, 294
  and feature geometry, 164–72
  and visual pathways, 312
Prosodic phoneme, 23
Prosodic phrase, and prosodic structure, 23
Prosodic structure, 23–24
Prosodic units, and movement, 211
Prosodic word, 1, 7, 70–74, 81
  and constraints, 281
  and handshape, 160
  and prosodic structure, 23
  and syllable, 206, 225
PROSODIC WORD = 1 ≤ 2σ (PWd), 232, 234,
  300
Prosodies
  and autosegmental status, 24
  and contrast, 24
  restrictions on, 24
  and timing, 24
Prosody, 23
[Protractive] aspect, 172, 200–1
[Proximal], 152
Proximal joint, 69, 75, 133, 245
  definition of, 30
Proximal movement, 173
  and syllable nuclei, 168

Proximilization, 30–33, 133–35, 220–24
  and physiology, 31–33
  definition of, 134
Prunet, J.-F., 78, 110
Psycholinguistics, 105, 258–59
Pulleyblank, D., 162
[Punctual] aspect, 197, 200
PUT-ON-SHOE, 101, 278, 283
Püschel, D., 307

'Q', 296
QUIET, 57–61, 249–50, 268–69, 270
  'characteristically' QUIET, 57–61
  [['characteristically' QUIET-'ish'], 57
  ['characteristically' [QUIET-'ish']], 57
  'characteristically-X', 258
  QUIET-'ish', 57, 58–61

'R', 300
RABBIT, 85
RAINBOW, 132, 136
READ, 14, 141, 143, 167, 197, 200, 274
READ^CHECK, 140, 280
READING, 14
REBEL, 43, 45, 103, 156
Redundancy, 6–7, 22, 69, 131, 204, 219,
    267, 291
  and aperture setting, 164
  and features geometry, 117–19
  and handshape, 103
  in handshape, 257
  and handshape contour, 159
  and lexicon, 53
  and nondominant hand (H_2), 280
  and thumb, 113–114
  and two-handed sign, 255
  and types of signs, 252
  and Weak Drop, 249–50
Redundancy Rule, 104, 110
Redundant features, 69, 287, 289
Reduplication, and markedness, 70
Reilly, J., 2
Releasing, 165
REMEMBER, 7, 273
REMOVE, 186
[Repeat], 133, 136–37, 206
Representation. See Feature geometry
REQUEST, 17–18, 267–69, 268–69
RESPECT, 143, 146
RESPONSIBILITY, 122
RESTRAINED-FEELINGS, 251
RESTROOM, 154
Retina, 307
REVENGE, 260
RIGHT/CORRECT, 252, 259–60
Ring finger, 112, 234

ROLL-OVER-LAUGHING, 170
Ross, J. R., 243
Routinized sequences, 235–36
Rubbing, 165
RUN, 114–115, 143
RUN-OUT-OF, 100, 172, 196–197, 200–1
RUSSIA, 123

'S', 9, 105, 112, 126, 161–62, 173
Sagey, E., 63–64, 95, 265
Sainburg, R., 30
SALAD, 110
Salience, 133, 160, 216, 224
Sandler, W., 5, 7, 10, 19–20, 33, 35, 42, 45,
    64, 71, 75–76, 86–87, 94, 98, 102, 110,
    117, 131, 136, 142–43, 159, 178, 193,
    195, 204, 248, 253–55, 265, 282–83, 306
SARCASTIC, 112
SATURDAY, 108
SAY-NO, 170
SAY-NOTHING, 122
Schick, B., 21
SCIENCE, 298
Scobbie, J. M., 55
SCOTCH, 123
Secondary movement, 164. See also Trilled
    movement (TM)
Secondary path. See Trilled movement
    (TM)
SEE, 110
Segment, 1, 159, 313
  and backward signing, 207–8
  definition of, 28
  and deletion, 189
  in Dependency Phonology Model (DP), 90
  and feature geometry, 64, 136
  and language acquisition, 304
  and movement, 88, 129, 142, 180–93, 289
  and nominals, 241
  and ordering, 183–84
  relation to inherent and prosodic features,
    51
  and representation, 304
  and sonority, 74
  as static unit, 204
  and syllable, 71, 206
  vs. syllable, 304
  and timing units, 177–80
Selected fingers, 7, 9, 42–43, 68, 209, 211,
    235–36, 267
  and constraints, 300
  and feature geometry, 102–6, 163, 287
  fingers$_0$, 110–12
  fingers$_1$, 110–12
  and handshape, 117
  in Moraic Model (μ Model), 88

Selected fingers (*cont.*)
  and prosodic word, 304
  separate from joints, 113
SELECTED FINGERS (SF), 232, 236, 304
  SF (A), 300
  SF (B), 300
Selkirk, E., 23, 76, 78
Semantics, 197, 200
  and abbreviate sign, 298
SENATE, 154
SEND, 66–67, 147–48
Senghas, A., 292
SEPARATE, 114–15
Sequential movement, 205–11, 214
Serbo-Croatian, 243
Setting, 42–43, 136, 191–92
  change in, 4, 62, 80, 133, 135, 151–55, 167,
    182–83, 194, 225 as movement, 129
  change in and output, 152, 155
  changes different from other path
    movements, 152–55
  and feature geometry, 201, 204
  in Hold-Movement model (HM), 178
  and metathesis, 152–54
  and morphology, 204
  and static units, 194
Setting changes, and default joints, 30
Shadow signs, 252
Shaw, P., 238
Sherrick, C. E., 306
SHOOT-A-GUN, 114
Shoulder, 30, 69, 75, 133, 219
  and circling, 165
  as default movement, 151
  and movement, 131
  and path movement, 4, 129
  and tremor, 165
SHOW, 257
SHOWER, 107
SHUT-UP, 66–67
SICK, 141
Side-to-side movement, 156
Sieklecki, T., 117
Sign, 83. *See also* Abbreviated sign;
    Arbitrary name sign; Classifier name
    sign; Double contact sign; Double place
    sign; Handshape, change in; Initialized
    sign; Mirror sign; Name signs; Shadow
    sign
  errors in, 94, 117, 215, 220, 259
  and historical change, 259–60
  and local proper names, 11
  types of, 7
Sign Language of the Netherlands, 15
Signal transmission, 306
Signing space, 15–18

Simple movement, 130, 215, 237–43, 306
  definition of, 237
SINCE, 7, 251–252
SIT, 5–7, 143, 206, 214, 252
SLAVE, 123, 132
SLEEP, 126, 197, 200
SLEEP^CLOTHES, 282
Smith, W., 15, 19, 71
Smolensky, P., 3, 54–55, 74–76, 79, 225,
    227, 269
SNAP-PHOTOGRAPH, 240
SNOW, 169
"Snowflake" (Valli), 249
SNOWFLAKE, 249
SNOWFLAKE-FALLS, 249
SOCIAL-WORK, 187, 205
Sociolinguistics, 293
[Sonorant], 69, 95, 133, 180
Sonority, 26, 75–77, 88, 205, 213–37. *See
    also* Derived sonority; Inherent sonority;
    Visual sonority
  definition of, 27–28
  and minimal syllable, 227
  and phonetics, 216–24
  and prosodic features, 165
  and syllable, 305
  and Trilled Movement (TM), 201
Sonority Sequencing Constraint (SSC), 76–
    77
SORRY, 29, 122, 130, 136, 141, 143
Sound Pattern of English, 53–54, 65, 71,
    304
Sound waves, 307
Spanish, 80
Speech errors, 109
Split-ergative language, 144
Spoken language, 225
  and constraints, 55
  and feature geometry, 95
  and mora, 246
  and phonological theory, 55
  and sign language, 76–80
  vs. sign language, 28, 64–66, 180, 193,
    215–16, 246–47, 313
  similar to sign language, 1, 10, 24, 46, 55–
    56, 67, 69, 72, 74–76, 89, 95, 98, 109–10,
    112, 131, 133, 144–45, 153, 163, 225,
    227, 238, 255, 279, 285, 303–6, 308–13
[Spread], 95, 110, 126, 167
Spreading, 32–33, 63, 131
  and aperture and tone, 189
  and feature geometry, 135
  and inherent features, 184, 187
  and joints, 30
  local to path movement, 135
  and timing slots, 186

and Trilled Movement (TM), 165
and verbs, 147
Stability
and handshape, 42
and orientation, 44
and place, 43, 98
Stack, K., 4, 34–35, 131, 142, 178–79, 181, 204, 286
[Stacked], 110, 126, 296
STAGE, 123
STAND, 110
STAPLE, 241
STAPLER, 241
START, 257
Stasis, 84, 130–31, 227
and morphology, 204
and predictability, 178, 194
and Trilled Movement (TM), 204
Static units, 177–80, 178
STATISTICS, 298
STEAL, 156, 185
Stem, 82, 98, 120, 145, 180, 197, 227, 238, 280
and activity noun, 242
and constraints, 54, 299
and contact predictability, 205
and [delayed completive], 200
and derivational rules, 57–58
and direction, 200, 143–51
and handshape, 105, 161, 224
and movement, 72, 135–36, 182, 201
and nominals, 238
and nondominant hand (H_2) restrictions, 282
and orientation, 150
and place of articulation, 43
and Trilled Movement (TM), 200–2, 204
two movements, 186–93
and verb, 147
Steriade, D., 79
Stevens, K., 3, 69, 133, 222
S-T-O-C-K M-A-R-K-E-T, 301
Stokoe, W., 19, 42, 70–71, 83, 85–86, 123, 135, 159, 237, 251–53, 253–54, 308
Storytelling, 10
[Straight], 131, 185–86
Straight movement, 15, 142–43, 155, 190–91, 206, 225, 298
as default movement, 131
and feature geometry, 131–33
Straight + circle movement, 72
Stratification, 297–303
Stress, 23, 28, 67, 78–79
[Strident], 69, 133
STRIKE-MATCH, 240
STUNNED, 173, 224

Subject, 143, 145, 147
Subordinate conceptual function, 143–45
SUBSCRIBE, 136, 145–146
Subsyllabic forms, 305
Subsyllablic units, 68, 72, 237–46
SUMMER, 308
SUN + B-U-R-N, 298
SUNDAY, 108, 249, 270
Supalla, S., 302
Supalla, T., 4, 11, 18, 21, 84, 190, 238–40, 294, 302
[Supination], 51, 97
Surface forms, 55, 141–42
and constraints, 58
and well-formedness, 54
Swedish Sign Language, 15
Swiss German Sign Language, 15
Syllabification, 76, 79, 304
Syllable, 1, 55–56, 70–74, 159, 313. *See also* minimal syllable; Mora
and asymmetry, 77
bimoraic, 61–62, 225
and constraints, 54, 299
and constraints on nondominant hand (H_2), 279
and counting, 6, 209
definition of, 71–72, 205–6
and feature geometry, 77–80, 213–15
and fingerspelling, 230–37
and handshape, 160
heavy, 78–81, 225
light, 78–81, 225
and monomorphemic forms, 208
and moraic structure, 77–80
and movement, 72–73, 80–81, 213, 237–46
and prosodic structure, 23
relation to inherent and prosodic features, 51
vs. segment, 304
and sequential movement, 205–11
and setting, 62
in sign and spoken language, 303
and sonority, 76–81, 224–37
and stress, 67
and tone, 80
and V syllable, 74
and vowel, 74
weight of, 306
and weight units, 237–46
Syllable nuclei, 73–77, 168, 171, 205, 227, 245
and constraints, 232
and movement, 211
Syllable peak, 164
[+Syllabic], 305
[−Syllabic], 305

[Symmetrical], 126, 261–63, 266–67, 269–70
Symmetry Condition, 252–53, 257
Synchronic forms, 256–57
Synchronic operations, and feature
    geometry, 262–63
Synchronic variation, 248
Synchronous movement, 251, 265, 267
Syntax
    and assigning of class, 18
    and systematicity, 22
    and verb stems, 143–44

Tab, 83. *See also* Place of articulation
Taiwanese Sign Language, 15, 19
TAKE, 14, 30, 65, 131, 200
TAKE-OFF, 136
TAKE-UP, 66–67
*TAKING, 14
Takkinen, R., 215
Tallal, P., 311
Tateishi, K., 23
TEACH, 107
Telic meaning, 197
TELL, 131, 145–46
Tense markers, 135
Theory of Constraints and Repair
    Strategies, 55
THIEF, 122
THING, 96, 125, 154
THINK, 75, 140–42, 180, 227
THINK^SELF, 19, 98, 120
Three-slot account, 195
Three-slot structure, 289
THROW, 5, 14, 42, 70, 80, 114, 131, 206,
    214
*THROWING, 14
Thumb, 98, 105–106, 112, 234
    as articulator, 113
    and base joint, 114, 116
    and constraints, 117
    and contact, 104, 163
    and contact with body, 115
    and contact with selected fingers, 116–17
    and feature geometry, 113–17
    and metacarpal joint, 114
    and nonbase joint, 116
    and predictability, 117
    and specification, 113–17, 119
Thumb specification, 255
Tier Conflation, 204, 289
Tier. *See* Feature geometry
TIME, 140–141
Time lines. *See* Grammar
Timing, 63–64, 88, 90, 156
    and feature geometry, 136, 286
    and nonmanual prosodic features, 173
    and prosodies, 24

Timing units, 288–289, 308
    definition of, 177–80
    and feature geometry, 179–82, 304–5
    and morphophoneme, 196–205
    and phrase-final lengthening, 193–96
    and sonority, 217–18
    and uniformity of movement, 183
TOILET, 167
Tone, 23, 80, 131
Tone language, 23–24, 61, 80
Tone melodies, 24, 46, 131
Tone-bearing unit (TBU), 61–62, 65
Tongue, 165
    and handshape, 98
Tongue wagging, 100, 165, 167, 172–73,
    197
[Top], 152–53
Topicalization, 243
Torso, 224
    as passive articulator, 98
TOUCH, 7, 252
[Tracing], 33, 51, 125, 133, 136, 140–41,
    142, 180, 192, 222, 225, 266, 290
Transitional movement, 130, 155, 226
Transitivity, 143
Transverse plane, 31–32, 97, 119–20, 150,
    152, 274
TRAVEL-AROUND, 132
TREE, 102–103, 167
Tremor, 165, 167
TRIGONOMETRY, 298
[Trilled movement], 64, 201, 205, 218, 242,
    244, 258, 294
    and feature geometry, 164–72
Trilled movement (TM), 7, 13–14, 57, 88,
    130, 162, 197
    and arbitrary name signs, 298–99
    classification according to articulatory site,
        167
    and direction, 200
    and morphology, 204
    as movement, 129
    nonmanual, 173
    and predictability, 165
    and sonority, 218
Trubetzkoy, N., 70, 79
TRY-ON, 101, 278, 282
TWENTY-ONE, 114
Twisting, 165
Two-handed signs, 7–10, 55, 123, 173, 247–
    83
    and [alternating], 126
    and derivation, 58
    and differences among models, 290–92
    and feature geometry, 247–48, 256–65,
        277–82
    and historical change, 259–60

and movement, 58
and nondominant hand (H₂), 251–55
and place of articulation, 120
and restrictions on, 251–55
as simple structure, 256–65, 277–82
and Weak Drop, 265–77
Two-movement form, 206
Two-slot structure, 195, 286, 289
Type 1 signs, 58, 186–87, 249, 252–53, 255,
     258, 260, 265
  definition of, 7
  and differences among models, 291–92
  and feature geometry, 256, 261–65
  and nondominant hand (H₂), 254
Type 2 signs, 186–87, 189, 251–52, 252–53,
     255, 257–260, 265, 272, 282
  definition of, 7
  and differences among models, 291–92
  and feature geometry, 256, 261–65
Type 3 signs, 46, 123, 186–87, 189, 252–53,
     255, 257–60, 265, 267, 272, 280
  and constraints, 277
  definition of, 7
  and differences among models, 291–92
  and feature geometry, 256, 261–65
  and Weak Drop, 274–77
Type 4 signs, 190
Type C signs, 7, 9, 252

'U', 296
UGLY, 308
[Ulnar], 112, 287
UNDERSTAND, 5, 80, 117, 130–31, 134,
     136, 181–82, 194, 196–197, 20–1, 206,
     214
Ungerleider, L., 311–12
Ungrammatical Signs
  *CHECK^READ, 281
  *CHECK^VOTE, 280
  *Impossible Sign, 9
  *TAKING, 14
  *THROWING, 14
  *WITH, One-Handed form, 250, 270
  *WORD^HELP, 280
Unidirectionality, 238
Universal grammar, 1, 313
[Unopposed], 113
[unrealized inceptive] aspect, 244
Upright-being-move-forward, 308
Uyechi, L., 33–35, 45, 72, 90, 104, 106, 120,
     131, 142, 152, 165, 167, 204, 286

'V', 145, 296, 298
Valli, C., 94, 209, 231, 249
VANISH, 173, 224
Venda, 131

Vendler, Z., 14, 197, 242
Vennemann, T., 71
Ventral plane. See Frontal plane
Verb, 11–15, 21, 238, 242, 258, 294. See also
     Classifier predicates
  and "verb sandwich," 244–45
  and agreement, 15–18, 147–48, 180, 289
  and direction, 143–51
  and movement, 137
  and semantic component, 146
  spatial loci, 145
  and syntactic component, 147
[Vertical plane], 287
Vertical visual processing, 306
Visual cortex, 311–12
Visual Phonology Model (VP), 90–92, 96,
     123–24, 142, 178, 181–82, 204
Visual processing, 2, 80, 306–13
  different from audition, 306–7
  and sonority, 216–17
Visual sonority, 213–37
  definition of, 215–24
  and syllable, 224–37
Vocal tract, 216
Vogel, I., 23
[Voice], 23, 69, 95, 113
Vowel, 68, 85, 95, 112, 305–6
  and feature geometry, 304
  and syllable, 73
  and syllabic structure, 78
Vowel epenthesis, 227
Vowel height, 65

WAIT, 169
Wallin, L., 4, 15, 21
WANT, 109, 114, 163
WAY, 125
WE, 155
Weak Drop, 55, 58–60, 123, 126, 248, 254,
     265–77, 283
  definition of, 249
Weak Freeze, 258, 265
  and feature geometry, 262–63, 265
Weak Prop, 282
WEDDING, 139, 141, 250
Weight unit, 28, 91, 213, 241–46, 287, 305–6
  and mora, 245–46
  and nominals, 241–43
  sentence-final position, 243–46
  and syllable, 206
Well-formedness, 54, 58, 85, 129, 155, 164,
     178, 182, 190, 211, 225–26, 231, 236,
     242, 265, 274
  and compounds, 280
  and constraints, 60–61, 73–74
  and lexical innovation, 293

Well-formedness (*cont.*)
  and movement, 205
  and prosodic word, 70
  and syllable, 70, 75, 303
  and visual sonority, 213
WET, 116
WHAT, 298
What system, 311–13
WHAT'S-UP, 141
WHEN, 72, 131–32, 273–74
WHERE, 167
Where system, 311–13
WHICH, 251
WHISKEY, 259–60
WHITE, 215, 249
Whittemore, G., 117
WHY, 113
Wiesel, T. N., 311
Wiggling, 165, 167, 169, 172, 197
Wilbur, R. B., 4, 6, 20, 33–34, 41, 58, 64, 88,
    102, 165, 179, 206
Willerman, R., 71
WILLING, 219
Wiltshire, C., 71, 78, 255
WINDOW, 11
Wirth, J., 69
WITH, 250, 252, 269–70
WITHOUT, 250
WOLF, 215
Woodward, J., 117
WORD, 29
WORD BLOW-BY-EYES MISS SORRY,
    29
Word formation, 237
Word length, 208–11
Word-level, 61
*WORD^HELP, 280
WORLD, 259–60
WOULD, 298
Wrist, 30, 45, 69, 133, 217, 219, 222
  and circling, 165
  and constraints, 236
  and contrast, 102
  and distalization, 134
  and fingers, 223
  flexion, 234
  and local movement, 4–5, 167
  and movement, 130–31, 156
  and phonetic enhancement, 173
  and orientation, 43
  and orientation change, 155–58
  and tremor, 165
  and Trilled Movement (TM), 165
Wrist nod, 234
WRITE, 163
WRONG, 140

'X', 163
X dimension (plane). *See* Frontal plane
X-slots, 136, 183–93, 194–195, 197, 204,
    206–8, 287, 305
  definition of, 183
  and trilled movement (TM), 201

Y dimension (plane). *See* Transverse plane
YEAR, 132, 142
YES, 43, 156

'Z', 232
Z dimension (plane). *See* Midsagittal plane
Zec, D., 71, 74–75, 79–80, 227, 243
Ziolkowski, M., 71
ZOOM-OFF, 197